FOUNDING GARDENERS

FOUNDING GARDENERS

The Revolutionary Generation,
Nature, and the Shaping
of the American Nation

ANDREA WULF

 Alfred A. Knopf · New York · 2011

Library of Congress Cataloging-in-Publication Data

Wulf, Andrea.
Founding gardeners : the revolutionary generation, nature, and the shaping of the American nation / Andrea Wulf.—1st ed.
p. cm.
Summary: "From the author of the acclaimed The Brother Gardeners, a fascinating look at the founding fathers from the unique and intimate perspective of their lives as gardeners, plantsmen, and farmers. For the founding fathers, gardening, agriculture, and botany were elemental passions, as deeply ingrained in their characters as their belief in liberty for the nation they were creating. Andrea Wulf reveals for the first time this aspect of the revolutionary generation. She describes how, even as British ships gathered off Staten Island, George Washington wrote his estate manager about the garden at Mount Vernon; how a tour of English gardens renewed Thomas Jefferson's and John Adams's faith in their fledgling nation; how a trip to the great botanist John Bartram's garden helped the delegates of the Constitutional Congress break their deadlock; and why James Madison is the forgotten father of American environmentalism. These and other stories reveal a guiding but previously overlooked ideology of the American Revolution. Founding Gardeners adds depth and nuance to our understanding of the American experiment, and provides us with a portrait of the founding fathers as they've never before been seen."—Provided by publisher.

ISBN 978-0-307-26990-4 (hardback)
1. Gardening—United States—History—18th century.   2. Gardens, American—History—18th century.   3. Gardening—Political aspects.   4. Founding Fathers of the United States.   5. Political activists—United States—Biography.   6. Conduct of life.   7. National characteristics, American—History.   I. Title.
SB451.3.W85 2011
712.0973'09033—dc22   2010052920

Jacket images: (clockwise, upper left, details) Steuartia by Mark Catesby, 1754, The New York Public Library / Art Resource, NY; Magnolia virginiana by Mark Catesby, 1731–43, Wellcome Library, London; Rhododendron maximum, 1806, Curtis's Botanical Magazine, Wellcome Library, London; Kalmia angustifolia by Mark Catesby, 1731–43, Wellcome Library, London; (center top to bottom) George Washington, Thomas Jefferson, John Adams, James Madison, The Granger Collection, New York

Jacket design by Barbara de Wilde

Manufactured in the United States of America

FIRST AMERICAN EDITION

TO JULIA

And though the vegetable sleep will continue longer on some trees and plants than on others, and though some of them may not blossom for two or three years, all will be in leaf in the summer, except those which are rotten. What pace the political summer may keep with the natural, no human foresight can determine. It is, however, not difficult to perceive that the spring is begun.

—THOMAS PAINE, *The Rights of Man*

CONTENTS

7
"Empire of Liberty"
Jefferson's Western Expansion 154

8
"Tho' an old man, I am but a young gardener"
Thomas Jefferson at Monticello 173

9
"Balance of Nature"
James Madison at Montpelier 190

Epilogue 213

AUTHOR'S NOTE

THROUGHOUT the book I use the word "garden" in its broadest sense rather than in the narrow meaning of "kitchen garden"—it also includes lawns, groves and flowerbeds, as well as the larger cultivated ornamental landscape of an estate.

Similarly, I have also used "gardener" and "gardening" in an extended meaning. When the founding fathers are "gardening," they might not actually be kneeling in the flowerbeds weeding, but they were involved in laying out their gardens, choosing plants (sometimes planting themselves) and directing their gardeners.

IN ORDER to avoid the unwieldy use in the text of both the common and Latin names of plants, I have used either one or the other, depending on the name by which a plant is most likely to be known. However, every plant is listed in the index under its common name (with the Latin name in parentheses) and under its Latin name (with its common name in parentheses).

FOUNDING GARDENERS

PROLOGUE

My first impressions of America were shaped when I went as a young woman on a seven-week road trip across the States, from Washington, D.C., to San Francisco. We drove hundreds of miles on roads that never curved, along a grid that mankind had imposed on nature. Some days we passed sprawling factories that were pumping out clouds of billowing smoke; other days we saw vast fields that seemed to go on forever. Everything differed in scale from Europe, even suburban America, where rows and rows of painted clapboard houses sit proudly on large open plots of immaculately shorn lawns. America exuded a confidence that seemed to be rooted in its power to harness nature to man's will and I thought of it as an industrial, larger-than-life country. I certainly never thought of it in terms of gardening—whereas in Britain, everybody seems to be obsessed with their herbaceous borders and vegetable plots. In America, I believed, I was more likely to see someone driving a riding-mower than pruning roses.

Then, in 2006, I went to visit Monticello, Thomas Jefferson's mountaintop home in Virginia, and began to understand how wrong I had been. On a sunny October morning, I stood on Jefferson's vegetable terrace, with straight lines of cabbages and squashes at my feet, and saw man and nature in perfect harmony. In the distance the horizon seemed to stretch into infinity; behind me was a manicured lawn lined with ribbons of flowers and, below, a romantic forest that crept into the gardens. The magnificent view from the terrace across the arboreal sea of autumnal reds and oranges of red maples, oaks, hickories and tulip poplars brought together Jefferson's neat plots of cultivated vegetables and sublime scenery of the Blue Ridge Mountains. Jefferson had combined beauty with utility, the untamed wilderness of the forest with the orderly lines of apples, pears and cherries in the orchard, and colorful native and exotic flowers with a sweeping panorama across Virginia's spectacular landscape. If nature had been dominated by man, it seemed it was only in order to celebrate it.

Later, I couldn't put Monticello out of my mind. I was in the midst of writing about the eighteenth-century American farmer and plant collector John Bartram, the British obsession with gardens and the introduction of non-native plants into the English landscape—many of which had been sent by Bartram from the American colonies. The more I learned about Bartram, the more fascinated I became by the American relationship to nature during the eighteenth century.

I pored over the correspondence between John Bartram and Benjamin Franklin, and after my visit to Monticello, I learned that Thomas Jefferson and George Washington had also ordered plants from Bartram, and that James Madison had visited Bartram's garden just before the Great Compromise of the Constitutional Convention in the summer of 1787. I read in John Adams's diaries how much he enjoyed working in his garden, fork in hand. Slowly, through records, letters and diaries, I came to see how vegetable plots, ornamental plants, landscapes and forests had played a crucial role in America's struggle for national identity and in the lives of the founding fathers.* Golden cornfields and endless rows of cotton plants became symbols for America's economic independence from Britain; towering trees became a reflection of a strong and vigorous nation; native species were imbued with patriotism and proudly planted in gardens, while metaphors drawn from the natural world brought plants and gardening into politics.

The founding fathers' passion for nature, plants, gardens and agriculture is woven deeply into the fabric of America and aligned with their political thought, both reflecting and influencing it. In fact, I believe, it's impossible to understand the making of America without looking at the founding fathers as farmers and gardeners.

Founding Gardeners examines the creation of the American nation and the lives of Washington, Adams, Jefferson and Madison through the lens of gardens, landscapes, nature and agriculture. Part of this is played out in Washington's Mount Vernon, Jefferson's Monticello and Madison's Montpelier—all large plantations in Virginia—as well as Adams's much smaller farm, Peacefield, in Quincy near Boston. But it was Benjamin Franklin who was the first of the revolutionaries to place plants at the heart of the country's struggle.

In response to the tensions between Britain and America, Franklin turned to plants and agriculture. In his "Positions to be examined con-

---

* The term "founding fathers" describes a group with a fluctuating membership. When I refer to the four main protagonists of this book as a group—George Washington, Thomas Jefferson, John Adams and James Madison—I have taken the liberty of using the term "founding fathers."

cerning National Wealth," Franklin listed in 1769 the three ways by which a nation might acquire wealth, and gave his opinion on each: "The first is by *War* . . . This is *Robbery*. The second by *Commerce* which is generally *Cheating*. The third by *Agriculture* the only *honest Way*." Eleven years before the thirteen colonies threw off the yoke of Britain's rule in 1776, the controversial Stamp Act had been given Royal Assent by King George III. This tax on paper affected almost every colonist, for it was applied to newspapers, legal documents, liquor licenses, books and every deck of cards. It was a desperate attempt to fill Britain's depleted coffers, run low by the Seven Years' War, which had seen Britain fight against the French on North American soil.* When the war had come to an end in 1763, the British economy lay in crisis, riddled with war debts and plagued by a series of bad harvests. Britain's solution was to make the colonists pay.

As news of the ratification of the Stamp Act reached America, colonists rallied together to protest against Parliament's rule. The Virginia House of Burgesses—the legislative assembly of colonial Virginia—declared the tax illegal. Throughout the colonies, riots broke out. The protesters burned effigies and raided the houses of British officials—on the way drinking their wine cellars dry—insisting that the British had no right to levy such taxes on the colonies. In Boston, an effigy of Andrew Oliver (the man who collected the stamp duty) and of the devil holding a copy of the Stamp Act were hung from an ancient elm tree near the town common. In the evening, 3,000 people marched through the streets, smashing the windows of Oliver's house before beheading and burning his effigy on a bonfire made from his furniture.

Franklin was in London at the time, having arrived in December 1764 on behalf of the Pennsylvania Assembly. His mission was to change the governance of Pennsylvania which was controlled by the so-called "proprietors," the heirs of William Penn, who had founded the colony in the seventeenth century. It was his third visit to the British capital, a place he loved for the intellectual stimulation and sociability. But during this visit, his relationship with Britain underwent a seismic shift—a shift that not only led to his assured signature on the Declaration of Independence, but that is also mirrored in his changing attitude toward seeds and crops. Indeed, his involvement with plants can be seen as a kind of barometer of his political convictions.

---

* The Seven Years' War was a global war in which Britain fought for dominance over India, sugar production in the West Indies and the slave trade in West Africa, as well as battling French power in North America.

Benjamin Franklin, 1767

For a long time Franklin had been interested in plants, both for their scientific and economic value. Part of a lively network of letter-writers who exchanged seeds with each other, he corresponded with farmers, gardeners and botanists in America and Europe, and experimented in his Philadelphia garden with different vegetables and crops. From London, he regularly sent seeds home to his wife, Deborah, helped by his British scientific and gardening friends. When one of them couldn't procure a new species of grain that Franklin wanted, another offered the entire produce of the previous year (clearly realizing how keen Franklin was). Franklin sent a new kind of oat and barley to Deborah to distribute among the plantsmen in Philadelphia, as well as sending vegetable seeds and Chinese rhubarb, which was valued for its medicinal properties. As the political troubles intensified, so did Franklin's agricultural interest.

The outbreak of the anti–Stamp Act protests in America had forced Franklin to become the unofficial ambassador for the colonies in Britain. He met the Lord Treasurer, Lord Grenville, in an attempt to persuade him to abandon the scheme but to no avail. Grenville, Franklin said, was "besotted" with it. Yet, though Franklin thought the Act to be unconstitutional and believed that the colonies had to be represented in Parliament, he did not, at this point, contemplate the possibility of independence. A "faithful Adherence to the Government of this Nation," Franklin insisted as houses were burned in Philadelphia, "will always be the wisest Course." But he misjudged how much his fellow colonists hated the impositions. In Pennsylvania, Franklin's steadfast defense of Britain was held against him and in late September 1765, furious rioters threatened to destroy his house in Philadelphia.

Britain had always nurtured the colonies as her greatest export market—paper, nails, glass, clothes and linen were all produced in Britain's burgeoning manufacturing sector and sold in American markets. In addition to staples, luxury products such as silverware, porcelain, carpets and silk became an important British export. The trade of hundreds of ships connected London, Bristol and Liverpool with Boston, Philadelphia and New York. Between 1730 and 1760, exports to the North American colonies quadrupled, filling the purses of British merchants and manufacturers. At the same time laws, regulations and duties imposed by the British and a lack of labor prevented the colonists from developing their own manufacturing sector. With plenty of fertile soil, the colonies instead became the fields of the mother-country—shipping grain, corn and tobacco to Britain. Consequently almost all colonists lived off the land. They fought against the wilderness, draining swampy soil and snatching plots from the rugged embrace of the forest. As they wrested their fields from the forest, trees fell in the thousands, clearing the way for cash crops such as tobacco, rice and indigo.

Franklin believed that the colonists' reliance on agriculture for their main income, combined with the seemingly endless resources of land, could be turned to their advantage. America could be self-sufficient. And as tension over the Stamp Act grew, Franklin argued that the colonies would be able to pressure the British by boycotting their goods. "I do not know a single article," Franklin told MPs, that the colonies couldn't either "do without or make themselves." It was his four-hour testimony in front of Parliament, many believed, that led to the repeal of the Stamp Act a few weeks later. But it soon became clear that the British had no intention of offering the colonies representation in Parliament. Instead, more duties were imposed, including on tea, paint and glass—all imported products that the colonists were only allowed to buy from Britain.

For the next three years Franklin tried to persuade both the colonists and the British politicians to reach a compromise. In essays and letters in newspapers, he was constantly explaining, moderating, smoothing and arguing. But when the government refused to compromise, he finally had to admit that words were no longer enough. In January 1769, he rallied behind the colonists' call for a sweeping boycott of British goods.

The boycott made Franklin's seed collecting all the more urgent. Not only was he sending larger amounts of seeds and more varieties home, but these were now for America's profit alone, not for Britain's. Every time someone told Franklin about a new edible plant, he was thrilled by the possibility of its economic potential. "I wish it may be found of Use with us," he told one correspondent when he forwarded seeds for a new crop, and when he heard of tofu, it so excited his curiosity, he said, that he procured a recipe from China, dispatching it together with chickpeas to a friend in Philadelphia.* These dried seeds carried the possibility of a new world and political freedom. In the coming years he sent upland rice and tallow tree† from China and seeds of "useful Plants" from India and Turkey, as well as introducing kohlrabi and Scottish kale, among many others, to America.

Franklin, who had been the "chairman of British Colonies" of the Society for the Encouragement of Arts Manufacturers and Commerce in London, now rarely went to the Society's meetings. The Society had tried to encourage colonists to grow commercial crops by paying premiums and awards, but by 1770 Franklin accused the Society of betraying the new nation, claiming that the "true Spirit of all your Bounties" were in the interest of Britain, not America. No longer was America to be a colonial grain store, or a market for Britain's goods. America, Franklin was convinced, could provide all the necessaries herself and they would just have to renounce the luxuries they couldn't produce. He echoed what John Adams had written in Boston's newspapers under the rustic pseudonym Humphrey Ploughjogger. In response to the Stamp Act, Adams had suggested that colonists should wear coats made of the hides of their own oxen rather than woollen ones from Britain. Adams promised that he

---

* Franklin dispatched the wrong "vegetables," because he sent "Chinese caravances," which most certainly were chickpeas (also called "garbanzos"). The process for making tofu was correct, but it is of course made of soybeans.
† The wax of the seeds of the tallow tree was used in China to make candles.

would not buy "one shilling worth of any thing that comes from old England." As such, self-sufficiency became a weapon in the fight for parliamentary representation and against British economic restrictions. Slowly colonists began to equate home production and agriculture with the upholding of domestic liberty.

To Franklin's regret, the boycott did not pressure Parliament into relinquishing authority over the colonies. Nothing was achieved, and in May 1771 Franklin wrote that "the seeds [are] sown of a total disunion of the two countries," while at the same time urging patience in order to postpone "this catastrophe."

Franklin continued to plead for moderation, but it became clear that Britain would never accept an empire that would give the colonial assemblies the same rights as Parliament. As the clashes between Britain and her colonies escalated, Franklin became the voice of American rights in Britain and the scapegoat for the troubles. At the end of January 1774, six weeks after a group of colonists dumped more than three hundred chests of tea into Boston's harbor in protest against the tax on tea—known as the Boston Tea Party—Franklin was questioned and attacked in the Privy Council about the colonial affairs. As the abuse was hurled at him, the sixty-eight-year-old Franklin, dressed in a blue suit made of Manchester velvet, stood motionless and with his head held high before the British accusers.

Three days later he wrote to his son William that "my Office of Deputy-Postmaster is taken from me." The British government had stripped him of the post that he had held for almost twenty years, severing their connection with Franklin. In this briefest of letters, Franklin then advised William, who was the royal governor of New Jersey, to give up his position in order to become a farmer: "I wish you were well settled in your Farm. 'Tis an honester and a more honourable because a more independent Employment." It was a turning point for Franklin, who for so long had clung to the idea that Britain would recognize the rights of the colonists. Farmers, he now believed, held the key to America's future because they, not the henchmen of the British empire, would create a new nation.

For one more year Franklin tried to facilitate a compromise, but then he realized that it was time to return home. With no reason to stay any longer in "this old rotten State," he boarded an American ship in March 1775, never to return to Britain. When he arrived in Philadelphia a little more than six weeks later, the Second Continental Congress was convening and the following day Franklin was made a delegate. "We should be prepared to repel force by force, which I think, united, we are well able to do," Franklin wrote to a gardening friend shortly after his arrival. He described the atmosphere in Philadelphia as one of mounting belligerence, containing "all Ranks of People in Arms." The next day George Washington, with his military uniform packed in his trunks, arrived in the city. The colonists were preparing to fight the British.

Franklin believed firmly in America's ability to survive. America would rise, Franklin wrote to an old friend in Britain in September 1775, because "it will itself by its Fertility enable us to defend it. Agriculture is the great Source of Wealth and Plenty. By cutting off our Trade you have thrown us *to the Earth,* whence like *Antaeus* we shall rise yearly with fresh Strength and Vigour."

The other founding fathers shared his belief. Agriculture and the independent small-scale farmer were, in their eyes, the building blocks of the new nation. Ploughing, planting and vegetable gardening were more than profitable and enjoyable occupations: they were political acts, bringing freedom and independence. When, after the War of Independence in 1783, the former colonies had to mature from being a war alliance to being a united nation, nature also became a unifying force. It was the Constitution that welded them together politically, legally and economically, but it was nature that provided a transcendent feeling of nationhood. America's endless horizons, fertile soil and floral abundance became the perfect articulation of a distinct national identity—of a country that was young and strong.

The founding fathers' passion for nature and plants can still be seen today for it shaped America in all its contradictions—from the rise of industrial agriculture in the Midwest to the protected wilderness in the national parks. America's most revered patriotic songs revel in images drawn from nature: the "amber waves of grain, / For purple mountain majesties / Above the fruited plain!" in "America the Beautiful"; in "God Bless America," "From the mountains, to the prairies, / To the oceans, white with foam"; and in Woody Guthrie's "This Land Is Your Land," with its chorus of "From the redwood forest, to the Gulf Stream waters / This land was made for you and me." Today's slowly changing attitude toward local produce, home-grown vegetables and inner-city gardening in the United States are part of the same endeavor. The new "food movements" (accompanied by a flurry of books and initiatives)—ranging from the promotion of urban agriculture to the preservation of farmland, from the first lady's vegetable garden at the White House to the returning interest of native species in ornamental gardens—can be placed in the context of the founding fathers' legacy.

For me, one of the greatest surprises was that the cradle of the environmental movement did not lie in the mid-nineteenth century with men like Henry David Thoreau or John Muir, but that it could be traced back to the birth of the nation and the founding fathers. The protection of the environment, James Madison had already said in a widely circulated speech in 1818, was essential for the survival of the United States. The founding fathers might not have romanticized nature as later generations did, but they were equally passionate about it. Madison did not suggest living in misty-eyed harmony with nature but living off it in the long term. He condemned the Virginians for their ruthless exploitation of the soil and the forests, fearing that nature's equilibrium would be unbalanced. Humankind, Madison said, could not expect nature to be "made subservient to the use of man." Man, he believed, has to find a place within the "symmetry of nature" without destroying it—words that remain as important today as they were when he spoke them.

In politics, the founding fathers have been evoked by almost every politician across a wide spectrum. This book offers a window into a new and important aspect of the lives of the founding fathers. It is significant that the old elm in Boston, from which the effigy of the loathed stamp distributor had dangled, was renamed the Liberty Tree. America's landscape, soil and plants played a crucial role in the creation of the nation and became steeped with political ideology but also with hope for the future. Jefferson, for example, crafted the grounds at Monticello as carefully as his words—it became a living tapestry of the themes that made America after the revolution. Every time I visit Monticello now, I go first to the vegetable terrace. Each time, no matter how often I see it, the contrast between the breathtaking view and the orderly rows of vegetables stirs me. I pick up a handful of the red soil and let it run through my fingers and I feel a visceral connection to the founding fathers and to their vision for this country.

1

"THE CINCINNATUS OF THE WEST"

George Washington's American Garden at Mount Vernon

By the summer of 1776, Manhattan had been transformed into an armed camp. American soldiers drilled in the wide tree-lined streets and troops took over the elegant brick mansions normally occupied by the New York elite. Huge wooden barricades were erected where fashionable women had promenaded only weeks earlier, and forts were built around the tiny hamlet of Brooklyn to defend the city. New York faced 32,000 British troops—more than one and a half times the city's entire peacetime population and the largest enemy fleet ever to reach American shores. The prospects of victory were slim. The commander-in-chief, General George Washington, had less than half the manpower, with his numbers declining even further as smallpox spread through the camps. Many of his officers had yet to experience the field of battle; those who had, had certainly never seen warships as menacing as those that approached New York—the combined firepower of just five of these was enough to outgun all the American cannons onshore. On the first day alone, more than one hundred enemy vessels had anchored in a bay south of the city, turning the water into a forest of looming masts.

New York was "in commotion" one observer said, as the frightened inhabitants of Manhattan fled. Over the next few weeks seventy-three

British warships and almost 400 transport vessels sailed into the bay. Washington inspected the forts, observed the enemy movements as they encamped on Staten Island and rallied his men, reminding them that they were "Freemen, fighting for the blessings of Liberty." Then, as the British troops were preparing their ferocious onslaught, Washington brushed aside his generals and his military maps, sat in the flicker of candlelight with his quill and wrote a long letter to his estate manager and cousin Lund Washington at Mount Vernon, his plantation in Virginia. As the city braced itself, Washington pondered the voluptuous blossom of rhododendron, the sculptural flowers of mountain laurel and the perfect pink of crab apple. These "clever kind[s] of Trees (especially flowering ones)," he instructed, should be planted in two groves by either side of his house.

It may seem baffling that amid this unprecedented crisis the commander-in-chief was designing new ornamental groves for his pleasure ground. But his horticultural letter is perhaps easier to understand when we consider the trees Washington was insisting be planted: soaring white pines and tulip poplars, glorious alabaster dogwood and stately red cedars. Only American natives should be used, he instructed, and all could be transplanted from the forests of Mount Vernon. As the young nation faced its first military confrontation in the name of liberty, Washington decided that Mount Vernon was to be an American garden where English trees were not allowed.

As the war intensified in the months and years that followed the battle of New York, Washington's dedication to his garden and plants did not abate. Sometimes new planting schemes seemed to occupy his thoughts more than the desperate situation of his country and men. In December 1776 he wrote, "I tremble for Philadelphia," but a few lines later in the same letter, "it runs in my head that I have heard of some objection to the Sycamore." Washington always longed for his estate manager's "infinitely amusing" letters because they included detailed horticultural reports on how his grounds were progressing, from digging up some flowerbeds to descriptions of the groves. Even during the terrible winter at Valley Forge two years later, when his army was hungry and sick, Washington urged Lund to continue work on his estate because such improvements were the "principal objects I have in view during these troubles." It was almost as if Washington escaped from the trials of war by imagining fields of healthy corn swaying in the wind and thinking of the promises of spring when "the Buds of every kind of tree & Shrub are swelling."

Nor was this love for gardens and nature restricted to Mount Vernon. In his General Orders, for example, Washington recommended that the troops make "regimental Gardens" in order to produce vegetables for army rations and also because he believed it would be healthy and comforting for his men—what we would call therapeutic. If the soldiers gardened, Washington was sure, "it will become a matter of amusement and of emulation." Even as his army trudged through blizzards and deep snow, he remained open to the allure of nature. Only days after describing how the men struggled through conditions so severe they "exceeded anything of the kind that had ever been experienced in this climate before," Washington reflected not on the hardship of this icicled embrace but noted in his diary that "the Trees and Earth being glazed looked beautiful."

For Washington, trees were both a glorious expression of America's beauty and a political trope. It was a tree that had become the most striking emblem of the revolution—the Liberty Tree, which, as Thomas Paine wrote in his eponymous poem, was the "temple" of the revolutionaries. So significant was the old elm in Boston that many old specimens in towns across America had been designated as Liberty Trees. Similarly, during the early years of the war, the schooners with which Washington defended Boston against the British carried flags that depicted a green pine tree with the inscription "An Appeal to Heaven." And when Washington described his lack of funds to pay his soldiers as "an Ax at the Tree of our Safety Interest & Liberty," he used trees as metaphors in the struggle for independence. Later, in August 1777, he roused his army by ordering every soldier to march through Philadelphia with "their heads adorned with green branches" as a sign of hope.

By the end of the war Washington had become, for many, the greatest of heroes, a man who had led his men across the icy Delaware to surprise the British army in a daring attack and who sat upright on his horse as bullets whizzed past him. Washington, however, did not think of himself in such a heroic way. The war had been a long-drawn-out ordeal. His soldiers starved, were regularly forced to serve without pay and had walked barefoot through snow. More men died of disease than at the hands of the enemy. Washington himself spent the whole war in the field with his army, waiving his pay and wrestling with Congress for supplies. He was tired after so many years away from his fields and garden. He had walked over the broken earth of battlefields and seen his army almost extinguished by the British. Instead of the young green of Indian corn pushing through the furrows of Mount Vernon's freshly ploughed fields, he had seen the blood of wounded soldiers staining America's soil.

The only time he saw his beloved Mount Vernon during the whole eight years was on a short stopover on the way to the last, decisive battle in Yorktown in October 1781. But even after this victory he could not go home. Two years later, frustrated and impatient to "quit the walks of public life," Washington was still waiting for the official end of the war, first in Princeton, New Jersey, where Congress had convened, and later at West Point (Garrison, New York). It wasn't until November 1783 that he at last received the news he had so longed for: the Treaty of Paris had been signed, and the British troops had ended their seven-year occupation of New York and Long Island. The war was officially over. Washington, exhausted but elated, had achieved the unthinkable, leading the thirteen colonies to victory and securing the birth of a new nation.

Washington the soldier had done his duty and delivered victory, but this was not the only legacy he wished to leave his country. The commander-in-chief saw the future of America as a country peopled not by soldiers but by farmers—an agrarian society that would be industrious and happy, where "our Swords and Spears have given place to the plough share and pruning hook." The general who had defeated the British army idealized not the military tactician or the political revolutionary, but the farmer. "The life of a Husbandman of all others," he believed, "is the most delectable," both "honorable" and "amusing." Again and again he had written of his wish to sit "under my own Vine & my own Fig tree"— using metaphors that the prophet Micah had invoked when referring to the messianic kingdom of peace.

This biblical image of peaceful rural retirement after the ravages of war appealed to Washington, but not all of his officers shared his vision. Rather than a tearful farewell and comradely embraces, they wanted to bow before their general and put a crown on his head. During the war, as supply chains of food, ammunition, clothes, tents and money collapsed, there had been calls to invest Washington "with dictatorial power" and to appoint him "sole Dictator of America" to bring order to the chaos. One officer wrote that he believed that postwar America needed to be ruled by Washington with "the title of king." Washington, though, was shocked when he heard that "such ideas exist in the Army," believing them to be "the greatest mischiefs that can befall my Country."

Washington chose the plough instead of command. He dreamed of a "whole world in peace" and wished to "clip the wings of some of [the] young soldiers who are soaring after glory." For most military leaders victory would have meant power and authority, but for Washington it meant a simple yet fulfilled life as a farmer and plantsman. "I can truly say I had rather be at Mount Vernon," he said, "than to be attended at the Seat of Government by the Officers of State and the Representatives of every Power in Europe."

The general was to become known as much for the surrender of power as for its execution. Unlike Caesar and Alexander the Great, who had been "wading to the conquest of the world through seas of blood," one of his admirers commented, Washington was "pure and virtuous." In refusing the continued lure of power he followed the model of the Roman hero Cincinnatus, summoned from his plough to save his country. After his victory, Cincinnatus had relinquished the offer of dictatorship in order to return to his farm. With his retirement to Mount Vernon, Washington advertised his own lack of interest in power—it was a sign of his true republican character.

As Washington rode south from the fort at West Point toward Mount Vernon, the citizens of the new American nation lined the decorated streets to glimpse their hero. At six foot two and a half and muscularly built, his body always held "perfectly straight," fifty-one-year-old Washington certainly looked the part, dwarfing his fellow soldiers and citizens and radiating strength, confidence, dignity and "something uncommonly majestic and commanding." And though the crowds that filled the streets of the cities and villages along his 300-mile homeward journey saw a warrior hero, the condition of his soil and the new shoots of spring were far closer to Washington's heart than any strategy of war.

His love for his country was deeply rooted in his passion for nature, agriculture and gardens. As early as 1748, as a sixteen-year-old surveyor in the Appalachian Mountains, Washington had gazed in wonder at the "most beautiful Groves" and had spent days "admiring the Trees & richness of the Land." During his long absences from home, he continued to follow his interest, observing the new landscapes as a farmer would—investigating the soil, noting species of trees and agricultural practices. In turn the thriving plants and fields became for him a symbol of the future of the young nation. "We have now a goodly field before us," Washington wrote shortly after the war, a field that the Americans now had to cultivate in order to "reap a fruitful Harvest."

Like Benjamin Franklin, Washington saw in the cultivated soil the country's wealth and independence. But there was a crucial difference in their understanding of the world of plants. Franklin (like the first settlers) equated the value of a plant with its productivity: useful plants would feed the American people and trees were valuable sources for fuel and building materials. Washington would have agreed, but being a generation younger he was also more susceptible to the sheer beauty of the American flora.

On 23 December 1783, five weeks after he had set out from West Point, Washington returned his commission as commander-in-chief in Annapolis, some fifty miles from Mount Vernon. There "was hardly a member of Congress who did not drop tears," one congressman observed, and at his farewell ball women queued to dance with him, just to "get a touch of him." As soon as the speeches were over Washington excused himself, "intent upon eating his christmas dinner at home." Less than forty-eight hours later, as he stood on the ferry, he could see his house across the Potomac River, perched 125 feet high on the steep wooded slope, rising above the snow-dusted forest. Finally he had returned to what he called his "philosophical retreat."

MOUNT VERNON WAS more than just fields that provided Washington's livelihood, it was also an expression of his social standing within Virginia society. For centuries European estates and houses had been public articulations of their owners' status, taste and politics, and gardens in particular had long been utilized as a sign of the owner's wealth and power. At Mount Vernon, Washington's rising position in society had been similarly imprinted on his 8,000-acre estate, which had changed radically from the 2,500-acre plantation he had inherited almost three decades previously. Just before his marriage in 1759 to Martha Custis, the wealthiest widow in Virginia, he had marked his move into the upper echelons of society by completely rebuilding the house. He had added another story to the seven-room farmhouse, extended the estate and built two walled gardens for flowers, fruit trees and vegetables. He had also turned the orientation of the house from east to west. By the time Washington brought his wife home, the principal entrance and rooms faced not to the ocean and Britain beyond it but to the west, toward the interior of the country. By turning his back to the Old World, Washington had expressed his belief that the future of the colonies lay in the west beyond the Appalachian Mountains. The final touch had been a straight half-mile vista, which Washington cut through the dense forest, opening a spectacular view from his parlor and dining room toward the fertile lands beyond the frontier, "the Land of promise, with milk & honey."

The next spur of building activity had begun in 1773, after Martha's sixteen-year-old daughter Patsy (from her first marriage) died. As a consequence, half of Patsy's substantial inheritance went to Martha and only a month later Washington ordered his first batch of building materials. He added wings to both sides of the house, as well as a large central pediment and a cupola as ornamental focus points, and a spectacular colonnaded double-height porch—the so-called piazza—overlooking the Potomac, the river that Washington believed connected the country to the western interior.

Now, RETURNING FROM war after eight years of absence, Washington could finally look upon his land. Snow, however, covered his fields and gardens. The cold blanket turned the ground into a white canvas on which only the lines of walls, walkways, and the edges of flower and vegetable beds remained. No color or scent could distract from these outlines. It was a garden ruled by geometry, the landscape of a surveyor's mind—Washington's former profession—tidy and ordered with patterns imposed on nature's unruly shapes. A straight road led to the house, terminating in the so-called Circle, an oval driveway. On each side of this road was a large square walled garden containing fruit and nut trees, vegetable plots and some ornamental flowerbeds. The symmetry continued with the outhouses that extended neatly from the two walled gardens to each side of the house.

Yet something wasn't right. As Washington surveyed his garden, he was struck by the austere formality, the straight driveway and sense of confinement. The brick walls around the two square gardens enclosed much of the ground that lay in front of the house; by contrast, the outhouses and mansion, which sat exposed on the highest ground, seemed almost naked against the large expanse of the lawn at the back. During Washington's absence his estate manager had planted the flowering shrubs and trees as he had instructed, in two groves "without any order or regularity." But the young native trees were still not mature enough to have a real impact on the landscape. The gardens around the house were rigid and, as one visitor who had come during the war remarked, "barren."

Washington had left in 1775 as a wealthy Virginia colonist, but he had returned as a war hero who had transformed his country and freed his people from tyranny. Standing in Mount Vernon, he realized that what had been perfect for a successful plantation owner was now woefully inadequate. Fresh from revolutionary triumph, he resolved to tear up the driveway, pull down the walls and dig up the hedges to liberate his garden from its claustrophobic corset of geometry, just as he had freed his country from Britain's imperial yoke. As he returned victoriously from the battlefield to the plough, Washington would transform Mount Vernon once again. This time it wouldn't just be the estate of a Virginia planter—it would be the landscape garden of a revolutionary.

"I AM BECOME a private citizen on the banks of the Potomac," Washington wrote in February 1784, five weeks after his return. "Free from the bustle of a camp & the busy scenes of public life, I am solacing myself with those tranquil enjoyments." It was indeed quiet at Mount Vernon. The snow and ice cut the plantation off from the rest of the world. No letters arrived and few visitors made their way through the freezing winter landscape. As the cold weather slowed down the pace of daily life, Washington had time to consider not just his landscape, gardens and fields, but his future. "The tranquil walks of domestic life are now unfolding to my view; & promise a rich harvest of pleasing contemplation," he wrote to his friend and fellow soldier Comte de Rochambeau. He felt like a "wearied Traveller," and his future, he said in private as he had done in public, was in agriculture.

The war hero became a farmer once again. Benjamin Rush, one of his fellow revolutionaries, described how Washington assumed "the dress and manners of a Virginia planter," including a weathered old gray coat. "His simplicity is truly sublime," Washington's protégé Lafayette said, remarking that in his retirement he was "even greater than he was during the Revolution." Every day he rose at five o'clock and, after an early breakfast of Indian hoecakes made with cornmeal soaked in butter and honey, rode the twenty miles across his plantation,* regardless of whether icy gales whipped across the fields or the fog rolled thick through the trees (such determination would cause his death fifteen years later when he refused to change his wet clothes before dinner after a five-hour ride across his estate during a winter storm). He was "completely involved with all the details of his lands," another visitor noted, while others were surprised when they were greeted by their hero dressed in a plain coat and mud-splattered boots.

---

* Washington had divided his plantation into five farms: Muddy Hole, Dogue Run, River, Ferry (also called Union) and Home House (or Mansion House). Each had its own overseer and slave work crew.

Washington also spent many reluctant hours in his study, desperately trying to bring order to his papers. Countless times during the war, they had been bundled up and hidden "out of the way of the Enemy" at a moment's notice, and the result was utter chaos. Instead of planting and redesigning his gardens, Washington suddenly found himself surrounded by piles and piles of papers—not just army accounts and expenses, but also the leases and tenant agreements for his tens of thousands of acres of land in the Ohio valley. The papers were in such confusion that Washington was at a loss as to what land was his and what wasn't. From surveyors he requested maps, boundary details and information on "the state of the Lands which I am entitled to in my own right." Some of the forests had been cleared and turned into fields, but because of the remoteness of the land across the Allegheny Mountains and Washington's long absence, tenants had failed to send a share of the profits.

By the close of summer 1784, Washington had given up on bringing order to his tenant affairs and resolved that he must travel to the West himself, on what he called "a tour of business." In September he set off toward western Pennsylvania and the "fertile plains of the Ohio." Here, he explained, "the poor, the needy & the oppressed of the Earth" could settle in peace and "Increase & Multiply." With thousands of acres to his name this would also conveniently make Washington a very wealthy landowner. Riding through the wilderness, it was the first time since his days as a surveyor that Washington saw the landscape as a civilian and not as a military commander. He could admire trees just for their intrinsic beauty rather than worry about the timber supply for stockades and fuel for his soldiers. At last mountains were not obstacles for the movements of the troops but majestic landscapes that allowed glorious views across the bountiful land.

He returned truly inspired from his 700-mile trip in the beginning of October. With the soil and plants holding the hope of America's future, Washington decided to "diversify the scene" by bringing nature from across the United States into his gardens. Species from the north and the south, from the mountains in the west and the coastal plains in the east would grow together in horticultural union at Mount Vernon, shaping the first truly American garden. "I shall hope to receive the Balsam trees; or any others which you may think curious, and exoticks with us," he wrote to his old friend George Clinton, the governor of New York.* Two weeks later he asked for white pines, the tallest of the northeastern

---

* Balsam firs were "exoticks" for Washington because the tall conifers grew only in the northern states.

conifers, and for eastern hemlocks, elegant trees with softly arching branches and shallow roots that make them the perfect mountain tree, as they can cling to rocks, ravines and the stony embankments of waterfalls. From the southern states he wanted live oak, the embodiment of the South, adored for its wide low-slung and almost horizontal branches on which Spanish moss swayed like abandoned feather boas. From his nephew George Augustine Washington in South Carolina he ordered *Magnolia grandiflora* because he had read in his garden books that it "flowers early, & is a beautiful tree" and requested umbrella magnolia with its huge leaves and white blossoms. The evergreens would make the gardens attractive during the winter months and the magnolias would bring glorious blooms. These ornamental trees and shrubs, Washington wrote to a friend, "are now become my amusement."

At the same time Washington began to assemble a collection of trees and shrubs that he found in the forests on his own estate. "Road [*sic*] to my Mill Swamp & to other place," Washington wrote in his diary, "in search of the sort of Trees I shall want for my walks, groves, & Wildernesses." He knew that the steadily increasing stream of visitors and strangers who came to Mount Vernon would first see this part of the garden. And it seemed that he was now deliberately choosing native evergreens, conifers and flowering trees to make a statement. By doing so, the gardens in front of the house would be an expression of his vision of republican simplicity, and his personal statement of independence.

Washington's new garden was to be truly American, a radical departure from the traditional colonial plots, for it was the first ornamental garden to be planted almost exclusively with native species. Since the first settlers had arrived in 1607 in Virginia, colonists had tried to re-create the gardens that they had left behind in Britain, including old-world species, which often cost a fortune to procure and cultivate. John Custis, for example, Martha Washington's father-in-law from her first marriage, had grown English yews and hollies clipped into balls and pyramids in his garden in Williamsburg, and his English friends had regularly dispatched to him European plants, including tulips, foxgloves, Guernsey lilies, tuberose and lilacs. Colonial gardeners such as Custis would have thought it pointless to plant American native trees and shrubs when these were growing in abundance, almost like weeds, in the wilderness just outside their garden gates. Since most American gardeners remained wedded to their old European plants and traditional plots, Washington's adoration for native species was revolutionary.

Ironically, though, Washington was reading a British publication in order to choose these American species: Philip Miller's best-selling *Gardeners Dictionary*. First published in 1731, it was the most important horticultural publication of the eighteenth century—the first and only comprehensive manual of practical gardening in Europe. Every species that was available in Britain was listed alphabetically, together with advice on how to propagate and cultivate it. Miller had been the head of the Chelsea Physic Garden in London and had more horticultural knowledge about American species than any other gardener except John Bartram, a Pennsylvania farmer who had supplied English plant lovers from the 1730s with hundreds of seed boxes from America. Unlike Washington, who was familiar with Virginian species and some others that he had noticed during his military campaigns, Miller had received and cultivated plants from all thirteen of the former colonies.

Whenever Washington wanted to know something about American trees and shrubs, he consulted the *Dictionary*. "In looking into Millers Gardeners Dictionary," Washington wrote to Clinton, he learned that the Northeastern conifers were more easily raised from seed than by cuttings (which made the transport from New York to Mount Vernon less complicated). Until his death Washington used the *Dictionary* regularly, preferring such practical books to political works or classical texts. For easy access, he always kept the *Dictionary* on the table in his study, together with the other agricultural and gardening books he used the most— Washington read only books on "agriculture and English history," Thomas Jefferson remarked later. On his return journey from West Point after the war, Washington had even found time to stop in New York to order the latest agricultural works (the bookseller knew exactly what his famous customer wanted).

Exactly a year after he had returned home from war, Washington finally decided to implement these ideas and reinvent his grounds. Undeterred by the snow, he set to work. On 12 January 1785, a week after he had written to his nephew George Augustine to order species from South Carolina, Washington scoured his forest for trees. An icy wind was lashing across the fields as he zigzagged the estate. Here and there he stopped, marking the trees he wanted to be dug up: he found thriving ash trees, "a great abundance of the red-bud of all sizes," pines and cockspur hawthorn, which he admired because they were "full of the red Berries." Even in the depths of winter as the deciduous trees stood naked in the forest, Washington recognized the many different flowering species by their shape and bark. He chose crab apple, which in spring would be covered in clusters of soft pink blossoms, and the scented fringe tree with its

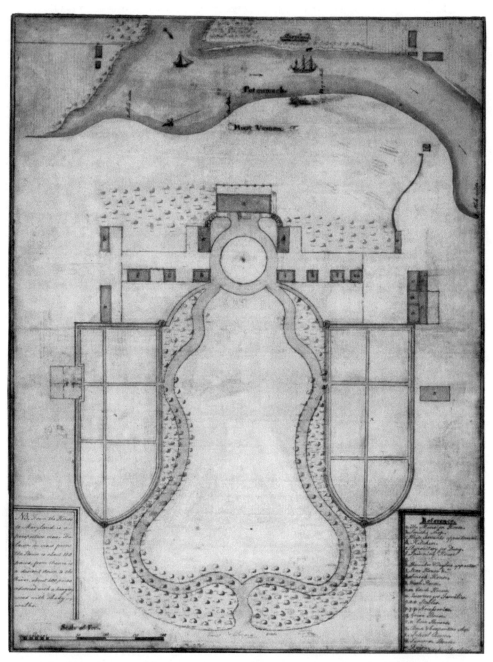

Samuel Vaughan visited Mount Vernon in August 1787. His drawing is the only plan of the bowling green, the winding walk along the shrubberies and the two bullet-shaped enclosed gardens. He also depicted the two groves next to the mansion that Washington had planned in the summer of 1776 just before the Battle of New York.

plumes of dangling white flowers. When he returned home, he noted every species and their location—one of the longest entries in his diary. A week later, the work began in earnest and Washington was "Employed until dinner in laying out my Serpentine road & Shrubberies."

In front of his house, where the straight driveway and the adjoining two-walled kitchen and fruit gardens covered most of the ground, he planned a large bell-shaped tract of lawn instead—the "bowling green"—hugged by a winding walk on both sides along which he envisaged hundreds of American trees and shrubs planted in irregular drifts and heights. In order to create the sinuous openness of the bowling green, he altered the shape of the enclosed gardens by reducing them to almost half of their original width and adding a curved wall to extend their length. With this Washington would turn the two square gardens that had dominated the front into two slim bullet-shaped sections at the edge of the central lawn. The walls would disappear behind the irregularly planted trees and shrubs.

Having gathered his chosen trees, the eager Washington ordered his slaves to remove the snow and begin digging holes immediately. He admitted it was "exceeding miry & bad working" but, determined to see his vision of an all-American garden realized, pressed on regardless. The new walk, his "serpentine road," which circled the bowling green, was lined with trees that were placed "promiscuously without Order," as Miller instructed. He planted tall trees such as black gum, American linden—which Clinton had sent from New York—and aspen, which he had procured from Fairfax, Virginia. As undergrowth he chose mountain laurels, which in spring open their puckered pink flowers like mini-umbrellas. Many of the species that Washington collected in the surrounding forests were spring-flowering shrubs that would also look magnificent in autumn. Sassafras, for example, paraded exquisite yellow flowers on its naked branches in early spring and colorful leaves in autumn. Similarly the flowering dogwood, one of Washington's favorites, impressed with its perfect alabaster blossom in April and May and its brilliant red foliage in October.

Painting with his trees, Washington contrasted the smooth white bark of the aspen against the furrowed trunk of black gum, and set the fluttering large leaves of maples against the tiny droplet-like leaves of honey locust. The rigid conical shape of young red cedars provided vertical brushstrokes, while the mountain laurels spread in looser, more horizontal lines. In autumn the buttery yellow of the tulip poplar and aspen would make a wonderful background to the fiery reds of black gum and maples. All his life Washington had observed the landscape around him and now this intimate horticultural knowledge helped him to place the trees and shrubs in groups that would show off their beauty in the most effective way.

If the plants provided the colors and shapes with which Washington was creating his floral painting, the garden books he had studied over the past months instructed him how to sketch. In addition to the *Dictionary* (because "Miller . . . seems to understand the culture of Trees equal to any other writer I have met with"), Washington also admired Batty Langley's *New Principles of Gardening,* a book he had bought years earlier, in 1759. Langley, like Miller, advocated gardens "after Nature's own Manner." Following their instructions, Washington created two "shrubberies"—plantations of ornamental shrubs and trees—between the bowling green and the walled gardens. Like the seats in an amphitheater, the lowest specimens were placed at the front and the tallest at the back. "The Trees should rise gradually one above another," as well as trailing the twisting shape of the walks, Miller advised in his *Dictionary.* Some of the larger trees such as the maples and tulip poplars Washington placed on the bowling green itself, almost as if the densely planted shrubbery was tapering out into single trees on the lawn—once again taking Miller's word as inspiration, for in the *Dictionary* it said trees should be planted "forwarder upon the lawn than others, whereby the regularity of the lawn will be broken."

Unlike other gardeners, Washington did not distinguish between the rare and the common. He did not care, for instance, that tulip poplars grew in almost every forest of the thirteen states. He cherished their upright white-orange flowers as much as the rarer satin blossom of the *Magnolia grandiflora,* which was native to the Southern states only. The plants were American and that was all that counted because this part of the garden celebrated America, irrespective of the rarity of the plants.

Every day Washington could be found outside marking his trees and overseeing the planting. It seemed his persistence reached near-obsessive levels. Too often, however, he was interrupted with requests for letters of introduction and certificates for servicemen, or his army accounts. He longed to be "relieved from the drudgery of the pen" so that he could give his full attention to these cherished gardening amusements. The "raising of shrubberies &c" was now his favorite occupation but instead every "Dick, Tom, and Harry" pestered him with "references of a thousand old matters with which I *ought* not to be troubled, more than the Great Mogul." But even when he was not holed up in his study, he was distracted by the stream of visitors who arrived from across the United States and Europe to see the hero of the revolution.

Eighteenth-century hospitality demanded that he welcome and feed such strangers. His house, he complained to his mother, "may be compared to a well resorted tavern, as scarcely any strangers who are going from north to south, or from south to north do not spend a day or two at it." Sometimes even his sleep was disturbed when strangers knocked on the door in the middle of the night* or when he considerately served cups of tea to ill guests. So many people came to Mount Vernon that one and a half years after his return Washington wrote in amazement in his diary that he: "dined with only Mrs. Washington which I believe is the first instance of it since my retirement from public life."

Mount Vernon had become the most visited private house in the country. "No pilgrim ever approached Mecca with deeper enthusiasm," one visitor said, while another marveled that so many people turned up "from all parts of the world; hardly a day passes without." At the end of February 1785, as Washington was laying out the Serpentine Walk, he suffered yet another typical day of interruptions: "first by the coming in of Mr. Michael Stone about 10 oclock (who went away before noon)— then by the arrival of Colo. Hooe, Mr. Chas. Alexander, & Mr. Chs. Lee before dinner and Mr. Crawford, his Bride & sister after it." The following morning Washington decided he had had enough of the continuous entertainment he was expected to perform and went outside to mark the ground at the bowling green, which was "hard froze," instructing his slaves to dig holes for the trees no matter how difficult it was. Washington did not just oversee the planting and digging, he often worked alongside his men, stripping off his coat and laboring "like a common man," visitors noted in surprise. He talked proudly of the trees "which my hands have planted."

Throughout these cold winter weeks, Washington continued the work in the Serpentine Walk, noting every detail in his diary. He planted many more clumps of native trees and asked his former general and chief of artillery, Henry Knox, to inquire about the design of "public walks" in Boston because he wasn't sure if gravel would "resist the impression of the wheels." If there was "a better composition," Washington wrote, he would like to use them for his Serpentine Walk. And as his slaves and gardeners created an American garden, Washington trailed them with his knife eagerly poised, "pruning and shaping the young plantation." Yet within a week his impatience had been punished, as heavy sleet encrusted the branches of the trees and shrubs in half-inch-thick "tubes of Ice." As

---

* This was the sculptor Jean-Antoine Houdon and his three assistants, who had been sent by Franklin and Jefferson from Paris to make Washington's bust.

he looked outside, he saw that most of the young trees were bent, many with broken branches. His enthusiasm had, on this occasion, gotten the better of him, having harmed rather than nurtured the young trees.

In the middle of the shrubberies on each side of the bowling green Washington built a "necessary"—an outside toilet. Each looked like a little octagonal temple, painted white with a red bell-shaped roof. Following the advice of British garden writers, Washington laid out narrow gravel paths winding past the trees and bushes. But by terminating the path with a toilet instead of a pavilion or a statue as was fashionable in Britain, he combined beauty with utility in a fresh and original way, which would become typical in America's gardens.

Along the paths toward the two necessaries, Washington planted his most scented flowers, which included a few non-native species. In early summer, he hoped, two different species of lilacs (*Syringa vulgaris* and *Syringa × persica*)—one from Europe and one from Asia—would spread their perfume, their mauve blossoms competing with the white pompoms of English guelder rose and the fragrant white blossom of mock orange. The reason Washington used some non-native species in this small area had a practical purpose, because their scent would mask the smell. But he also planted the native trumpet honeysuckle, so that the twining climber would scramble up the white walls. Not only would sweet-smelling red flowers cover any unpleasant odors but their prime attraction to Washington may well have been Langley's romantic assertion that they were "a Plant of Liberty."

By mid-March, the main planting of the two shrubberies was finished. Snaking along each side of the bulging outline of the bowling green that stretched away from the house, the shrubberies framed the long vista toward the West Gate. Only the round end of the bowling green where the two sides met had remained empty, because Washington did not envisage this as an area planted with flowering species. Here to the left and right of the entrance to the bowling green he wanted a "wilderness." Instead of plants that spread color and perfume across the garden, he chose only conifers to create a more shaded space.

This would be part of Washington's carefully orchestrated one-mile approach to the house, which led along a meandering road. The route was a theatrical masterpiece of hide-and-seek by which the mansion tantalizingly appeared and disappeared as the road dipped in and out of the forest. The wilderness and shrubbery was a continuation of the approach that led from the dense forest through thickets with occasional openings to the entrance of the sinuous bowling green. From here visitors would first pass the shady plantation of conifers and then the flowering shrubs, which—once mature—would be tinged in brilliant hues. The wilderness provided the link between the forest outside the garden and the ornamental trees and bushes near the house—it was the transition between dark and light, the wild and the domestic.

Unlike the two shrubberies through which the Serpentine Walk wove, each wilderness featured separate twisting gravel paths where family and visitors would be able to find refuge from the scorching Virginian sun. It was a manicured and dwarf version of an American pine forest, highly stylized into two "Pine labyrinths," as Washington called the area, or the "Miniature Labyrinth" as another of his visitors later described it. The idea was a combination of Langley's designs, which showed many varieties of groves laid out as labyrinths, and Miller's instructions that deciduous and evergreen species should not be mixed in a wilderness.

Once again Washington searched his estate for trees, and three days after he had laid out the twisting walks, he marked three wagonloads of pines and had them immediately planted, undeterred as ever by an icy March rain. The next day the weather worsened and many of the pines, Washington noticed in the morning, "yielded to the Wind & Wet, and required propping." But this was not the only problem. As he was staking the flattened trees, Washington was called back to public duty.

During the War of Independence, Virginia and Maryland had temporarily suspended their dispute over the navigation rights of the Chesapeake Bay and the Potomac. But now that the common enemy, Britain, had been defeated, the two states had returned to their old conflict. Despite their union during the war, in the wake of victory the thirteen states began to act more as independent countries rather than as one nation. People across America regarded themselves as belonging foremost to their own state, not so much as Americans—just as Washington considered trees from New York as "exoticks" because they were not from his Virginia.

Maryland and Virginia had authorized three and four commissioners respectively to deal with the claims, and Washington invited the agents from both parties to meet at Mount Vernon for the negotiations. One of the commissioners was his old friend George Mason, who lived some twenty miles away in Gunston Hall. Like Washington, Mason was passionate about plants and, knowing how delighted his host would be, brought some along. Washington had rushed the work in his garden so that it would be finished before the commissioners arrived, but on inspecting his new wilderness on 24 March 1785, the day he expected Mason, he decided to double the number of pines because he found them "rather too thin."

Over the next few days the men discussed and settled the jurisdiction of the navigation and fishing rights, signing their final agreement on 28 March. The success of the so-called Mount Vernon Conference was more than the end of a parochial conflict. For some it also heralded the possibility of a broader solution between the thirteen states—if Maryland and Virginia were able to find an arrangement, maybe the other states would too. As he presided over the negotiations in Mount Vernon, Washington as always found time to talk about matters of planting. So passionate had Washington been about his new garden that several of the commissioners dispatched trees to Mount Vernon once they had returned to their estates. Mason traveled home to Gunston Hall in Washington's carriage and sent it back filled with cuttings from his gardens, and Maryland representative Daniel of St. Thomas Jenifer sent several hundred fruit trees later that year.

As spring slowly arrived, Washington strolled along his new trees and bushes, noting every change, reveling in the rebirth of his plants. "All nature seemed alive," he mused while looking at his creation. Washington was not a man of many words, even when writing his diary, which hardly contained more than a line about the weather or the name of a guest who had joined him for dinner. But during the spring of 1785, inspired by the new plants, the color, scent and beauty of his garden filled its pages. "The tender leaves of many had unfolded," he wrote, "the Dogwood had swelled into buttons" while another tree was "shedding its fragrant perfume." Since the end of the war the glory of his plants had only been in his imagination, but now Washington admired the different hues of maple blossom—"some being of a deep scarlet, bordering upon Crimson—others of a pale red, approaching yellow." The vibrant spring colors were everywhere—on the bare branches of sassafras clung delicate yellow flowers, which Washington thought "would look very pretty" mixed with the glowing pink of the eastern redbud. And whenever he saw a beautiful blossom in the forest he noted that it "deserves a place in my Shrubberies."

By mid-May, however, Washington's initial joy had been replaced with disappointment. "Most of my transplanted trees have a sickly look," he noted despondently. They were "withering" and "bereft of their leaves," and the small pines in the wilderness were "entirely dead," only the larger ones managing to cling on. A quick count of the casualties revealed that "half the Trees in the Shrubberies, & many in the Walks, are dead & declin[in]g." A few months later, he put shades over some of the remaining trees to protect them from the parching summer heat, but by August he could see that much had been lost: "In a word nature had put on a melancholy look—everything seeming to droop." But Washington was a pragmatic plantsman as he had been a pragmatic military leader, famed for his glacial self-control and stoic resilience. He had not lost his nerve during the war, and he wasn't about to lose it in his garden. His trees needed nurturing just as the new nation did. When he described how the pleasure of planting lay with seeing "the work of ones own hands, fostered by care and attention, rising to maturity," he might have been speaking about his own contribution to the creation of the United States.

"Once he has begun anything," one visitor observed shortly after the mass dying in the garden, "no obstacle or difficulty can come in his way." And so he started again, spending much of the next winter replanting. There were many other things to do: the lawn of the bowling green was sown, he fenced eighteen acres of the steep and wooded slope between the Potomac and the lawn that lay behind the house in order to create a deer park, the two enclosed gardens were replanted with fruits, flowers and vegetables, and new walls had to be erected.

Washington was a hands-on gardener who was involved in every detail, from searching for trees in his forests to drawing the layout of his new greenhouse. He knew exactly what he wanted and instructed his correspondents how to pack the seeds that they were sending from across the United States, "in dry sand as soon as they are gathered." When he read a "recipe" on how to protect plants from pests by using seaweed because the "Salt is pernicious to most Insects," he forwarded it to the *Virginia Journal and Alexandria Advertiser* to share the knowledge with fellow gardeners. He also enclosed a small area between the house and one of the walled gardens (the Upper Garden) as an experimental nursery where he could work away from the crowds of visitors, which still showed no signs of abating. In this more intimate enclosure, the so-called Botanical Garden, Washington spent more time than in any other part of the garden.

He counted his plants and kept a record of when and how they perished. To keep track of them all, he chipped different numbers of little notches into sticks as substitute labels according to a key code that he noted in his diary. He also took detailed records of dates and locations of planting, which he kept safe in his study with the seeds. He ran his estate, according to one congressman, like a military operation—"Not a day's work but is noted; what, by whom, and where done . . . Thus the etiquette and arrangement of an army are preserved on his farm."

Washington's sense of pragmatism and his entrepreneurial spirit could also be seen in areas of his garden that took on a more utilitarian purpose. He believed that "experiments by intelligent and observant farmers" were the backbone of agriculture, and saw the Botanical Garden as the ideal location for such investigations since the seeds that he wanted to test would not survive in fields or meadows, where "(if not forgot) they are neglected; or swallowed up." So it was in the Botanical Garden, the old vineyard,* and to some extent in the two walled gardens, that a slightly different approach was taken. Here Washington experimented with non-native plants and seeds. He planted European orchard grass (Dactylis glomerata), which was used for hay, and "bird grass" (*Poa trivialis*), which was recommended for pasture; seeds from the West Indies and even from China as well as "Wheat from the Cape" and guinea grass (a native to Africa that was successfully grown in the West Indies as animal fodder). In the walled gardens he grew English walnuts and cherries, French pears and grapes, as well as peach trees from Portugal. These plants served a different purpose from the ornamental natives in front of the house (the most visible area). Washington grew them not as patriotic statements or living symbols but for their economic potential and possible future use in American agriculture.

The reasons for Washington's constant search for new crops, fodder and green manure lay in the soil of his plantation, in the history of Virginia and in his belief in the future of the country. Since the days of the early settlers, Virginians had grown tobacco, a crop that was coveted on the European market but that also exhausted the soil. The cultivation of tobacco was ruinous not only because it depleted the fertility of the land but because it had made America dependent on Britain. Every year the crop had been shipped across the ocean to be sold and marketed by British merchant agents. Plantation owners like Washington and Jefferson had no control over the sales of their own harvests and had felt the pain of the economic chains. Washington had stopped growing tobacco in 1766 and was trying to find alternatives in the hope that the new crops would break this dependence by supplying the home market in America instead.

Part of the problem was also the "ruinous" outmoded agricultural methods in America to which most farmers, Washington bemoaned, steadfastly clung. Nothing much had changed since the first settlers had arrived and American farmers continued to work their soil as their fathers and grandfathers had done. If America wanted to be economically independent, this had to change, as "Nothing in my opinion would con-

---

* The old vineyard was fifty yards beyond the walls of the Lower Garden. In spring 1785, Washington turned it into an experimental "nursery" for large-scale experiments.

tribute more to the welfare of these States, than the proper management of our Lands," Washington wrote to a fellow plantation owner. Because of the disastrous effect of tobacco cultivation, his foremost endeavor when he returned to Mount Vernon was the replenishment of the ground.

Washington tried many different methods because "every experiment is a treasure." He scattered different amounts of gypsum—"Plaister of Paris"—on his lawn to examine its viability as a fertilizer. He believed that the mud from riverbeds might be used as manure and when he heard of a dredge in Philadelphia—"Mr. Donaldson's Hippopotamus"—he decided in autumn 1785 "to make a full experiment upon a small scale," digging up the mud from the Potomac and spreading it on a field. He tested marl (similar to lime), ash and "fish heads, guts &ca." and later built a dung depository. He used the human waste from the necessaries, corresponded extensively about manure and bought the latest agricultural publications from Britain (because "no Country has carried the improvment [sic] of Land & the benefits of Agriculture to greater perfection than England"). In fact, he was so obsessed with manure and the improvement of the soil that he was actively seeking a farm manager who, "Midas-like," could "convert every thing he touches into manure, as the first transmutation towards Gold."* He was so innovative in his agricultural methods that many regarded him as "the first farmer in America."

Washington had at last achieved what he had set out to accomplish. As he spread manure on his fields or planted a tree that he had found in his forest, he gave physical embodiment to his belief that the future of America lay in the fields and forests. The recent experiments in the utilitarian parts of the estate were aimed at improving agriculture, while the plantations of ornamental native species in front of the house carried a symbolic message that this new nation would be independent, self-sufficient and strong. Both areas, in their own way, illustrated Washington's fervent patriotism.

Mount Vernon was his private statement of independence and republican simplicity, wrought from the soil and trees of his country. European visitors accustomed to the pomp of their courts were divided in their judgment—the Prussian Baron von Steuben, for example, who had fought with Washington in the War of Independence, was dismissive about what he thought was a modest estate. Others, however, understood that this simplicity was "quite in keeping with the idea we have of Cincin-

---

* Less than a year later, on 21 April 1786, Washington's new farm manager James Bloxham arrived in Mount Vernon from Britain.

natus and of those other great commanders of the Roman Republic."
Mount Vernon, with its many outbuildings and neat gardens, looked like
"a rural village." Everything was as Washington liked it—"trim, handsome & thriving"—tidy fences, scythed lawns, gently winding paths, and
woods that had been cleared from its messy undergrowth. This was his
vision of the United States of America. After the chaos of the revolution
and the war, Washington and his "brother farmers" were bringing order
to the land. Agriculture and planting, Washington was hopeful, were to
be his only occupations until his death: "I wish most devoutly to glide
silently and unnoticed through the remainder of life."

2

"GARDENS, PECULIARLY WORTH THE ATTENTION OF AN AMERICAN"

THOMAS JEFFERSON'S AND JOHN ADAMS'S ENGLISH GARDEN TOUR

SPRING HAD DUSTED the trees and shrubs with the first specks of green, a glimpse of the glorious spectacle that would soon follow. As Thomas Jefferson left the noisy streets of London behind one morning in early April 1786, he could see the English countryside unfold its undulating patchwork of fields, hedgerows and narrow lanes. Robins were building their nests and small wagtails were just arriving back from their long migration to Africa. The hornbeam's dangling light-yellow catkins were dancing in the sun and the soft leaves were slowly uncurling on the naked branches, while the blackthorn was already wrapped in white blooms. Lining the roads were swaths of the tiny bright yellow lesser celandine—also sometimes called "spring messenger" because they are one of the first flowers to blossom. In the forest the oaks and beech trees were still without leaves but alabaster white wood anemones and pale yellow primroses lit up the ground. Nature was slowly awakening from its long hibernation and Jefferson was excited to finally see the quiet signs of spring after the hectic cacophony of London life.

Forty-two-year-old Jefferson was the American Minister to France but his colleague John Adams, the American Minister to the court at St. James's Palace, had asked him in February for help with some difficult trade negotiations in London. "Come here without loss of time," Adams had begged, because the discussions between Britain and the United States that he had been heading had completely stalled, as had the fraught negotiations with the Barbary States—Tripoli, Morocco, Algiers and Tunis—that controlled navigation in the Mediterranean (asking for a hefty "tribute" for allowing American ships to pass unmolested). "I dare not communicate to Congress what has passed without your Concurrence," Adams had told Jefferson a few weeks previously. He trusted Jefferson and desperately needed his support, for Britain's refusal to cooperate threatened the United States of America's very survival.

The two men had first met in Philadelphia, during the long months before the Declaration of Independence, where Adams had led the heated discussions while Jefferson silently watched. Jefferson was no orator but had proven his sharp mind and exquisite writing style when he wrote the new Constitution of Virginia. It was Adams who had suggested that the quiet Virginian should write the Declaration of Independence, but they only became close friends years later, when their paths crossed again in Paris, where Adams was instrumental in securing the peace treaty after the War of Independence. Jefferson's wife, Martha, had died before his appointment to Europe, and in Adams the grieving diplomat found both support and comfort. Jefferson had joined him in Paris at the end of 1784, but Adams was then relocated to London a few months later, with his famously independent wife, Abigail, and their nineteen-year-old daughter in tow.

Adams had many reasons to be worried. When the war had ended, the joy of victory was almost immediately tempered by the sheer destruction left in its wake. Thousands of farms had been torched and entire counties in New York, Pennsylvania and the Carolinas had been plundered. A need for iron during the war had left great swaths of forest denuded of the wood that was required as fuel for America's foundries, and the crops in the northern states had been blighted. Moreover, as if this agrarian devastation had not been enough, fire had also consumed much of Charleston and New York. The United States was heavily in debt and paper money was worthless.

As farmers had slowly begun to recover, they relied on foreign markets to trade their surplus produce. But all ports in Britain and her colonies had been closed to American ships in a deliberate attempt to thwart the young nation's chances of success. It was against this bleak background of looming economic catastrophe that Adams the straight-talking lawyer and farmer from New England and his Virginian fellow revolutionary Jefferson had been ordered by Congress to forge a set of commercial treaties that would allow the United States to resume her trade with Europe. But the old oppressor was standing by, predicting that the United States would have to return to the colonial fold. "There is a strong propensity in this people to believe that America is weary of her Independence," Adams had quickly discovered on arriving in London, before adding that those who believed such nonsense were "Sufficiently insane."

Jefferson's arrival in London on 11 March 1786 had failed to advance things further. And so, after three weeks of wasting his time in London, the restless Jefferson had been so frustrated that he decided to go on a garden tour instead, leaving Adams behind in case the British changed their mind. Jefferson's disgruntlement about the enforced inactivity was unsurprising because he hated to be idle. He needed to be constantly occupied—reading, recording flowering times of shrubs, measuring or inventing mechanical gadgets. Whenever circumstances stopped him from work, he would occupy himself with something else—from calculating how long it would take to pay back the national debt to constructing a letter-copying machine. "Ennui," he warned his oldest daughter, was "the most dangerous poison of life."

When Jefferson left his lodgings in Golden Square on 2 April, he was joining the hordes of tourists who traveled the length and breadth of the country to visit England's landscape gardens during spring and summer, when landowners from Shropshire to Kent opened their estates to the public. Everybody wanted to see the most fashionable gardens in Europe. The English taste in gardening "doubtless is the best," one Swedish botanist declared after touring the country, while Catherine the Great had ordered her landscape architect to "visit all the notable gardens" of England, "and, having seen them, to lay out similar ones here." Tourists with a taste for gardening would not miss the opportunity to visit the famed landscapes—Franklin too had seen them during his time in England, and Jefferson was to be no exception.

The learned Jefferson had been excited to travel to Europe in the name of his country, "combining," as he said, "public service with private gratification." Paris and London were after all the greatest cities in the world—centers of art, learning and science. Gardens in particular fascinated Jefferson. He had an "affection in every bud that opens," he said, and previous to his visit he had already ordered from London a "pair of slippers of waxed leather, rather thick, for walking in the garden." For years he had studied British horticultural books to learn about the art of planting and designing such landscapes. Despite his disdain for the country, he had to concede that the English had created the most magnificent landscapes in Europe.

Even as the colonies had prepared to declare their independence ten years earlier, while Jefferson labored over the words of the Virginia constitution and the Declaration of Independence, he had found time to order British garden books. The one he admired most was the best-selling *Observations on Modern Gardening* by Thomas Whately, who—in a twist of irony—had also been one of the authors and defenders of the controversial Stamp Act. As patriots across the colonies were boycotting British goods, Jefferson had disloyally dreamed of an English garden. Over the years he constantly drew extensive plans of new improvements for his garden at his plantation Monticello in Virginia: elaborate planting schemes, waterworks, poetic inscriptions, and fanciful Gothic temples and Chinese pavilions, all inspired by the latest English fashions. He had even tried to find a British gardener but without any success, and so it was mostly in his mind that he moved hills and forests, let water cascade from rocks and lounged in ornamental temples that were never built.

When Adams asked Jefferson to join him in Britain, the Virginian finally had the opportunity to see what he had only read and dreamed about. On the first day of his garden tour he saw no less than five* and stayed the night in Weybridge in Surrey, some twenty miles to the west of London, so that he could see the famous Wooburn Farm the next morning. As with all English gardens, the entry to Wooburn Farm was free. Except for a small gratuity for the servants or guides, visitors simply had to sign in at the entrance lodge. As this was just a formality, Jefferson was perplexed when the gardener refused him entry on the grounds that his master had ordered him not to admit anybody who might be English. "But I am not an English man," replied the bewildered (and no doubt slightly offended) Jefferson, before the gate was opened. Asked to explain why "the English" were not allowed to visit, the gardener explained that the owner "cannot trust them, [as] they will take something with them." It was not just theft that the owner was worried about—with the increasing number of garden tourists across England, vandalism was also rising as visitors stole plants, broke things and even graffitied the pavilions and alcoves. At Wooburn Farm the disturbances had been particularly bad and the Catholic proprietor had been forced to close his garden for "the savages, who came as connoisseurs, scribbled a thousand brutalities."

Walking along the sandy path in long strides, Jefferson could immedi-

---

* Jefferson saw Alexander Pope's garden at Twickenham, as well as Chiswick, Hampton Court, Esher Place and Painshill.

ately see why Wooburn Farm was one of the most celebrated gardens in England. Instead of immaculately shorn lawns or rolling parkland, there were pastures with "spotted cows," vegetable plots and the dark lines of freshly ploughed fields. Wooburn was a *ferme ornée* (a so-called ornamented or ornamental farm), a style of garden that combined the beauty of a pleasure ground with the agricultural elements of a working farm. It was this fusion that so intrigued and attracted Jefferson. He had read about it in Whately's *Observations,* which had praised the merging of the "simple delights" of country life with the elegance of groves of flowering shrubs and trees. Whately had described the "bleating of the sheep," the "tinklings of the bell-wether" and the "clucking of poultry" that animated the scene.

The "ornamented" part of Wooburn consisted of groves and shrubberies that bordered the paths, which were woven around the fields and meadows like colorful ribbons. According to garden fashions, the shrubberies graduated gently from low-growing scented flowers at the front to tall trees at the back, just as Washington had done in Mount Vernon. And though early April was not the most spectacular season to admire the diversity of the planting, Jefferson could already see a hint of what would come. He had missed the flowering of the snowdrops and crocuses but instead there were graceful bluish purple Canterbury bells, bright yellow *Narcissus jonquilla* and the paler primroses. Most of the shrubs were still naked and neither the rambling honeysuckles nor jasmines were yet in flower, but the crab apples in the last row of the border were covered in white blossom and the alders were dripping with yellowish pendulant catkins.

When Philip Southcote had designed Wooburn Farm in the 1730s, he had been the first to coalesce the necessities of farm life with the seemingly incongruous fashions of pleasure gardens. Across the Atlantic Washington had made a step toward this when he had decided to place his kitchen gardens next to the bowling green and shrubberies in Mount Vernon, but he had shied away from integrating vegetable plots and fields among his shrubberies. In fact, just as Jefferson was admiring Wooburn's blend of the aesthetic and the practical, Washington's slaves were raising, brick by brick, the new walls of the bullet-shaped Upper and Lower Gardens—the demarcation between the flowering shrubs around the bowling green and the fruit trees and vegetables. Wooburn's unique combination of beautiful groves with tidy farmland struck a chord with Jefferson's vision of America as a continent of both sublime beauty and vast lands that would feed the nation. The grandeur and majesty of forests was united with the fertile lands that, divided into neat fields, would bring wealth to the country. On a small scale Wooburn combined just that—beautiful groves with tidy farmland.

But Wooburn was also a horticultural reflection of the dichotomy of Jefferson's own character: his lifelong quest for moneymaking crops and useful vegetables versus his delight in ornamental plants; the contrast between the farmer and the connoisseur; and the tension between his attempts to run a profitable plantation and his insatiable love for beautiful things, just as he idealized a simple agrarian society while indulging in prodigal shopping trips in London and Paris.

Thomas Jefferson has often been described as an enigma. He was a slave owner who declared that all men were equal; a man who insisted he had no political ambition yet spent much of his life in politics. He would become the president of the United States but he saw himself foremost as farmer, gardener and philosopher. His character was so multilayered and often contradictory that successive generations have celebrated and identified with utterly different aspects of him, while leaders from every corner of the political spectrum have been able to claim "their" part of Jefferson for their own agenda. Jefferson himself famously described the conflicting forces inside him in a love letter that took the form of a long dialogue between the "Heart" and the "Head." While on the surface this letter revealed the internal battle of a man enchanted by a woman, it also helps us to understand Jefferson's attitude toward nature and his plantation.

When the Heart talked about the garden at Monticello, Jefferson described a place of breathtaking beauty: "With what majesty do we there ride above the storms! How sublime to look down into the workhouse of nature, to see her clouds, hail, snow, rain, thunder, all fabricated at our feet! And the glorious Sun, when rising as if out of a distant water, just gilding the tops of the mountains, and giving life to all nature!" This was not a description of a working plantation but a rapturous eulogy on America's landscape. Yet his Head asserted, soberly, that "Everything in this world is [a] matter of calculation," advising the Heart to "Advance then with caution, the balance in your hand." And just as the Heart and the Head were torn between emotions and reason, so Jefferson was torn at Monticello between beauty and utility.

Jefferson needed to run a profitable agricultural operation in order to pay off his debts and to sustain his expensive lifestyle, but he also wanted to create something aesthetically impressive. Like Washington, Jefferson belonged to the upper strata of Virginia society. He was a large landowner, having inherited several thousand acres from his father, to which he had added another 5,000 acres when he had married the wealthy widow Martha Wayles Skelton in 1772. Reputedly, his first memory was of being carried on a pillow by a slave and he owned almost 200 slaves. But instead of building his house and plantation in the fertile land of the valley, Jefferson had placed it on the top of a mountain with no water supply. No sensible plantation owner would have done so—plantations from Virginia to Georgia lined rivers on which the harvest was carried to the trading towns and from there to the European markets. Instead of rich yields and easy access to Richmond and Fredericksburg, Jefferson had chosen glorious views over the seemingly endless lines of the Blue Ridge Mountains that stood as the western signposts for the wilderness beyond. By moving onto a mountain, the Heart had triumphed over the Head: Jefferson had sacrificed profit for beauty, seemingly unable to hold on to both.

At Wooburn Farm, however, he saw for the first time how the beautiful could coexist with, indeed complement, the practical. It would be decades before he implemented what he had learned here and in other English gardens, but for the rest of his life Jefferson planned his ornamental farm at Monticello with fields of pasture that were nestled around the mountain like pearls on a necklace next to groves of trees and flowering shrubs—a garden in which colorful flowers vied with experimental crops and vegetable plots for the attention of the visitors. He admired Wooburn so much that he resolved to come back with Adams to show him how the English had masterfully integrated agriculture into the pleasure ground. But before he could even propose the idea, he had to return to London because the British foreign secretary, Lord Carmarthen, had suddenly requested a new draft of the commercial treaty.

ONCE AGAIN Adams and Jefferson labored over the details and wording of a treaty that they knew was unlikely ever to be signed by the British. Adams was frustrated because he had not accomplished much in the past year. Not only was he trying to negotiate with the British about their trade but he also had to deal with the unfulfilled agreements from the peace treaty. There was the issue of compensation for the slaves and property that the British had confiscated during the war, as well as the continuous presence of the British in areas of the United States where they still occupied their garrisons. There had been little progress because the British were reluctant to deal at all with their former colonies and for the most part Lord Carmarthen refused even to acknowledge Adams's and Jefferson's letters.

The negotiations with His Excellency Abdrahaman, envoy of the sultan of Tripoli and representative of the Barbary States, had been equally humiliating. Adams had met him several times and had gone to great lengths to please him, smoking a two-meter-long pipe "in aweful Pomp, reciprocating Whiff for Whiff" so perfectly that he had been praised: "Monsieur, votes etes un Turk." But while arousing this admiration in such woefully undignified circumstances, it had dawned on Adams that the $80,000 Congress had granted for the "tribute" was far from enough. If America did not increase the budget, Adams feared, there would be "a universal and horrible War." Only in the previous week, just before Jefferson had gone on his garden tour, Abdrahaman warned them that the Barbary States were ready to attack American vessels, for "it was written in their Koran" and therefore their duty to fight the enemies of Islam.

Nor was the British public in any mood to help its former colonies: "An ambassador from America! Good heavens what a sound!" the *London Public Advertiser* had scoffed upon Adams's arrival in London the previous summer. Adams had been right to be anxious about his new post: the British hated the Americans. "This People cannot look me in the Face," he wrote after attending a ball—"there is a conscious Guilt and Shame in their Countenances." Everybody, Jefferson agreed, was pugnacious toward the Americans—the king, the newspapers, and the courtiers. Even the British government and the opposition agreed for once in their hostility. Putting forward a slightly eccentric theory, Jefferson mused if it was "the quantity of animal food" consumed by the British that "renders their character insusceptible of civilisation." Jefferson for his part had an aversion toward the British as well, which had deep roots from long before the War of Independence. Like George Washington and other Virginia planters, he had been caught in a tangle of debts and spiraling interest payments with the British tobacco merchants.* To him England was corrupt and her government despotic. It was a nation that perpetuated inequality, ruled by "nobility, wealth, and pomp," he sneered. Their rude manners and unwillingness to cooperate with the United States of America had only strengthened this animosity.

Despite their misgivings, Jefferson and Adams went back to the trade treaty, but once they had dispatched the new draft on 4 April, there was nothing much to do other than wait for a reply. Jefferson was keen to

---

* While he was in England, Jefferson also wrote to one of the merchants, claiming that "To pay that debt at once then is a physical impossibility." Having lost much of his harvests because of the war, Jefferson ended his letter, writing "We deem your nation the aggressors."

continue his excursions. In London, he said, "I have lost a great deal of time in ceremony, returning visits &c." and knowing that he might never return to Britain, he wanted to inspect as many of the famous gardens as possible.

Adams was a willing companion. Over the previous weeks he would have heard much praise about the English garden because Jefferson was not the only American garden enthusiast in London. Adams and Jefferson had met William Hamilton, a fellow gardener from Philadelphia who had toured England to get some ideas for his own estate, The Woodlands. Jefferson would later describe it as "the only rival I have known in America to what may be seen in England." Gardens were probably the only topic the three men were able to talk about, as Hamilton had not been a supporter of the revolutionary cause and in 1778 he had even been tried for treason.

Unlike Jefferson and Hamilton, the frugal John Adams never intended to re-create the grand gardens that he visited. Despite being ambitious, he simply would not have been able to afford it because he was not a wealthy landowner. Adams had inherited forty acres in the village of Braintree (which would later become incorporated in the town of Quincy), a few miles outside Boston to which he had added several small parcels over the years. Until his appointments in France and Britain, his main income had come from his work as a lawyer. His garden was not so much an elegant ornamental landscape as a typical kitchen garden with an orchard that supplied fruits and vegetables for his family. Far from being any less appreciative of beautiful gardens, the impetuous and sometimes short-tempered Adams found they had a powerful and therapeutic effect on him. The sturdy trunks of trees with sinuous roots clawed into the soil, wind rustling through the leaves, branches laden with fruit and sweet-smelling flowers created a peaceful world of "tranquil Walks" that Adams found enchantingly relaxing.

Throughout his life Adams felt that cities, with their "putrid Streets," were harmful to health and mind. He always made it a priority to find time for rural excursions, particularly when the pressures of politics became too much. Like Jefferson and Washington, Adams regarded himself as a farmer first and always preferred being in his fields or in his garden to other pursuits. It was the "zeal at my Heart, for my country," Adams said, that kept him in politics, not a particular love for it.

When the Continental Congress had discussed the future of the thirteen colonies in 1775, Adams had escaped as often as possible to visit the country estates outside the city. "Such Excursions are very necessary to preserve our Health, amidst the suffocating Heats of the City, and the wasting, exhausting Debates of the Congress," he had written to Abigail, who had stayed behind to manage the farm. Over the years he had seen many of America's finest gardens and his diary was peppered with effusive descriptions of what he had seen. In London he and Abigail always invited sea captains from Boston for dinner to hear news from home and in particular "how the Trees flourish in the common."

Gardens but also forests, fields and meadows were places where Adams could be himself. He was never happier than when planting, pruning apple trees or getting his hands dirty in the "old swamp . . . digging stumps and Roots." The sturdy New Englander made an awkward figure at Court. He never learned the art of flattery, gracious dancing or small talk and felt more comfortable delving into ditches or ploughing his fields than conversing with European ambassadors in gilded drawing rooms. Social life in Europe, he felt, was "an insipid round of hairdressing and play," and he would have preferred to return home "to Farming."

On 4 April 1786, less than twenty-four hours since Jefferson had walked among the meadows of Wooburn Farm, he and Adams set off in a hired post chaise with their two servants. They drove along the Thames toward the west, passing the villas and gardens that hugged the river. They made quick progress as the network of roads lacing the English countryside was the best in Europe—much envied by foreign tourists who thought that traveling in England was far preferable to continental travel. Their first stop was Wooburn Farm—Jefferson must have talked so enthusiastically about it that Adams was eager to see it too. He agreed that Wooburn Farm was "beautifull," and couldn't wait to tell Abigail about it. For, unlike the grand formal parterres they had seen at the aristocratic estates in France, the rustic and modest *fermes ornées* were more suitable gardens for an agrarian republic. Though certainly enjoyable, the garden tour was not a leisurely excursion. Most days Adams and Jefferson traveled between forty and fifty miles, often visiting several gardens. Some of these covered hundreds of acres, meaning there was little time to stroll along serpentine paths or sit on one of the many alcoves that were scattered around the pleasure grounds. Instead the two enthusiasts hurried to see as many gardens as possible. Jefferson in particular thought that too much detail during sightseeing "will load the memory with trifles, fatique the attention" and thus be a complete waste of time. He was not here to admire tranquil groves and sweet-smelling shrubs for the sake of their beauty but to gather as much knowledge as he could.

Talking to gardeners, Jefferson insisted, was a much more useful occupation than to "waste my time on good dinners and good society." As a guidebook Jefferson and Adams relied on Whately's *Observations,* which described the gardens they wanted to see in great detail as well as explaining the general design principles of the English garden. The descriptions, Jefferson thought, were "remarkeable for their exactness" and "models of perfect elegance." He carried his copy with him, scribbling comments in the margins as well as taking notes so that he could apply these lessons to his garden at Monticello.*

As Adams and Jefferson walked together through the gardens, they made an odd pair. Where Jefferson was tall and thin, almost gangly, Adams was shorter and rounder—reputedly they had once been compared to a candlestick and a cannonball. At six feet two and a half inches, Jefferson towered about seven inches over the stout Adams, who had put on so much weight that his wife pitied the horse that had to carry him. Jefferson's powdered hair and elegant Parisian clothes gave him the air of a polished diplomat. He accentuated his sophistication with striped silk waistcoats, starched ruffles and cravats. During their garden tour he even went to the hairdresser. Adams preferred a plainer style. At heart he was a farmer and, unlike the other ambassadors at the courts in Versailles and St. James's, who were swaddled in ribbons, wrapped in lace and decorated with expensive jewels, Adams wore sturdy broadcloth. He proudly carried the aura of simple republican life and said that he had no drop of blood in his veins "but what is American."

These differences in appearance reflected deeper contrasts in character. Adams was confrontational, assertive and direct. Franklin thought that Adams was "always an honest Man, often a Wise One, but sometimes and in some things, absolutely out of his Senses." Many people respected Adams for being forthright but even friends like Jefferson admitted he was sometimes "vain" and "irritable" (though Jefferson also insisted that nothing else was "ill" about his friend). By contrast Jefferson avoided conflict wherever possible because he felt an "abhorrence of dispute." He was astonished at what Adams had to endure during the protracted treaty negotiations: "Indeed the man must be of rock, who can stand all this," he confided to Abigail. "It would have illy suited me. I do not love difficulties." He was intensely private ("I keep what I feel to myself"), a characteristic that Adams had seen firsthand the previous year when Jefferson withdrew from society for several months after receiving the tragic news that his two-year-old daughter, Lucy (who had remained in Virginia), had died of whooping cough. Exhausted with grief, he "confined

---

* Adams also bought a copy of the book, noting in the margins which gardens he had visited with Jefferson.

himself from the world," just as he had done when his wife, Martha, had died in 1782 after Lucy's birth.

Jefferson was a quiet, thoughtful man. His composure was always controlled and never "ruffled," as a contemporary observed. Where he was reserved, Adams was openhearted and chatty. Adams talked a lot—too much, he often realized—and sometimes envied Washington, Franklin and Jefferson for their ability to hold their tongue. Even when he read, Adams entered into a dialogue—with the author—scribbling in his books "Fool! Fool!" or an approving "Excellent!" Adams's diary was infused with his innermost anxieties, emotions and hopes, while Jefferson's summaries of the day consisted of detailed account books. "Nothing was too small for him to keep an account of," his overseer at Monticello later said, as Jefferson filled row after row with neat lists of even his most trivial expenses. In his diary Adams recounted the conversations of the dinner parties he attended, while Jefferson calculated the average cost of the meal per person.

But they also had much in common: their love for the young republic, an insatiable curiosity for the world around them, as well as a passion for books, learning, agriculture and, of course, gardens. While the two had lived in France, Adams's house in Auteuil had become almost a second home for the widowed Jefferson, and when the Adamses left for London, the lonely Jefferson missed them terribly: "The departure of your family has left me in the dumps," he wrote to Adams, adding "my afternoons hang heavily on me." Now at last the two friends had time to enjoy each other's company once again.

On the second day of their tour Adams and Jefferson headed to the village of Buckingham. Having seen the beauty of the English landscape fused with agricultural utility, they now wanted to see a garden that brought landscape and politics together: Stowe, one of the most famous gardens in England. Stowe had been created fifty years earlier by Lord Cobham,* who had set out to celebrate liberty, honor and civic duty as well as the strength of a free England. He had turned against the geometrical baroque gardens in which swirling arabesques had been cut into turf and trees had been trimmed into stiff globes, cones and pyramids. Cobham celebrated nature as it was (albeit stylized), with trees left unclipped and paths snaking sinuously through irregularly planted thickets.

He had been a staunch member of the Whigs, a political group that had

---

* Cobham had also employed some of the most famous landscape designers in Britain, including Charles Bridgeman, William Kent and Lancelot "Capability" Brown.

greatly influenced Adams's and Jefferson's political thinking by opposing monarchical tyranny in the name of liberty. In the late seventeenth century the Whigs in Britain had created a constitutional arrangement in which monarchical power was restrained by an elected parliament, thereby elevating the principle of individual liberty above the God-given rights of kings.

At the same time, some of the Whigs had begun to use their gardens to express these political ideas. Mirroring their rejection of tyranny, they had turned against the rigid designs, geometrical patterns and clipped shapes associated with Louis XIV's lavish Versailles (for them the home of absolutism and despotic rule). Over the course of the eighteenth century they had exchanged the artifice of straight canals and immaculately sheared hedges for serpentine lakes and clumps of unpruned trees. The irregularity of nature had become a symbol of liberty, or, as one of the most influential garden writers would tell Washington a few years later, it "opposes a kind of systematic despotism." Whig gardeners literally liberated the garden, and in so doing, "Freedom was given to the forms of trees," Horace Walpole—Britain's first garden historian—wrote in 1780. Jefferson adored this style, having read about it extensively in his many gardening books, and complained whenever an owner had not embraced it wholeheartedly enough—one garden "shews still too much of art," elsewhere a "straight walk" spoiled the landscape, having "an ill effect."

Stowe was particularly explicit in its political posturing, as Cobham had in the 1730s turned parts of it into a denunciation of Robert Walpole, the first prime minister of Britain. Cobham turned against the centralized power around the court and government, accusing Walpole of corruption and debauchery. In line with this, Cobham's garden told a story of the choices between virtue and vice, between reason and passion and between civic duty and vanity. His intention was to distance himself from the immorality and flaws associated with Walpole and the court.

Jefferson, who liked to be prepared, purchased a guidebook that illustrated Cobham's landscapes and monuments. At the entrance to Stowe, visitors faced the choice between a path of vice or virtue. This was a moral dilemma popularized by the classical tale of the Choice of Hercules, in which Hercules was tempted by the Goddess of Pleasure to follow the easy path of dissipation and by Virtue, who promised glory after a life of hardship. At Stowe the path of vice led to the Temple of Venus, which featured busts of famous adulteresses, and to the Temple of Bacchus, with scenes of "Mysterious Orgies"—all of which the frugal Adams thought to be "quite unnecessary as Mankind have no need of artificial Incitements, to such Amuzements." Not surprisingly he preferred the garden of virtue. This part of the garden had been inspired by a famous essay that both Adams and Jefferson had read. Written by Joseph Addison, an English Whig, it described a dream set in an ideal garden presided over by the Goddess of Liberty herself.

Addison's imaginary garden was an allegory of honor and virtue, values that the revolutionary generation held dear. He had described, for instance, a Temple of Honour to which men who had promoted "the good of their country" could retire—a sentiment that Adams and Jefferson shared. What Cobham had done at Stowe was to make Addison's allegorical landscape real. As Adams and Jefferson strolled along the gravel paths, past dozens of temples and statues, they walked through a story of political dissent.

On a grass mound and enveloped in evergreen laurel, just as Addison had described it, stood the flawless classical Temple of Ancient Virtue housing Greek philosophers, lawgivers and thinkers that embodied wisdom, virtue and moderation. Opposite it and within sight—as if engaged in a political dialogue—was the Temple of Modern Virtue. Cobham had deliberately built it as a ruin to illustrate the moral decline caused by the prime minister's corruption and political hold over Parliament. And if this allusion was not strong enough, Cobham had also placed a headless statue dressed in contemporary clothes next to the ruin—it did not take a huge leap of imagination to identify the figure as the prime minister Robert Walpole.

Anything that criticized the British government as depraved would have delighted Adams and Jefferson, for whom "it was certainly the most corrupt and unprincipled government on earth." Yet what Cobham had created in Stowe went even further, for it aligned the venality and debauchery of England with an inevitable collapse of the entire country. If England followed her path of vice, she would fall just like the crumbling structure of the Temple of Modern Virtue.

Such a message would have resonated with the two statesmen, for despite their optimism about the new republic both were aware that just as the mighty Roman republic had fallen through debauchery, gluttony and corruption, America too could succumb to such evils if it was not careful. Everywhere in Europe Jefferson and Adams had been appalled by the love for luxury and utter laxity of morals that they feared could easily descend on their young nation and bring about its downfall. "My dear Country men! how shall I perswade you, to avoid the Plague of Europe?," Adams wrote home, as if the vice of Europe was somehow infectious. Young men and women were particularly susceptible to the seductions of the Old World. It was wrong to send them to England and

The crumbling ruin of the Temple of Modern Virtue with the headless statue
to the far left and the elegant Temple of Ancient Virtue at Stowe—
illustrations from Stowe's guidebook

France for their education, Jefferson warned, because "There is a great
deal of ill to be learnt here." Luxury had "bewitching Charms," Adams
echoed, declaring that if he had the power he would banish from America
"all Gold, silver, precious stones, Alabaster, Marble, Silk, Velvet and
Lace." Americans should lead a simpler life away from the hedonistic
excesses of Europe and follow a path of civic duty, not individual gratification. The indulgence in luxury made people weak and effeminate,
thereby corrupting a society, while public virtue, Adams insisted, was
"the only Foundation of Republics."

As Adams and Jefferson walked along, these fundamental beliefs of the
revolutionary generation were reflected in Cobham's garden. Opposite
the Temple of Modern Virtue, on the far bank of a snaking river, they saw
the Temple of British Worthies, which eulogized those who had stood for
such public virtue. This was Cobham's answer to the "Temple of Honour" in Addison's essay. In sixteen niches, Cobham had placed busts of
British heroes divided into men of action and of ideas, including King
Alfred, Edward the "Black Prince," and William III—all embodiments of
the Whig ideals, representing freedom and liberty, for they had fought
against the shackles of tyranny.* Adams admired the celebration of virtu-

* In Cobham's Temple of British Worthies, the seven men (and one woman) of
action were King Alfred, Prince Edward, Elizabeth I, William III, Walter Raleigh,
Francis Drake, parliamentarian John Hampden, merchant and politician John
Barnard. The eight men of ideas were poet Alexander Pope, financier and philan-
thropist Thomas Gresham, architect Inigo Jones, John Milton, William Shake-

The Temple of British Worthies at Stowe

ous exemplars who served the public good. And Jefferson, with his passion for Enlightenment thinking and science, realized that this kind of monument to leaders and thinkers was exactly what he wanted for Monticello: a pantheon of heroes who stood for liberty and virtue as well as lauding the advances of science, political philosophy and exploration.

A few months after the visit to Stowe, Jefferson began to compile his own collection. Like Cobham, he acquired Francis Bacon, Isaac Newton and John Locke ("my trinity of the three greatest men the world had ever produced," Jefferson said), as well as William Shakespeare, seventeenth-century parliamentarian John Hampden and explorer Walter Raleigh. To Raleigh he would later add Columbus, Magellan, Vespucci and Cortez, as "our country should not be without the portraits of its first discoverers." And because he would celebrate America's revolutionaries instead of princes and kings, Jefferson asked Adams for his portrait "to add it to those of other principal American characters which I have or shall have." Among many others that he acquired were portraits and busts of Franklin, Washington, Madison and Thomas Paine. Probably inspired by Cobham's temple, Jefferson would later call his paintings and busts "my American worthies"—the largest private collection of American heroes in the country.

---

speare, John Locke, Isaac Newton and Francis Bacon. John Locke in particular was important for the American revolutionaries because his famous *Second Treatise of Civil Government* with its argument of natural rights and social contract had influenced much of their political thinking.

Continuing their tour of Stowe, Adams and Jefferson found yet more inspiration when they came across sheep which seemed to be grazing in the midst of the garden. Only when they came closer did they see how these pastures had been separated from the pleasure grounds by a deep ditch that encircled the entire garden. This was a ha-ha,* the most revolutionary gardening device of the eighteenth century. Because cattle couldn't cross the ditch, a ha-ha provided the same security as a fence or a wall (keeping the animals outside the ornamental garden) without spoiling the views. Instead of high walls that screened the wider landscape from the garden, the ha-ha allowed panoramic vistas across the surrounding countryside. Across England, the ha-ha had liberated gardens from their brick corsets. And in the United States Washington had already built one in Mount Vernon at the back of his house in the months after the Declaration of Independence and was about to begin the construction of another at the front of his garden. Both Adams and Jefferson would follow, building their own to incorporate vistas of the rugged American landscape—as well as pastures, farm buildings and orchards—into their garden views.

When Adams and Jefferson had finished their tour, they thought Stowe to be so "superb" that they spontaneously decided to go further north to visit more gardens. "We have Seen Magnificence, Elegance and Taste enough to excite an Inclination to see more," Adams wrote to Abigail, and with no word from Carmarthen about the draft treaty there was nothing stopping them from extending their tour further. They leafed through their garden guide deciding where to go and as the checkerboard of manured fields and pastures passed their carriage window, they had hours during which they could discuss their farms back in America—Adams's modest homestead in New England and Jefferson's large plantation in Virginia.

In the evenings over veal chops, jellies and sherry in the taverns, they could also reflect on the gardens they'd seen. Jefferson, the obsessive list maker, noted how many gardeners and laborers were needed in order "to estimate the expence of making and maintaining a garden in that style," while Adams just enjoyed the pleasure of walking through the gardens, thinking that they "were the highest Entertainment." Now he and Jefferson wanted to see The Leasowes near Birmingham, Adams wrote to Abigail, the garden created by William Shenstone, a poet and gardener

---

* The ha-ha was a French invention but had become popular in England earlier in the eighteenth century. In France it had been called an "Ah, Ah" because the French, when they first saw it, had exclaimed "Ah! Ah!" in surprise.

whom Jefferson much admired for his pastoral verse that hailed rural life.

For most tourists, however, the most popular attraction in the Midlands was Matthew Boulton's famous Soho factory in Birmingham and the beginnings of the industrial revolution. They came from around the world to see Boulton's assembly-line production of toys, candlesticks and other metal objects as well Josiah Wedgwood's labor-saving manufacture at the pottery works Etruria in Stoke-on-Trent. "I had lords and ladies to wait on yesterday," Boulton had boasted some years previously, "I have Spaniards today; and tomorrow I shall have Germans, Russians and Norwegians." But for Adams and Jefferson a quick look around the city and a brief stop at a "manufactory of Paintings upon Paper" was quite enough. They didn't envisage America as an industrial country and therefore had no time for factories or manufacturers—"it would be a waste," Jefferson said. He liked to get out of cities as quickly as possible. "I make a job of it," he explained, "and generally gulp it all down in a day." Instead they headed west to The Leasowes.

Like Wooburn Farm, The Leasowes revealed its status as an ornamental farm through its name—*laeswe* was Old English for "pasture" or "meadow," and Leasowes is pronounced like "meadows." It was, however, not just an exercise in rusticity. Inspired by classical poetry, The Leasowes was a metaphor for a republican and simple way of life, influenced by the writings of Homer and Virgil, for whom working the soil was a model of republican virtue. The poet Alexander Pope—read by both Adams and Jefferson—had popularized these pastoral verses when he translated them to English. Toward the end of the eighteenth century, as industrialization, emerging sprawling cities and the boom in manufacturing threatened rural life, the notion of a bucolic world became even more potent in Britain. The industrious farmer untainted by avarice became the hope for the future—a world of ordered simplicity and Arcadian rhythm.

Jefferson was familiar with Shenstone's ideas and work, having copied lines from the poems into his garden notebook, and he had read Shenstone's *Unconnected Thoughts on Gardening*. From the early 1740s until his death in 1763, Shenstone had created a garden that consisted of a farm with a circuit walk studded with seats, urns and pastoral inscriptions evoking a bucolic idyll. Once again Jefferson had come prepared, reading not only Whately's account in the *Observations* but also Joseph Heely's *Letters on the Beauties of Hagley, Envil and the Leasowes* and William Shenstone's works, which included Robert Dodsley's *Description of The Leasowes*. Equipped with these books, reading while walking, Jefferson compared the writing with reality and took note of what he did and didn't like. Together with Adams, he walked up a hill that formed the southern boundary of the garden to find an octagonal seat among a circle of firs on the highest point. The landscape rolled out toward Wales in the northwest to the "blue distant mountains that skirt the horizon." The view must have reminded Jefferson of the prospect from Monticello's summit, where he was able to see the Blue Ridge Mountains that lay like crooked spines along the western border of Virginia.

They followed exactly Dodsley's map, which numbered the points of interest and Jefferson commented in his journal that the "landscape at No. 18. and prospect at 32. are fine." But Jefferson was disappointed to discover that Shenstone had not been bolder in integrating the agricultural element. "This is not even an ornamented farm," he complained, "it is only a grazing farm with a path round it," because instead of vegetable plots and fields, there were only pastures and meadows. Adams by contrast adored the "Variety of Beauties" on such a small scale. It was "the simplest and plainest," he wrote, and "the most rural of all."

As they reflected on what they had seen, the most exciting revelation of all was that the English garden was not really English at all. For the gardens they had explored during their tour were densely populated with American trees and shrubs. There were tall white pines, with their long feathery plumes of needles, and shortleaf pine, the most common yellow pine in the former colonies. Familiar shrubs such as rhododendrons and mountain laurels provided the green backbone to the shrubberies during the winter months and brought sculptured blooms in late spring. These were the groves and clumps that had grown from John Bartram's seeds and cones over the previous five decades.

Wherever Adams and Jefferson visited, they encountered scores of trees and shrubs that reminded them of home, ranging from the flowering dogwoods, which were already wrapped in virginal white blossoms, to American sycamores and birches that were bursting into spring leaf. There were many coniferous trees, such as graceful eastern hemlock and the columnar red cedar, which the Philadelphia farmer and plantsman John Bartram had always included in the seed boxes that he had sent from America to England between the 1730s and his death more than four decades later. At Stowe grew the southern catalpa, found by Bartram in the southern states, as well as the purple-flowering raspberry and mapleleaf viburnum, which, like so many other American forest species, seem to be on fire in autumn. Unlike the more subdued indigenous English species, many of these American imports were prized for the way they created a fiery spectacle when the bloodied foliage of black tupelo would compete with the reds of the maples and the aubergine purple of sweetgums.

John Bartram's American seed boxes had provided the English gardener with a new palette of hues and shapes that brought variety and colors even to the winter garden. The flowering shrubs, trees and evergreens had completely transformed the English garden and by now, Jefferson and Adams saw, the British were obsessed with American species. Having admired the English garden for so long in his books, it was only now that Jefferson realized how easy it would be to carve such gardens from the American forests, at practically no expense at all, Jefferson said, because "We have only to cut out the superabundant plants." Adams was similarly thrilled to see so many "rare Shrubbs and Trees, to which Collection America has furnished her full Share" in the English garden. Also at The Leasowes were the ubiquitous tulip poplars and black locusts that laced the sky with a delicate pattern of fresh spring green. Both trees had been introduced to Britain in the 1630s but only when Bartram had sent thousands of seeds had the trees slowly become common in the English parkland. There was arborvitae, one of the first North American coniferous trees to arrive in Europe (in the 1530s), but like the tulip poplar, it had only became widely and cheaply available when Bartram dispatched it regularly.

THE LEASOWES WAS the most northern point of their journey. Heading back south over the next few days, Adams and Jefferson managed to visit Hagley, a 1,000-acre park that Lord Cobham's nephew George Lyttelton had built in the mid-eighteenth century, and Blenheim, one of the grandest estates in Britain. Here a team of fifty were employed to maintain the pleasure ground alone, Jefferson noted studiously in his journal. These sights made such an impression on them that Adams, years later, advised his son to see the gardens when visiting England, for these estates, he said, "are the greatest Curiosities." What they had seen, Jefferson wrote to a friend, "indeed went far beyond my ideas."

By 10 April, just under a week since they had set off, they were back in London, "charmd with the beauties." They were not so taken, however, with the lack of news from the British ministers. Jefferson dismissed all attempts to negotiate a deal with Britain as "absolutely fruitless." Instead he went shopping for books, chessmen, ribbons, toothbrushes, muslin and breeches. Because the English were famed for their mechanical arts, he also purchased several instruments that were necessary for architectural drawings and for laying out a landscape garden: a pocket level, a pantograph to enlarge and reduce drawings, a small theodolite, protractors, as well as a pocket graphometer used to transpose drawings onto the landscape, and—continuing the gardening theme—a "botanical microscope." In between shopping expeditions, Jefferson accompanied Adams and the rest of the family on a day trip to the gardens at Osterley House and Syon House just outside London. Meandering walks led through landscapes that once again featured a great number of American species. "All the Evergreens, Trees and Shrubbs were here," Adams noted in his diary.

After almost two weeks of waiting for a response from Carmarthen, Jefferson had done all his shopping and seen all the gardens he had wanted to see. "6 weeks have elapsed," he wrote in frustration, "without one scrip of a pen, or one word from a minister." Yet although this particular political mission was futile, for Jefferson it ultimately didn't matter, because "We are young, and can survive them; but their rotten machine must crush under the trial."

On 25 April, Adams and Jefferson wrote to John Jay, the United States secretary of foreign affairs, summarizing what had been achieved (or not). That day the Portuguese Minister with whom they had also negotiated had accepted their commercial treaty and would send it to Lisbon to be ratified (which it never was), but at the same time they had to accept that no one in Britain was interested in signing a treaty with the United States. Adams and Jefferson also feared that the deal with the Barbary States would be "very tedious and expensive" and "without success." With no leeway to negotiate because the budget Congress had authorized was so small, there was not much that they could do—it was a mere "drop in the bucket," Jefferson complained.*

It was time for Jefferson to return to Paris, but not before one last shopping trip at The Vineyard in Hammersmith just outside the city, one of the most prized nurseries in the country. Founded by Lewis Kennedy and James Lee more than four decades previously, the nursery was famed for its vast choice of foreign species. They had received some of the few and precious seeds that Joseph Banks had brought from the *Endeavour*

---

* In January 1787, Adams signed a treaty of protection with Morocco, paid for by "gifts" to the Emperor of Morocco. When Washington became president, he spent around 15 percent of the annual national budget on the Barbary States. Only in 1816, when the British and Dutch attacked Algiers, did the threat of the Barbary pirates stop.

voyage from Australia in 1771 (they raised the first eucalyptus tree in Britain), while plant collectors from Kew Gardens regularly supplied South African and Asian seeds and bulbs.

Yet none of these precious exotics interested Jefferson—all he wanted to buy were American plants for his friends in France. If the French wanted to create *le jardin anglais,* they needed the glossy evergreens, spring-flowering shrubs and towering trees of Jefferson's native forests. When he left for Paris he had in his luggage the seed catalogue of The Vineyard nursery and had ordered more than seventy American plants. It was easier for Jefferson to procure these seeds and saplings from a London nursery than directly from America—only a few months later he would realize just how difficult it was, when the seeds that he had ordered from South Carolina traveled on a roundabout way from Charleston to Paris via New York, Lorient and Le Havre.

The irony was that the English garden was in fact American. "It is now a fashion in England," one German garden lover observed, "to create plantations which consist almost entirely of seeds from America." In a strange twist, at the very moment that the colonies had become independent, American species had become the mainstays of the most fashionable English groves and shrubberies. Adams was delighted, and over the next two summers, he and his family visited as many gardens as they could. With Jefferson gone, Adams bought his own copy of Whately's *Observations.* But they missed Jefferson and his horticultural knowledge. "We wished for your Company," Adams wrote to Paris two months after Jefferson had left, bombarding his friend with questions about the gardens in France and how they compared with the ones they had seen during their tour.

Adams went on his own to Thorndon in Essex, where the late Lord Petre had planted John Bartram's first seeds more than fifty years before. Petre had been hailed as the most innovative landscape designer of his age when he had created the parkland in the 1730s. He had drawn with Bartram's trees as if they were "Living Pencils," using their height, foliage and texture like brushstrokes in a vast landscape painting. Instead of enforcing patterns on nature with pruning shears, the American trees themselves provided the shapes and color. By the early 1740s there were so many American plants in Thorndon that one of the visitors had written, "when I walk amongst them, One cannot well help thinking He is in North American thickets—there are such Quantities."

Adams was so impressed by the way the English used American native species that he made "a List of these Trees, Shrubbs and Flours," because "Larches, Cydresses, Laurells are here as they are every where." It was almost as if the English adoration of American plants made him appreciate their beauty more. What he did not understand, however, was why the owners spent so little time on their estates. They seemed, Adams said, "very indifferent to their Beauties." Why have a place like this, he asked, if the "beauty, Convenience, and Utility . . . are not enjoyed by the owners"? For a man who relished every minute that he could spend in a garden, it seemed absurd to create such picturesque landscapes and never walk among the groves.

Both Jefferson and Adams were profoundly inspired by these pleasure grounds. For now, though, their gardens flourished only in their imagination, nourished by garden books and visits—Adams in Britain, Jefferson having to make do with France. When the Adamses left London in late spring 1788, they packed books, seeds and plant lists of American trees, shrubs and flowers in the English garden, all of which would be indispensable once they had returned to their own farm. Back home, there were "many places" where ornamental farms such as those they had admired at Wooburn Farm and The Leasowes could be constructed. England's gardens were an inspiration, but in America they would be able to take them even further and for less money, because "Nature has been more liberal" to America than to "most of the places here," the Adamses said. Just before their departure, Abigail wrote to Jefferson that they couldn't wait to return: "improveing my Garden has more charms for my fancy, than residing at the court of Saint Jame's where I seldom meet with Characters So innofensive as my Hens & chickings, or minds so well improved as my Garden."

O F E V E R Y T H I N G one could see in England, Jefferson believed, gardens in particular were important for Americans. They might have failed to negotiate a trade treaty with Britain and the Barbary States, but they had discovered how important America had been in the creation of the gardens of the old enemy. Now it was easy for Jefferson to admit that the English garden "surpasses all the earth"—he could wholeheartedly embrace them without feeling unpatriotic because they were populated with American plants and shaped by ideas of liberty. When Adams and Jefferson returned to the United States, they would lay out gardens that were directly inspired by what they had seen in England.

3

"A NURSERY OF
AMERICAN STATESMEN"

The Constitutional Convention in 1787
and a Garden Visit

WHEN THE BELLS CHIMED their brassy melody on 13 May 1787, Philadelphia's citizens rushed into the streets despite the unusually cold and wet weather. The men of the First City Troop of Light Horse, in their smart white-and-black uniforms, sat on their horses in straight formation at the edge of the Schuylkill River. As the elegant carriage crossed the river at Gray's Ferry, the men raised their hands and saluted George Washington. When the carriage rolled on, they rode beside it to the city center, where the artillery waited to welcome the hero with celebratory gunfire. Looking through the window, Washington could see the crowds that lined the streets in the rain, cheering and waving.

He had been on the road for the past five days, having left Mount Vernon while his slaves planted corn. It had been an exhausting journey because rain had hindered his progress and strong winds had made the crossing of rivers dangerous. But Washington was not the only one who had left home that month. Eleven years after they had declared independence, delegates from across the states traveled once again to Philadelphia.*

---

* Delegates were sent by eleven states, with the exception of Rhode Island, which refused to attend altogether, and New Hampshire, which would send delegates later because they couldn't afford the travel expenses at this time.

Some rode across the mountains and others came by carriage down the muddy roads. It was rough traveling, for America's roads were notoriously bad—"every minute you run the risk of turning over," as one French tourist complained. Several weeks passed before the full number of delegates had at last arrived, and it would take four months of heated discussions, long speeches and circular arguments before they would be able to return home again. During those long summer months they would assemble every day except Sundays behind closed doors and windows to argue about the future of the Union.

The reason for their gathering was that many had lost confidence in the Articles of Confederation, the first Constitution of the United States. This had been drafted in the months following the Declaration of Independence and adopted five years later, in 1781. Because the Union had been formed as a war alliance, the Articles of Confederation had granted Congress no real power to make decisions about the day-to-day running with regard to the levying of taxes and managing foreign affairs. As a result, after the war ended in 1783, the states had retreated into parochialism, often pursuing their own narrow interests at the expense of others in a determined attempt to restore local economies ravaged by the war.

New York, for example, now imposed duties on vessels coming from New Jersey, and many states were still using non-interchangeable currencies. No money was paid into the public treasury, and when people spoke of "my country," they usually meant their state rather than the United States. The Declaration of Independence had spawned only two national institutions: the army, which had been reduced to a handful of regulars after the war, and Congress, which now found itself impotent. When a group of farmers in Massachusetts rebelled against tax and debt collections late in the summer of 1786, many began to fear that anarchy might spread across the states unless Congress was given more legislative and administrative muscle.

Some of the men who had united the colonies in the fight for independence now saw the need to make the alliance stronger, believing that the former colonies had to become one nation if they wanted to survive. George Washington, for example, was certain that if nothing changed it would "be our downfal as a Nation," adding that this was as obvious to him as "the A.B.C." John Adams, who was still in London and who felt the lack of congressional power whenever he tried to negotiate on the Union's behalf in Europe, agreed that something had to be done because to his mind Congress had been reduced to nothing more than "a diplomatic assembly." Writing to Washington, John Jay, the secretary of foreign affairs, similarly warned that the failure to change the Articles would "threaten to blast the Fruit we expected from our 'Tree of Liberty.' " Many were disheartened, but among all of them one stood out—Thomas Jefferson's most loyal friend and fellow Virginian, James Madison.*

A mere five foot six—slight even by eighteenth-century standards and "no bigger," as one contemporary put it, "than half a piece of soap"—the frail and quiet Madison faced the threat of being eclipsed by the more dynamic, colorful orators of the revolution. But his appearance belied an iron will and a legislative genius. "Never have I seen so much mind in so little matter," one observer marveled, and his wife, Dolley, would later call him "great little Madison." A congressman for Virginia and son of a plantation owner who had long voiced concerns about what he saw as "dangerous defects in the Confederation," Madison had relentlessly lobbied for the convention and spent months preparing for it. The assiduous thirty-six-year-old who had studied law, among other subjects, at Princeton University, had approached the task with a tenacious diligence. He had ordered from Jefferson a trunkful of books from London and Paris in order to study the governments of modern and ancient republics, and as a result had written two essays, "Notes on Ancient and Modern Confederacies" and "Vices of the Political System of the United States," neat summaries to which he could refer during the sessions in the coming months.

He favored a single, strong federal government over a many-tentacled confederacy of independent states because the rivalry between the states threatened to unbalance the Union. North Carolina, for example, was "a patient bleeding at both Arms," taxed by Virginia and South Carolina. New Jersey was in a similar predicament, being taxed by both Pennsylvania and New York. The competing states therefore needed something like a "disinterested & dispassionate umpire," Madison believed, which would require much more than merely amending the Articles of Confederation. What Madison sought to secure at the convention was nothing less than a brand-new constitution that would form the foundation of the American nation.

Unsurprisingly, as the driving force behind the convention Madison had been the first to arrive in Philadelphia, on 5 May 1787.† It had also been he who had managed to lure Washington away from his garden and

---

* Jefferson and Madison had first met in 1776 and had become friends in 1779 when Jefferson was governor of Virginia and Madison his adviser in the Executive Council.

† The delegates were scheduled to meet on 14 May 1787, but it was not until 25 May that a quorum was reached.

fields in Mount Vernon, in the belief that the hero of the revolution would imbue the convention with the necessary patriotic gravitas. It had taken Madison many months of persistent arguing, but after much reluctance, Washington had finally relented.

The summer of 1787 was one of the most important moments in the history of the United States. During these weeks the fifty-five delegates of the Constitutional Convention overcame their differences—temperamental, political, regional and economic—to forge a legal framework on which the country would be built. While most ordinary Americans did not see the states as one nation, many of these men understood that they had to become one country, economically and culturally. "Let us look to our National character," Washington said to Madison, for "We are either a United people, or we are not."

Such rhetoric was crucial, for, as they arrived from across the United States the delegates made an incongruous group, both in terms of their respective states' agendas and their own backgrounds. Some had degrees from the best universities in America, while others had no formal education at all. There were wealthy slave owners, financiers and city lawyers as well as small farmers and land speculators. They were from the South and the North, some protecting the rights of the small states that feared being squashed by the large ones, others zealously fighting for slavery. Some were pompous, others were plain, some were silent during the debates, others were enthusiastic orators. The youngest delegate was twenty-six years and the oldest—Benjamin Franklin—was eighty-one.

But there were also similarities: of the fifty-five delegates more than half were farmers or came from a planter's background. For many of them, agriculture, plants and politics were parts of one single endeavor—the creation of a country that was independent, industrious and virtuous, a country that would not succumb to the same corruption, decadence and tyranny that had destroyed ancient republics and Europe. They believed that farmers were the backbone of society. Husbandmen, as Madison said, were "the best basis of public liberty, and the strongest bulwark of public safety." At the same time, the delegates' interest in plants, agriculture and gardens granted a welcome relief from the tedium of the protracted and fraught discussions, as many of them escaped together on excursions to country estates and gardens. One of these visits in particular—to John Bartram's magnificent garden on the outskirts of Philadelphia, halfway through the convention—arguably had an even more important part to play in the birth of the Constitution.

· · ·

As the delegates in Philadelphia began the painstaking work of thrashing out a new constitution, Jefferson—who, like Adams, sent advice from Europe throughout the discussions—was fighting another battle in Paris. It too would involve plants and nature, and was part of his crusade to give America a strong national image and identity. Unlike the delegates in Philadelphia, however, the tools he used were native trees, the weights of American mammals, a pelt of a panther and the bones and skin of a moose.

For the past few years the accomplished Virginian had been seeking to refute the French theory of the "degeneracy of America." Noting how European grains, vegetables and fruits often grew quickly but then failed to mature in America, and how imported animals did not thrive, some French scientists insisted that flora and fauna degenerated when "transplanted" from the Old to the New World. America's native species fared no better because they were fewer and all of them inferior, the scientists argued. To make matters worse, some also insisted that even humans did not mature properly in the New World—they had children early and their health declined while still young. One of these scientists was Georges-Louis Leclerc, comte de Buffon, the most famous French naturalist of his age. He wrote that in America all things "shrink and diminish under a niggardly sky and unprolific land."

As these theories and arguments spread, the natural world of the United States became a metaphor for its political and cultural significance. So, by the same logic, Jefferson reasoned, if he could prove that everything was in fact larger and grander in the New World, he would elevate his country above those in Europe. Nature had thus become a weapon of political battles and patriotic endeavors. Jefferson had consulted written accounts, including John Bartram's travel journal and Humphry Marshall's recently published *Arbustrum Americanum: The American Grove*, the first botanical book about America's plants to be written by an American and published in the United States. He also asked friends and acquaintances to send him the biggest specimens of different mammals from across the thirteen states, compiled a list of measurements to correct Buffon, and requested details from his former guardian, Thomas Walker, of "the heaviest weights of our animals . . . from the mouse to the mammoth." *

Jefferson was not the first American to take up the dispute. Before his

---

* Jefferson also kept a weather diary in America because Buffon blamed the climate for the degeneracy. In spring 1784, Jefferson encouraged Madison to do the same and both men continued these records for the rest of their lives.

return from Paris to Philadelphia in 1785, Benjamin Franklin had found his own, typically striking way to refute the French theory. While still in Paris as the American minister, he had attended a dinner party together with Abbé Raynal, one of the offending scientists. As Raynal was elaborating his favorite subject, Franklin noted that all the American guests were sitting on one side of the table with the French opposite. Seizing the opportunity to make his point with as much flair as possible, he offered his challenge: "Let both parties rise, and we will see on which side nature had degenerated." As it happened, Franklin had told Jefferson, all the Americans were of the "finest stature," while the French were all diminutive—in particular Raynal, "a mere shrimp."

Franklin's argument might have been charming, but Jefferson approached the challenge more scientifically. Before leaving for France, he had packed an "uncommonly large panther skin" in preparation for his fight and ordered a moose from Vermont to show Buffon its enormous size. Even Madison had found time to assist during his intensive studies of ancient republics and dissected animals to provide Jefferson with detailed measurements of organs, bones and even the "length of nails" of a weasel. Part of this battle for America was a short book that Jefferson wrote (the only one he ever published): *Notes on the State of Virginia*, first published in French in 1785. Jefferson was finally preparing the first English edition just as the delegates in Philadelphia were arguing about the Union's future.

Notes on the State of Virginia was much more than a description of Virginia. It was a celebration of the whole of North America through its flora and fauna, because Jefferson believed that there was "nothing so charming as our own country." Not only was the United States of America magnificent, it was also "made on an improved plan," for Europe was only "a first idea, a crude production, before the maker knew his trade," Jefferson wrote. Adams agreed, insisting that the French scientists had conjured up "despicable dreams," and praising Jefferson in public for having "exposed the mistakes." Adams so thoroughly approved of the *Notes* that when he had his portrait painted he posed with a copy of it.*

In Jefferson's book the flora and fauna of the continent became the foot soldiers of a patriotic battle to prove that America was vigorous and strong. Under the banner of the-bigger-the-better, he listed the weights of bears, buffalos and panthers to prove his point. Even the weasel, he wrote, courtesy of Madison's measurements, was "larger in America than

---

* This was Mather Brown's portrait of Adams, in which he changed the title to *Jefferson Hist. of Virginia*.

in Europe." The Scandinavian reindeer was so small, Jefferson was reported to have boasted to Buffon, that it "could walk under the belly of our moose." Best of all, however, was the American "mammoth"—the mastodon—which according to Jefferson was the largest of all animals. Though only bones had been found of this relative of modern elephants, Jefferson included it in his list because he believed that it was still roaming somewhere in the unexplored West. Its gargantuan proportions made it the perfect symbol for the powerful and independent nation. Jefferson also added a long catalogue of native plants, dividing them into four categories—medicinal, edible, useful and ornamental—at the same time demonstrating his impeccable botanical knowledge by recording all plants by both their common and Latin names.*

None of the ornamental plants that Jefferson listed were small wildflowers. Instead his line-up included magnificent trees such as tulip poplar, flowering shrubs such as eastern redbud and climbers such as trumpet honeysuckle. The only exception in this list was Spanish moss, which, though neither a tree, shrub nor climber, added to the majestic appearance of trees such as live oak in the South. But there were no lady's slipper orchids with their pouchlike blossom or bloodroot, which grew like carpets of white petals across all thirteen states. Pretty as they might have been, delicate forest flowers had no place in Jefferson's portrayal of this mighty nation.

In the *Notes* Jefferson was also the first to provide a botanical description of the stately pecan tree. Today it is one of the most valuable cultivated native trees, but British and French botanists knew little about it and had not been able to describe it accurately because only the nuts were known. Jefferson was desperate to parade it in France and asked Madison to "procure and send me an hundred or two" of the nuts. Native to the mainly unsettled Mississippi Valley, it was almost impossible to obtain—even Bartram did not grow them in his nursery. For months Madison tried to find a supplier and the amount he finally received was only a fraction of what Jefferson had wanted. Madison sent them on to Jefferson via Adams in London but continued his search. On 15 May, just as the first delegates were arriving in Philadelphia, Madison finally received another box of nuts, which he immediately dispatched to France. The news of the arrival of the horticultural treasure spread

---

* Apart from his own observations, Jefferson also referred to his botanical books in order to compile this list, which included Carl Linnaeus's work, Frederick Gronovious's *Flora Virginica* and Philip Miller's *Gardeners Dictionary*. He might have also included local knowledge about medicinal plants as used by Native American tribes.

quickly among the delegates and ten days later Washington sent some pecans to Mount Vernon, advising his new estate manager and nephew George Augustine Washington to "plant as soon as you can."*

The delegates' interest in new plants was not surprising because, unlike other farmers in the thirteen states, many of them experimented with new agricultural methods, exchanged seeds and created fashionable gardens. Franklin might have called them *"une assemblée des notables"* for their political clout, but he could equally have been referring to their progressive attitude to agriculture and gardening. Several were members of the two (brand-new) agricultural societies in the United States of America that had been founded specifically to improve agricultural methods—a "purely patriotic" goal, as one of the members explained. Washington had been elected to both societies and wished that "every State in the Union would institute similar ones." Of the representatives for Pennsylvania, four were members of the Philadelphia society, including Franklin and George Clymer, another signatory of the Declaration of Independence. Two of the delegates from South Carolina were founding members of the South Carolina Agricultural Society, and Caleb Strong, a delegate from Massachusetts, would become the president of the future Massachusetts Society for Promoting Agriculture.

Other delegates with a keen interest in plants and agriculture were George Mason from Virginia and Daniel of St. Thomas Jenifer from Maryland, who both had large gardens at their plantations and had sent trees to Washington after the Mount Vernon conference in spring 1785. There was also the lawyer and Virginia plantation owner George Wythe, Jefferson's old teacher and friend, who swapped fruits and crops with him and John Dickinson, a wealthy plantation owner and the author of *Letters from a Farmer in Pennsylvania*. Adams had admired Dickinson's "fine Gardens" at Fairhill, just outside Philadelphia, before they had been destroyed during the War of Independence. Even Robert Morris, the "financier" of the American Revolution, had switched his interest to agriculture and horticulture, dispatching Bartram's seed boxes to Jefferson in France and redesigning his estate, The Hills.

As the Constitutional Convention got under way, many of the delegates seized the opportunity to exchange horticultural tips—Mason from Virginia, for example, quizzed Hugh Williamson from North Carolina about the price of crop seeds in the South. Studious and comprehensive as always, Madison approached it more systematically and after a quick survey among the delegates was delighted to report back to his father at

---

* Today the pecans in Mount Vernon are the oldest trees on the estate.

their plantation Montpelier that "as far as I can learn," the crops in Pennsylvania and elsewhere in the thirteen states "have been remarkably fine," while Robert Morris asked Washington for a model of the latest plough in Mount Vernon.

Much of their time, however, was spent in the East Room of the State House—the room in which some of them had declared independence eleven years previously. They sat for at least five hours a day, six days a week, at small tables that were arranged like an opening fan around Washington, who had been unanimously voted as presiding president of the Convention. Madison had secured himself a table in the front row that oversaw the whole room so that he could see and hear everything, for he had decided to take notes of every argument, discussion and vote. Every night he transcribed the lengthy notes from these convoluted meetings, an arduous task that "almost killed" him, he admitted, but nothing would stop him from recording this historic moment. Madison, a fellow delegate observed, was "the best informed Man of any point in debate."

The delegates were sworn to secrecy. Guards were posted outside, and despite the summer heat the windows were kept shut so that no one could eavesdrop. The stakes were high—success would breathe new life into the ailing body politic, but failure would lead to a schism in the Union before it had even set foot upon the world stage. As Franklin wrote to Jefferson in Paris, failure to revise the Articles of Confederation "will show that we have not Wisdom enough among us to govern ourselves." Behind sealed doors, the delegates began to discuss America's future, and the particular issue of how power should be shared and exercised within the Union.

If there was to be a strong government, most agreed, it should be controlled by a separation of powers between the legislative, executive and judiciary branches. Adams had already carved it into the constitution of Massachusetts, and many of the delegates, if not all, were reading Adams's *A Defence of the Constitutions of Government of the United States of America,* which had been published in London in January 1787 and had just arrived to the booksellers in Philadelphia. The *Defence* advocated a system of checks and balances to keep the forces of power in equilibrium—a notion that had its roots in nature and physics. Tellingly, the epigraph that Adams chose for the title page of the book was a quote from Alexander Pope: "All Nature's difference keeps all Nature's peace."

Adams's inspiration for the political architecture of America came not only from the political philosophers whose work he admired and the lessons he had taken from ancient republics but also from the insights he had gained from his life as a husbandman. A farmer who had to drive a heavy wagon down a steep hill, he wrote in the *Defence,* would place one pair of oxen in front of the cart and one pair behind to counterbalance the pull from the load. Just as the farmer divided the forces of the oxen—"checking one power by another"—so the forces of the legislature had to be divided into two assemblies. The balance of nature, Adams insisted, was a model from which a people could learn.

In Philadelphia the delegates were discussing similar issues, and within days of their first meeting they voted that the national government was to be divided into legislative, judiciary and executive branches and that the legislature should consist of two houses (later called the House of Representatives and Senate). Yet many delegates opposed Madison's idea of a strong government for fear that too much centralized power would stop the individual states controlling their own state matters. The discussions raged on for weeks, with one of the most controversial points being how power should be distributed between the larger and smaller states. The Articles of Confederation had given each state one vote regardless of size or population, but Madison and other delegates from the larger states favored a proportional representation that would give them greater leverage in Congress. Unsurprisingly, the smaller states, such as Delaware and New Jersey, wanted to keep the one-state-one-vote system.

Some delegates believed that the representation of the states should be based on their wealth (and contribution to the Union), while others felt the determining factor should be population. Both arguments centered around the question of whether slaves were to be counted as property or as inhabitants, or not at all. As a compromise, one delegate suggested a proportional representation according to the number of free citizens to which slaves should be added, with each one counting as three-fifths of a person. This did not mean that delegates believed that slaves were only three-fifths human—instead this ratio was proposed as a measurement of the wealth that a slave brought to the economy of the different states, thus reducing them to mere numbers in the calculation of political power.

Over the next weeks the debates became more heated and with everybody at loggerheads, some state delegations were even split internally. One by one, each of the several proposals on the table was rejected. Previous decisions were overturned and debates collapsed into dead-end arguments. There were speeches that lasted a day or longer, and by the end of June everyone was complaining about the lack of progress.

"We move slowly in our business," one delegate mused, "it is indeed a work of great delicacy and difficulty, impeded at every step by jealousies and jarring interests." Another wrote that they were "still in such a stage as to render the Result very dubious." Locked up in the airless room, the delegates found the process grinding. Even the noise of the carriages passing in front of the State House seemed too much, and so the city's street commissioners were asked to put gravel down to muffle the sound. On 28 June, Franklin even suggested opening the Convention every morning with a prayer because of the lack of progress and the disagreements "on almost every Question."

Sometimes a group of delegates met at Franklin's garden, only a few blocks from the State House, to talk in private and in the fresh air. On his return from Paris in 1785 Franklin had transformed the vegetable plots behind his town house into a small walled ornamental garden consisting of a lawn surrounded by trees and flowering shrubs and gravel walks. With his retirement from the diplomatic duties in France, Franklin now had time for his "private Amusements," he said—"Conversation, Books, my Garden, and *Cribbidge*." Natural history and botany were his favorite subjects, he told a visitor during the summer of the convention. He was particularly proud of his botanical books and enjoyed showing them to visitors. For his garden Franklin had used the same gardener who had worked in the recently designed State House Yard, ensuring that the work would be executed according to the most fashionable standard. The previous summer workmen had delivered many loads of gravel, earth and sod to transform the small garden into a green oasis. Franklin had also bought seeds from Bartram's nursery and a garden roller to keep the paths and lawn perfectly smooth. Here, in the shade of the mulberry trees, the delegates found respite from the sheer tedium of constitutional debate in the State House.

As for Washington, he relaxed only when he rode into the countryside to explore farms and gardens. He visited a farmer to "see the effect of the plaister of Paris" as manure, which he had tested himself at Mount Vernon, and inspected a vineyard. He questioned so many farmers that he quickly gained a reputation as a "sturdy farmer . . . more interested in agricultural topics than in matters of strategy or politics." When the convention came to a complete deadlock over the one-state-one-vote system in the Senate, Washington went to the Agricultural Society in Carpenter's Hall, where he would have seen a display of all kinds of innovative farming implements including ploughs, hoes and carts, as well as models of mills and other agricultural machinery and buildings.

Despite his daily duty as the president of the Constitutional Convention, Washington continued to run his estate from Philadelphia. He had brought his notes and observations from the previous harvest, and every Sunday he wrote long and detailed instructions to his estate manager (expecting equally extensive reports in return). His obsession with agriculture and plants did not stop at the fields and groves. On 1 July, he wrote from Philadelphia how to finish the new dining room at Mount Vernon. The ceiling and walls of the most elegant room in the house were to be decorated with moldings of fashionable plaster swags and garlands, but instead of the typical Etruscan vases or antique urns, Washington chose wreaths shaped of interwoven wheat stalks and agricultural tools. A marble mantelpiece with carved farming scenes continued the agricultural theme.

The other delegates also found relief in the picturesque surroundings during these fraught negotiations. The city was renowned for its beautiful country estates and pleasure grounds that nestled along the winding Schuylkill River. Having to spend six days a week cooped up in the State House, the delegates of the Constitutional Convention used every opportunity to escape the stifling air. They had tea and cake at Gray's Ferry tavern on the river, which was set in a beautiful garden. Here they meandered along serpentine walks that wove through irregularly planted groves. This was America's first public pleasure park and featured shady arbors, waterfalls, artificial grottoes and even several hermitages. It had been designed by Samuel Vaughan, a wealthy London merchant and Jamaican plantation owner, shortly after his arrival in Philadelphia in the early 1780s. Vaughan had also created another garden that the delegates much enjoyed: the new State House garden, laid out just below the windows where the men were shaping the Constitution. Here they delighted in the "pensive wandering through these rural scenes," starting a tradition that a visitor still observed a few years later, when the members of the Pennsylvania House of Representatives used the garden "to compose their thoughts, or refresh themselves after any fatique of business, or confer together and converse." Washington may have felt reminded of home because, like Mount Vernon, the State House garden was laid out in meandering gravel paths, sinuous clumps and shrubberies, all planted with native species.

Even the frantically busy Madison found time to join his fellow delegates on these garden visits. Together with John Rutledge from South Carolina and Washington, Madison rode to The Woodlands to see William Hamilton's ornamental garden, which Hamilton had begun after his return from England (where he met Adams and Jefferson before they set off on their garden tour). They also went to Belmont, where the owner, Richard Peters, was experimenting with seed drills, new recipes for manures and other agricultural innovations. Both Madison and Washington corresponded with Peters on agricultural and horticultural matters after this visit and even Alexander Hamilton, the most urban of all delegates, was so impressed by Peters that he consulted him years later when laying out a garden at his house The Grange (in today's Harlem, then just outside New York).*

While Washington, Madison and their fellow delegates were finding solace in their botanical excursions, Jefferson was making sweeping plans for the future of America by fighting Buffon and forensically examining the agricultural landscape of southern Europe. On the same day that Washington instructed his estate manager about the agricultural moldings in Mount Vernon's dining room, Jefferson wrote from Paris to Adams in London about his tour of France and Italy. His doctors had recommended the waters in Aix-en-Provence to heal his broken wrist—an injury sustained from enthusiastically jumping over a large kettle in someone's backyard—and the Virginian had used the opportunity to turn the sojourn into a patriotic quest for new crops that might flourish on American farms.

Jefferson believed that every journey should be also educational, and for that purpose had compiled some instructions for American tourists in Europe. This included a list of "Objects of Attention for an American," with agriculture as number one. Following his own suggestions Jefferson had spent several months questioning farmers and gardeners along the way, trying to learn about their plants and agricultural methods. "I have courted the society of gardeners, vignerons, coopers, farmers & c.," he wrote to a friend, explaining to another that he had been "examining the culture and cultivator." After several months in France, Jefferson had gone on a three-week detour across the Alps to find out what kind of rice the Italians were growing, hoping that it would thrive in South Carolina. Under threat of the death penalty, he had smuggled "as much as my coat and surtout pockets would hold."

Today it might seem extraordinary that Jefferson risked imprisonment—and his life—for a few grains of rice, but he truly believed that they might hold the seeds of America's future. "Agriculture," Jefferson wrote that summer, was "the surest road to affluence and best preservative of morals." At the same time, horticultural espionage seemed to fill Jefferson with joy, for he described the journey as a "continued feast on objects of agriculture, new to me, and, some of them at least, susceptible

---

* Hamilton moved into The Grange in 1802. He created a garden and joked, "A garden, you know, is a very usual refuge of a disappointed politician." In December of the same year, he asked Peters for some agricultural and horticultural advice for this new arrangement because "I am as little fitted as Jefferson to guide the helm of the UStates." Peters's reply was "Spare no Expence to destroy Weeds . . . Weeds are the Jacobins of Agriculture. If you do not destroy them, they will certainly ruin you."

of adoption in America." He examined vineyards (there were more important crops for America, he decided), almonds (too "precarious") and capers (easily cultivated), but it was the olive tree that was most promising. "Of all the gifts of heaven to man, it is next to the most precious, if it be not the most precious," Jefferson wrote enthusiastically to his American friends—"this is the object for the patriots."*

Jefferson was so impatient about any new and potentially lucrative plants that he not only dispatched them to America but also tested them in his own garden in Paris. He grew, for example, sulla, which he had received from Malta, to determine its viability as animal fodder in the States. Madison also received some of these seeds during the sitting of the Convention and shared them with Washington.

In Philadelphia, meanwhile, little had been achieved. In the past seven weeks the delegates had agreed to replace the Articles of Confederation instead of simply amending them and determined that government should consist of three branches, but that was all. They had failed to make any decision about the thorny issue of representation of the states in the two houses. "It is impossible to say when the Convention will rise," one delegate wrote to his wife in New Jersey. Finally, on 5 July, a committee presented a compromise, the so-called Connecticut Plan:† in the House of Representatives the number of representatives for each state was to be in proportion to its population, while in the Senate each state would have an equal vote. However, the large states, with Virginia leading, remained opposed to the suggestion. By 10 July, Washington wrote to Alexander Hamilton (who had temporarily left the Convention to attend to some business in New York), "I wish you were back. The crisis is equally important and alarming." Franklin, as so often, alluded to nature to explain the predicament, comparing the situation with a two-headed snake (true to form, the scientifically minded Franklin had one on display in a jar) that was trying to move forward with one head around one side of a bush and the second head around the other side. The future of America depended on one head moving with the other—but with no delegate willing to change, there seemed to be no way around the impasse.

Then, late at night on Friday, 13 July, with the Convention on the verge of collapse, the botanist and Ohio land speculator Manasseh Cutler

* When John Rutledge's son traveled to France, Jefferson instructed, "I must press on you, my dear Sir, a very particular attention to the climate and culture of the Olive tree."
† It became known as the Connecticut Plan because it had originally been suggested by Connecticut delegate Roger Sherman in June when it had been rejected.

joined Madison and some other delegates for a drink after dinner at the Indian Queen, the tavern where they were boarding. When the delegates heard that Cutler had planned an excursion to Bartram's Garden for the following morning, they decided to accompany him. Known among European gardeners as an unrivaled storehouse of American flora, the nursery had more recently become famous through St. John de Crève-coeur's charming portrayal of John Bartram in his international best seller *Letters from an American Farmer*—a work that today is hailed as the "first work of American literature." We can only imagine that the delegates hoped that a day surrounded by America's magnificent trees and shrubs would calm matters and remind them just what would be at stake when they cast their votes, once again, on the following Monday.

On Saturday, 14 July, just as the sun was rising at five o'clock, James Madison, Alexander Hamilton (who had just returned from New York), Alexander Martin and Hugh Williamson from North Carolina, John Rutledge from South Carolina, Caleb Strong from Massachusetts and George Mason and his son from Virginia, together with Cutler, two Philadelphians and Samuel Vaughan, the garden designer of the State House Yard, boarded their carriages at the Indian Queen. Franklin, who had always enjoyed visits to Bartram's Garden, was not able to accompany them because his kidney stones were troubling him. They drove out of town, crossing the Schuylkill River at the floating bridge at Gray's Ferry as the morning mist veiled the surface. For the first time in weeks the temperature had dropped to a mere 61°F. The air was crisp and the dew still clung when the carriages stopped outside the gray stone house that Franklin's old friend John Bartram had built with his own hands.

Sixty years earlier the land on which the delegates now stood had been fields, but since then it had been nurtured into the country's most comprehensive collection of mature American trees and shrubs. John Bartram had died a decade earlier, in 1777, at the age of seventy-eight, but his sons John and William continued the business.

A talented botanical artist, William Bartram was also one of the most knowledgeable naturalists in America—he had "a library within himself," one fellow botanist enthused. He had received a thorough education at the Philadelphia Academy, where his teacher had used "every possible occasion, to instil republican principles into the minds of his youthful pupils." William was well known among the founding fathers. During the War of Independence, Franklin had offered to use his position as the American minister to flout the American embargo on trade with Britain by having Bartram's seed boxes sent to Paris and distributing them to Britain, as well as overseeing the printing of the French plant catalogue. A few weeks before the delegates descended on the nursery, Washington had visited* and he would later order hundreds of trees and shrubs for the garden at Mount Vernon. Jefferson, too, had always found time to see the garden when he was in Philadelphia—even while writing the Declaration of Independence—and had sent regular orders from Paris for seed boxes so that he could disperse them among French gardeners. Jefferson recommended the nursery to his friends and, knowing how much the Bartrams craved the latest plant books, he dispatched publications from Europe such as the English translations of Carl Linnaeus's botanical books.

With his connections to the leading men of his day, William was used to visits from wealthy landowners, revolutionary leaders, international botanists and tourists from across the world, but nothing had prepared him for the early-morning visit of the delegates of the Convention. As the carriages rolled to a stop outside the house, William was at work in the garden. The smartly dressed delegates found him barefoot, with his sleeves rolled up, hoeing the flowerbeds. "He at first stared at us," Cutler said, taken by surprise by so "large and gay a company so early in the morning," but within moments William's initial embarrassment was forgotten as the delegates began to question him about the trees and shrubs in the five-acre garden.

Together with William, the men strolled down the gentle slope toward the river. The forty-eight-year-old William had to walk carefully because he was still suffering from complications of a compound fracture of his leg. In the previous year he had fallen out of a twenty-foot cypress tree in the garden as he was gathering seeds from the top branches. As they walked along the softly rippling land, they could see the small glades and scoops that John Bartram Senior had laid out in an attempt to imitate the natural habitats where he had first found the plants. At the same time, the undulating lie of the land provided protective pockets that sheltered the more tender plants and created microclimates, allowing the Bartrams to grow such trees as the glorious evergreen *Magnolia grandiflora*, which John Bartram had collected in the Carolinas and which normally perished so far north. There was a little stream and an artificial pond for the collection of aquatic plants. The land was uniquely suited for growing species from a wide variety of habitats because it lay on the dividing line between the sandy soil of the coastal plains and the rocky outcrop to the west.

It was the perfect garden for a plant collector and William had fol-

---

* Washington went again on 2 September 1787, two weeks before he returned home to Mount Vernon.

A Draught of John Bartram's House and Garden as it appears from the River 1758   Sent to P Collenson

1. my Studey
2. Common Flower Garden
3. upper Kitchen Garden
4. the Lower Kitchen Garden
5.6. Walks 150 yards long of a moderate decent

A new flower Garden 25 yards long & 10 broad

A Pond or Spring head   conveid underground to the spring or milk House

The Course of the Fence is Northwest & south east

Schuilkiln River 400 Yards wide

lowed his father's footsteps—one of the Native American tribes whom he had befriended during his travels had even named him "Pug Puggy," the "flower hunter."* But unlike John Bartram, William saw more in the natural world than a treasure trove of ornamental or potentially useful plants—his perception of America's landscape was that of a scientist *and* an artist. Whereas John Bartram Senior's published travel accounts read like dry observations of soils, plants and potential agricultural uses of the frontier land, William Bartram's journal revealed a man enraptured by the grandeur of America: forests were "sublime," trees were "transcendent" and plains were "Elysian fields." When he saw the natural world of his country his mind was "suspended" and "beheld with rapture and astonishment."

William had tried to publish the journal of his travels in the previous year but failed to procure enough subscriptions. When *Travels* was eventually published, in 1791, it was far more successful in Europe, where it went through nine editions in the first decade. Romantic poets such as Samuel Taylor Coleridge, William Wordsworth and François-René de Chateaubriand were inspired by his vivid descriptions of the southern states, but in America the response was more muted.† Although most Americans were not ready for such nature writing, the founding fathers most definitely were. Like Jefferson in *Notes on the State of Virginia*, William Bartram described an America that was sublime, magnificent and certainly not inferior to Europe. Neither Washington, Jefferson nor Adams left any letters or accounts that described their appreciation for William's writing, but they all put their names on the subscription list of the *Travels* in summer 1790.‡ Madison liked William's work so much that he and his future wife, Dolley, would visit the garden often, also adding William's portrait to the gallery of "worthies" in the dining room at Montpelier.

---

* *Pak·pv·ku·ce* is the Creek word for "flower" and is pronounced pakpak-oci— which William Bartram translated as "flower hunter," although that would be *Pak·pv·ku·ce fayv* (pronounced pakpak-oci fa:y-a).
† Success came only in the nineteenth century, when the Transcendentalists, inspired by the English romantics, turned to William Bartram's writing. Henry David Thoreau admired William's work for its balance of poetry and science and Ralph Waldo Emerson was nudged by Thomas Carlyle in 1851 to discover true American nature writing with "a wondrous kind of floundering eloquence in it."
‡ Franklin's name is missing from the list because he had died a few months before the subscription.

Facing Page: Bartram's house and garden, drawn by William Bartram in 1758. The figure on the path is probably John Bartram Senior. By the time the delegates visited almost three decades later, many more trees would have been planted.

Walking along a tree-lined path that led from the house toward the river at the end of the garden, the delegates could see many of the trees that William would later describe in the *Travels*. Wherever they turned they encountered yet another specimen from yet another part of the country. America's entire flora, it seemed, was assembled here—from trees that John Bartram had collected far north near Lake Ontario to flowering shrubs that William had brought from Florida. Some were rare; others were common. There was *Pinus pungens,* a pine that grew only in the Appalachian mountains, as well as aspen, the most widespread of all North American trees. Live oak from the Deep South was side by side with tamarack, one of the northernmost trees in America.

There was the wonderful fringe tree, one of the most showy American shrubs. When Madison and the North and South Carolina delegates had traveled to Philadelphia two months previously, they had seen its dangling feathery tassels of white blossom in the thickets that lined the roads—but Caleb Strong, a delegate for Massachusetts, had probably never encountered it, because it grew naturally only in the states south of New Jersey. Similarly, George Mason, who had never in his life left the area around the Potomac River and Chesapeake Bay, must have been excited to see conifers from the northern regions of the Union, such as mature balsam firs, which John Bartram had collected in the 1740s in the Catskills, or the trees that came from the Carolinas, such as *Halesia carolina,* which was also called silverbell for its drooping clusters of white bell-shaped blossoms. One visitor had recently commented on the many "species of which very little is generally known."

In Bartram's Garden, the delegates could see how the manifold flora of each state thrived together, their branches intertwined in a flourishing horticultural union. John Bartram Senior had been the first to bring together trees and shrubs from all thirteen states, but he had done so for commercial reasons in order to supply his British customers and out of scientific curiosity. By contrast, Washington had been the first to unite the trees and shrubs from across the thirteen states as a visual expression of the young nation. Since then—and inspired by Washington—the idea had also been taken up by Samuel Vaughan,* who had planted the garden of

---

* When Washington and Vaughan had first met in Philadelphia in December 1783, they had quickly discovered their shared love for gardens and native species. During the summer of the Convention they met regularly—most certainly discussing the designs and plantings of their gardens. In August (while Washington was still in Philadelphia), Vaughan visited Mount Vernon, drawing a plan of Washington's new gardens and shrubberies (see Chapter 1, p. 24).

the State House (which was, after all, the birthplace of the Union) with the declared purpose of having "a specimen of every sort in America."*

The delegates walked in the shade of the willow oaks, tulip poplars and pines that Bartram had grown from seeds sixty years previously, and stepped around the innumerable tubs of saplings that the Bartrams raised for sale. This was, above all, a working garden, which some visitors failed to understand when they criticized how rare specimens were "covered over w^t weeds" and beautiful trees "lost in common thicket." Washington himself, who had visited just a couple of weeks earlier, had commented that the garden "was not laid off with much taste," while nonetheless greatly admiring the "curious plts, Shrubs & trees." Cutler equally complained that everything seemed to be "jumbled together in heaps." But taste was not the point: what had concerned John Bartram, and now his sons, was that the greatest possible variety of American plants should thrive here, however southern their origin—and if that meant sheltering a rare and tender shrub in a protective grove, so be it.

As the men made their way down to the river's edge, they were seemingly unconcerned with order or layout. Beauty was all around them and they were above all relieved to be freed from the heat, frustration and locked doors of the State House. They reveled in inspecting plants they had never seen before and took a particular pleasure in the exquisite white flowers of *Franklinia alatamaha,* a small tree that William had recently named after Benjamin Franklin. The Franklin tree was the rarest of all American plants in the garden, because it could be found only in one particular location in Georgia.† William had discovered it with his father in 1765 but had only managed to collect ripe seeds on his later travels. The tree was such a horticultural wonder that botanists pilgrimaged to Philadelphia to see it. Only the British were awkward about the discovery, preferring the name *Gordonia pubescens* and refusing to accept *Franklinia alatamaha*—which was probably not surprising, given Franklin's role in the American Revolution.

The men could immediately see why Bartram's Garden was famed for its flowering shrubs and trees. The Franklinia was just part of this mag-

---

* Most plants in the State House Yard had come from the Bartrams. Vaughan had ordered fifty-five species from the nursery and continued to replace dead trees and shrubs from their stock.
† In 1803, less than four decades after John and William Bartram had found the tree in Georgia, it was spotted for the last time in the wild. Humphry Marshall described it as *Franklinia alatamaha* in his *Arbustrum Americanum* in 1785, crediting William with naming it.

nificent show—there was also southern catalpa, which John Bartram had collected in the Carolinas. With its large, translucent, light green leaves and white summer blossoms, it would have been new to the Northerners Strong and Mason. Another flowering rarity from the South was *Stewartia malacodendron,* admired for its white camellia-like blooms (hence its common name, silky camellia).

The delegates, so Cutler observed, were "very free and sociable," forgetting as they talked with Bartram and wandered along the paths the weight of expectation that lay upon their shoulders. Alexander Martin, for example, a delegate from North Carolina, didn't say much at all during the Convention, but now quizzed Bartram about the trees and shrubs in the garden. Like William Bartram, the other North Carolina delegate, Hugh Williamson, had been educated at the Academy of Philadelphia and was well known as a man interested in natural history. A member of the American Philosophical Society, Williamson also published his observations in the society's journal and had sent seeds and dried plants for their collection. Just a week earlier he had written home requesting news on the crops in North Carolina, exasperated that "nobody thinks it worth while to mention such a subject." He would have certainly appreciated the towering trees in Bartram's Garden, because, like Jefferson, he thought that America's rivers, mountains and plants were on "a scale of more magnificence than those of the old world." Even Alexander Hamilton, who was neither a farmer nor particularly interested in botany or gardening, understood that nature could have a political or at least a symbolical meaning. Years after the visit to Bartram's Garden, when he created his first and only garden, he planted a row of thirteen sweetgums at his house The Grange to honor the original thirteen colonies.

After three hours the delegates bid their good-byes. Never in their entire lives had they seen so many different species of trees and shrubs. The plants had arrived in Philadelphia from across the thirteen states where they had all thrived in their native habitats, but here they flourished together. The graciously bowing branches of eastern hemlock from the northern states protected southern shrubs. Beautyberry, which John Bartram had brought from South Carolina and which would parade its clusters of bright purple berries on its naked branches in autumn, flourished under the spreading canopy of pin oak that grew as far north as Vermont. Here in Bartram's Garden, America's spectacular flora prospered in a vigorous horticultural embrace.

Two days later, on Monday, 16 July, the delegates assembled at the State House for the final vote on the Connecticut Plan. As always, Madison sat at his table in the front, recording everything that was said and decided. They had already agreed that Congress would be divided into two chambers—the House of Representatives and the Senate—but they had failed to come to any resolution on the distribution of power. Until now the larger states had voted that the number of representatives in both houses should be proportional according to the population of each state, giving the larger states more power. The Southern states, regardless of size, had rallied behind Virginia to defend the institution of slavery. The smaller states wanted to continue the one-state-one-vote method that gave each state, no matter how small, equal say in national matters. The Connecticut Plan combined the two, with one house based on proportional representation and the other based on one-state-one-vote.

As the voting started, one by one the delegates called out "aye" or "no" to approve or disapprove the Connecticut Plan. There were only ten states voting—neither Rhode Island nor New Hampshire had sent delegates yet and with only Alexander Hamilton present, New York did not have the required quorum. Massachusetts was called first. Two delegates said "no" and two said "aye"—the vote would not count, for it was divided. Everybody must have listened, surprised, because as a large state Massachusetts had always voted for proportional representation. Only two weeks previously, on 2 July, Massachusetts had voted "no" to each state having one vote in the Senate. But Caleb Strong, one of the delegates who had been at Bartram's Garden, called out "aye" and, by switching sides, had split the vote.

Now five "ayes" were needed for the Connecticut Plan to be adopted. Tensions rose as the vote swung first one way, then another. When Virginia was called as the seventh state, all small states had cast their "ayes"—four in total—but this would not be enough. As the largest state, Virginia with Madison as their leader voted a predictable "no." There were three more states left, North Carolina, South Carolina and Georgia—all slaveholding states that usually voted with Virginia. In the previous days and weeks they all had stood against the Connecticut Plan.

North Carolina was called next, and—contrary to all expectations—voted "aye." There must have been a moment of silence, while the implications of this about-turn were fully registered: with North Carolina's voting with the small states and not with Virginia, the necessary five "ayes" for the Connecticut Plan had been cast. A compromise had finally been reached and the way for a new Constitution was paved. As much as Madison was frustrated about the outcome of the voting, at least the small states were now prepared to consider his grand vision of a stronger national government. And, as he later admitted during the ratification process, it was the Great Compromise that made the government of the

United States unique, because the proportional representation in the House of Representatives made the government "national" while at the same time the distribution of the states' power in the Senate made it "federal."

But the question remains—why did North Carolina's delegates and Caleb Strong change sides? On the afternoon after the visit to Bartram's Garden, Strong had warned his colleagues that "If no Accommodation takes place, the Union itself must soon be dissolved," and North Carolina's delegates must have realized the same truth: that if the Union was to survive, they had to compromise. The smaller states would have never given all the power to the larger states because they needed at least one house that gave each state equal votes, "as a security for their political existence," one delegate later explained. Like Strong, Williamson and Martin could only have decided this after their visit to Bartram's Garden because until then they had always voted against one-state-one-vote in the Senate.

It can only be speculation that a three-hour walk on a cool summer morning among the United States of America's most glorious trees and shrubs influenced these men. But what we do know is that the three men who changed sides and made the Great Compromise possible that day had all been there and marveled at what they saw. What we also know is that Massachusetts's and North Carolina's switch of vote turned the thirteen states into one nation. The young country was like a growing tree, as one contemporary said, and the "Union is the vital sap that nourishes the tree. If we reject the Constitution . . . we girdle the tree, its leaves will wither, its branches drop off, and the mouldering trunk will be torn down by the tempest."

4

"PARTIES AND POLITICKS"

James Madison's and Thomas Jefferson's Tour of New England

As winter passed the baton to spring and the lilacs readied themselves for their scented bloom, Thomas Jefferson ached for nature. Every week he wrote from Philadelphia, the temporary capital of the United States, to his two girls, twelve-year-old Mary and eighteen-year-old Martha, firing questions about the garden in Monticello—when are the peas up, has the manure been put on the beds, which shrubs and flowers are blooming? "I suppose you are busily engaged in your garden," he wrote to Martha in March 1791, "I expect full details from you on that subject." Their descriptions were his lifeline to the place he loved more than any other. "Have you noted the first appearance of these things at Monticello?" he asked Mary, before insisting that she record any leaf or blossom that "indicates the approach of spring." In return he described the awakening of spring in Philadelphia, sending lists of dates, from the leafing of the willows to the blooms of flowering dogwoods.* He also dispatched rare seeds of beautiful flowers, reminding them to nourish them with their own hands. "I shall envy your occupations in the feilds [sic] and garden," he wrote to Martha, "while I am shut up drudging within four walls." He chided and cajoled them to write more regularly, accus-

---

* The noting of botanical dates such as times of blossoming and leafing was also part of his long study of the American climate.

ing them of being too "lazy" to fulfill his botanical requests. When little Mary failed to report that the frost had killed some fruits, he complained, "I find I have counted too much on you as a Botanical and zoological correspondent."* If he couldn't be at Monticello, he at least wanted to follow the unfurling of every leaf and the opening of every bud through Martha's and Mary's descriptions—it was as close as he could get to being among his blossoming fruit trees or smelling the sweet scent of guelder rose, for he had to stay in Philadelphia where Congress sat.

When Jefferson had returned to the United States of America from Paris in late 1789 he had found himself appointed secretary of state—a position he had only reluctantly accepted, for all he wanted was to be in Monticello. Much had changed since he had left the country five years previously. Instead of thirteen states that were only loosely connected through the Articles of Confederation, the new Constitution bound the Union together with a strong central government that for the first time could levy taxes and mint money. It was a government that had authority over America's foreign affairs and regulated commerce between the states. At the same time the Constitution was a framework that allowed—even encouraged—the continuous negotiation between the states and the federal government because "the seeds of amendment," as George Washington explained by using a horticultural analogy, were "engrafted in the Constitution." The ravaged country that Jefferson had left behind after the war was slowly recovering. Foreigners admired the "well-cultivated fields" and the "extensive and industrious farming." Everywhere in the country mills had been built, and in New England small-scale manufacturers thrived, producing cloth, rope and leather.

Since March 1789 Washington had stood at the helm of the new United States after unanimously being elected as the first president. John Adams, who had returned from London the previous year, was his vice president, Washington's former aide-de-camp Alexander Hamilton was secretary of the treasury, and Madison remained a leading member of Congress. But it was a reluctant coterie: Washington would have preferred to look after his fields and gardens at Mount Vernon, Jefferson would also have happily exchanged his political life with that of a farmer, and Adams hated his office as vice president, which he described, with characteristic hyperbole, as "the most insignificant Office that ever the Invention of Man contrived." Only Madison and Hamilton seemed to enjoy their political clout.

---

* A month later Mary wrote back, telling her father that in fact she hadn't failed him because the "fruit was not killed as you thought."

Though Madison was painfully shy among strangers, he had emerged as one of the most brilliant legal minds in the United States. Together with Hamilton, he had been instrumental in the long-drawn-out ratification process of the Constitution when they wrote the *Federalist Papers*—eighty-five essays that explained and defended the new legal framework of the United States.* But they were an unlikely pair: the pale Madison and the dashingly handsome Hamilton, born the illegitimate son of a West Indian merchant of Scottish origin. Always dressed in black and sickly looking, Madison was almost invisible next to the charming Hamilton, with his penchant for fine tailored coats and brightly colored clothes. But they shared an obsessive work ethic and were known for their almost frenzied determination. Just as Madison had recorded every word of the Constitutional Convention and devoured all the information he could find on theories of governments, Hamilton had a reputation for working ferociously at a relentless pace. The speed with which they churned out the *Federalist Papers* in the year after the Constitutional Convention was a testimony to their energy and dedication.

Since the early days of the revolution, the founding fathers had fought together for the future of their country. But in the years since, divisions had slowly begun to form between them that, once hardened, would lead to the formation of the United States of America's first political parties. Key to their emergence were fundamental differences in what the revolutionary generation believed ought to be the fabric of American society—the dream of a nation of farmers versus the vision of a merchant and trader elite. On the one side were the so-called Federalists such as Hamilton and Adams, who favored a strong central government and commercial links with Britain, and on the other Jefferson's and Madison's Republicans, with an emphasis on the rights and powers of states and a promotion of individual liberty.†

The first fissures appeared in January 1790, when Hamilton as secretary of the treasury introduced a financial strategy that would deal with domestic and international debts, and which favored merchants and

---

* Originally *The Federalist: A Collection of Essays, Written in Favour of the New Constitution, as agreed upon by the Federal Convention, September 17, 1787.* Of the eighty-five essays, Madison wrote twenty-nine, Hamilton fifty-one and John Jay five.
† The Jeffersonian Republicans—sometimes also called Democrats by their enemies—later split and became the modern Democratic Party. The Jeffersonian Republicans were also called "Antifederalists" and the Federalists were called "Antirepublicans." Although parties had not been formally established in 1791, for the sake of consistency, they will be called "Republicans" and "Federalists" throughout this chapter.

speculators as the gatekeepers to a healthy economy. The proposal seemed to have its provenance in Hamilton's own background. Unlike the landowners Madison and Jefferson, Hamilton had to work as a lawyer to earn a living and had long been part of the mercantile world of New York. With trade in his blood, Hamilton's idea of the future of the United States of America was unsurprisingly industrial: "The spirit of enterprise," he said, "be less in a nation of mere cultivators, than in a nation of cultivators and merchants." An entrepreneurial urban elite, he believed, should be the backbone of America's society, because the wealth of the country depended on commerce and, crucially, on close trading relationships with Britain.

The core of Hamilton's Assumption Plan was to consolidate the separate debts of the thirteen states into one that was to be controlled by the government, making it more powerful than ever before. This would also ensure that the nation's numerous wealthy merchants would support the new government. When Hamilton announced his intention to place the fiscal levers of the whole country in the hands of the federal government and move the United States of America closer to Britain, Madison publicly denounced the plan, and one of the most inspired political partnerships of the era ended.

As these divisions appeared, the political landscape changed forever. Today we believe that political parties are the foundation of democratic societies, but most of the revolutionaries thought that their emergence threatened the very existence of republics. Madison had vehemently condemned the division of the republic into two parties, while Adams stressed that there "is nothing which I dread So much."

But with the specter of commerce looming over the country, Madison saw no other choice than to fight Hamilton and his vision of America. This shift from fervently defending the idea of a strong central government during the Constitutional Convention to leading an opposition that favored the rights and powers of the individual states might seem like a retraction of Madison's political beliefs, but when viewed through the lens of agriculture and his background as the son of a Virginia planter, it was a logical position. Madison was not so much opposing a strong government per se but the idea of a mercantile empire bound to Britain (and to merchants that had shackled Virginia tobacco farmers in a spiral of debts before the revolution). The old enemy, Madison said, would put the new nation "in commercial manacles."

Madison's comrade in this battle was his old friend and fellow Virginian Thomas Jefferson. Like Madison, Jefferson was dismayed by Hamilton's financial plans and worried about the fate of agriculture in Hamilton's world of speculators and "stock-jobbers." "Wealth acquired by speculation," Jefferson said, "is fugacious . . . and fills society with the spirit of gambling."* Both Madison and Jefferson defended their vision of the United States of America as an agrarian republic—a country of independent farmers untainted by the corrupting influence of Britain. Botany would play a prominent role in this battle because useful crops would ensure America's independence and self-sufficiency. Madison insisted that "Experiments for introducing these valuable productions are strongly recommended," while Jefferson went even further, claiming that the "greatest service which can be rendered any country, is to add an useful plant to it's culture." Botany "I rank with the most valuable sciences," he continued, because it bettered life—culinary, medical, economic and aesthetic.

Jefferson now sought to apply the agricultural lessons that he had learned in Europe in the United States of America. One example was his effort to change rice cultivation in the South. Ever since the day he had courageously smuggled some grains out of Italy in 1787, Jefferson had believed that upland rice—grown in dry fields instead of flooded paddy fields—would enable southern farmers to leave their malaria-infested swamps and move up onto the healthier plateaus to the west. Every opportunity was therefore explored to procure it. Correspondents from England and the West Indies sent the precious grains, a seven-year-old prince from Cochinchina (part of today's Vietnam) also promised to provide some, and Jefferson even received rice that Captain William Bligh had managed to bring back to London from his treacherous voyage after the mutiny on the *Bounty* in the South Pacific.

In June 1790, in the midst of the disputes over Hamilton's financial plans, Jefferson planted the prized grains in flowerpots on the windowsills in the house he had rented in New York, where Congress was temporarily meeting. He also gave some to Madison, who forwarded them on to his father with detailed planting instructions and later gave some African rice to William Bartram and to the members of the South Carolina Agricultural Society. More often than not they failed to germi-

---

* Years later, in 1816, Jefferson was so appalled by the commercialization of the United States that he talked about a separation between the industrial North and the agricultural South. "I have no hesitation in saying, 'let us separate,' " Jefferson wrote. "I would rather the States should withdraw, which are for unlimited commerce and war, and confederate with those alone which are for peace and agriculture."

nate, but Jefferson never gave up, understanding that "Botany is the school for patience." If he managed to cultivate one new species out of one hundred that he procured, Jefferson told one of his botanical correspondents, then "the ninety nine found otherwise are more than paid for." And so he distributed the rice as widely as he could.*

Now, with the increasing threat of Hamilton's mercantilism and a nation once again tied to Britain, his botanical projects gained greater urgency. If America's orchards were laden with fruits and the fields groaning with crops, the country would be wealthy and young men would not be tempted to turn to commerce. As he peered into the little earthen pots to see the first green blades of the rice plants pushing through the soil, his mind was on the propagation of the nation. And though his own rice experiments failed, the seeds that he distributed to the farmers in Georgia flourished. This success, he insisted when judging his services to the country later, was so important that he added it to the same list that also included the Declaration of Independence (as well as the introduction of olive tree saplings).

But gardening and planting were more than patriotic occupations to Jefferson—they were also a refuge from the wranglings of politics. As the dispute with Hamilton wore on and the rift between the old revolutionaries deepened, Jefferson became increasingly troubled. Political quarrels in particular burdened him because he hated conflicts and arguments that were, he grumbled to Washington, "against my love of silence and quiet." Instead he longed for nature and whenever he thought of his garden, he said, "I feel with redoubled ardor my desire to return home." This wish was exacerbated by the lack of outside space at the house he had rented in Philadelphia, where Congress had moved from New York in December 1790.† Without his daily rounds through his garden and across his fields, Jefferson felt deprived and unhappy. He was yearning to leave Philadelphia, where he was "labouring without pleasure."

Without pleasure, and also without success, for by the end of February 1791 Congress had passed Hamilton's momentous bank bill. Modeled on

---

* Jefferson continued his endeavor and during his retirement dispatched rice to the governor of Georgia. By 1813 he was proud to report that rice was successfully cultivated in the upper parts of Georgia and Kentucky.

† As Jefferson prepared to move from New York to Philadelphia, he asked Franklin's grandson William Temple Franklin to find a house for him with a garden—in fact, he wanted two houses as "to assign the lower floor of both to my public offices, and the first floor and both gardens entirely to my own use." In the end he couldn't afford this and moved to a house with no garden at all.

the Bank of England, a federal bank would be founded that would concentrate the country's capital to provide credit and regulate commerce. Though imbued with national economic powers the bank was funded largely by private investors—a financial aristocracy, Jefferson and Madison believed, who would effectively run the country. The bank, Jefferson later wrote, was "invented for the purposes of corruption" based on the "rotten" model of Britain.

Just days after the bank was chartered, the downhearted pair resolved to escape to nature and take a botanical ramble up the Hudson River valley. Apart from anything else, Jefferson hoped that some time off would rid him of the furious headache that had become a recurring ailment. Madison too felt ill and believed that the best remedy in the world was "a long journey, at a mild season, thro' a pleasant Country."

Yet, as they prepared for their departure to the Hudson River valley, Jefferson unwittingly found himself embroiled in another political storm, one that threatened to splinter the unity of the founding fathers even further. At the center of this dispute was the pamphlet *Rights of Man,* written by Thomas Paine. An Englishman who had transcended his nationality, Paine had become an American hero fifteen years earlier, when his widely read *Common Sense* had convinced many colonists to seek independence from Britain. This latest publication was Paine's response to Edmund Burke's condemnation of the French Revolution,* widely praised as a clarion call to the American people, imploring them never to forget the essence of their own revolution. To Jefferson, however, it was also a timely attack on an old friend who in recent years, he believed, had come to betray the very spirit of 1776: Vice President John Adams.

Since their garden tour in England five years previously, Adams and Jefferson had moved apart in their political thought. Where Jefferson was an Anglophobe, Adams had come to regard the British constitution as "the most stupendous fabric of human invention."† In the *Defence of the Constitutions of Government of the United States of America,* which Adams had written during his time in London, he declared that the bal-

---

* Edmund Burke's *Reflections on the Revolution in France* was published in November 1790.
† Adams had written about this in the *Defence* but also talked about it during a cabinet meeting in April 1791. Adams had said, Jefferson later recalled, that if some of its defects were corrected, the British constitution "would be the most perfect constitution of government ever devised by man." Abigail had rightly worried that "they will think in America that he [Adams] is for sitting up a King."

ance of power inscribed in the British constitution was a model that the United States of America should applaud. Their opposing opinions about the French Revolution only intensified the disagreement. Paine, Jefferson and Madison had greeted it with enthusiasm—Jefferson had witnessed the birth pangs of the revolution during his last summer in Paris and had even helped Lafayette draft the French *Declaration of Rights*. And though shocked by the riots and the violence that led to the storming of the Bastille on 14 July 1789, he had never once questioned the revolution's legitimacy. "We are not to expect to be translated from despotism to liberty, in a feather-bed," Jefferson mused, certain that other countries in Europe would soon follow suit with the United States of America as the model for all these new republics.

By contrast, Adams with his background as a lawyer feared the fury of uncontrolled mobs and fundamentally disagreed with Jefferson, Madison and Paine, condemning the revolution as nothing more than a "shambles." In response to the French Revolution he had published a series of essays that warned against the dangers of unchecked democracy and the perils of turbulent passions. To Adams's mind it would lead to anarchy and tyranny for the simple reason that the French revolutionaries were out of control. They were, he said, like men "flushed with recent pay or prize Money, mounted on wild Horses, lashing and speerring [*sic*], till they would kill the Horses and break their own Necks."

These essays went to the core of an ideological disagreement between the old revolutionaries. Jefferson and Madison, like so many other Virginia tobacco planters, despised the British and had interpreted Adams's polemic against uncontrolled democracy in France as a yearning for a monarchy in the United States of America. It did not help that Adams had tried to introduce monarchical titles to the American republic, suggesting for example that Washington be addressed "His Highness the President of the U.S."—according to Jefferson the "most superlatively ridiculous thing I ever heard" and a sign that Adams was "absolutely mad."

The row had been rumbling on in private for some time, with the irascible Adams denouncing Madison as a "creature of French puffs" and Jefferson accusing Adams of a pernicious obsession with monarchy. By 3 May 1791, however, these thoughts erupted onto the public stage. As the first American edition of Paine's pamphlet rolled off the printing presses in Philadelphia, every reader saw Jefferson's words on the first page— words that he had written in a personal note to the printer and that had never been meant for public consumption. The *Rights of Man*, so Jefferson's unintended endorsement read, was the answer to "the political heresies which have sprung up amongst us." Everybody who read these words understood that the secretary of state of the United States had turned against the vice president.

Within a few days the book's endorsement, as it passed from hand to hand in the taverns of Philadelphia and New York, created a political scandal. Hamilton was "open mouthed against me," Jefferson wrote to Madison, and Washington's secretary warned that Jefferson's note would put the secretary of state in direct opposition to Adams. The intensely private Jefferson was "mortified" and "thunderstruck" about the printer's incompetence and indiscretion. He had never made a secret of being anti-monarchical, he wrote to Washington by way of excuse, and said he would not mind telling Adams to his face that he believed him to be a heretic. But to have his opinions ping-ponged publicly in pamphlets and newspapers was not what Jefferson had intended. Adams, Jefferson correctly concluded, would be "displeased" to say the least.

In the midst of this dispute Jefferson found comfort in the thought of his and Madison's imminent botanical excursion, but at the same time he also subtly shifted its scope by injecting politics into the itinerary. On 9 May, Jefferson wrote to Madison suggesting they travel north along the Hudson River valley, and that instead of coming back the same way they go east into Vermont before turning south into Massachusetts and Connecticut. The trip that had originally been conceived as a ramble along the Hudson River valley would thus become a tour of the northern states. As well as examining the forests and fields in Vermont, which had become the fourteenth state only two months earlier, the detour would also allow them to meet some of the local political leaders.

The controversy over *Rights of Man* ossified the division of the young administration and marked a dramatic change, because until then political disagreements had been played out on a local or regional level. Within a few years, however, this would turn into concerted party action between the Federalists and the Republicans in the national arena. As the divisions crystallized, Jefferson and Madison delayed their tour and instead of immediately heading north they met some political allies in New York. One of them was Madison's old friend the poet Philip Freneau, whom they tried to persuade to establish a national newspaper— the mouthpiece of what would become the Republican party and a counterpart to the *Gazette of the United States*, which supported Hamilton and his policies.

They also met the chancellor of New York, Robert Livingston, yet another experimental farmer who corresponded with Jefferson about innovative agriculture and politics, and whom Jefferson later called his "brother agriculturalist," and Aaron Burr, who fifteen years later would kill Hamilton in a duel. Livingston and Burr had already joined forces with the governor of New York, George Clinton*—a coalition through which Burr had recently won the seat of Hamilton's father-in-law in the Senate. Unsurprisingly, Hamilton's supporters accused Jefferson and Madison of pursuing "a pasionate courtship" with his opponents.

Although there wasn't yet a coherent national opposition, Jefferson knew that Livingston was also worried about Hamilton's fiscal policies, and had written to him earlier in the year to discuss Hamilton's bank bill. Their meetings in New York did not go unnoticed, Hamilton's supporters reporting the "twistings, combinations, and maneuvres" as well as, even more worryingly, the "Ghost of Antifederalism."

Only after these political meetings did Jefferson and Madison finally leave New York, on 21 May, equipped with a list of the best taverns along their route. Just as Jefferson had escaped from the tedious trade negotiations with the British in 1786 on a garden tour with Adams, he was once again turning to nature for comfort and inspiration. This time, however, he would not be visiting staged garden scenes laced with political meaning but rather, some of the United States of America's most spectacular landscapes—rugged nature that decades later would inspire the first generation of American painters and poets (the Hudson River School) to celebrate the American wilderness.

Averaging an impressive thirty miles a day, they bumped along the rough mud roads in Jefferson's phaeton, talking botany and politics as they passed the forested mountain ranges of the Catskills and Adirondacks. Now and again, they stopped and wandered on foot into the forest to investigate. These were the moments when party politics vanished from their minds, because "you should . . . not permit yourself even to think while you walk," Jefferson insisted. Madison hoped that the tour would satisfy his considerable botanical curiosity, and he was not to be disappointed. Throughout the trip he and Jefferson diligently documented observations in their journals, particularly their admiration for trees that were "either unknown or rare in Virginia."[†]

There was the dense conical conifer arborvitae, for example, the northern bayberry with its fragrant leaves and a flowering shrub that would make a wonderful addition to gardens because it was "loaded richly with large flowers of a strong, pink fragrance." Its delicately

---

* Clinton had called Hamilton an "upstart attorney" and "a superficial, self-conceited coxcomb."
† Meticulous as always, Jefferson also listed the exact daily mileage, as well as rating the inns along the way as " *good," "+middling" or "−bad."

sculpted, deep red blossom greatly intrigued them and Jefferson thought it was "the richest shrub I have ever seen." It was an azalea, he was certain, but it could not be the pinxterbloom azalea which he knew from Virginia. When he looked through his botanical books on his return to Philadelphia he thought it might be *Azalea viscosa* (today's *Rhododendron viscosum*), but he couldn't be entirely sure.*

A week after leaving New York they reached Lake George, nestled in the Adirondacks. The heat was stultifying, the embankments were alive with rattlesnakes (two of which they killed to examine more closely) and they were besieged by swarms of mosquitoes and other insects. But despite nature's assaults, they were enchanted by Lake George, marveling at what was "unquestionably the most beautiful water" they had ever seen, clear "as chrystal." This long finger of a lake stretched for miles, weaving in and out of the surrounding forested mountains. As sea gulls circled above the lake, Jefferson and Madison walked in the shade of rich groves of arborvitae, white pine and aspen. There were wild gooseberries (probably *Ribes cynosbati* or *Ribes hirellum*) loaded with black fruit, a species of wild cherry (probably *Prunus pensylvanica*) that they had never seen before and wild strawberries in abundance underfoot. They were amazed to find the "honey suckle of the gardens" (most certainly *Lonicera canadensis*) growing wild on the banks of one lake. When they found paper birches, Jefferson stopped to peel off some bark on which he wrote letters to his daughters. The trees and shrubs reminded him of his own garden, which never left his mind, and throughout the trip he sent instructions to Monticello on pruning, grafting and other essential horticultural tasks.

They also visited some old battlefields from the revolution but, as Jefferson wrote to his son-in-law, they infinitely preferred "the botanical objects which continually presented themselves." The headache that had been a constant companion throughout the past months had by this time disappeared completely, proof enough that "the drudgery of business" was to blame.

Plants and agriculture had always been a part of the friendship

---

* After their return Jefferson wrote to Madison, "I am sorry we did not bring with us some leaves of the different plants which struck our attention," because without the leaves he was finding it difficult to identify them. It was unsurprising that Jefferson was struggling because it was a different species from the only two that had been classified at that time—*R. periclymenoides* and *R. viscosum*. They had probably seen *R. prinophyllum*, which has a spicy clove-like fragrance. The other northern species with deep red blooms is rhodora (*R. canadensis*), but it's not noted for its scent and it has a different number of stamens from the other species, which Jefferson would have certainly noticed.

Lake George

between Madison and Jefferson, and their letters abounded with remarks about seeds, trees and crops. Even when Madison was in the midst of crafting the Constitution, he had found time to organize seeds for Jefferson and to dispatch the rare pecan nuts, maple and honey locust seeds, dozens of cuttings of apple trees and other American shrubs for Jefferson's French friends. At the same time Jefferson had used Madison's position as a member of Congress to gain access to other congressmen, sending seed boxes to his friend to distribute among the politicians.

And once again, as they traveled through New England, the old friends observed the landscape as gardeners and plantsmen. As the countryside unfolded they also saw a republic of farmers spread out before them, a nation that to their mind was endangered by Hamilton's plans. This was how most white Americans lived—on farms spread across the United States. Only one in twenty of the population lived in towns. No city was larger than 50,000 people and, except for New York and Philadelphia, no city had more than 25,000 inhabitants. "Each man," one foreigner remarked, "owns the house he lives in and the lands which he cultivates, and every one appears to be in a happy state of mediocrity." The scenery was one of "meadows, newly snatched from uncultivated nature," and a "mixture of romantic wilderness and cultivated beauty."

But as Jefferson and Madison reveled in this scenery, they also investigated it scientifically. Equipped with a questionnaire, they asked farmers and landowners about an insect that had been ravaging the wheat harvest.* The Hessian fly, so called because it was originally thought (though wrongly) to have arrived in the straw bedding of the Hessian troops during the Revolutionary War, had spread from Long Island to Pennsylvania and as far south as Mount Vernon's fields. The larvae of the fly sucked the sap from the green wheat and stunted the growth of the plants, destroying the crops. No method had been found to halt its destructive path, and farmers across the United States were terrified, predicting that "the whole continent will be over-run—a calamity more to be lamented than the ravages of war." Such was the danger to America's economy that Jefferson had called a meeting of the American Philosophical Society (of which he and Madison were members) six days before he set out on the tour. He had offered to conduct a survey about the pest and how it had spread, he told them, if they could provide him with a questionnaire.

The insect had also become a political issue when, on the advice of Joseph Banks, the president of the Royal Society in London, Britain closed its ports to American wheat for fear of introducing the fly to their fields. Even Thomas Paine became involved, telling Banks that he believed the embargo was "only a political manoeuvre." Jefferson thought it was yet again a British plot "to do us injury," while Banks warned that "obloquy" would descend on Americans if they would "wilfully bring over the Fly" in revenge against the British. The former British prime minister, the duke of Grafton, even believed that the Americans deserved the Hessian fly—a "scourge of Heaven . . . upon such ungratefull colonies and rebellious people."

In the meantime, rumors continued to spread that they were not just on a nature vacation but were clandestinely nurturing a political agenda. Furthermore, the British consul general in the United States dispatched a warning to London, writing that Jefferson and Madison had gone north "to proselyte as far as they are able to a commercial war with Great Britain." Another British diplomat sent reports to London accusing them of touring the north to advocate their "favorite objects on behalf of France." There was some truth to these allegations, in that Jefferson wanted to shift more trade from Britain to France (as he had already tried

---

* Jefferson and Madison asked farmers about the life cycle of the Hessian fly. How many eggs were on one stalk, when had the insect first appeared and, most important of all, could the eggs, larvae and flies be found in the grain? In order to save their wheat exports they needed to prove that the fly could not cross the ocean in the harvested grain.

to do during his time as American Minister in Paris). On their way up the Hudson River valley, for example, they stopped at the small port town of Hudson, where Jefferson tried to persuade a large distillery owner that wine imported from France would produce better spirits than the molasses from the British West Indies. The advantage was that Americans would be able to deal with French rather than British merchants.

In addition Jefferson had been concocting a plan that would allow him to outmaneuver Hamilton, who had been working to strengthen the commercial relationship between America and Britain. His weapon would be a botanical one: the native sugar maple. Not only was this a magnificent tree that turned the northern mountains into a kaleidoscope of reds and oranges in autumn, but Jefferson believed it also could be of great economic and political value. American sugar maple orchards chimed with Jefferson's and Madison's vision of a country of small farmers, because the tree had the potential to rid America of its dependence on British West Indies sugarcane. It was an ideal crop for small-scale home production because it didn't require large plantations and slave labor as sugarcane did. Instead the tree's sap could easily be harvested by the wives and children of American farmers during the weeks when not much work could be done on the fields.

Not only might the United States "supply themselves sugar for their own consumption," Jefferson wrote, "but be great exporters." He had been thinking about this for some time and had asked for facts and figures on maple sugar production in New England, where small orchards were cultivated for domestic use. He had also requested some sugar samples which he forwarded to Washington, knowing that the president was always keen to learn about new crops. Only a few days before his departure, Jefferson had asked his old revolutionary friend Benjamin Rush to write an account of the tree, its locations and the tapping and yield of sugar, as well as the possible cultivation of the tree in an orchard and the process of turning the sap into sugar. Having assembled all the facts that he possibly could, Jefferson would use his botanical tour to talk to local growers and gain as much firsthand knowledge as possible.

On 4 June, about halfway through their trip, he and Madison arrived in Bennington, a town in Vermont at the foot of a hill that was entirely covered with maple trees. They had reached the heart of sugar maple country and the home of Moses Robinson, who had just recently been elected to the U.S. Senate. Like the two Virginians, Robinson opposed Hamilton's economic plans and would become a steadfast member of the Republican party. Here, during their two-day stay, party politics and botany wove together. Robinson entertained Jefferson and Madison at his house, inviting other leading citizens and local Antifederalists, including Joseph Fay, the former secretary of state for Vermont. They walked in the garden and the two friends found yet more trees they hadn't seen before. Madison admired one, which was releasing clumps of downy seeds that sailed in the wind like delicate cotton balls, but had to wait until Jefferson consulted his botanical books back in Philadelphia to learn that it was balsam poplar, the northernmost hardwood in North America.

The conversation then turned to the economic possibilities of expanding the small-scale New England sugar production to a national level. Sensing that they were in the presence of a kindred spirit, Madison and Jefferson bombarded their host and other guests with questions and passionately advocated the plan. Fay happily agreed to promote the project. He would examine his "young groves," he promised, to calculate the number of maples per acre and he would plant an orchard "to encourage others." Their enthusiasm for patriotic orchards was clearly infectious. When they talked to Anthony Haswell, another fervent Republican and the printer of the *Vermont Gazette,* he was quickly convinced and ran a piece in his paper declaring that "attention to our sugar orchards is essentially necessary to secure the independence of our country."

There may have been other motives behind the stopover at Bennington besides the sugar maples, for Jefferson added it to their itinerary only after the *Rights of Man* scandal erupted. One British diplomat correctly suspected that Jefferson's and Madison's intentions "have been to feel the pulse of the country." Although they were not formally establishing a fully organized party apparatus, their discussions with Robinson, Haswell and Fay certainly hint at an attempt to gauge possible party loyalties. Indeed Madison had by this time emerged as the opposition leader, after a local newspaper in Albany described him as "the Charles Fox of America," referring to the leader of the opposition in the British government. When the article was republished in other parts of the country the idea of parties echoed across America's political landscape.

Politics, Madison wrote to a friend, "entered of course into our itinerary conversations." Jefferson certainly had party politics on his mind—or "party Jugglings" as one of Hamilton's friends called it—because he had asked that the *Gazette of the United States* be sent to him during the tour. Jefferson hated the Federalists' mouthpiece for "disseminating the doctrines of monarchy," he said, but it was important to know what their rivals were thinking.

At Bennington Jefferson and Madison praised Paine's *Rights of Man* and reflected on the "defects of British Government." Though Fay was not immediately convinced by their position, he quickly changed his mind on reading Paine. All of them—Robinson, Haswell and Fay— remained lifelong Republicans and supporters of Jefferson. Haswell later reported in the *Vermont Gazette* that Jefferson and Madison "secured to themselves a fund of political knowledge" in Bennington.

After their politically charged weekend in Vermont, Jefferson and Madison traveled south through Massachusetts and Connecticut, where their attention turned back to agriculture and plants. Madison recorded everything from soil types, crops, sizes of farms, the price of land and the different species of forest trees. His journal read like an agricultural survey: "soil good but often very sandy," "farms vary from 50 to 200 acres," "useful growth Sugar maple, white pine, White Cedar," "An acre of good land yields 30 bushs. Indian Corn Rye, potatoes." Passing through Connecticut, however, they now entered the heartland of the staunch advocates of Hamilton's plans. Their trip had not gone unnoticed and the local politicians and landowners "ridiculed, J___n & M__n's Tour." John Trumbull, for example, the state attorney, had sardonically written to Adams after Hamilton's bank bill passed that Madison had "dwindled . . . to the insignificant leader of an impotent Minority." Later that year, as party divisions intensified, Trumbull would tell friends that he planned to write a satire about the Virginia politicians and the strength of the Federalists.

From Connecticut Jefferson and Madison sailed to Oysterpond Point (today's Orient Point) at the northeastern tail of Long Island for the last leg of their journey. Their final stop was William Prince's nursery in Flushing, a visit that once again brought politics and gardening together. Just as the old revolutionaries frequented Bartram's Garden when Congress met in Philadelphia, they had all discovered the nursery when New York had been the temporary capital of the United States. Madison had bought trees here in the past, while Adams and Washington had visited together in 1789, during the first year of the presidency. Being accustomed to Bartram's vast selection, Washington was disappointed, noting in his diary that the "shrubs were trifling and the flowers not numerous"; only the "young fruit Trees" had fulfilled his expectations.

Jefferson, however, was not interested in variety on this occasion, rather he wanted to buy a few of the trees that they had seen during their tour. Most of all he wanted sugar maples—not just some but "all you have," he told Prince with characteristic extravagance. The thriving sugar orchards in the northern states together with Hamilton's continuing mercantile overtures to Britain convinced Jefferson that he needed to act fast if he was to reduce American dependency on British sugar. It was as if the formations of orderly rows upon rows of upright saplings were symbols of America's defiance against Britain, an arboreal army fighting for economic independence.

Jefferson's urgency was matched by that of Hamilton, for the secretary of the treasury had been steadily working on his rival version of America's future. In April he had supported the foundation of the Society for Establishing Useful Manufactures and was now canvassing for America's first industrial city, which would supply Americans and customers across the world with paper, linen, cotton, blankets, carpets and other products.* In the summer, as Jefferson and Madison returned from their tour, Hamilton sent two agents to find a suitable site for this shining new city. A few weeks later they reported to have found "one of the finest situations in the world," the Great Falls of the Passaic River. Such natural wonders had always impressed Jefferson, who had declared Niagara Falls so stupendous that they were "worth a voiage across the Atlantic," but Hamilton was not interested in awe-inspiring nature. The roaring water that plunged more than two hundred feet into a narrow gorge might have looked magnificent, but the real beauty was that it could be harnessed to power the mills.†

As Hamilton worked on his industrial dream, Jefferson continued to campaign for sugar maple orchards across the country. He was so efficient in promoting this American sugar (asking people to taste it in order to convince them to plant the orchards) that it quickly became impossible to procure even a few grams from anywhere in the United States. At Monticello he planted an entire grove from Prince's delivery, but in the end he failed to produce sugar due to the climate. Despite the setbacks he continued to order seeds and saplings, for it "is too hopeful an object to be abandoned."

At the same time the tour of the northern states had also been of great personal benefit—when Jefferson arrived back in Philadelphia on 19 June, a little more than a month after he had left, he told Washington that

---

* Since February Hamilton had been systematically working on his "Report on Manufactures," which he presented to Congress in December. The report laid out how the federal government should support and finance large-scale manufacturing. Even children could be employed, Hamilton enthused, because many were working in Britain's cotton mills at "a very tender age." In the end the report was never translated into legislation, but Jefferson and Madison regarded it as another attempt to place more power in the hands of the federal government and to undermine the agrarian republic. Adams believed that the encouragement of manufacturers should only be "discreet" and only in the "general Interest of Agriculture."

† The manufacturing town on the Passaic River was never completed, and by early 1796, all that was left were a few abandoned and derelict buildings.

"Mr. Madison's health is very visibly mended." Of his own health, he was able to report that his headache had disappeared. Jefferson probably also hoped that the furor about his attack on John Adams had finally died down, but instead he found that it had flared. In the midst of the tour, on 8 June, the first of eleven essays criticizing Paine's *Rights of Man* (and by extension Jefferson) had been published under the pseudonym Publicola* and reprinted in newspapers across the country, from Massachusetts to South Carolina. At the same time, Hamilton's new national bank opened. Investors scrambled for stocks, selling them on within one hour to the highest bidders. Madison was appalled by the "eternal buzz [of] the gamblers" and Hamilton's "Bank-Jobbers"—men who made their money by shifting paper rather than soil. Banks, Jefferson warned, would sweep away the fortunes and morals of the people.

The old revolutionary friends and colleagues had drifted apart. And though the new alliances were complex and sometimes even contradictory, the once subtle divisions hardened. Adams, for example, was regarded as a Federalist (in fact he would become the first and only Federalist president), but at the same time he also mistrusted Hamilton and the financial coterie around him. Like Jefferson and Madison, Adams believed that the soil held the future of the United States of America, and when Abigail suggested he buy stocks in the new national bank he refused to invest. Had he followed her advice, they would have earned more money than they ever made through their farm.

Washington was left in the middle, despairing about the fissures within his own administration. "I regret—deeply regret—the difference in opinions which have arisen, and divided you and another principal Officer of the Government," he wrote to Jefferson. By autumn the Republicans had their very own national partisan newspaper. In early August Freneau sent the proposal for the new paper to Jefferson, "the hint of which you, Sir," he wrote to Jefferson, "in conjunction with Mr. Madison were pleased to mention to me in May last."

During those four weeks in May and June 1791, Jefferson and Madison aligned politics and plants so closely that it is impossible to consider them separately. Sometimes plants were the reminder of their vision of the United States of America; sometimes nature provided a place of solitude, an escape from the political quarrels in Philadelphia; and sometimes a plant such as the sugar maple tree held the promise of changing the political and economic landscape.

---

* Many readers, including Jefferson, thought that Adams was "Publicola," but it was Adams's son, the future president John Quincy Adams.

Hamilton's son would later write that Jefferson and Madison used "the pretext of a botanical excursion" to rally party support. Continuing the botanical theme, he claimed that they sowed "tares" along the way— comparing their political ideas with weeds that could overtake productive grain fields. He might have exaggerated, as the tour did not create a coherent party overnight, but it certainly was the beginning of Republican allegiances—only five years later a presidential election was fought with smear campaigns along the new party lines. Above all, however, the tour cemented Jefferson's and Madison's friendship and political alliance. Almost forty years later, Madison would remember the botanical ramble as an occasion that "made us immediate companions." Their friendship "was for life, and . . . never interrupted in the slightest degree for a single moment."

5

"POLITICAL PLANTS
GROW IN THE SHADE"

The Summer of 1796

"I will not sit here in summer," Vice President John Adams moaned in April 1796, "I would sooner resign my Office." His sullen mood was the result of having been holed up in Philadelphia, the temporary capital of the United States. Over the past seven years, whenever Adams had to attend to his office during the congressional sessions, he had missed his fields, his long walks and of course his wife, Abigail, who often remained behind to run the farm in Quincy in his absence. "I long for rural sceanes," he wailed, "I want to take a Walk with you in the Garden." From Philadelphia he instructed her on agricultural matters and complained bitterly when she failed to mention the farm. Abigail's replies tended to combine reports on manures, clover, ploughs and pruning with sage political advice. His outcries when her letters were delayed revealed just how much he needed them: "No Letter for The Vice President," he would sulk. "All Day in bad humour—dirty Weather—wet walking—nothing good—nothing right . . . Smooked I know not how many Segars."

THE FRUSTRATION HE FELT during his time in Philadelphia was rooted in his visceral experience of nature. He had always loved the feel of the wind in his face, as well as picking plants when he went on long rambles in the woods, fields, meadows, and by rivers and lakes. Away from his beloved farm, he dreamed of being home pruning apple trees or planting cabbages. When the lack of fresh air and gardens in Philadelphia became too much, he visited the country estates outside the city to observe new methods of husbandry and gardening, but nothing compared to seeing his own land. "Oh my farm when shall I see thee," he lamented, "there will be no End of my tragic Oh's and tragic Ah's."

That spring Adams had missed seeing the meadows transform into colorful carpets of wildflowers. Instead he had watched the Federalists and Republicans battle over the Jay Treaty, a landmark agreement so controversial that John Jay, who negotiated the deal, later claimed that he could have traveled the whole country by the light of burning effigies of himself. Commercially the treaty further aligned the United States of America with the British Empire, effectively rejecting the French-American alliance that had been formed during the War of Independence. Britain had finally agreed to vacate the forts in the western territory and the threat of war was at last dispelled. Adams stood by Washington and the Federalists, who welcomed the closer links to Britain, but Madison, Jefferson and their fellow Republicans deeply disapproved of the pro-British turn.

The Senate had ratified the treaty the previous summer, but in spring 1796 the House of Representatives needed to decide whether to fund it or not. In his role as vice president, Adams was relegated to being a mere spectator during the long debates and so his mind frequently wandered back to his farm at Quincy. He also took pleasure in using agricultural metaphors to make his point. The Jay Treaty, he wrote to a fellow Federalist, was like making manure—like the lime he mixed with earth, mud and straw, it "occasions some smoke and some Dust and some hissing but will end in reducing all to one rich mould." As the disagreement intensified, he once again used the metaphor of the cart with pairs of oxen at the front and back with which he had so vividly explained the checks and balances of government almost a decade earlier. Only this time the wagon was stuck "in the Mire" and with the oxen pulling in opposite directions, the "Wheels Stand Still."

After a protracted and acrimonious battle, the House of Representatives passed the appropriation bill for the treaty by the smallest margin on 30 April 1796. Adams was relieved that the debates were over and desperate to return to his garden, "the Ultimate Object of all my Hopes, Wishes and Expectations, for myself." There was no reason to stay in Philadelphia a moment longer than he had to. He requested leave of absence and less than a week later he was on the road home.

Coming six years after Alexander Hamilton's Assumption Plan, the Jay Treaty (now finally passed) was a triumph for the Federalists' economic plans, and with America now firmly allied with Britain, exports of grains and other products rose rapidly. Staunch Republicans, on the other hand, stood against it on pure principle, unmoved by the soaring economy. Appalled that the prosperity of his country now relied on commerce with Britain, James Madison, who had put all his political clout behind the battle, condemned the treaty as "the most worrying and vexatious that I have ever encountered." The debate, which should have managed to "fortify the Republican cause," he wrote to Jefferson, "has left it in a very crippled condition." A number of moderate Republicans had spoken out in favor of the treaty, and when they began to abandon Madison, he lost his majority in Congress. Federalist newspapers were jubilant, one declaring the politician "absolutely deceased, cold, stiff and buried in oblivion for ever and ever." When Madison left Philadelphia in June, he was defeated and tired, and desperately longed for Montpelier. Until now he had focused on his political career, but the prospect of being a full-time farmer was becoming increasingly attractive.

Madison and Adams were not the only ones who felt worn out after the battle. President Washington was exhausted but also felt betrayed, as his support for the Jay Treaty had provoked vicious attacks from his opponents. Republican newspapers censured Washington for acting like a king and a traitor. For the first time, the man who had united the people of the United States of America was treated like a mere mortal and not a hero. Only four years previously Jefferson had begged him to run as president for a second term, confident that "North and South will hang together, if they have you to hang on," but now Jefferson privately accused Washington of betraying his country.* "Be upon your guard," an anonymous letter had warned Washington about Jefferson. "You have cherished in your Bosom a Serpent, and he is now endeavouring to sting you [to] death." The president had managed to brush off such tittle-tattle but found it hard to sidestep the slanderous articles. The "Old Hero

---

* Jefferson's accusation was that Washington and his administration had had "their heads shorn by the harlot England." This letter, which Jefferson had written in private to his gardening friend Philip Mazzei in April 1796, was published a few months later in newspapers in France and America. If Washington did have any doubts before, the letter proved that Jefferson had turned against him. Bemoaning that America was ruled by Federalists and their monarchical principles, Jefferson had written that "it would give you a fever were I to name to you the apostates who have gone over to these heresies, men who were Samsons in the field and Solomons in the council." And though he had not named Washington, everybody knew whom he meant.

looks very grave of late," Adams confided to Abigail, "the turpitude of their attacks touches him more nearly than he owns in Words." There was nothing that Washington wanted more than to resign and to return to Mount Vernon for good.

That spring one man was missing from Philadelphia: Thomas Jefferson, who had resigned as secretary of state at the end of 1793. Jefferson was the only one of the founding fathers who could enjoy these months without the attrition of desperately long congressional discussions. He kept a low public profile, living on his mountaintop, as he described it, "like an Antediluvian patriarch among my children and grand children, and tilling my soil." Again and again he insisted that he had no interest in politics and party matters. When Adams sent him a book on the French Revolution (still a contentious subject between them), Jefferson wrote that he couldn't promise to read it for it was "on politics, a subject I never loved, and now hate." Visitors, he claimed, could look forward to being entertained from morning until night with agricultural discussions but would have to look elsewhere for political conversations. Though he convincingly played his role as a retired farmer, he wrote of his dismay about the "execrable" treaty in private letters to his political allies, many of whom agreed that it was an alliance between England and misguided politicians "against the legislature and people of the United states."

By the summer of 1796, Adams, Madison, Washington and Jefferson had all repaired to their farms and plantations, where agriculture, planting and gardening took precedence over politics. The founding fathers have often been cast as the haloed demigods of the American Revolution—some cerebral and literary, others brave and heroic—but what has long been missing from this picture is their lives as farmers and gardeners, which both reflected and influenced their political thinking and patriotism. Consequently their farms, fields and gardens can be read like their diaries and letters, and so the summer of 1796 provides a window into this part of their lives.

There was Adams with an axe in his hand felling trees next to his hired laborer, a New England farmer with a modest estate, a Federalist, but one who hated merchants and banks and who, to his wife's frustration, "never saved any thing but what he vested in Land." Madison, who had married the vivacious Dolley two years previously, had yet to inherit Montpelier, but during the summer of 1796 he began to prepare for the future—on the one hand his life as a plantation owner, on the other the first election campaign in American history. Also in Virginia was Jefferson, riding across his plantation as his slaves harvested the wheat, a man who conjured up many visionary farming methods and fanciful gardening schemes that never made it from the notebooks to the plantation. And then there was Washington, who applied the same rigorous discipline and management to Mount Vernon as he had to his army, turning it into a large business enterprise that comprised not only plantations but also a commercial gristmill, lucrative fisheries and later a whiskey distillery.

It was a summer in which the president discussed the culture of pineapples with the Spanish ambassador and entertained his guests with long talks on the merits of different types of ploughs, while the vice president was happily mixing manure in his own yard. A keen Madison oversaw the construction of a new mill in Montpelier, finding distraction from the painful defeat over the Jay Treaty. Adams was out in his fields every day, and Jefferson was trying his agricultural inventions at Monticello. All were testing new agricultural implements, sowing new crops and comparing the yields of their fields. At a time when the political party lines had hardened, agriculture and its importance for the future of the United States of America remained the one topic all four agreed upon and continued to correspond about.

The summer of 1796 stands between the battle over the Jay Treaty and the official announcement of Washington's retirement in September. Played out on the estates among plants, ploughs and fields but also bracketed by important political shifts, the summer was at once typical and extraordinary. The men ran their farms and planted as they did every year, focusing on what they enjoyed most. When Adams had told Jefferson two years previously that "I have Spent my Summer So deliciously in farming that I return to the Old Story of Politicks with great Reluctance," any of the four men could have said the same.

But something was different about the summer of 1796, because it was the last one that would see the United States of America led by a unanimously elected president. After the political abuse that he had endured during his second term there was nothing, not even his elevated and unerring sense of duty, that would make Washington stay on for another term. This decision made the summer of 1796 exceptional, for it was the calm before the political storm. "This has been the most quiet Summer I ever knew, in Politicks," Adams wrote at the end of it, capturing the strange lull. It was as if the United States of America was holding her breath for what was about to follow.

WHEN ADAMS ARRIVED in Quincy in early May 1796, his sour mood immediately evaporated. Instead of quarreling politicians and busy city life, he now saw the roses that were growing under the window of the parlor and the beautiful lilacs that perfumed the air. From this window Adams could see the old-fashioned flower garden that was divided in rectangular grass plots bordered by ribbons of flowers and sharply clipped low box hedges. In layout it was similar to many other colonial gardens throughout the seventeenth and eighteenth centuries and had been planted decades before the Adamses moved in. Adams would have seen the last daffodils that freckled the grass plots with yellow dots and the red columbines with their blooms of dangling bells. These were the flowers that Abigail compared to a "humble citizen," in contrast to the stately crown imperial, which was banned from the garden because "it bears to[o] monarchical a Name." There were also little grass plots in front of the house and an ancient orchard nearby with the fruit trees in full blossom—peaches, "saint Germain pears" and Russet apples. Behind the house, where the land gently dipped, they had established a kitchen garden with potatoes, large asparagus beds, lettuces and strawberries.

Adams had always maintained that he could only be happy when working the soil. "I should prefer the Delights of a Garden to the Dominion of a World," he had declared nearly twenty years earlier, "I had rather build stone Wall upon Penns Hill, than be the first Prince in Europe, the first General, or first senator in America." But that summer Adams embraced his life as a farmer with more passion than ever before. For the first time in more than a decade he dug out his diary and filled it with nothing other than accounts of his farming activities, almost as if he had decided to leave some record of this part of his life to posterity. Within days he had pushed aside the memories of the "unpleasant Moments" in Philadelphia and immersed himself instead in his "rural Amusements."

Adams's farm was so modest that, according to one French visitor, "no Paris advocate of the lowest rank" would live there. It was certainly small compared to the several thousand acres that Washington and Jefferson owned and that Madison would soon possess, but since inheriting the first 40 acres after his father's death in 1761, Adams had increased his property to about 500 acres. The white clapboard house of two stories with six chambers was not grand by any means but was at least bigger than the small saltbox cottage he had shared with Abigail before leaving for Europe. They had bought the new house in 1787 while the family had still been in Britain, but Abigail had been disappointed on their return.* It

---

* Both John and Abigail had seen the house before they left for Europe, but evidently their time in London and Paris had made them accustomed to more luxurious and larger dwellings. When they returned they were surprised how small the house was compared to what they remembered.

John Adams's farm at Quincy in the early nineteenth century. The flower garden was to the left. Note the ornamental trees to the right of the house.

was so small, she wrote, that "it feels like a wren's house," warning her daughter not to wear feathers on her hat and her son-in-law to avoid heels "or he will not be able to walk upright."

When they bought the house, the garden was a "wilderness" and the fields completely overgrown, but the orchard had the best collection of fruit in the neighborhood. Despite his constant frustration and anxiety about lack of money, Adams adored his land, particularly the "two or three spots" that he claimed offered "the most beautiful Prospects in the world." Whenever he bought another small parcel of land, Adams looked forward to working and improving it. "My Farm gallops like a gay hobby Horse," he enthused, delighted in the transformation of the land into neat fields, vegetable plots and flowerbeds. Over the years Adams had built stone walls, constructed a corncrib, drained some land, planted a large vegetable garden and put two additional windows in the parlor so that they could see the flowers below.

As a couple they divided their duties—Adams was in charge of the farm (when he was at home), the trees and the earth-moving garden work, while Abigail looked after the flowerbeds. She had left the overall layout as it was when they first moved in but added many of the flowers they had collected in England. She admired the tall blue candles of larkspur blossom, the orange flowers of nasturtiums and the bright yellow spring dress of daffodils and cowslips. A few years later, their son Thomas would bring flowers and fruits from his diplomatic mission in Europe, knowing how much his parents treasured them.

Adams and Abigail had acquired a more sophisticated taste in gardens during their time in Paris and London. In France they had fallen in love with the ornamental grounds at the house they had rented in Auteuil, just outside Paris. So besotted was Adams with it that he immediately began to worry that wherever they lived next would lack such beautiful surroundings. Abigail too dreaded the day they would have to leave, writing to her niece that "I shall mourn my garden more than any other object." But on arriving at the fashionable Grosvenor Square in London, they had been pleasantly surprised. The house was "in as good an Air as this fat greasy Metropolis, can afford," Adams said, or, as Abigail put it a little more politely, it was "one of the pleasantest squares of London," full of shrubberies and meandering walks. Their tours of England's gardens had also inspired them with ideas for their own, because Adams had deeply admired the ornamental farms such as The Leasowes and Wooburn Farm for their fusion of beauty and utility.

In the years since their return in 1788, Adams had never found time to implement any of these ideas, but now, as summer arrived, he began to bring the farmland, the gardens and the countryside into one unified whole. As he had seen with Jefferson on their visit to Stowe, the best way to do this was with a ha-ha—the ditch that allowed sweeping views across pastures and the countryside yet prevented cattle from walking into the garden, making walls and fences—which Adams thought were "a folly"—obsolete. It had been exactly ten years since Adams had seen the ha-ha in Stowe, but by July 1796 he was finally ready to remove some walls and dig his own.

"An ornamented Farm, appears to me an Innocent and desirable object," Abigail believed, and though they might cost a fortune in England, where she had admired them with her husband, at home it would be cheap because a farm nestled in America's spectacular landscape was already much like a *ferme ornée*. It would be easy to follow Joseph Addison's directions, which had inspired so many English gardeners. Adams had read the essay in which Addison had railed against rigid shapes and patterns that garden shears and rulers imposed on nature. He had, like Jefferson, also bought Thomas Whately's *Observations on Modern Gar-*

dening, which was filled with instructions on how to create such ornamental farms. He and Abigail admired Whately so much that they had also given the book as a present to some of their relatives.

"To blend the useful with the agreeable," Whately advised his readers, was the goal of such improvements, a notion that chimed with Adams's vision for his farm. He had enjoyed the orchestrated vistas in the English gardens, which guided the eye to the most important elements of the surrounding landscape, but in England the focal points were often temples. Adams wanted to emphasize instead the agricultural parts of his farm and the hills in the distance. "We have opened the Prospect," Adams wrote in his diary in July, "so that the Meadows and Western Mountain may distinctively be seen," following Whately's directions of "opening the garden to the country." Just as Mount Vernon's vista led from the house across the rolling land toward the west, Adams was now creating such views (although much shorter than Washington's half-mile opening—Adams only had to fell fifty cedars to create this view). The garden in Quincy would never be as grand as the ones in Mount Vernon, Monticello and Montpelier, both because Adams could not afford it* and because he thought such elaborate designs "mere Ostentations of Vanity." His estate might have been small, but he took great pride in it because it was, more than anything, "the farm of a Patriot."

By the end of the summer, almost a decade after he had bought the house and farm, he finally decided to name it, calling it Peacefield, in commemoration of the 1783 Peace Treaty that he had helped to forge, the years of peace that the United States of America had enjoyed since the War of Independence and the solace that Adams felt when he was at home. The name united Adams's passions—his country, his politics, his garden and his fields. It showed how much politics and plants, the United States of America and agriculture, and peace and soil belonged together in his world.

One of the reasons why Adams was concerned with the naming of his estate and the appearance of his garden that summer might have been that he was preparing for a new stage in his life. Early in January he had heard the first rumors that Washington was determined to resign the following spring after the end of his second term, and Martha Washington had implied as much herself, Adams wrote to Abigail. Within a few days he had dashed off the next letter, telling Abigail that he was now certain

---

* Unlike Jefferson, who despite his huge debts was in the process of demolishing his house in Monticello in order to build a more sophisticated one, Adams never lived above his means.

of Washington's decision, but that he would not be vice president under anybody else—most certainly not under Jefferson. In his many letters to Abigail he went endlessly back and forth about how he should proceed, and clearly needed her opinion—"Think of it and say nothing to any one but your J.A." By the end of January he had confided to his wife that he was considering the presidency himself but seemed to be playing the reluctant suitor. "I hate to live in Philadelphia," "I hate Levees," "I hate to Speak to a 1000 people to whom I have nothing to say," he protested. But for all his outward hesitation and Abigail's own ambivalence toward the idea, his ambition also shone through, convincing him that "all this I can do."

Never exhibiting the reserved control that Jefferson or Washington had achieved, he refused to suffer in silence—"I sighed, sobbed, & groaned, and sometimes screeched and screamed, And I must confess to my shame and sorrow, that I sometimes swore." His temperament might have been volatile, but it was not malicious, and when writing to Abigail, his vanity, emotions, fears and excitement would flow from the pages, deliberating, retracting, accusing and sometimes simply showing off. Adams knew only two ways of releasing tension—conversing with Abigail and working in his garden, where he took his shovel or pruning knife and disappeared for hours. He needed the physical work, the dirt between his fingers or the strong handle of a scythe in his hands. "My Time," he said when feeling paralyzed by politics, "might have been improved to some Purpose, in mowing Grass, raking Hay, or hoeing Corn, weeding Carrotts, picking or shelling Peas." Working the soil, Abigail told their son, "keeps his Spirits in action, and gives him Health." Without the digging and scything at home, Abigail believed, he "could not endure" life in Philadelphia. And Adams had never worked with so much vigor in his garden and on his farm as in the summer 1796 as he debated—by way of digging and planting—what the future might hold for him.

At the same time, some 500 miles away in Montpelier, Madison was slowly recovering from losing the battle over the Jay Treaty. Madison might have looked "pale, withered, haggard," as Adams commented when he left Philadelphia, but once again his delicate constitution belied the steely determination that drove him. He wasn't going to give up, and so while Adams contemplated the presidency, Madison was planning the Republican counterattack. As he rode across the plantation every day, he was not only investigating the fields and talking to the overseers but also trying to work out how he could convince a reluctant Jefferson to exchange his beloved farming pursuits at Monticello for a life in the President's House. It wouldn't be an easy task, because Jefferson once again protested that he no longer had any interest in politics—"the little spice of ambition, which I had in my younger days," he asserted, "has long since evaporated." The best strategy, Madison decided, was not to see Jefferson at all during the summer (despite Montpelier only being a short day's ride from Monticello). "I have not seen Jefferson," he wrote to James Monroe, in code so that no Federalist could discover their plans if the letters were intercepted, "and have thought it best to present him no opportunity of protesting to his friend[s] against being embarked in the contest."

While Jefferson pretended not to be involved, Washington planned his retirement, dreaming of sowing, growing and sitting under his vine and fig tree. There were no provisions made in the Constitution for a limited number of terms, and he knew that most Americans assumed that he would serve for life, but he had other plans. Throughout his presidency Washington had been aware that he was walking on "untrodden ground," and fully realized that as the first in his office, whatever he did would establish a precedent. So when he decided to retire in order to return to farming and gardening, Washington knew that he would leave an enduring stamp on American politics. For the irony is that what we interpret as a necessary check on, and curtailment of, executive power— the two-term presidency that would become a cornerstone of America's democracy*—had its seed in the president's refusal to brook any further delay in his return to his fields and flowerbeds.

Washington left Philadelphia for Mount Vernon at the end of June for his last summer as president. He arrived to see a garden that had been prepared by his estate manager for a string of prestigious and important visitors expected over the coming weeks. A month earlier Washington had instructed that everything should be in "prime order"—the necessaries spotless, the lawn rolled, the paths raked and a new front gate built. "I shall expect an abundance of every thing in the Gardens," Washington ordered, for the house will be "crowded with company . . . as the ministers of France, Great Britain, and Portugal, in succession, intend to be here—besides other strangers."

The garden that he had planted more than a decade earlier had matured into colorful shrubberies and shady walks filled with American native species. Along the serpentine walk in front of the house, rosebays paraded their origamied white blossoms, taking over from the pink-

---

* Only Franklin Delano Roosevelt broke this precedent, but in 1951 the two-term presidency was written into law with the Twenty-second Amendment.

tinged blooms of mountain laurel. Walking along the neatly raked paths Washington would have been able to smell the sweet fragrance of the last spidery flowers of Carolina allspice. Southern catalpa was at its best, almost concealing its large leaves with its abundant floral white dress, and the tulip poplars had just shed the last of their yellow-orange petals, as had the black locusts. The huge white cups of *Magnolia grandiflora* were still clinging to the branches next to the shiny leaves. "A thousand other bushes," one visitor said, "all covered with flowers of different colors, all planted in a manner to produce the most beautiful hues."

Since planting the garden in early 1785, Washington had also created six large oval beds on the bowling green in front of the house with the trees and shrubs that he had admired in Bartram's Garden during the Constitutional Convention in 1787. Since then, William Bartram had sent more than one hundred varieties—conifers, deciduous trees and many shrubs including the lavish southern species that Washington had seen flowering at Bartram's such as *Franklinia alatamaha*, silky camellia and the Carolina silverbell. Once again Washington had followed Philip Miller's instructions in the *Gardeners Dictionary* by creating "rising clumps"—the ovals were thickly planted with dwarf varieties at the edge climbing to a stately white pine at the center.* Crimson cardinals and Baltimore orioles with their beautifully contrasted orange and black plumage were flying in and out of the trees, adding dancing spots of bright color and delighting with their songs. The gardens looked glorious.

While at Mount Vernon, Washington received a letter from Alexander Hamilton that contained a draft for the president's final words to the American people. Six months previously, he had asked Hamilton to write his Farewell Address, sending him the draft that the diligent Madison had prepared for the possible retirement at the end of the first term as well as a few paragraphs that addressed the "considerable changes" that had occurred in his second term. He left it to Hamilton to either revise or prepare an entirely new one—his only stipulation was that it be "honest; unaffected; simple garb."

In tandem with this Farewell Address, Washington also arranged the agricultural aspect of his retirement, having decided to radically change the management of his plantation. If successful, it would make his fields

---

* Lawns dotted with clumps and oval flowerbeds—many planted with American species—were fashionable in England. Washington had probably also been inspired by another publication that he owned—*The Seats of the Nobility and Gentry* by William Watts—which featured almost one hundred engravings, many showing landscape gardens and shrubberies.

more productive and provide a stable income, but the main incentive was to reduce slave labor on his land. Instead of one plantation run by one master and worked by his slaves, Washington proposed that most of his arable land be divided into smaller lots to be leased to tenants who were encouraged to refrain from using slave labor. Washington planned to keep only the farm operation associated with the mansion, and that only "for amusement." The idea was "to separate the Negroes from the Land." What he should do with the surplus slaves remained a problem, so he asked his estate manager, William Pearce, to compile lists of all his slaves with information on how they were related to each other and "the Neighbouring Negros," as he wanted to avoid splitting up families. At the same time he planned to sell his vast tracts of land in the Ohio territory. The money from the sales, he explained, would allow him "to liberate a certain species of property which I possess, very repugnantly to my own feelings." Advertisements of the terms and conditions for the leases were dispatched across America from Ohio and Kentucky to Hartford and Alexandria.*

Washington was in search of a particular breed of tenant. He had no intention of leasing his land to "the slovenly farmers of this country" who ruined the soil by cultivating their land with the same methods and tools that had been used since the Middle Ages. For centuries, farmers had yoked their oxen and horses to wooden ploughs to turn the soil into the familiar ridges and furrows. Most still cast their seeds by hand instead of with new seed drills—animal-drawn machines that dropped seeds in regular rows†—an invention that had been "violently opposed." Virginia farmers (if they didn't grow tobacco) planted their fields on a three-year cycle, starting with Indian corn, then wheat and then a year fallow—after which it started again. With no understanding of nutrients or fertilizers, farmers slowly destroyed the soil. In a country where land was plentiful and labor dear, farmers just cleared a new plot of land to start all over again.

Adams had called the Massachusetts farmers "a lazy, ignorant sett" and Washington was equally frustrated about the "abuse" of the land. In England, however, where land was scarce, scientifically inclined agriculturists had begun to restore the soil's fertility in the early eighteenth century by introducing crop rotation. Farmers across England worked on a

---

* Once he got a response to the advertisements, Washington hoped, "I shall be able to take more decisive measures" and plan how to reduce the number of slaves.
† Jethro Tull had invented his seed drill in England in 1701 but many farmers had refused to use it—critics said that it required long experience to handle the implement efficiently.

four-field cycle that introduced fodder crops such as turnips. Since then the idea had developed into five-, six-, seven- and eight-year methods based on the same principle. Leguminous plants like clover, buckwheat and winter vetch acted as "green manure," which, when ploughed under, added organic matter and released nitrogen into the soil, while grazing crops brought cattle and much-needed manure to the fields.

For the past decade Washington had kept abreast of the latest innovations by corresponding with England's leading agriculturalist, Arthur Young, who sent him publications, new seeds, ploughs and plans for farm buildings. Washington had tested these new farming methods and wanted tenants who would follow his visionary six-year crop rotation and also give their word that not an inch of his land would be used to cultivate tobacco. To find tenants who were acquainted with the most up-to-date practice, Washington wrote to his agricultural correspondents abroad for men "particularly from Great Britain."*

Washington had studied the latest agricultural books and discussed his experiments with friends and correspondents. "His favourite subject is agriculture," visitors at Mount Vernon remarked again and again, surprised to be lectured at great length by the president of the United States about crops, ploughs, "a very minute account of the Hessian fly" and other pressing farming issues. Even when he led 13,000 troops to crush the so-called Whiskey Rebellion in 1794, which saw several thousand grain farmers protesting against the tax on whiskey, Washington examined the fields en route and relayed his observations back to his estate manager. "Our welfare and prosperity depend upon the cultivation of our lands," he wrote, reiterating that the "common farmer will not depart from the *old* road 'till the *new* one is made so plain and easy that he is sure it cannot be mistaken."

Despite his more modest means, Adams shared this zeal for innovative agriculture. He had previously published an essay that stressed the importance of "making Experiments, upon Soils and Manures, Grains and Grasses, Trees and Bushes." He had introduced clover and grasses to his meadows and had grown hemp in his garden to test it as a possible crop. Jefferson was also busy learning the new methods—"the few who can afford it," he wrote to Madison, "should incur the risk & expense of all new improvements."

Since his retirement Jefferson had been studying crop rotation, and in

* A few years earlier, Washington had already employed an English farmer as manager, because he wanted his plantation run according to the latest agricultural methods.

spring 1796, as Congress had battled over the Jay Treaty, he had sent questionnaires to a number of his fellow farmers about fodder crops. For some time he had been corresponding with "the best farmers of all," including Washington and Madison, in order to determine how best to implement crop cycles. He sent diagrams for an eight-year plan and asked for their opinions. Madison was more than happy to oblige, sending Jefferson a new pamphlet on the subject, and Washington, having experimented for years with crop rotation, was also delighted to advise Jefferson on different crops and methods.

The condition of their respective fields when they retired was an indicator of how differently each of the founding fathers ran their farms. Jefferson's were in the least impressive state, ravaged by overseers and suffering from a decade of neglect while he had been in office. While Jefferson blamed his long absences from home for the losses, Washington had successfully managed to run his plantation from the same distance. Every Sunday without fail during his eight years as president he wrote explicit instructions to his estate manager—the longest of all his letters during this period. Washington's innovative farming techniques had gained him the reputation as "best Farmer in the State," while the cerebral Jefferson was regarded as something of a failure because his agricultural knowledge was based too much on theory rather than practice. Since the beginning of his retirement, however, Jefferson had embraced farming wholeheartedly, determined to turn his depleted land into lush fields. "I am but a learner," he wrote to a friend, "an eager one indeed but yet desperate." He relished his new life away from politics and spent the summer of 1796 on horseback all day out in the fields, as one visitor noted in June, despite the scorching heat of the sun. The red soil of Monticello had become the main interest in his life. "I have made researches into nothing but what is connected to agriculture," he wrote in July, for "I am entirely a farmer, soul and body."

Equally Madison, who until recently had mainly been occupied with politics, had begun to focus on the day-to-day operation of farming. As the eldest son he was expecting to inherit several thousand acres in Orange County in Virginia, but with his father still alive, Madison had long searched for another vocation. He acquired two farms near Montpelier and when his brother (who had managed the plantation with the father) died, in 1793, Madison took over more responsibilities. Like Adams and Washington, he had written long farming letters from Philadelphia during the Jay Treaty debates that showed him to be a similarly innovative farmer. He built his own mill, studied crop rotation and, despite his frailty, also enjoyed the physical work such as chopping wood. Jefferson was delighted that his closest friend was "now immersed in farming." Their letters had always included weather and farm reports, and now they could compare yields, crops and tools. Jefferson arranged for a new plough from one of the members of the agricultural society in Philadelphia for Madison and quizzed him about Jethro Tull's horse-drawn hoe. Madison in turn reported about a *"patent plow"* that was "worth your looking at."

The improvement of agricultural methods and crops was not only an immediate economic necessity. While at a more prosaic level, farming provided a basic livelihood for most Americans, for the founding fathers, free husbandmen with small self-sufficient farms would be the foot soldiers of the infant nation.

This was not a new idea—Aristotle had claimed that for a republic "an Agrarian people is the best" and the Romans had elevated the farmer as the most virtuous kind of citizen, imbuing the hardworking peasant at his plough with patriotic pride. Virgil's poem *Georgics* had been admired as a celebration of virtuous country life, while Cicero had written that "of all the occupations by which gain is secured, none is better than agriculture, none more profitable, none more delightful, none more becoming to a freeman."* This emphasis on farmers as the foundation of a free society had its origin in the belief that republics were the most fragile form of government. With the removal of the monarchy, the traditional control mechanisms of society—which were based on fear and force—had to be replaced by self-control, moral integrity and industry. "Only a virtuous people are capable of freedom," Franklin had written, "as nations become corrupt and vicious, they have more need of masters." As such the strength of a republic—the people—was also its weakness. People's selfishness, ambition, avarice and vanity in America posed such a threat that Adams worried "whether there is public Virtue enough to support a Republic."

To put the common good before one's private interests, the founding

---

* American revolutionaries were not the only ones who injected pastoral associations into the republican endeavor. French revolutionaries had translated this vision into their new republican calendar, creating names for months that were inspired by the agricultural year rather than by Roman gods. The calendar was divided into periods such as Prairial (French, *prairie* or "pasture"), Messidor (Latin, *messis* or "harvest") and Fructidor (Latin, *fructus* or "fruit"). And instead of saint days, each day was now associated with crops, vegetables, fruits, farm animals and agricultural tools.

fathers believed, was the foundation of a nontyrannical and nonmonar-
chical government (again a notion lifted from classical literature), and the
only basis on which a republic could be founded. Closely linked to the
concept of "public virtue" was that of "private virtue," described as
being frugal, temperate and uncorrupted—traits that the founding
fathers ascribed to farmers. "Cultivators of the earth," Jefferson wrote,
"are the most vigorous, the most independent, the most virtuous." They
elevated the independent yeoman to an elemental place in American life.
Hardworking and independent farmers were the pillars of American society because only a virtuous and industrious people would be able to hold
together the republic.

As LONG AS a man had a piece of land of his own that was sufficient
to support his family, Franklin had said, he was independent.* Jefferson
went even further, arguing that only farmers should be elected congress-
men because more than any others they were "the true representatives of
the great American interest." A man who cultivated his own soil was
immune to moral corruption, Jefferson said, unlike the deplorable merchants who "have no country" and therefore no real attachment to their
nation. Laborers employed in manufacturing and factories would never
be bound to their country as farmers who worked the soil were. "The
small landholders are the most precious part of a state," Jefferson
insisted, and had written into his draft for the Virginia Constitution that
every free person was to be entitled to fifty acres of land (he had failed to
get it passed). Madison agreed and published an article in the *National
Gazette* declaring that the greater the proportion of husbandmen, "the
more free, the more independent, and the more happy must be the society
itself."

The well-tended fields of small farms became a symbol for America's
future as an agrarian republic. John Adams had been the first to provide
a legal base for the elevation of agriculture when he chiseled the promotion of useful arts (of which agriculture was regarded the most important) into the constitution of Massachusetts in 1779. He had included a
section stating that the government should encourage societies and

---

* This was a sentiment that Madison later applied to emigrants, insisting that farmers would be more easily integrated than merchants who "are less tied . . . to their
new Country by the nature of their property & pursuits." Adams equally disliked
merchants because they were "living in Such Pomp and Such Expence upon Property of others, giving Charities, making feasts, Signing Subscriptions, blaring away
with Furniture, Equipage &c."

awards that promoted agriculture and other useful arts. Eight years later the framers wrote into the Constitution that the federal government had the duty "To promote the Progress of Science and useful Arts."

It was easy for Adams and Franklin to proselytize based on the idea of the independent yeoman farmer, but it was more problematic for the slave-owning Washington, Jefferson and Madison. On a political and economic level they might have been fighting for their dream of a nation of free farmers, but back at Mount Vernon, Monticello and Montpelier, hundreds of slaves were harvesting wheat and corn, working from dawn to dusk six days a week.* Despite this contradiction, Washington, Jefferson and Madison still firmly believed that widespread small-scale farming in principle fostered an independent people.

With the elevation of the small farmer as the guardian of liberty, seemingly mundane tasks such as collecting manure, planting seeds and devising crop rotations became elemental parts of nation-building, and the founding fathers' political rhetoric became ever more infused with agricultural imagery. Jefferson for example said the accounts of the United States "may be, made, as simple as those of a common farmer." After a summer of happy farming, Adams told Jefferson that the "Earth is grateful . . . I wish We could both say the Same of its Inhabitants." Even Washington's political motto of "slow and sure," Jefferson wrote, "is not less a good one in agriculture than in politics."

If agricultural improvements had become political acts, then experimental farmers, Madison argued, were "patriotic individuals." Every advance the founding fathers made would make America stronger and more independent. They were, as Madison quipped, "worshippers of Ceres," the Roman goddess of agriculture. Their agricultural correspondence zigzagged the country and crossed the ocean. They exchanged the latest books, shared valuable seeds of new crops, reported about the yields of their harvests and compared their experiments. Madison tried out a new species of wheat from Italy that Washington passed on to him,

---

* In the past Jefferson had even thought that small-scale farming held the possibility of ending slavery at Monticello. While still in Europe he had considered settling German farmers "intermingled" with his slaves on farms of fifty acres each. The Germans whom he had met were "absolutely incorruptible by money"—the epitome of the virtuous farmer. The slaves would remain his property but their children would be free, and by being brought up in the proximity of the German farmers, Jefferson believed, they "will be good citizens." Jefferson never implemented this scheme (nor any other along these lines), and when he returned to his plantation, he abandoned his plans to free his slaves. During his life he freed only three slaves and a further five through his will, while Madison never freed any of his slaves. Only Washington freed the slaves who belonged to him after his death.

as well as some new varieties of beans from Mount Vernon's garden. Adams heard about a new sort of wheat and forwarded a paper describing it to the American Academy of Arts and Sciences, where he was president. He and Washington also encouraged a farmer to pursue the cultivation of a vineyard and Jefferson was so "delighted" by a new Indian corn that he packed it in his luggage on his way home to present to his friends, including Madison. On his journey into his retirement, Jefferson had acted as Washington's courier, dropping off some pecan nuts at the post office in Alexandria on his way from Philadelphia to Monticello. Madison dispatched a new crop from Jamaica ("where it forms a great proportion of the food of the Slaves") to Jefferson, and when Washington received chicory seeds from an agricultural writer in Britain, he shared them with Jefferson, who declared "it as one of the greatest acquisitions a farmer can have."

They kept up-to-date with innovative methods by reading gardening and agricultural books, mostly from Britain. In the summer of 1796, Jefferson, for example, consulted Miller's *Gardeners Dictionary* in order to find new species of winter vetch for his crop rotation. Washington kept a whole collection of gardening and farming books open on the table in his study, including old favorites such as the *Gardeners Dictionary* and the latest publications from agricultural writer Arthur Young. Whenever an American agricultural book or pamphlet was published (which was still rare), they enthusiastically bought those too. In the previous summer, for example, they had all eagerly read John Bordley's *Sketches on Rotations of Crops,* the first American treatise on the subject.

They were also fascinated by new agricultural technology. Threshing machines in particular excited them because for millennia farmers had separated the grains from the chaff by hand or by letting their horses trample over the wheat (neither efficient nor very hygienic, as the grain mixed with dirt and excrement). Washington had constructed an innovative sixteen-sided barn at Mount Vernon, in which horses ran in circles "treading" on the upper floor, the clean grain falling through narrow gaps onto the floor below. Washington and Jefferson had together inspected a threshing machine on a farm just outside Philadelphia, and Jefferson had become so interested that he had ordered a model from Britain through the American minister in London. Like an excited child, he had constantly updated Madison about his progress—"I expect every day to receive it," "I have not yet received my threshing machine," it had at last "arrived at New York." When he finally constructed and tried it in August 1796, it was a "great success."

That summer Jefferson was also ploughing his fields with his newly invented "mould-board of least resistance." He had a knack for mechanics and could spend years brooding over a single invention. Ever since he had seen the badly designed ploughs in the Netherlands and France, he had thought about making a more efficient moldboard (the wooden part of a plough that lifts and turns the sod). The plough, Jefferson believed, was the most important agricultural tool, "to the farmer what the wand is to the sorcerer."* With his inveterate fondness for science, Jefferson had created a mathematically perfect moldboard. When it was finished, his slaves yoked the oxen to the plough and watched their master draw it through the red soil with ease.

While Jefferson only dirtied his hands for a scientific experiment like this, Adams stood in a pile of compost that was rising in his yard—seemingly one of his most favorite spots, because no other subject was mentioned so frequently in his diary that summer. In fact, the only correspondence that Adams thought worth noting at all was a letter about a "report on manures" from Britain, which Jefferson, Madison and Washington also had received. Mundane as it seems, manure was of the greatest concern to all four of them, for one of the reasons why yields in the United States of America were declining so drastically was the lack of manuring. Since the first settlers had arrived in the early seventeenth century, American farmers had let their livestock roam freely in the forests, where they scattered their manure miles away from the fields.

Over the years Adams had experimented extensively with dung, mixing it with mud, lime and seaweed, which was easily available from the nearby shore. One of the most charming images from Adams's life—and proof of how different he was from the powdered and bejeweled diplomats in Europe—was his close investigation of a manure heap just outside London. Teasing apart the straw and dung, the American Minister to the court at St. James's Palace "carefully examined" the stinking pile and clearly didn't mind the muck on his hands. He noted the exact contents and ingredients, before announcing with glee that it was "not equal to mine."

While Adams had his arms up to the elbow in the dung, the studious Madison used pen, paper and numbers to tackle the problem. In spring 1796, in the midst of the Jay Treaty controversy, he had managed to find time to calculate precisely how many wagonloads of manure were

---

* In 1807 Jefferson received a gold medal from the Society of Agriculture in Paris for his moldboard. He never patented his plough because he believed that every improvement should be shared with other farmers. A patent, Jefferson said, was "doing a great deal more harm than good."

needed to produce a healthy harvest of potatoes and dispatched instructions to Montpelier to cover the fields with dung. Unsurprisingly, Madison approached agriculture with the same attention to detail as he approached legal and political issues.

Somewhat ironically, these steaming piles of dung became icons of the founding fathers' agricultural vision. While other farmers let their cattle and hogs drop the nutritious dung far away from the plantations, Washington was the first American to build a stercorary—a covered dung depository where manure could be stored, aged and mixed. "Nothing, is more wanting in this Country," Washington wrote to Jefferson, asking him to share all knowledge on manures with his friends. Jefferson thought a British pamphlet on the subject so delectable that he declared it a "charming treatise." In the summer of 1796 they all received a pamphlet on manure from John Sinclair, the president of the British Board of Agriculture, who knew that they were not only the most powerful political figures in the United States of America but also the most innovative farmers.* All agreed with Washington that "the profit of every Farm is greater, or less in proportion to the quantity of manure which is made thereon."

The downside of being so groundbreaking, however, was that many American farmers found their ideas controversial. Manuring was labor-intensive because the dung had to be collected, stored, mixed and then carted to and spread across the fields. Their fellow farmers needed to be convinced that it was worth all the effort. One of the problems, the revolutionaries felt, was that there was no American equivalent to bodies such as the newly established British Board of Agriculture, which encouraged (through medals and awards) and disseminated (through publications) innovative methods and their advantages.

For years they had tried in vain to get agriculture onto the political agenda. Adams had suggested as far back as 1771 that a society to encourage agriculture in Massachusetts be established, and five years later had convinced Congress to adopt a resolution to establish "in each and every Colony" a society for the improvement of agriculture and other useful arts. But nothing had happened on a national level. Washington and Jefferson were honorary members of the agricultural societies in Philadelphia and South Carolina, and Adams was a member of the

---

* When Adams was made an honorary member of the British Board of Agriculture, he wrote, "I am not much charmed with the honor of being elected a member of any Society in Europe especially in England," while Jefferson (who accused Adams of being pro-British) did not have such qualms when he was offered the membership.

recently founded Massachusetts Society for Promoting Agriculture*—but none of these had national outreach.

Washington now began to make this goal a political priority. With his retirement only months away, he felt a greater urgency to leave a legacy in the shape of such a national board. At the opening of the congressional session at the end of the year—"the last I shall ever address"—Washington wanted to recommend "an Agricultural establishment" that would serve the national interest. In December he told Congress that it "will not be doubted, that with reference either to individual, or National Welfare, Agriculture is of primary importance." It was to no avail—Washington would never see the establishment of a National Board of Agriculture. "I am sorry to add," he told John Sinclair two days after he had left office, "that nothing *final*, in Congress, has been decided respecting the institution of a National board of Agriculture, recommended by me, at the opening of the Session."†

"OF ALL THE SUMMERS in my life, this has been the freest from Care, Anxiety and Vexation to me," Adams wrote in August, not knowing that all this was about to change. On 19 September 1796, Washington left Philadelphia for Mount Vernon, and as he boarded his coach, the nation opened their newspapers to find his Farewell Address printed across one and a half pages. Washington declared his intention not to stand for another term—once again, just as he had done after the War of Independence, he turned away from power. He urged his compatriots to rein in the "spirit of Party" and unite in a federal government, the great strength of the United States, "a main pillar in the edifice of your real independence." Yet his Farewell Address was, as one contemporary described it, "a signal, like dropping a hat, for the party racers to start." The summer of 1796 was over.

The two front-runners were Adams and Jefferson, but both remained on their farms—seemingly untouched by the electioneering—with Jefferson pretending for weeks not to be aware that he was a candidate and even Adams keeping unusually quiet. It was the first American election that was fought between two parties that, as one commentator observed, "mutually accuse each other of perfidy and treason." The Federalists

---

* The first award that the Massachusetts Society for Promoting Agriculture gave was for two essays on manure.
† In 1803, Madison became the president of the short-lived National Board of Agriculture in Washington, D.C., but it was only in 1852 that a nationwide agricultural society was successfully established.

denounced the Republicans as being puppets of the French and the Republicans attacked the Federalists for their alleged obsession with monarchy. The Republican press portrayed Adams as an "advocate for hereditary Governments," and even the Federalists turned against him, attacking him for his "enemity . . . to Banks and funding systems."

Like Adams and Jefferson, Madison had also remained on his estate and only returned to Philadelphia in late November for the beginning of the congressional session in December. Once there he began to update Jefferson with predictions for the outcome of the election. It was possible, Madison wrote to his friend in Monticello on 5 December, that Adams might not win because Hamilton was working against his own candidate, favoring the second Federalist nominee, Thomas Pinckney. Then, five days later, with the results still unclear, he prepared Jefferson for the possibility of the vice presidency. But Jefferson remained reluctant, replying that he wished Madison himself had been put on the ballot, finishing the letter with a discussion of agricultural matters instead of politics. Meanwhile, Adams prepared himself for defeat, "then for Frugality and Independence. Poverty and Patriotism. Love and a Carrot bed." Finally, when the electoral votes were counted, Adams had won by just three—he had received 71, Jefferson 68, South Carolina's Thomas Pinckney 59 and New York's Republican candidate Aaron Burr 30 votes.

As the vice president (and therefore the president of the Senate), Adams found himself in the peculiar situation of being the one who officially announced the result in February 1797. He would be the second president of the United States and his vice president would be Jefferson, for he had the second-most votes.* Not only did Adams face the unenviable and profoundly daunting task of following Washington, the hero of the American Revolution, he would also have to govern with a vice president who was not from his own party. Jefferson continued to insist that he had "no ambition to govern men" and quoted Virgil: "flumina amo, sylvasque inglorius"—"[though] inglorius, I love rivers and woods." He seemed much more delighted about another election altogether. As Adams was announced president-elect of the United States, Jefferson was voted president of the American Philosophical Society, "the most flattering incident of my life," he wrote.

By the time of Adams's inauguration in March 1797, they had all traded places, as if playing a game of musical chairs. Washington

---

* The rule that the candidate with the second-most votes became vice president was changed in 1803 with the Twelfth Amendment because of the problems in the 1796 and 1800 elections.

"Seemed to me to enjoy a Tryumph over me," Adams wrote to Abigail. "Methought I heard him think Ay! I am fairly out and you fairly in! See which of Us will be happiest." And as Jefferson rode toward Philadelphia, once again leaving behind his fields and gardens, his ploughs and threshing machine, Madison, who had refused a diplomatic post in Europe and a reelection to Congress, was looking forward to his own retirement at Montpelier. "It Seems, the Mode of becoming great is to retire," Adams said. "Madison I Suppose after a Retirement of a few Years is to be President or V. P. . . . It is marvellous how political Plants grow in the shade. Continual Day light and sun shine, Show our Faults and record them."

6

"CITY OF MAGNIFICENT INTENTIONS"

The Creation of Washington, D.C., and the White House

ON 1 NOVEMBER 1800, President John Adams arrived at Washington, D.C., the new capital of the United States. But instead of magnificent tree-lined avenues, elegant houses, shaded gardens and thriving shops, his carriage passed marshy fields and forests, dodging filthy deep puddles and ruts along the way. Where roads should have been, cattle grazed in pastures divided by fences, and none of the streets he had seen on the large map that the city's architect had drawn were recognizable. The only signs that this scrubland might one day be divided into an urban grid were the overgrown quarry stones, each bearing the name or number of a street.

The first government clerks had arrived five months earlier, bringing with them a bewildering array of crates, papers, files and furniture from Philadelphia, which had been the seat of government for the last decade and where Adams lived in the President's House in Market Street. Everyone had been struck by the sharp difference between life in Philadelphia, the largest and most metropolitan city in the United States of America, and the new capital, which offered only a few hundred "small miserable huts" as houses. "We have the name of a city but nothing else," one congressman griped. Not a single thing about Washington exuded the atmosphere of a city—quails perched in the bushes, bullfrogs serenaded lonely riders and turtles sheltered under a web of roots of the sycamores along the river. Pennsylvania Avenue, the road that connected the Capitol to Adams's new home, was hidden by a thorny veil of briars and described by one contemporary as impenetrable, nothing more than a "deep morass." The avenue that was designed for grand parades, another visitor scoffed, "is as much a wilderness as Kentucky." Just below the Capitol the avenue wasn't even opened yet because a farmer was growing crops there—carriages, he offered, could take the path through his fields.

As Adams's carriage jostled along, he saw to his dismay that the Capitol stood only half-finished, even though Congress was due to convene there for the first time in less than three weeks. "The City of Magnificent Distances," Charles Dickens would later write, Washington "might with greater propriety be termed the City of Magnificent Intentions."

When Adams's coach rolled to a stop at his new residence, the President's House, which soon would be called the White House,* his reception committee consisted of a group of workmen who had spent the day plastering some of the rooms. The building that Adams saw—bar the east and west wings and the porticos, which were added later—still stands today, but it was a work in progress to say the least. The secretary of the treasury, Oliver Wolcott, had been so shocked on first inspecting it four months earlier that he declared, "I cannot but consider our Presidents as very unfortunate men, if they must live in this dwelling."

To enter the house Adams had to traverse some wooden planks that precariously bridged the one-story gap over the basement between the front door and the ground below. Six of the thirty rooms had been prepared for the president's arrival, but not a single one was completely finished and furnished. There were not enough lamps to light the rooms and what little furniture had arrived from Philadelphia was dwarfed by the vast, empty spaces. To reach his private apartments on the first floor the rotund Adams had to climb a small, twisting back stair, because where the main staircase should have been was a gaping void. The White House might have been the biggest house in the United States, but when Adams moved in, it was cold and horribly uncomfortable, with every room reeking of wet lime and horsehair from the fresh plaster.

In the evening, as the fires roared to drive the damp out, Adams tried to take his mind off his miserable surroundings and thought instead of his

---

* For the sake of consistency, the President's House will be called the White House throughout the chapter. However, the first recorded use of the name "White House" was only in 1811.

country's future. "May none but honest and wise Men ever rule under this roof," he wrote to Abigail, who had stayed behind at their farm and whom he missed desperately. His letters had always been infused with love—"Yours, Yours, Yours, ever, ever, ever yours," he had written from France twenty years earlier—and his affection showed no sign of abating: "I am with tenderness inexpressible ever yours," he still wrote. His wife of thirty-six years was the only one who understood him, and for some time had been worrying about the political pressure the presidency put on her husband. "He is made of the oak instead of the willow," she explained to her sister, "he may be torn up by the Roots, or break, but he will never bend." As he sat at his table in this enormous empty building the day after arriving, the sixty-five-year-old Adams wrote to his wife to invite her to join him. The house was "habitable," he promised, but knowing that she had been concerned about unfinished rooms and the cold, he wisely refrained from mentioning any of the missing details.

The outside, it transpired, was even worse than the interior. The vast grounds that surrounded the White House were ornamented with brick kilns instead of fountains, workers' shacks instead of pavilions, and construction debris instead of finely raked gravel paths. No vegetable plots or fruit trees would provide any produce for the president's kitchen, nor was there a private area that the family could use as a garden. In an attempt to clear up the mess the commissioners had tried—and failed—to evict the carpenters who were living in wooden sheds on the grounds. The carpenters had warned that the president's new home would remain unfinished if they were forced to leave because there was no other accommodation in the city. Only two days before Adams's arrival, the commissioners had written more letters asking workmen to remove their temporary houses, but the orders had been ignored.

Nothing had changed when Abigail arrived three weeks later. "This place," she wrote to her sister, echoing the scornful congressman, is "known by the name of the city, and the Name is all that you can call so." Abigail's coachman had been forced to jump off the carriage again and again to cut overhanging branches so that they could pass after losing their way in the thick woods. Determined to find something positive amid such depressing circumstances, Abigail praised the views from the house across the wide, romantic expanse of the Potomac and the forests beyond. The marshy edge of the Tiber Creek (a small arm of the Potomac south of the grounds) appeared like the glinting surface of a lake and the wooded hills seemed to stretch on into infinity.

Others, however, were less forgiving or appreciative of the landscape. Some called it a "mere swamp," while many government officials could find neither accommodation nor workspaces. The Treasury Building to the east of the White House was the only completed office building; the War, Navy and State offices had to rent temporary rooms; the Supreme Court was still looking for a home two months after its occupants had all arrived; and the House of Representatives had to meet in the rooms allocated to the Library of Congress. There weren't even enough water closets: with only days before Congress convened, the doorkeeper of the House of Representatives cautiously suggested that they erect one in the center lobby for the members of Congress "who are at such a distance from the ground floor that it might be difficult to reach the journey's end in time."

THAT THE SEAT of government should have been situated in such an uninspiring location, somewhere in the middle of nowhere, was a reflection of the tensions within the Union—between the North and the South, the rural and the urban, the farmer and the merchant, as well as the wider differences between the Federalists and the Republicans. American politics in all its subtleties was played out in the layout, design and location of the city and, in particular, in the way in which the White House gardens developed over the years.

To understand why the capital was placed where it was, we have to return to the summer of 1790, when New York served as the temporary seat of government and the first political fissures quivered through the Union. During that summer two issues paralyzed Congress: the future location of the nation's capital and the question of how America's finances and debts should be handled—"two of the most irritating questions," as Jefferson remarked.

One after another, more than a dozen potential sites for the new capital had been proposed and then rejected as each different state held to its own parochial agenda. The Northern states pressed for a capital in one of the commercial centers, such as New York, while the Southern states insisted on a location more proximate to their own soil. Countless arguments and justifications were batted back and forth—James Madison, for example, had appealed to science to prove that Virginia would be the best home for the capital, by presenting a geographical calculation which placed the Potomac and Washington's Mount Vernon at the country's exact center.

"We pity the poor congress-men, thus kicked and cuffed about from post to pillar," the *New York Advertiser* wrote with mock concern, "where can they find a home?" But the dilemma was serious, and seemingly intractable. Washington later said that the dispute proved "more in danger of having convulsed the government" than any other event.

The other congressional gridlock that summer stemmed from Alexander Hamilton's finance plan for the United States, proposed in January 1790, whereby the Revolutionary War debts of each of the thirteen states would be "assumed" by the federal government into one national deficit. This would allow the government to deal with one centralized debt rather than with thirteen different ledgers. As well as exacerbating the divide between the mercantile Federalists and the agrarian Republicans, however, the so-called Assumption Plan also triggered vehement opposition from the large Southern states because most of them—unlike their Northern equivalents—had already paid back much of what they owed, and they resisted the idea of giving power over their state economies to central government. As the congressional debates raged on, all refused to compromise. The Southern states, led by Madison (who had been nicknamed "Big Knife" for his battle-hardy political skills and in defiance of his size), had staunchly opposed Hamilton's proposal, bringing the discussions to a deadlock in the early summer.

That June, Jefferson—reluctant to accept Hamilton's plan but convinced that "a mutual sacrifice . . . [was] the duty of every one" invited Madison and Hamilton to his New York house in Maiden Lane. There, over a meal cooked according to the latest French recipes and helped along by bottles of fine wine, he brokered a deal between the two opponents. By the time the dinner ended, Jefferson later claimed, Madison had agreed to stop blocking Hamilton's fiscal plan (though he wouldn't vote for it). In return—because "the pill would be a bitter one to the Southern states"—Hamilton would support the capital's new location on the Potomac River along the Maryland and Virginia border.* Clearly the location of the seat of government was so important to Jefferson and Madison that they were willing to trade it for an economic strategy they despised.

Shortly afterward the Assumption Bill and the Residence Act were passed. With these, Hamilton's economic vision was enacted while Philadelphia would be the temporary capital for ten years until the new city was built. To avoid further conflict it was decided that Washington, who still tried to maintain an impartial role in the new party politics, would determine the new capital's exact site (but only after Jefferson

---

* In telling the story about this bargain, Jefferson simplified the situation. Over the previous weeks there had in fact been several secret meetings and the so-called Dinner Table Bargain was only the culmination.

and Madison had crisscrossed Maryland and Virginia on an assessment mission).*

Both Jefferson and Madison produced detailed memorandums on how to proceed, and in January 1791 Washington announced the capital's location. By placing it on the banks of the Potomac—the river that for many Virginians was the gateway to the West—the city was turned toward the future of the country. And even more important, by choosing a site away from the commercial centers, the three men proclaimed their vision of the United States of America as an agrarian republic. The capital would be far away from Hamilton's odious merchants, speculators and corrupt, money-obsessed cities. Cities, according to Jefferson, also were the source of anti-Republican sentiment because Federalists "all live in cities."

Although they agreed on the location of the capital, when it came to the actual design of the city and the public buildings, Jefferson and Washington were of very different minds. This was because of their conflicting beliefs about what the role of the federal government should be. And though Washington had tried to stay clear of the emerging battles between the Federalists and Republicans, he had been vocal about the importance of a strong government. By contrast Jefferson had always insisted that the central government should not have too much power over the states. They agreed, however, that the capital was to reflect the government and its power (or lack of power) and that it needed to be designed accordingly. Consequently, Washington envisaged a grand imposing city, while Jefferson wanted it to be as unobtrusive and out of the way as possible. As such the struggle over how the capital should be designed was not so much an aesthetic or architectural disagreement but an important political battle.

In his first memorandum to Washington, Jefferson made explicit what he held to be the most important issues: the capital should be a small town laid out on a rectangular grid that would grow organically over time, spreading out from its center. Two squares should be allocated for the president's house and garden, one for the Capitol, one for a market and nine for "public walks"—far from being a celebration of the seat of government, the capital of the United States should be a city of gardens. Some 1,500 acres, he suggested to Washington, would be needed in total, of which 300 would be for public buildings and parks, and the rest should be laid out in the future. It would be a republican city—on an inti-

---

* In the following year, in 1791, the new capital was named "Washington" after the president.

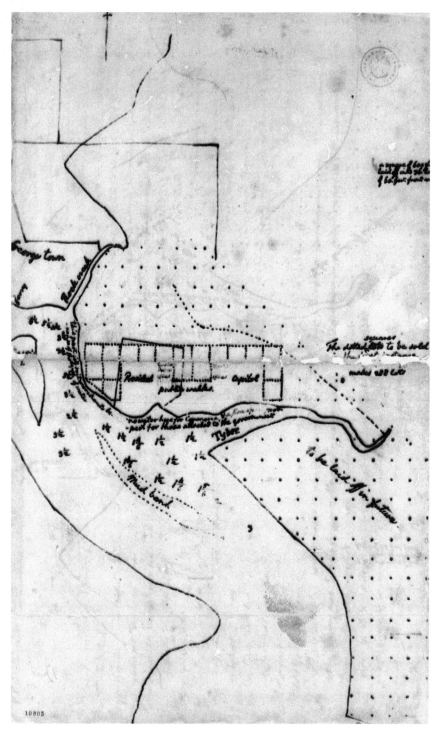

In 1791 Jefferson sketched his vision of the new capital, already underlining the need for parks and gardens when he scribbled "public walks" on the plan. The city was to grow organically from the small center around the President's House and the Capitol, while the areas marked with dots were to be laid out at a later stage.

mate scale, virtuous and simple. "A government continually at a distance and out of sight," Hamilton had warned in *The Federalist Papers,* "can hardly be expected to interest the sensations of people"—exactly what the Republicans had in mind for the new capital.

By contrast, the magnificent city that Washington and his chosen designer, the French Major Charles Pierre L'Enfant, dreamed up would proclaim a mighty, dominant central government. L'Enfant was the Federalists' favorite architect, having transformed New York's City Hall into the splendid Federal Hall—the home of Congress during New York's time as capital—resplendent with a frieze of thirteen stars and a pediment filled with the great American eagle, clutching thirteen arrows and an olive branch. Over the years L'Enfant had also staged spectacular patriotic events and parades, mastering the language of monumental symbols and gestures. He derided layouts like Jefferson's, which were based on a rectangular and regular grid, as "tiresome and insipide." Instead the capital, L'Enfant told a receptive Washington, was to be built on an "enlarged plan," with sweeping avenues that cut like sunrays through the city.

At 5,000 acres, L'Enfant's design would be almost four times what Jefferson had in mind—larger than New York, Philadelphia and Boston combined. Where Jefferson had scribbled on a small piece of paper a small town bounded between Georgetown and Rock Creek to the north, Tiber Creek to the south and the Potomac to the west, L'Enfant's map of the city was so enormous and unwieldy that it was difficult to carry around to present at meetings.

Jefferson was not alone in his objections to Washington's "Hobbyhorsical federal City." L'Enfant's plan was on "too large a scale," one of the commissioners complained, explaining that this "may suit the genius of a Despotic government" but certainly not a republic. Yet, as so often, once he had made up his mind, Washington stood resolute—he wanted a city that would be imbued with the tenets of the Constitution, the Union and the American Revolution. The plan and buildings had to be impressive, he argued, because they "shou'd look beyond the present day." The new capital would be the nexus of America, binding together not only the Northern and Southern states, "but the trans-Alleghenians with the Atlantic states."

L'Enfant understood that Washington's vision required the layout of the capital to be infused with political ideology. He therefore drew the balance of power—the executive versus the legislative and the states versus the federal government—onto his master plan of the city. The two most prominent buildings in the capital, the White House and the Capitol, would house the executive and legislative powers respectively. Connected by Pennsylvania Avenue (named after the state where the Declaration of Independence had been signed and the Constitution written), the executive and legislative were linked and yet apart. At the same time the broad avenues that pierced vistas through the city were named after the original thirteen states. They were arranged geographically with New Hampshire and Connecticut avenues to the north, South Carolina and Georgia avenues to the south and Maryland and Pennsylvania avenues in the middle.*

The separation of power was not the only political gesture written into the map of the capital. The sheer importance and strength of the federal government was also crucial to Washington's vision, meaning that everything in the new city was to be magnificent. The buzzword was clearly "grand"—there would be "grand fountains," a "Grand Cascade" one hundred feet wide with a forty-foot drop, vast public parks and, of course, a "Grand Avenue," the Mall, which connected Congress, the garden south of the President's House and an equestrian statue of George Washington. Congress would assemble on a hill that was, L'Enfant enthused, "a pedestal waiting for a monument." One and a half miles westward, placed on a ridge overlooking the Potomac with views of the entire city, was the president's home. Washington's city, L'Enfant said, would be "a monument to national genious and munificence."

L'Enfant's plan also appealed to Washington as a landscape designer. Like Washington, who had carefully staged his house within the grounds at Mount Vernon to take advantage of the long vista toward the west and views across the Potomac in the east, L'Enfant placed the public buildings on "the most advantageous ground" with the best prospects across the city and the countryside. His plan combined the language of French baroque grandeur and formality with the sensibilities of English picturesque garden design.

On paper the radiating avenues and straight lines had imposed a formal grid of squares and diagonals onto the city, but like an accomplished landscape designer L'Enfant had also integrated the undulating lie of the land. Instead of leveling the city and forcing it into a one-dimensional frame of geometry, L'Enfant used the billowing hills and valleys, the broken ground and dips, to create the irregularity and variety that according to the school of English landscape gardens were hailed as picturesque. From the wooded ridges to the plains at the river, L'Enfant exulted, the

---

* The three avenues that were named after the most populous states, Pennsylvania, Virginia and Massachusetts, were also the avenues that cut through the whole city.

hills were like "the waves of a tempestuous sea." When he remarked that "nature had done much for it, and with the aid of art it will become the wonder of the world," he used the same language as English gardeners. Just as irregularity in the English garden had replaced the formality that had symbolized French absolutism, L'Enfant was introducing the same ideas to the capital of the United States. But where the vistas in the English garden culminated in temples and statues that celebrated virtues and heroes, L'Enfant's avenues were designed to end at real symbols of liberty—the Capitol and the White House. The metaphors of liberty that had been used in the eighteenth-century English gardens such as Stowe would be translated into a city.

Contrary to these ideas was L'Enfant's notion of the "sumptuousness of a palace" for the house of the president. Clearly visible in his map, it measured almost 700 feet by a little more than 200 feet (four times bigger than the White House that was eventually built). Washington told Jefferson that he wanted the house "upon a scale far superior to any thing in this Country," and the enormous footprint of the palace epitomized what Jefferson feared. The secretary of state who during his time in Paris had developed a taste for elegant furniture, fashionable clothes and other luxury goods, was more austere when it came to his country's capital. Instead of L'Enfant's palace, he preferred a more modestly sized house based on the country villas his favorite architect, Andrea Palladio, had designed in sixteenth-century Italy. Elegant but simple, a Palladian villa celebrated country life and was, for Jefferson, the most suitable building for an American president.

Unsurprisingly, the conflict-averse Jefferson never openly opposed Washington's plans for his magnificent federal city, opting instead for a less direct approach, when he tried to steer the president toward a simpler design and sent suggestions and drawings of his more intimate layout. Similarly reluctant to engage in an open dispute, Washington pretended not to be aware of any disagreement, but did not move at all from his original ideas, steadfastly clinging to the majestic designs. He politely forwarded one of Jefferson's drawings to L'Enfant, but left no doubt what he thought by adding, "I do not conceive that you will derive any material advantage from an examination of the enclosed papers." The frustrated Jefferson was in luck, however, for in the end it was L'Enfant who brought about his own downfall.

The debacle began in November 1791, when L'Enfant, without authorization, demolished the house of Daniel Carroll, one of the most powerful landowners in the district. Surprised that his house had been razed, Carroll bombarded Washington and Jefferson with complaints, but L'Enfant maintained that he was not at fault. Carroll's house stood in the middle of a main street, an indignant L'Enfant told Jefferson, and therefore it simply had to be destroyed. Jefferson coolly observed that "there is as yet no such thing as a street" and that L'Enfant had no right to remove houses on streets that only existed in plan. This was the difference between a city that grew organically from its center, as Jefferson envisaged, and L'Enfant's master plan, which saw the matrix of the biggest city in America superimposed onto a wilderness. When L'Enfant refused to submit to the authority of the commissioners, Jefferson must have been delighted to inform him that his services were no longer required. Even Washington, who had tried to defend his architect to the end, had to admit that L'Enfant's behavior "astonishes me beyond measure!"*

Following L'Enfant's forced resignation in February 1792, Jefferson, sensing another opportunity to influence matters, suggested that an architectural competition be held for the design of the President's House. Some historians believe that Jefferson not only wrote the advertisement for the competition but also anonymously submitted his own design, modeled on Palladio's famous Villa Rotonda, a small country house. Others think that the drawings were entered by builder John Collins, who had been encouraged by Jefferson. Either way, Jefferson seemed to have been involved to some degree in reducing the size of the original plan. In the end, however, it was Washington who was once again victorious, because James Hoban, his favorite and the architect whom he had introduced to the commissioners, won the competition with a larger design (though much smaller than L'Enfant's original footprint).

Over the next two years Jefferson continued to scheme and succeeded in removing from the Capitol a tomb space for Washington and the president's chamber. Both designs were at odds with his ideas of a republican city—one turned the Capitol into a shrine, while the presence of a president's chamber was an intrusion of the executive into the legislative. Exploiting the jealousy between the two architects William Thornton (who had won the architectural competition for the Capitol) and Stephen Hallet (who had lost it) allowed Jefferson to instigate these changes—after Hallet found several mistakes in Thornton's drawings, he was put in charge as site architect and eliminated the president's chamber and the tomb. Jefferson, who corresponded with Hallet in French, must have sug-

---

* L'Enfant went on to plan another city that also ended in failure: Alexander Hamilton's manufacturing city Paterson at the Great Falls of the Passaic River, where Hamilton envisaged industry and factories instead of agrarian idylls.

gested these changes. When Washington finally discovered all these alterations months later, during an inspection of the foundations, it was too late to reverse them. Despite his reputation of glacial cool, Washington was furious that such drastic changes had been made behind his back, and lost his temper, forcing the commissioners to fire Hallet.* Despite all Jefferson's efforts, much of the original plans were still on the table. Instead of a small, self-effacing republican town, L'Enfant's huge city had prevailed. By the time he resigned as secretary of state in late 1793, Jefferson had grown to rue his role in the Dinner Table Bargain bitterly— "of all the errors of my political life, this has occasioned me the deepest regret," he admitted.

After his refusal to take power at the end of the War of Independence and his reluctance to become president, Washington's apparent obsession with grand designs might seem out of character. But the man who preferred being the master of his crops to being the leader of the American people had not suddenly changed. Quite the contrary, Washington simply believed that the unity of the states and therefore the nation depended on a strong central government—and he would make sure that his eponymous city was a reflection of this.

One project, in particular, the commissioners realized, was "an object which the President has much at heart": the first national university and botanic garden. In the summer of 1796, as he prepared himself for retirement and Hamilton wrote the Farewell Address, Washington became engrossed with the idea. Visitors at Mount Vernon noted that the conversations were either about agriculture or about the establishment of the university in the new capital.

The importance of a national university and an adjacent botanic garden was not so much about the education of young men per se (there were several state universities across the United States) but, as ever with Washington, for the purpose of national unity. As men from across the different states would study together at a young age "when friendships are formed," he explained, they would understand that there was no reason for the "jealousies & prejudices which one part of the union had imbided agains[t] another part." Their loyalties would be to the nation rather than to their states. At the same time a national botanic garden would bring together a "forrest of the different trees of America," just as Washington himself had attempted at Mount Vernon. Thornton, the architect of the Capitol, believed that the trees in the botanic garden

---

* Washington later instructed Thornton to reinstate the tomb space but it was never built because of the slow building progress.

could "serve as parent-trees" to supply nurseries across the states. In September and October 1796, a flurry of letters scuttled between Washington and Hamilton, the commissioners, Thornton and Madison. Washington wanted the need for a university added to the Farewell Address, but Hamilton thought that the president's last speech to Congress would be a more appropriate vehicle. "It will be felt as the last request of a departing Friend," one of the commissioners wrote to Madison.

At the same time the restless Washington began to search for the best site for the botanic garden. The commissioners suggested that the grand gardens that L'Enfant had designed between the president's park and the Capitol (today's Mall) would be "extremely well calculated for this purpose," but others disagreed. With so little basic infrastructure in place, many thought it was a little premature even to think about a botanic garden. But the president saw the political importance of the project and remained unmoved. He reiterated that a botanic garden would be "a good appendage" to the university and pressed for a final decision to be made. But nothing could be agreed during his presidency—his last public project in the federal city would depend on his successors.*

SIX MONTHS LATER, in March 1797, John Adams was inaugurated as the second president of the United States and assumed responsibility for the federal city. Unlike Washington, Madison and Jefferson, Adams had never been particularly interested in the removal of the capital to the Potomac. A shining city in the wilderness seemed absurd and against his parsimony. "I was strenuously opposed to the whole system in every grade of its progress," he commented later.† Friends had warned him back in 1789, when discussions on the locations began, that "you will probably be dragged in a few years to the banks of the Potowmac, where Negro slaves will be your servants by day, mosquitoes your sentinels by night." A project that drained public coffers when Congress wouldn't even increase his meager salary was not what the frugal Adams wanted.

---

* Washington's university and botanic garden were not built for many years. During his presidency Madison proposed a university to Congress three times and in 1816 Benjamin Henry Latrobe prepared a drawing of a university situated on the Mall between Thirteenth and Fifteenth streets (just east of today's Ellipse). In 1817, the Columbian Institute for the Promotion of Arts and Sciences proposed a botanic garden, and finally in 1820 Congress gave them five acres near the Capitol.
† Adams later bitterly complained that he was accused of having been involved in the creation of the capital. "Charge as much Ignorance, Folly, and Pride as you please upon the City of Washington," he wrote to Benjamin Rush in 1808, "but lay none of it to me. Not one shilling was spent upon it by me."

Washington, D.C., was the vision of Virginia men, not his. In fact, Adams would have preferred if the seat of government had moved every four years between Philadelphia and New York.

For the first three and a half years of his presidency, Adams governed from Philadelphia, the temporary capital, and the commissioners quickly learned that he had no intention of getting involved in the building of Washington. In the month after his inauguration Adams wrote to them that he would rely entirely on their expertise and experience because "the whole of this Business is so new to me." A few months and several pleading requests from the commissioners later, Adams realized he needed to be more explicit. "The Importance of the City to the Union, I fully understand," he explained exasperatedly, "but at present the Union is menaced, from other Causes and Quarters with more dangerous Portents."

The threat came from the French, who since the ratification of the Jay Treaty (and the Union's subsequent realignment with Britain) had begun to seize American merchant ships. Instead of creating a city of magnificent public buildings, Adams was building a navy and preparing for the possibility of war. The presidency and negotiations with the French government, Adams said to Abigail, would be neither "Beds of Roses nor Walks of Flowers." France not only threatened America at sea in the so-called Quasi-War (an undeclared war) but also humiliated the administration when a diplomatic delegation of three distinguished American politicians was refused a meeting with the French foreign minister in Paris. Adams struggled to maintain the United States of America's neutrality, uncomfortably stuck between the wishes of his own belligerent cabinet to declare war and the attacks from the pro-French Republicans who accused him of being a warmonger. Unlike Washington, who had been revered for most of his presidency, it seemed that Adams was assailed from all sides. The foreign crisis and political struggles kept him so busy that it took him almost a year even to glance at the map of the city. This was certainly no time to play architect, the overworked Adams insisted—the "Situation of the United States is uncommonly Critical."

As Adams governed from the presidential house in Philadelphia, building work in the capital was progressing only slowly. At the time of Adams's inauguration in March 1797, the White House still had no roof and the windows were empty holes in the walls. The Capitol was even more behind schedule. With the relocation of government to Washington, D.C., scheduled to take place in just three years' time, the commissioners had a daunting task before them. Their anxiety was exacerbated by the fact that funds had begun to run low. In October and November 1797 they wrote repeatedly to Adams, expressing their concern about the shortage of funds, but it took the president until December to reply. The wording of his letter made clear how little interest he had—though he granted them the power to borrow $150,000, he failed to specify where this would actually come from, suggesting instead they procure it "wherever you can find it." He refused to "make himself a Slave to the Federal City," he said in the following year—he would do what his official duty required of him "and no more."

Like Adams, the new vice president, Thomas Jefferson, was showing no interest whatsoever in the new capital. As the secretary of state under Washington, Jefferson had been constantly in contact with the commissioners, but now he went silent on the subject. The city as it was designed was still based on Washington's grand vision of sweeping avenues and enormous public buildings. Therefore, the less progress made, the closer it would come to Jefferson's original ideas. If the avenues remained mud roads, no glittering parades would be able to be held there; if the President's House remained roofless, the executive of the American nation would fail to reflect power and strength; and if plots were left undeveloped it would resemble a small country town rather than a buzzing metropolis. If Adams was not going to do anything about the city, Jefferson certainly wasn't going to either.

Building work was progressing so slowly that by March 1798, it seemed that there might not even be a home for the president in the new capital at all. Work came to a complete halt and "clashing interests" threatened Washington's dream. Some wanted to move the Supreme Court or even Congress into the White House, while others proposed that a smaller, more modest dwelling for the president be built on Capitol Hill. Adams still did not care, telling the commissioners that he would be perfectly happy just to rent a simple house. In despair, Alexander White, one of the commissioners, wrote to the retired Washington in Mount Vernon, explaining what was going on. Gossip began to circulate that Adams was trying to sabotage the new capital. For the first time since he had become vice president, Jefferson picked up his pen to write about the new city. It was rumored, so Jefferson told Madison, that Adams had no desire to keep the government in Washington for long. Once politicians and government employees lived in the unfinished city and experienced the lack of comfort, it would be easy to convince them to abandon Washington, D.C. They would return to Philadelphia and make it the capital instead, and that was certainly not what Jefferson had envisaged.

Adams, however, had no such intentions. The truth was that even if he had wanted a say in anything to do with the capital, he would have struggled to make much of an impact, for the commissioners sang a chorus of "the late President always," referring constantly to Washington's opinions as well as continuing to write to him. When Adams dared to suggest moving the War Office and Treasury away from the White House to the Capitol, for example, he was quickly overruled—Washington, who had personally sited them there, dismissed Adams's plans as "nothing short of insanity." He needn't have worried, because Adams quickly got bored by such backroom dealing and did not even answer the commissioners' letters. Only when they told him that they would proceed with the original plans did Adams reply. "Although I may have been inclined to an opinion," he finally wrote, with humility, he never intended "to give orders contrary to your unanimous Judgment." Government departments stayed where Washington had placed them, Congress would meet in the Capitol, and the president would live in the executive mansion.

Adams, having learned his lesson and now completely preoccupied with the threat of war, subsequently left all decisions to the commissioners, who dealt with the problems—dwindling funds, brickmakers who were digging holes and removing earth from Pennsylvania Avenue to make bricks, and agricultural squatters on public land. Washington also remained involved, monitoring the city's development with interest and employing Thornton to build some private houses for him in the new capital. In November 1799, the sixty-seven-year-old rode the sixteen miles from Mount Vernon to inspect Thornton's work. Satisfied that all was going to plan, and no doubt relieved that Adams had resumed his passive role, he returned home. Yet Washington would never see Congress move into the Capitol or attend a banquet in the White House, for this would be his final visit to the city he had long dreamed of building.

A week after his return to Mount Vernon, on 14 December, as a torrent of hail, rain and snow staged an icy spectacle, Washington inspected his farms for hours. The next day he woke feeling ill, but was determined to go out again to mark some trees on his back lawn "to be cut down in the improvement of that spot." That night he woke his wife, Martha, shivering and hardly able to speak, gasping that he was unwell. Doctors were hastily called and after they had finished their torturous cutting, bleeding (half a pint of blood at a time), purging and blistering, the hero of the American Revolution knew he did not have much time left. "Have me decently buried," he said with his last breath, "and do not let my body be put into the vault in less than three days after I am dead."

During the last days of his life he had two things on his mind: the new capital and his grounds at Mount Vernon. His last correspondence was a nineteen-page report to his estate manager, instructing once again on crop rotation and manures, and letters to the commissioners of Washington, D.C., and to Thornton.

As WASHINGTON'S DEATH WAS MOURNED across the country, Adams suddenly turned his attention to the capital. As long as Washington had been alive, the capital had remained his project, but now Adams must have felt for the first time that he could take charge. If the government was really to move to the new city within the following year, the building work needed to be stepped up a gear. But the first thing on Adams's mind was not streets or buildings—it was a garden. He told Benjamin Stoddert, the secretary of the navy, that he would move into the White House after all, even though he would have only a few months remaining of his term by the time of the move. Trees should be planted immediately, he told Stoddert, "so as to make it an agreeable place to walk." The president, Stoddert then instructed Thornton, who was not only the site architect but a passionate gardener himself, wanted a garden because that "large, naked, ugly looking building will be a very inconvenient residence for a family" without it.

What Adams envisaged was something like the Bingham garden, the most opulent garden in Philadelphia. A few years previously Adams had briefly rented rooms opposite Bingham's Mansion House on Third Street. Enclosed within a high fence, the grounds were laid out like an English garden, in irregular clumps of trees. The garden at the executive mansion seemed more important to Adams than the interior—probably because it was among plants that he was most relaxed, pruning his trees or picking insects off his roses. In the previous winter Abigail had even sent a small greenhouse to Philadelphia, so that he would not miss out on his horticultural joys in the cold months of the year. Gardening and working in his meadows was so important to Adams while he dealt with the pressures of government that he compared it to "Medicine."

Thornton was enthusiastic about the idea of planting trees and promised to do everything in his power to help in advance of Adams's arrival. He sketched rows of erect Lombardy poplars to extend like wings from the White House toward the Treasury and the War Office—similar to the lines of poplars that surrounded the Bingham house. But when he and his wife, Anna, inspected the site, they found the ground "in great confusion"—brick kilns, water pits for the bricklayers and all kinds of other refuse. The creation of a garden would not be helped, Thornton's wife commented, by the fact that funds were at an all-time low. Thornton

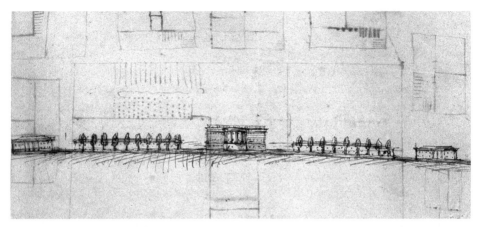

William Thornton's sketch of the White House with rows of trees as "arboreal wings,"
terminating in the War Office to the left and the Treasury to the right

could see that if he did not personally undertake to implement Adams's plan, "it will not be done at all," though he warned Stoddert that the "garden will be a work of much more difficulty and expense than was at first apprehended." They would not be able to do anything more than "levelling some of the ground," he wrote.

The commissioners were also being obstructive, protesting that everything was on "too extravagant a scale." There were more pressing issues than planting a few trees, they complained, because it wasn't until late February 1800 that they had the funds to begin to make the mansion habitable for the president's arrival from Philadelphia in a few months' time. They reported to Stoddert, who had to explain to an increasingly impatient Adams why so little had been achieved. Problems continued to mount: the carpenters had been forced to lay down their tools because not enough timber had been delivered, the roof was leaking, and the plastering took much longer than originally estimated.

With a stream of reports listing one disaster after another, Adams began to doubt that he'd be able to move to Washington in the winter. Abigail was also "discouraged" by the lack of progress and wanted him to find other accommodation because she feared it would be his death to move into such an unfinished building. In June, Adams visited the new capital for the first time, writing to Abigail that he liked it "very well," and four and a half months later, on 1 November 1800, he became the first president to move to Washington. Abigail had remained reluctant to join her husband because she doubted they would remain there beyond the end of Adams's presidential term, but soon followed her husband to their new home.

The first weeks in the White House were some of the hardest in Abigail and John Adams's lives as everything seemed to disintegrate around them. They lived in a damp and leaking palace with hardly any furniture. They couldn't afford the small army of servants that was needed to run what Abigail called the "Huge Castle" and in any case there were no bells to call them (the bell hanger had died suddenly). The main audience room—today's East Room—was undecorated and empty, except for the laundry lines that Abigail strung across to dry their clothes. Despite being surrounded by forests, it was impossible to get any firewood to heat the house, Abigail complained, "because people cannot be found to cut and cart it!" The lack of money and time, combined with the commissioners' reluctance, had made it impossible for Thornton to create a garden for the president—funds were so low that there was not even a vegetable plot or small flowerbed. Problems continued and only a week after Adams's arrival the temporary War Office burned down, destroying most of the records from the Revolutionary War. Then a month later, Abigail and John Adams heard that their alcoholic son Charles had died in New York.

Worst of all was the vicious political atmosphere that surrounded the presidential election of 1800—the first and only one in American history that was fought between the sitting president and his vice president. Newspapers were filled with malicious slander, and even Adams's own party, the Federalists, were split. Not only was Adams attacked by the opposition but, to the Republicans' delight, Alexander Hamilton published a pamphlet that was more injurious to the Federalists and Adams than anything they could have written themselves. In "Concerning the Public Conduct and Character of John Adams," Hamilton accused the president of "disgusting egotism," "eccentric tendencies" and an "ungovernable temper." It was clear, Adams said, that even his fellow Federalist Hamilton "would prefer Mr. J. [Jefferson] to me." Abigail heard so many smears and lies, she said, "that I am disgusted with the world."

The campaigning became even more venomous than the previous election, when a hack journalist (to whom Jefferson had provided some financial support) portrayed Adams as both mad and a "hideous hermaphroditical character which has neither the force nor firmness of a man, nor the gentleness and sensibility of a woman." Accused of being pro-monarchy, Adams was now also blamed for the grand designs of the capital, even though he had had nothing to do with them. Madison's old friend Philip Freneau, the Republican poet and former proprietor of the *National Gazette*, wrote:

An infant city grows apace
Intended for a ruling race,
Here capitols of awful height—
Already burst upon the sight,
And buildings, meant for embryo kings,
Display their fronts and spread their wings.

The first electoral colleges were called on 3 December, but the voting and counting of the results took several weeks. By the third week of December, Adams knew that he had lost his presidency, but because of a tie between the two Republican candidates, it would take until mid-February to confirm that Jefferson was president-elect.* "The only Question remaining with me is what I shall do with myself?," a defeated and dispirited Adams quietly pondered, but the answer was simple: "farmer John" would feed his cattle, "potter in my garden among the fruit Trees and Cucumbers, and plant a Potatoe Yard with my own hand."

The election campaign destroyed the last vestiges of friendship between Adams and Jefferson. The election had been fought with dirty tricks, Abigail railed in her last letter to Jefferson, accusing him of "the blackest calumny, and foulest falsehoods." Jefferson, she wrote, had masterminded a smear campaign of "the lowest and vilest Slander"—attacks that had suggested that her husband had not only tried to crown himself as king of America but that he was mentally deranged.†

ADAMS LEFT THE CITY by stagecoach at four o'clock in the morning on 4 March 1801, quietly absenting himself from Jefferson's inauguration. The swearing in of the third president of the United States was a plain affair but as carefully planned as Washington's elaborate parades. At noon Jefferson walked from the tavern where he had stayed the night to the Capitol to take his oath of office and to read his Inaugural Address in the Senate chamber. Dressed as a "plain citizen" without a dress sword, after giving his speech he returned to the tavern by foot. It was the first of many gestures that expressed his return to what he

---

* The two Republican candidates, Jefferson and Aaron Burr, had both received 73 votes. With Burr refusing to step down, the House of Representatives had to decide—it took thirty-five ballots before Jefferson was declared president-elect. After this election, the Twelfth Amendment separated the voting for president and vice president.
† It would come to haunt Jefferson when in 1802 the same journalist accused him of having fathered children by his slave Sally Hemings.

believed to be true republicanism—simple, virtuous and agrarian. His government, Jefferson wrote, would return to "the original simplicity of its form" and its "republican principles." The Inaugural Address made clear to all who heard and read it that Jefferson would make his government as invisible as possible, and many were expecting an extensive pruning of federal powers. During his presidency he would reduce the national debt and, he wrote to the Speaker of the House of Representatives in May, slice expenditures for the army, the navy (which he hated for its association with mercantilism), American diplomats in Europe, taxes, the bureaucracy and even his fellow government officials.

Republicans worried that Washington, D.C., had been conceived "upon a plan much too magnificent," but as it stood in 1801 it was, in a sense, the perfect republican capital, because it was no city at all. Nothing much had changed since Adams had moved into the White House four months earlier—anyone who had feared that power was coalescing at the heart of the federal government would have been heartened to watch the politicians gingerly sinking in the mud between the building sites. This was not how Washington had imagined the capital of the United States, but Jefferson was not going to change it.

Washington had tried to turn the capital into an expression of his beliefs, and Jefferson would now do the same by ostentatiously doing nothing much at all. The most pertinent symbol for this approach was the garden at the White House—or, to be more precise, the nonexistent garden. Instead of admiring L'Enfant's fountains, visitors now had to be careful not to "fall into a pit, or stumble over a heap of rubbish." Everywhere were pools in which there were "numerous dead carcasses left to putrified," Albert Gallatin, the secretary of the treasury, said. The grounds were divided from the surrounding fields only by a broken post and rail fence, which Jefferson's washerwoman—in full view of everybody—used to dry the presidential stockings and shirts. It's almost certain that Jefferson did not plant a single tree or shrub in the White House garden, for it was unlikely that the man who made lists of everything would have failed to record it.*

It might seem strange that this horticultural connoisseur, who his entire adult life had been deeply curious about all things botanical and

---

* Jefferson kept an extensive memorandum book for his expenses and a garden book in which he noted what and when his gardeners sowed and planted at Monticello—even counting the number of peas that would fill a pint. In Washington, he also began a list for his dinner guests at the White House (dividing them with taxonomic precision into columns of Federalists and Republicans) and recorded when vegetables appeared on the market in the capital.

passionate about gardens, did not create one at the most important house in the United States. The man who had said that "there is not a sprig of grass that shoots uninteresting to me," and that gardens "added wonderfully to my happiness" did not care that the grounds around the White House did not remotely resemble a garden. By deciding to leave the landscape as he found it, Jefferson's "presidential garden" would exude neither grandeur nor power—and that was exactly what he wanted.

One of the reasons for ignoring the grounds was the house itself, which, though much reduced from what L'Enfant had envisaged, was still far too palatial to Jefferson's mind. With his wife long dead and his two daughters married, the only other person in this cavernous palace was the president's secretary. Jefferson inhabited, one visitor remarked, "but a corner of the mansion," leaving the rest "to a state of uncleanly desolation." The mess was not disturbing him, for he had never minded living in the midst of a building site—five years previously he had demolished and begun to rebuild his house at Monticello, living that summer "under the tent of heaven."

There was nothing he could do about the size of the White House itself, or indeed the grand master plan of the surrounding city, but he could certainly create a different setting, and a radically more republican atmosphere, than Washington and L'Enfant had envisaged. If Jefferson's government was to be one that was neither seen nor felt, the grounds of the White House would need to be "designed" accordingly. He would not have a garden that was reminiscent of Versailles and Louis XIV. "Avoid palaces and the gardens of palaces," the site architect had already warned Washington during the early years of planning, "if you build a palace I will find you a king." Ten years previously Jefferson had fought and failed to reduce L'Enfant's "Palace" to a modest country house, but now he would make sure that any palatial associations would vanish from the landscape. And so his garden legacy at the White House would be the reduction of the grounds from L'Enfant's sixty acres to a modest five, turning the remaining land over to the public.

Slashing government expenditures and shrinking the presidential grounds were not the only expressions of the new president's republican ethos, Jefferson also used the presidency itself. From the day of his inauguration Jefferson began to demystify the office of president, disposing of strict social protocols and casting himself as a simple farmer. Where Washington had been the glorified hero of the nation, Jefferson became the president of the people. As president, the towering Washington had exuded an air of formality and grandeur, riding on a white stallion with a gold-trimmed saddle or stiffly addressing the people at balls and levees with his hand on his dress sword (and never shaking hands). By contrast, Jefferson eliminated any vestiges of pomp and monarchical rituals. The "Palace" was used like a modest country seat and he stopped all public performances. "Levees are done away," he told the Speaker of the House of Representatives—instead intimate dinner parties for a few but rarely more than twelve people were introduced (three times a week for members of Congress). Seated at a round table to avoid any hierarchical order, Jefferson also eschewed political topics, instead favoring subjects such as gardening and agriculture.

In this studied simplicity everything was done for a purpose: Adams's Levee Room (today's State Dining Room) was changed into Jefferson's private study and he signed his invitations simply "Th:Jefferson" instead of "The President of the United States" as Washington and Adams had done. As diplomats bowed to the formalized etiquette at courts in Europe, patiently maneuvering along the gilded ladder of status, Jefferson made the White House distinctly American. "When brought together in society," Jefferson laid out in a memorandum, "all are perfectly equal, whether foreign or domestic, titled or untitled, in or out of office."

The man who had worn elegant lace, ruffles and luxurious silk waistcoats during his diplomatic posting in Paris now deliberately dressed down to impress. Jefferson often used his attire to make a point—when reviewing the local militia, for example, he was asked why as chief of the military forces he was not wearing a uniform, to which he reputedly answered that it was to "show . . . that the civil is superior to the military power." As president he made a point of being "without any tincture of pomp." Rembrandt Peale's famous presidential portrait shows Jefferson as a country gentleman with ruddy red cheeks and unpowdered hair—in stark contrast to Gilbert Stuart's portrait of George Washington dressed elegantly and with his dress sword, conveying an almost royal aura.

Many commented on Jefferson's new style. His hair, the British diplomat Augustus John Foster remarked, was "neglected," while a Federalist senator called it "dissheiveled." They mentioned his slippers "down at the heel" and "with his toes out," the coat "thread bare" and the linen "much soiled." In short, he looked, Foster said, like "a tall large-boned farmer"—exactly the image that Jefferson was trying to convey.

Jefferson used the White House as a gentleman farmer would treat a rural retreat, and life in the capital only served to bolster this vision. Most of L'Enfant's city was still invisible except on paper, few houses had been built and there was the constant bang of rifle fire outside the Capitol as

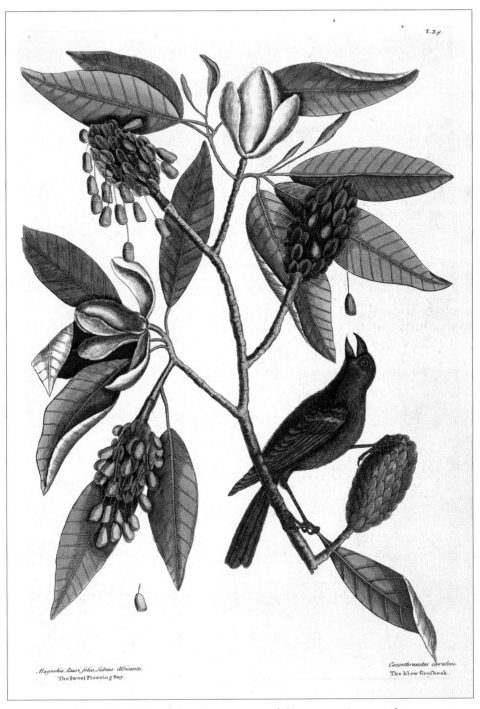

Magnolia virginiana. Sweetbay was one of the many native trees that
George Washington and Thomas Jefferson planted in their pleasure grounds.

RIGHT: George Washington as president, dressed elegantly and holding his dress sword, by Gilbert Stuart.

BELOW: This is the portrait that Mather Brown painted of John Adams in London. The depicted book is Jefferson's *Notes on the State of Virginia*.

ABOVE: Thomas Jefferson
during his first term as
president, looking purposefully "rustic" compared with
Washington in the Stuart
portrait.

LEFT: James Madison
dressed, as usual, in black

ABOVE: Mount Vernon as seen from the bowling green, with Washington,
his wife, Martha, and guests in the foreground. The small buildings to the left
of the mansion are the servants' hall and the gardener's house. The shrubs and trees
leading from the gardener's house away from the mansion mark the beginning
of the shrubberies, screening the walls of the gardens behind.

BELOW: Mount Vernon's east front, with the Potomac and the groves
next to the house. Washington enjoyed sitting on his piazza overlooking the river.

ABOVE: *Magnolia tripetala*. Umbrella magnolia was adored for its enormous leaves and flowers—it was native to the Carolinas.

BELOW: *Chionanthus virginicus*. With its delicate white tassels that flower in May, the fringe tree is one of the most stunning native American shrubs and small trees.

ABOVE: Designed by Samuel Vaughan, the State House garden was also planted with native species only. During the Constitutional Convention, many of the delegates used it as an escape from the stifling heat in the East Room.

BELOW: A romantic early twentieth-century depiction of John Bartram and George Washington at Bartram's Garden.

Pl. 59.

P. J. Redouté del.

Gabriel sculp.

Franklinia.

Gordonia pubescens.

John and William Bartram discovered the *Franklinia alatamaha* in Georgia in 1765. William later named it after their family friend Benjamin Franklin.

ABOVE: This painting of the Hudson River belonged to George Washington and was one of the many depictions of American landscapes that he collected.

BELOW: When Jefferson and Madison toured Vermont, they were keen to learn as much as possible about sugar maples in order to reduce America's dependency on sugar from the British West Indies.

Sugar Maple.
Acer saccharinum.

people shot quails and other birds. Washington, D.C., was reminiscent more of a country estate than a national capital. On the marshy land next to Pennsylvania Avenue and Capitol Hill, one English diplomat observed, there was "Excellent snipe shooting." Ducks were caught on the Potomac and the shoals of perch were so thick that in order to fish, people aimlessly shot into the water to "get a good dish full." The area of today's Mall was wetlands covered with reeds and swaths of American lotus that obscured the water surface—inhabitants caught many fish there.

With no gardening to be done outside, Jefferson brought some flowers inside to his private cabinet, the only room in the White House that he cared about. Shut away from the public, this was his sanctuary. In the drawers of a long table he kept a set of garden tools so that he could interrupt his long hours of writing to prune and deadhead his flowers. In the windows were pots of roses and geraniums, which were, his friend Margaret Bayard Smith remarked, "his delight to attend." Without his "darling grandchildren," whom he adored, she continued, the flowers became "objects of tender care."

It was in this room that Jefferson spent much of his presidency. He was practically invisible to the public and did not even deliver his Annual Message to Congress in person. One of his main concerns during these early years was the reduction of the enormous national debt (accumulated mainly through Hamilton's assumption of the state debts). During the first year alone, he received almost 2,000 letters and sent around 700 himself, not including the internal correspondence to and from his cabinet members. But for all the hours spent at his writing desk, he also needed to be close to nature, and so every day he would interrupt his correspondence at midday and go on long solitary rides through the countryside. Once in a while he stopped at farms to discuss "rural improvements," often bringing gifts of seeds that he had received from abroad. He also explored the thickly forested banks of the Potomac and the hills above the city. "Not a plant from the lowliest weed to the loftiest tree escaped his notice," Smith observed when Jefferson returned from his excursions with specimens that he had collected. Instead of holding public parades and parties, the third president waded through swamps and clambered up rocks in order to add a species to his collection. His love for botany was so widely recognized that the American botanist Benjamin Smith Barton even named a delicate flower—*Jeffersonia*—in his honor.

When he had first come to the district with Madison, now his secretary of state, more than a decade earlier, Jefferson had deeply admired the forests, and his ideas for the small capital town had always included large areas for public gardens and walks. He had therefore told the commissioners from the beginning that proprietors were not allowed to cut trees that the president (or the commissioners) thought to keep for ornamental purposes in the city. Even before the first houses had been built, Jefferson had suggested lining the avenues and streets with trees—after all, houses could always be erected quicker than a tree would grow to maturity.

Over the past decade, however, the commissioners had struggled to control the felling of trees for firewood and building materials. Again and again they wrote letters warning inhabitants about "cutting wood of any description" and asked that "ornamented Trees" remain standing in the public squares and on the grounds around the White House. Yet, with no guards to enforce these rules, trees continued to disappear. In a single night, one citizen recalled, seventy tulip poplars were "girdled" and afterward cut up for firewood. Thornton had also desperately tried to preserve the trees on the Mall but failed. By the time Jefferson became president, many trees had been lost. Most shocking of all, those on the grounds of the White House had been felled by Federalists after the accession of the Republicans, one observer noted, "out of spite to them who cherished it." Enraged by Jefferson's election, so the rumor went, his rivals had ordered the ancient trees to be cut down as a parting gesture, knowing how such vandalism would wound the new president, who regarded tree-felling as "a crime little short of murder." Jefferson was so furious at this unscrupulous destruction that shortly after he moved into the White House, the author of the Declaration of Independence was overheard making the rather surprising comment, "I wish I was a despot that I might save the noble, the beautiful trees that are daily falling."

Although Jefferson might have disliked L'Enfant's imposing city—the large White House and awe-inspiring formal gardens—he never wanted Washington to fail as a thriving and organically growing town. The problem was that L'Enfant's plan was so enormous that the city grew in several small clusters around important buildings such as the Capitol or the White House instead of around a single center. One of Jefferson's few improvements was therefore the work on roads to link these separate areas. The main link was Pennsylvania Avenue (still more a dirt road than an elegant boulevard), and though he was not planting trees in the White House garden, he was happy to order two double rows of Lombardy poplars along the avenue. Native willow oaks—one of his favorite trees—he said, should be planted in between so that they would eventually replace the fast-growing poplars.* As always, the meticulous Jefferson was involved in every detail, from drawing sketches of where to plant the trees to advising the superintendent of the city, Thomas Munroe, on how to protect them against grazing cattle (for cows were still wandering along the avenues of Washington).

Jefferson clearly felt that shaded footpaths for the public took precedence over spectacular presidential gardens. In the same vein he tried to democratize horticulture in the capital, encouraging gardening and opening a market for vegetables and other produce. He also requested that American diplomats across the world dispatch seeds from foreign ports to the White House—not for the president's use but for the citizens of the capital. Whenever a parcel arrived, Jefferson would visit local gardeners and nurserymen to distribute the seeds himself (together with his notes on how to cultivate them). He shared melon seeds from Malta, nuts from Kentucky and, from France, a species of wheat that was reputedly resistant to the destructive Hessian fly. On his daily rides, he regularly stopped to check on the progress. "This," one friend observed, "was the means of greatly improving our markets." Instead of planting his own vegetable garden at the White House, Jefferson patronized the Washington market, telling his steward to pay the highest prices for "the earliest and best products of these gardens" so as to encourage competition among the gardeners and an abundance of vegetables. In addition he would buy plants for Monticello whenever possible from nurserymen in the capital to support their business.

For six years Jefferson did nothing to the White House garden. Most of the money that Congress had appropriated was spent on roads and the Capitol building—as the seat of the Senate and the House of Representatives, it was much more important in Jefferson's political universe than the house of the executive. Some money was spent on the renovation of the White House (the roof was still leaking and the main staircase had to be installed), as well as on the construction of the east and west wings that Jefferson designed, but that was all.

Since Jefferson's inauguration in March 1801, the city of Washington had not changed much. Visitors continued to be surprised by the lack of

---

* Lombardy poplars were a good beginning as in Italy they were regarded as "a tree of liberty," because, as the eighteenth-century poet Victor Alfieri wrote, "the quivering of the leaves of this tree symbolized the prayers of those oppressed by despots." In the long term, Jefferson wanted American trees to shade the most important avenue in Washington, but there were not enough funds to replace the poplars with willow oaks.

urban atmosphere and complained about the rocks and the tree stumps that obstructed the roads, "often threaten[ing] your limbs with dislocation." Travelers who thought they had lost their way and asked for the capital were amazed to be told that they stood at its center. As foreign ambassadors paraded through the lavish rooms of the European courts, in Washington the ornate carriages of diplomats in full regalia got stuck in the avenues, the red mud clumped on the axles "like glue." Being stranded, one British diplomat drily commented, meant "either los[ing] one's shoes or one's patience." A group of congressmen got so lost one evening that they had to spend the rest of the night zigzagging through bogs and wasteland in search of Capitol Hill, several times almost overturning their carriage in the deep gullies that veined the ground. An accident in the middle of the night between the Capitol and the White House, another congressman worried, was dangerous because you were "out of sight or hearing of human habitation."

Then, one evening in spring 1807, Jefferson turned his attention for the first time to the garden at the White House. He and the Surveyor of the Public Buildings, the architect Benjamin Henry Latrobe, spent an entire evening discussing ideas for the grounds, not retiring until well after midnight—hours beyond Jefferson's usual bedtime. Exactly what piqued Jefferson's enthusiasm is unclear. Perhaps he felt that he should finally do something after six years of understated nothingness in the garden. Or maybe the popularity of the Republican party and the diminished Federalist threat made symbolic gestures less important.* Jefferson had won his second term by an impressive majority of 162 to 14 votes, and the Republicans were now so popular that even John Adams's son, the future president John Quincy Adams, joined the party. Or maybe, having decided to retire at the end of his second term, Jefferson thought it would be better to create a republican garden while he could, rather than risk his successors turning it into a mini-Versailles.

Whatever his reasons, the designs would not be lavish. Jefferson told Latrobe that he wanted changes that "require but a moderate sum." The first step was to enclose the five acres that Jefferson had allocated for the garden with walls and to open the remaining land to the public so that no future president could increase the grounds again. Jefferson first envisaged a circular garden—the most democratic of all shapes—but the surveyor calculated that the natural lie of the land lent itself to a slightly

---

* Jefferson also relaxed his strict "simple" clothes rule during his second term—for his second inauguration he did not dress as a "plain citizen" as he had in 1801 but "dressed in black and even in black silk stockings."

more oval shape. Jefferson also ordered that a professional gardener should be hired—though the work in the ornamental grounds would not justify a full-time employment—so Jefferson suggested finally laying out some vegetable plots "for the use of the Pts House."

Like Washington in Mount Vernon and Samuel Vaughan at the State House Yard in Philadelphia, Jefferson wanted to make a political statement with his choice of species. He envisaged an all-American garden, as Margaret Bayard Smith recalled, planted "exclusively with Trees, shrubs and flowers indigenous to our native soil." He made a long wish list—arranged according to the "forms and colours and the seasons in which they flourished." Categories included "Large trees for Single trees," "Clumps" and "Flowering Trees & Shrubs," to which Jefferson added the names of local nurserymen where they could be procured. This sudden burst of enthusiasm for the garden at the White House, however, was not matched by the public money available for such a creation. With the limited funds provided by Congress, there was not much that Jefferson and Latrobe could do.

When Jefferson left office two years later, he had not been able to plant a single tree or shrub. Instead he had to spend the budget on preparatory work—leveling most of the ground, enclosing it by walls and fences and adding the half-finished wings to the White House.* Latrobe had also built an arched gateway as entrance to the grounds from Pennsylvania Avenue, which, following Jefferson's rule of republican simplicity, was so restrained in its architectural detail that Thornton thought it was "scarcely fit for the entrance of a Stable Yard."

Jefferson's plans for the White House garden can only be gleaned from a sketch and a couple of Latrobe's drawings from 1807. According to these designs, radiating avenues would terminate at the entrance to the north of the house, with groves and weaving paths softening the formality of the straight lines. To the south, below today's oval reception room and portico, was to be a large rectangular plot (exactly the width of the house) bordered with trees, shrubs or flowers as well as an area designed along the lie of the land, following the dips and knolls. Paths would snake

---

* When James Madison became president, in March 1809, Latrobe hoped that the garden would be finished. Only ten days after the inauguration, Latrobe forwarded a plan that had been approved by Jefferson to Madison. "The principal work," he explained, "will be the planting of trees & shrubs." Two weeks later he sent a plant list based on Jefferson's suggestions, and two months after that Jefferson received an enthusiastic report: "If you were now at the Presidents house you would scarcely know it. The north front is become a wilderness of shrubry and trees." The planting wasn't very successful, and at the end of 1810, Latrobe reported that "the whole Area being at present without Shade."

around the small hillocks, clumps of trees and shrubs in a casual, informal way. Latrobe's drawings of the south and east front of the house also depicted thickly planted shrubberies enveloped by large trees.

But there was a place where Jefferson implemented his vision, another garden that he designed exactly at the same time: Poplar Forest, an estate he had inherited from his father-in-law that lay in Bedford County, in the foothills of the Blue Ridge Mountains, ninety miles west of Monticello. Knowing that Monticello would be crowded with visitors just as Washington had experienced in Mount Vernon, Jefferson decided to build a house and garden so far removed from the usual tourist itineraries that he would be able to live a more secluded life there. During his retirement Poplar Forest would become Jefferson's retreat, and much of what he was planning for the White House garden found its expression there instead.

At Poplar Forest, the house was placed in the middle of a five-acre circular enclosure—exactly the shape that Jefferson had originally wanted for the White House garden. Similarly, in June 1807, at around the same time that Jefferson and Latrobe were sketching the White House garden, Jefferson instructed his overseer in Poplar Forest to begin digging a sunken parterre to the south of the house—mirroring precisely the rectangular plot to the south of the White House. Years later, in 1812, Jefferson would plant a row of flowering native shrubs along both sides, again just as he had planned for the White House. Next to the house at Poplar Forest he placed clumps of native flowering shrubs such as *Robinia hispida,* with its dangling pink blossom, black locust, and eastern redbud—all of which were on the list that he had made for his Washington residence.

Other similarities were equally striking. At Poplar Forest, the east and west wings of the White House became two rows of trees flanking the house. And where Jefferson had designed (but never executed) two-story pavilions in the middle of these wings at the White House, at Poplar Forest they became planted mounds in the arboreal "wings." Next to the mounds, Jefferson built two small privies at Poplar Forest that were situated exactly where the buildings of the Treasury and War Office were standing next to the White House—quite possibly a symbol of Jefferson's aversion to the two departments.

Poplar Forest was the perfect republican retreat: far away from the commercial centers, turned toward the west, intimate, set amid agricultural activity and inspired by Palladio's country villas. Exactly what Jefferson had envisaged for the President's House and garden: his republican ideal writ into bricks, earth and trees.

At the White House Jefferson had not been able to translate all these ideas into the building and the grounds. And though the garden—

enclosed by its wall and fences—was much smaller than L'Enfant had wanted, Jefferson would never walk there in the patriotic shade of American trees. He had also failed to stop Washington's and L'Enfant's grand plans. However, because of the capital's remote location and the continuous lack of funds, it wasn't a bustling metropolis but remained for many years a small rural town where politicians battled with snakes and "vermin of all filths." As such, Jefferson had achieved what he wanted—if Washington, D.C., had been built as a reflection of the federal government, there was no need to worry. The city did not exude the atmosphere of a powerful central legislative or executive. The avenues might have looked grand on the map, but inhabitants still had to jump into the mud when their carriages got stuck. While others complained about the backwardness of the capital, Jefferson wrote about his life in the White House that it was "a very agreeable country residence . . . free from the noise, the heat, the stench, & the bustle of a close built town." For now it was a republican capital.

7

"EMPIRE OF LIBERTY"

Jefferson's Western Expansion

The sound of eighteen gunshots woke the citizens of Washington at dawn, announcing the arrival of Independence Day on 4 July 1803. As he did every year during his two-term presidency, Thomas Jefferson had organized a large party to celebrate "the only birthday I ever commemorate," ignoring his usual reticence against public appearances and show. At eleven o'clock orderly rows of soldiers and officers in shining uniforms marched along dusty Pennsylvania Avenue. The Lombardy poplars that had been planted only a few months earlier were still too small to provide any shade, and most looked sickly from being nibbled on by grazing cattle and deer.

The troops assembled at the White House to perform patriotic songs for the crowds. Tents and booths had been set up, transforming the land around the unfinished White House into a bustling, colorful and noisy fairground in which the teeming, well-dressed crowds jostled for space with cows and other livestock. Jefferson, together with his ministers and foreign diplomats, waited on the high steps of the White House to greet the soldiers. Tall, and with his long gray hair waving in the wind, Jefferson as always stood out from the smartly dressed and powdered politicians. Inside the house, servants scurried around placing wine, punch and cakes on tables set up in the large reception room. Once the music had stopped, the president invited his guests to food and drink, chatting and enjoying his favorite day of the year.

That day Jefferson was in a particularly festive mood because the previous evening, he had received news that Napoleon had agreed to sell the Territory of Louisiana to the United States, a vast amount of land covering more than 800,000 square miles, stretching west from the Mississippi to the Rocky Mountains and from Canada in the north to the Gulf of Mexico in the south, thus doubling the size of the country in one stroke. It was "the most important & beneficial transaction . . . since the declaration of Independence," one of Jefferson's contemporaries said. The deal would make Jefferson "immortal," according to the editor of the *National Intelligencer,* because not only New Orleans and Louisiana but also the entire Mississippi Valley, and indeed the whole of today's Midwest, now became part of the United States—for the bargain price of fifteen million dollars, around three cents per acre.

Not only had the country dramatically increased in size but France, the greatest military power in the world and a perpetual nuisance to the United States, had disappeared from the North American horizon. Since before the Declaration of Independence, the Mississippi had been controlled by Spain, Europe's weakest empire, but in 1800 Spain had ceded the land to France, a move that worried the Americans deeply. The moment France took possession of New Orleans, Jefferson had warned, "we must marry ourselves to the British fleet and nation"—a dramatic change of heart for a man who so despised the old oppressor. To avert a French empire in America, Jefferson had dispatched fellow Virginian James Monroe as a special envoy to Paris with the American offer to buy New Orleans and as much of the Mississippi Valley as the French would sell (at the same time asking Monroe to deliver a box of seeds to his French friends).

As it turned out, Jefferson got more than he had asked for. It wasn't so much Monroe's diplomatic skills as a successful slave rebellion in the French colony of Santo Domingo (today's Haiti), twinned with huge swarms of mosquitoes, that led France to give up the whole of the Louisiana Territory. Napoleon's plan had been to quash the Caribbean uprising with an army of 25,000 soldiers, who would then be transferred to New Orleans. The soldiers, however, never made it to Louisiana because almost all of them died, either in battle or from a devastating malaria epidemic. In the wake of this disastrous campaign, and with his army decimated, Napoleon abandoned the idea of a French colony in North America and decided to concentrate on Europe instead.

The timing of Napoleon's offer could not have been better, for it came on the eve not only of Independence Day but of the day that Jefferson's secretary, the former U.S. soldier Meriwether Lewis, was due to embark on the first ever overland journey across the whole of the North American continent. Originally conceived as an expedition through Spanish and French territory, Lewis's journey would now cross a continent largely free from European rivals.* The Louisiana Purchase, Jefferson later said, "increased infinitely the interest we felt in the expedition."

For months, Jefferson—the "man of letters and of science" who, as was rumored in diplomatic circles, dreamed of "distinguishing his Presidency by a discovery"—had gone to great lengths to make sure that the expedition was properly organized. Before Lewis departed, Jefferson handed him a letter authorizing his secretary to draw money and supplies on behalf of the United States from anybody across the world: an unlimited and unprecedented credit note. He also gave Lewis a cipher for his correspondence and a long list of instructions that he had compiled over the previous weeks. He had asked his secretary of state, James Madison, and Albert Gallatin, secretary of the treasury, to comment on a draft of these instructions, but except for some minor points—including the suggestion that Lewis be told to look out for "signs of the soil" and trees indicating "fertility"—they agreed that the fastidious president had covered everything. Today Jefferson's objectives for the expedition read like a blueprint for Enlightenment thought. Imploring Lewis to observe, collect, document and classify, they reveal a man who had been nurtured by rational enquiry and a passion for imposing order on nature.

"The object of your mission is to explore the Missouri river," Jefferson had written, in order to find a trade route across the continent to the Pacific. Lewis should also make maps of the new territory and gain knowledge about the Native Americans (including language, agriculture and customs) who inhabited these regions. At the same time he was to observe the climate, animals (including those "deemed rare or extinct"), minerals and "the soil & face of the country, it's growth & vegetable productions." These instructions had been shaped by Jefferson's own experiences: a lifelong study of natural history books and botanical inquiry, surveying, compiling records of Native American vocabulary, and his meticulous meteorological diary. Even his advice that Lewis should use "paper of the birch" to protect the writing from damp was the result of his own observations during his botanical ramble with Madison in the summer of 1791. Lewis was also to note "the dates in which particular plants put forth or lose their flower, or leafs," just as Jefferson had asked his daughters to do in their Monticello correspondence, only Lewis was being asked to chart the entire continent. Gaining all this knowledge was even

---

* Spain kept its claims to territory along the Pacific Coast and in the Southwest.

Meriwether Lewis

more important than actually reaching the Pacific, Jefferson asserted—and if threatened at any point, Lewis was to retreat rather than push forward, lest "the information you will have acquired" be lost.

Between the lines of these scientific instructions we can sense Jefferson's sheer excitement: soon he really might learn about this new world. Maybe Lewis would find the huge mastodon roaming across the plains, discover profitable crops, flowers in exotic shapes and sizes, and trees that would soar even higher than those already encountered. Jefferson planned this expedition in the name of science, but it would also be the beginning of a distinctly American glorification of the wilderness. The years after the expedition would see the awakening of an obsession with rugged nature, a passion that instilled the American landscape with patriotism and is still part of the national identity today.

For the past two years the widowed president and his secretary had lived alone in the White House "like two mice in a church." They had often talked about the journey and in the course of their many discussions had discovered their shared interest in botany and natural history. It was probably after Jefferson's daily rides through the countryside around Washington with his bags stuffed with plant specimens that Jefferson discovered Lewis's "remarkable store of accurate observation." Lewis was "no regular botanist," Jefferson noted, but with a mother who was an accomplished herbal healer, he had grown up with a tacit knowledge of plants. The president was sure that he had chosen the right man for the expedition—brave, strong and prudent but also "adapted to the woods," familiar with the native population and knowledgeable in the "three kingdoms" (plants, animals and minerals).

Lewis's intuitive grasp of the natural world notwithstanding, to prepare for the journey Jefferson had sent him to be tutored by America's leading naturalists and scientists in order to learn the arts of mapmaking and surveying, anatomy and fossil-hunting, as well as mathematics and botany. Andrew Ellicott, the Pennsylvania-based surveyor who had mapped Washington, agreed to teach Lewis how to take the necessary observations to make maps and advised on the best instruments to take. For nearly three weeks Lewis practiced measuring, calculating and using sextants, chronometers and a "portable horizon." In Philadelphia, Caspar Wistar, the professor of anatomy at the University of Pennsylvania and an authority on fossils, briefed Lewis about mastodons and the bones of the *Megalonyx* (an animal that Jefferson initially likened to a gigantic kind of lion)—both would symbolize the United States of America's strength if, as Jefferson hoped, they were living in the West.*

Lewis also consulted Benjamin Rush, a celebrated physician and signatory of the Declaration of Independence. Rush compiled a list of medicine that included hundreds of his famous pills, nicknamed "Thunderclappers," powerful laxatives consisting of mercury, chlorine and jalap which according to Rush would cure almost any illnesses. In addition he also wrote some "Rules of Health" and a long questionnaire about Native Americans, including questions about diseases, women's menstruation, food, vices, murder and death ("Is Suicide common among them," and, if so, "ever from love?"). Most important, the professor of botany at the University of Pennsylvania, Benjamin Smith Barton, polished Lewis's botanical knowledge, teaching him the intricacies of taxonomy and

---

* Jefferson had been the first to announce the discovery of the *Megalonyx* (or "great-claw" as he also called it) to the scientific world. In spring 1797 he sent his paper on the bones to the American Philosophical Society (published in the *Transactions* of 1799), and Wistar continued working on them. The symbolism invested in the *Megalonyx* failed because it was neither a giant lion nor a vicious carnivore, as Jefferson had hoped, but a ground sloth. Rather than attacking his prey with the great claws, the sloth had used them to climb trees.

botanical descriptions. Lewis also learned how to collect, dry, mount and label plant specimens, and how best to preserve seeds.

Jefferson's correspondence with these scientists reveals his excitement. If Lewis succeeded in his mission, he would bring home plants that would adorn America's flowerbeds and new vegetables and crops to feed the people of the United States. He would discover giant animals and trees that would symbolize the country's dominance and power. At the same time, he would convince the Native Americans to adopt the republican ideal of farming and cede their lands to the United States,* and he would show that the Missouri links the East to the Pacific.

Jefferson had long been intrigued by the West. When he had returned from France fourteen years earlier, he visited the ailing Benjamin Franklin to see the map that had been used to draw up the United States's western boundaries in the Paris peace talks after the War of Independence. Franklin, despite being bed-bound, explained the details and later sent Jefferson the map—his last letter before his death in April 1790. Over the past two decades Jefferson had also tried to organize explorations to the West on a number of occasions. The last time had been ten years previously, when he and some members of the American Philosophical Society had collected money to send the French botanist André Michaux across the continent. Washington, Adams and Madison had shared Jefferson's enthusiasm, all of them contributing between twenty and one hundred dollars. Unfortunately, despite the widespread support, the expedition failed because Michaux became tangled up in political problems among France, Spain and the United States.

This early interest in exploring the West was fired by more than just a yearning for knowledge. Basic economic concerns played their part—Franklin, Washington and Madison, for example, had all invested and speculated in huge tracts of lands in the western territories—but so too did the overriding feeling that the United States was to be an agrarian republic. Already before the Declaration of Independence Franklin had promoted settlements west of the Appalachian Mountains, explaining that westward expansion would protect the country from becoming a manufacturing society with all its vices. Americans were "placed in the most enviable condition," Washington echoed shortly after the War of Independence, for they were the "Proprietors of a vast Tract of Continent."

---

* Lewis and Clark knew that Jefferson wanted to turn the Native Americans into farmers and sent a long report about the different tribes of the "Eastern Indians," including information about the Mandan Indians, who "cultivate corn, beans, squashes and tobacco" as well as other tribes who though nomadic "might easily be induced to become stationary."

For long the Potomac River held the promise of the West.

Size mattered for an agrarian republic because a growing nation of farmers needed new fields to cultivate—and one day, Washington hoped, the
United States would become "a storehouse and granary For the world."
The West thus gradually become part of the political agenda. Jefferson
believed that the West would assure the agricultural and therefore republican future of the United States. "By enlarging the empire of liberty," he
famously claimed, "we multiply it's auxiliaries, & provide new sources of
renovation, should it's principles, at any time, degenerate." The West was
the guarantee of the United States and its people remaining virtuous. It
would secure liberty, Jefferson believed, for "millions yet unborn."

Most of the Federalists disagreed about the promises of the West, however. New Orleans was certainly of interest, because it was the port
through which much of the produce of the western territories had to pass,
but the additional acquisition of "a vast wilderness world" seemed ludi-
crous to them. It would "prove worse than useless to us," complained
one; another protested that they were being far too impetuous, rushing
"like a comet into infinite space." They were being asked to spend money
they did not have, one Federalist newspaper griped, "for land of which
we already have too much." Many opponents also feared that the expan-

sion westward would result in a sprawling, ungovernable country so enormous in size that no central government would be able to control it. But it was this vastness, the Republicans believed, that was America's asset. The larger the country, Jefferson said, "the less will it be shaken by local passions."

Lewis's expedition was met with equally strong reservations. Congress could only be convinced to finance it if Jefferson pretended it was for commerce, the president had told the Spanish, British and French ambassadors. In reality, Jefferson assured them, this expedition would be led in the name of science. The pretense, the president explained, was necessary because the Constitution had made no provisions for such scientific ventures. And even though the Federalists believed it a waste of money, they stood no chance against the congressional Republican majority. Despite being outnumbered, they continued to voice their objections—even after Lewis had set off. "The Feds.," Jefferson told Lewis, "treat it as philosophism, and would rejoice in it's failure."

Adams, though not active in politics anymore since his retirement to his farm in 1801, remained deeply interested in the nation's affairs. He had supported the Louisiana Purchase, because he believed it would bind the West to the East in one union,* but agreed with the Federalists about the futility of the expedition, writing that there were so many "Travellers in our Wilderness, which have proved in the end to be mere delusions, that I give little attention to them." Ten years earlier he had backed Michaux's failed expedition to the West but was now concerned that the "Country is explored and thinly planted much too fast." One of the reasons for his change of mind might have been the rift with Jefferson—it seems Adams was still smarting from the viciously fought election in 1800. In letters to friends Adams made his opinion of Jefferson's scientific interest in the West very clear: "I care not a farthing about all the Big Bones in Europe or America," he replied when one acquaintance inquired about the mastodon. "The spirit of party has seized upon the bones of this huge animal, because the head of a party [Jefferson] has written something about them," Adams mocked, but as long as no living specimen was found, "I feel little interest in them."

To Jefferson, however, a lot more was at stake than what Adams called "pitiful Bagatelles." On the contrary, the basis of Enlightenment thinking

---

* Adams thought that the control over the Mississippi and the transport of goods was essential for the union between the Western territories and the Eastern states. Without the Louisiana Purchase the United States would have lost this control and, he believed, the Western territories would have eventually become independent from the United States or united with England, France or Spain.

was to understand nature and nature's productions, be they fossils, plants or animals. Botany, horticulture, paleontology or any other aspect of natural history revealed a world to Jefferson that was orderly and governed by natural laws.* At the same time trees, fossils or an awe-inspiring landscape could contribute to an American narrative that endowed the country with attributes of strength and pride, associations that would become fundamental aspects of the national identity. In his *Notes on the State of Virginia,* Jefferson had rebutted Buffon's theory that America was degenerated; now Lewis's expedition along the Missouri and across the Rocky Mountains was about to add a new chapter to this story.

IN MAY 1804, after a winter spent just outside St. Louis, the center of the fur trade along the Missouri, Lewis began his 4,000-mile journey into the unknown and toward the Pacific Ocean. With him was his expedition partner, William Clark, with whom he had served in the army, and a party of more than forty men. Their provisions included one ton of dried pork, six hundred pounds of ammunition, canoes, surveying instruments, a microscope, and gifts for the indigenous population such as several kilos of colored beads, phosphorus and 144 "cheap looking Glasses." Amid this plethora of goods, Lewis and Clark also found room for America's first botanical textbook, the *Elements of Botany*—fresh from the printing press and written by Barton, who had taught Lewis in Philadelphia—and publications by the Swedish botanist Carl Linnaeus that explained the classification of plants and their botanical descriptions.

As private secretary to the president, Lewis had witnessed Jefferson's enthusiasm for plants firsthand, including the extensive botanical letters that arrived at the White House alongside all the usual political correspondence. The horticultural world was clearly excited to have a gardener president and Lewis would bear all of this in mind during his expedition. In Cincinnati, on his journey from Washington, D.C., to St. Louis, he asked a gardener to dispatch cuttings of fruit trees to Monticello, knowing how much Jefferson treasured his orchard. In St. Louis he procured "some slips of the Osages Plums and Apples"—the so-called Osage orange, a thorny tree from which Native Americans made bows. It could be clipped into impenetrable hedges and would, by the midnineteenth century, become the most commonly planted tree in America.

* This belief underpinned Jefferson's scientific and political thinking. Humans were also governed by natural laws—laws that implied natural rights such as freedom and equality.

He collected roots against snakebites, discovered a serviceberry that was superior in "flavor and size" to the one he knew from Virginia and thought the "yellow currant" (*Ribes aureum*) was "vastly preferable to those of our gardens." Like Jefferson, Lewis observed plants for their possible uses as edible or medicinal plants but also for their ornamental value.*

Over the next months the expedition members battled against the strong rapids and collapsing embankments of the Missouri River passing through today's Nebraska and Iowa. While Jefferson was mourning the death of his youngest daughter, Mary, who had died in childbirth, the Lewis and Clark expedition rowed along the Missouri, weaving through a landscape that promised to fulfill Jefferson's hopes. They saw prairies which seemed like a Garden of Eden abounding with buffalo herds and deer. The grass, Clark wrote in his journal, would make the "sweetest" hay, and stunningly colorful flowers were growing in a living tapestry as far as the eye could see. They gorged on delicious fruits, saving what they didn't eat for Jefferson's orchard, and were dazzled by the perfumed blossom swaying with the grass in the wind. Nature, Clark exulted, had "exerted herself"—the scenery was "magnificent," and the prairie, Lewis wrote, "fertile in the extreem." As they progressed on their northwesterly route into today's South and then North Dakota, the landscape changed, opening into vast plains with endless horizons. Lewis, who like Jefferson had been brought up in the mountains and forests of Albemarle County in Virginia, was struck by the immensity of the country that unfolded before them.

As Lewis and Clark traveled, they collected countless specimens and objects to send back to the White House: seeds of new vegetables, flowers and blossoms; dried, mounted and labeled specimens of plants (including information they had obtained from the Native Americans about their "virtues and properties"); skins of the animals they had shot; living birds and Indian artifacts such as buffalo robes. To ensure that their collections arrived safely in Washington, Lewis sent, in April 1805, a small group of his men from their winter quarters in Fort Mandan (in today's North Dakota) back to St. Louis, whence the trunks were dispatched to the White House. The men had also spent a whole day catching an animal

---

* Even in the wilderness, 2,000 miles away from home and many months into his journey, Lewis thought of gardens when he compared the lush grass of the plains with a "beatifull bowlinggreen in fine order." When he found a low-growing creeping juniper (*Juniperus horizontalis*), he thought it would "make very handsome edgings to the borders and walks of a garden," like box hedges only that it "would be much more easily propegated."

that was entirely new to scientists—the black-tailed prairie dog. It took five barrels of water and the whole expedition crew to chase the squirrel-like animal out of its labyrinthine warren.

Among the cargo was an ear of a variety of corn cultivated by the Mandan tribe, which Jefferson would grow for many years in Monticello. The Mandans were farmers, and their corn and other crops helped the expedition through their first winter. As temperatures dropped so low that the water in the cottonwoods froze and the trees exploded like cannons, Lewis bartered with the Mandans for food. Their choice to stay the winter near the village had been prudent because not only was the tribe hospitable toward the expedition members, but the village was also the central trading point in the northern plains.

When the boxes and trunks arrived at the White House in late summer 1805, Jefferson laid out the contents for inspection. The prairie dog and a magpie had surprisingly survived the long journey intact and were temporarily moved into the room where the president usually received his visitors.* The botanical specimens went straight to the American Philosophical Society and to the botanist Barton in Philadelphia, while Jefferson kept some of the artifacts "for an Indian Hall I am forming at Monticello." When Madison mentioned that William Hamilton (one of Jefferson's regular horticultural correspondents and the owner of The Woodlands in Philadelphia) was keen to receive rare plants from the expedition, Jefferson—always happy to share—dispatched several of the seeds, including "Mandan tobacco" (*Nicotiana quadrivolus*).

Jefferson packed, sent, delegated and examined—and though Congress had granted the money to the expedition, he alone was in charge of the scientific booty. With him as president, the White House had become the nexus of science, a control room of scientific inquiry. At dinner, botany, geography and explorations joined farming and agriculture as the favorite topics of conversation. The range of Jefferson's interest was huge—from lunar observations and the close examination of worms that attacked Lombardy poplars to practical experiments that entailed standing in the rain wearing a coat made from waterproof cloth. Jefferson used the East Room, which has subsequently been used for lavish state dinners, for something he thought much more important: the storage of fossils. Where today foreign dignitaries sip cocktails on the lawn,

---

* Jefferson then decided that the prairie dog and magpie should go to the naturalist, painter and collector Charles Willson Peale in Philadelphia.

Jefferson briefly kept two living grizzly bears that arrived from the West.* Thinkers and scientists across the United States were delighted to have "a Philosopher . . . at our Head." Jefferson was, one of William Bartram's protégés said, "the enlightened philosopher—the distinguished naturalist—the first statesman on earth, the friend, the ornament of science . . . the father of our Country, the faithful guardian of our liberties."

While Jefferson sorted and distributed the spoils from the expedition, Lewis and Clark pressed westward, equipped with as much information as they could gather about the lands beyond. Accompanied by a French-Canadian fur trapper and his Shoshone wife, Sacagawea,† whom they had hired as translators, they now followed the Missouri west through what is today North Dakota and then Montana. Almost exactly one year after they had left the buzzing trading port of St. Louis, the members of the expedition were enraptured by the Great Plains and the bountiful herds: the "country is as yesterday beatifull in the extreme," Lewis wrote on 5 May 1805. Three weeks later, they rowed beneath the majestic White Cliffs of the Missouri River Breaks, which had taken form during the Ice Age. Lewis thought that nature had carved these sandstone cliffs into huge buildings adorned with columns, alcoves, parapets and grotesque statuary, some ruined and crumbling. "So perfect indeed are those walls," he cried, "I should have thought that nature had attempted here to rival the human art."

After traveling more than 2,500 miles along the river from St. Louis they saw the snowcapped Rockies bounding the West in the distance with the fertile plains below. At the beginning of June 1805, three months into Jefferson's second term as president, Lewis and Clark described a pastoral idyll that would later entice settlers to the West: a "wide expance" boasting "innumerable herds of living anamals," "it's borders garished with one continued garden of roses" and "lofty and open forrests." The birds sang "most inchantingly" and the soil was rich. These were, Lewis said, "the most beatifully picteresque countries that I ever beheld."

---

* Jefferson received the two grizzly bears from Zebulon Pike, who had captured them at the Rio Grande. The president later passed them on to the naturalist Charles Willson Peale. According to Margaret Bayard Smith, Federalists enjoyed calling the grounds at the White House the "President's *bear-garden*."

† Sacagawea not only translated for the expedition but also negotiated with tribes and was an invaluable guide. Born Shoshone, she had been kidnapped as a girl, but by chance the party met her brother and the Shoshones almost 800 miles away from the Mandan village. This encounter allowed Lewis to trade for horses and a guide to cross the mountains.

Five days later Lewis, who had temporarily split off from the main group to reconnoiter, reached the first of the Great Falls of the Missouri. Nothing he had seen during the past year had prepared him for the noise of the roaring water, the rainbows that danced in the spray and the dramatic eighty-foot drop into the river. Lewis was lost for words, "disgusted" by his inability to express this transcendent sensation. He wished, he wrote in his journal, that he could draw like the landscape painter Salvator Rosa or use his pen like a poet. The scenery was enchantingly unique, Lewis enthused, a "sublimely grand specticle"—"sublime" being the only term that seemed appropriate to describe his feelings of awe and astonishment. Lewis's journal entry echoed Jefferson's language more than two decades earlier in his *Notes on the State of Virginia*, when he had described the Natural Bridge as "the most sublime of Nature's works" and the Potomac River's precipitous passage through the Blue Ridge Mountains as "one of the most stupendous scenes in nature."

Jefferson's fascination with the natural world and Lewis's awe at the magnificent new landscape came together in the idea of "the sublime," a concept that had been used since the mid-eighteenth century by English philosophers, poets and garden designers as an aesthetic category to describe landscapes. The idea was distinct from the "beautiful," which was applied to scenes or objects that were small, smooth, delicate and light. The "sublime," by contrast, was applied to the vast, rugged and dark. Mountains, in particular, merited this lofty term because seeing them supposedly induced "a sort of delightful horror" and astonishment in the onlooker.

The sublime was associated with breathtaking vastness, and although Europeans had invented the concept, in America, buoyed by the continent's scale, it would become distinctively patriotic. The Rockies were more commanding than the Alps, and the Potomac was more awe-inspiring than the Danube, Americans would soon proudly believe. Madison's friend Philip Freneau wrote that the Mississippi was a "prince of rivers in comparison of whom the Nile is but a small rivulet, and the Danube a ditch." Similarly Adams called the Thames "but a rivulet" compared with the majestic Hudson, and Abigail thought that nature was of "greater magnificence and sublimity in America than in any part of Europe." While in Europe Adams had even elevated the gentle hills around his farm in Quincy to the "the most sublime object in my Imagination," and as early as 1791 Jefferson had asked the American artist John Trumbull to paint Virginia's Natural Bridge so that he could present "to the world this singular landscape, which otherwise some bungling European will misrepresent." And Washington had encouraged William

Winstanley to paint the falls of the Potomac and other scenes, underlining that they should be depicted as "grand objects."*

Imbuing the grandeur and majesty of landscape with patriotic significance can be compared to the British tradition of using gardens as expressions of political ideology, as seen in Lord Cobham's garden at Stowe. "For these last forty years," one British garden writer had told Washington a few months before his death, "there has been a close resemblance between the prevailing system in politics, & that in gardening." If the natural or "picturesque" style of unclipped trees, soft lines and irregularly planted groves were used in England to express ideas of liberty, then America's endless horizons, fertile soil and floral abundance would be the perfect articulation of the nation's vigor and strength. The sublime "wildness" of the vast continent made North America uniquely different from Europe.

Already in 1776 Thomas Paine had aligned the importance of the revolution with the sheer size of North America. In *Common Sense* he had argued that a small island like England could never govern a continent as vast as America because nature had never "made the satellite larger than its primary planet." Underlining this was the popular notion that a people were influenced and determined by their surroundings. Similarly, J. Hector St. John de Crèvecoeur had written in his 1782 best seller, *Letters from an American Farmer,* that "Men are like plants. The goodness and flavour of the fruit proceeds from the peculiar soil and exposition in which they grow."† If America's wilderness shaped its people, so the argument went, they too would be powerful, spirited and unique.

When Lewis and Clark returned to St. Louis in September 1806, almost two and a half years after they had set off, they had crossed a continent alive with the contrasts of the sublime and the beautiful, of deep ravines and gently rolling land, of gushing waterfalls and meandering rivers, of large and small, cold and hot. The Great Falls, for example, had been awe-inspiring, but Lewis and his men also had endured seven-inch

---

* Sublime nature was apparently even used for party politics. Jefferson told a fellow Republican that Federalists had ordered the destruction of the rock from where one could see the passage of the Potomac through the Blue Ridge Mountains, which he had so rapturously described in the *Notes on the State of Virginia.* This had been attempted, Jefferson explained, "with the intention of falsifying his account and rendering it incredible."

† American scientist Benjamin Silliman said something similar after a tour through New England, noting that "national character often receives its peculiar cast from natural scenery." Almost one hundred years later, historian Frederick Jackson Turner would argue that the experience of the Western frontier defined Americans, creating a unique people who were stronger and freer than Europeans.

hailstones, the vicious thorns of cacti, and the prickly pear that tore their moccasins to shreds when they had to carry their boats around the Falls. Two months after they had heard the thunderous roar of the Great Falls, they had stood, a foot on each side, over the source of the river—the mighty Missouri had become a tiny gurgling stream. As they sweated in the heat of the intense August sun, they had looked across the vast plains at the glistening white snow of the mountains beyond, which suddenly seemed a daunting, impenetrable barrier. "I shudder with the expectation," Clark wrote when he thought of crossing "those Snowey tremendious mountains."*

The brutal journey through the snow-covered Rocky Mountains had almost killed them, but amid starvation, freezing temperatures and uncharted danger there had also been stunning beauty. Close to the snow fields they discovered pockets of colorful blossoms—nodding bluebells (*Mertensia paniculata*), exquisitely sculpted crimson columbines (*Aquilegia formosa*), yellow pealike flowers (*Thermopsis montana*) and the strongly scented licorice-root. And as they fought through three-foot-deep snow, they found carpets of yellow glacier lilies. Lewis saw great swaths of quamash of such brilliant blue that they shimmered like lakes in the distance. "So complete is this deseption that on first sight I could have swoarn it was water," he wrote in his diary.

"I RECIEVED, my dear Sir, with unspeakable joy your letter of Sep. 23 announcing the return of yourself, Capt. Clarke & your party in good health to St. Louis," Jefferson wrote to Lewis in late October 1806. The expedition had found a passage to the Pacific (albeit not an easy one), amassed valuable information about Native American tribes (including several "vocabularies"), and collected animal skins, bones (no mastodon, though) and what Lewis described as "a pretty extensive collection of plants." "Pretty extensive" was something of an understatement—Lewis had brought back a herbarium of around two hundred specimens in addition to the sixty he had sent back to St. Louis from their first winter quarters, almost none of which had ever been documented before.†

---

* Until then Lewis and Clark (and everybody else) had believed that the continent was symmetrical, assuming that a low and easily crossed mountain range mirroring the Appalachians would run along the Western side.
† A German botanist who spent some time in Philadelphia was paid by Lewis to arrange, describe and paint the collection. When Frederick Pursh left Philadelphia in spring 1809, he took his botanical drawings and also some of the dried speci-

The horticultural world was electrified. The plants that Lewis and Clark had discovered would line fields as hedges, add fruits to the American orchards and bring new shapes and color to flowerbeds. When Bernard McMahon, a Philadelphia nurseryman and author of *The American Gardener's Calendar*—the first practical horticultural book to deal exclusively with North America—heard of Lewis's arrival, he immediately dashed off a letter to Jefferson, anxious to procure a "small portion of every kind you could conveniently spare." Jefferson, who was drowning in presidential duties, was happy to share the seeds. With another war in Europe that once again saw England fighting against France, Jefferson was desperately trying to maintain the United States of America's neutrality, and closer to home there were additional problems. When Lewis and Clark returned to St. Louis, Jefferson was trying to make sense of the rumors that his former vice president, Aaron Burr, was plotting to attack the Spanish territories in the Southwest in order to create a new nation with Burr himself as a ruler. With all these troubles to deal with and yet another two years left of his second term as president, Jefferson had to admit that he was in no position to do the precious seeds "justice."

In spring 1807, as Aaron Burr was captured for his alleged conspiracy, the "public treasures" of the Lewis and Clark expedition were dispatched from the White House to McMahon and William Hamilton in Philadelphia. Within a week the first seedlings were pushing through the soil, reported McMahon, who had never seen seeds "in a better state of preservation." They held the promise of a new land. Dried, shriveled and unassuming, these seeds carried inside them a landscape that no white American other than the members of the Lewis and Clark expedition had ever seen. Once the leaves unfolded and the petals unfurled, gardeners in the East would be able to feast their eyes on the West. When the fruits ripened and the crops matured, they would be able to taste the prairies and the Mississippi Valley. These plants would bring the new American land to life, providing a uniquely visceral encounter with the vast continent that stretched all the way to the Pacific Ocean.

Jefferson was delighted by the sheer variety of the expedition's discoveries, reflecting that "Some of them are curious, some ornamental, some useful, and some may by culture be made acceptable on our table." McMahon was so excited that he sent Jefferson four letters in two weeks,

---

mens from Lewis's collection (even cutting off some parts of the plants). In 1814 he published *Flora Americae Septentrionalis,* in which he described 124 of Lewis's and Clark's plants. He named a genus *Lewisia* and another *Clarkia,* as well as three species: *Linum lewisii, Mimulus lewisii* and *Philadelphus lewisii.*

a running commentary on which plants were coming up—tobacco from the Mandans, prairie flax and four varieties of currants. Soon, he believed, he would be able to send Jefferson "plants of *every kind*" (almost thirty new species as it turned out). And though Jefferson had given away most of his seeds, that spring in Monticello, he sowed the few that he had kept, including Osage oranges, "Missouri great Salsafia," "flowering pea of Arkansa," and "Lilly, the yellow of the Columbia." He thought the yellow Arikara bean, which had fed the expedition team during their winter in North Dakota, to be "one of the most excellent we have," and Lewis's snowberry (*Symphorocarpos albus*) became one of his favorite shrubs—the alabaster berries that clung to the naked branches throughout winter, Jefferson said, were "some of the most beautiful berries I have ever seen."

The initial excitement surrounding Lewis's and Clark's return was a blend of relief, enthusiasm and pride in their achievement. The president himself could not have hoped for a better outcome, praising the "addition to our knowledge in every department" that resulted from the expedition, which had "entirely fulfilled" his expectations.* Yet the opening of the West also added a new chapter to the American narrative. Jefferson, Washington and Adams had long understood the potential importance of nature to the national identity but gradually over the next decades the idolization of the wilderness began to seep into the public imagination. Where previous generations had regarded America's untamed landscape as "hideous and desolate," a hostile environment that was an obstacle to farming and settlement, it now became an object of national pride.

This celebration of the American wilderness was entirely different from the roots of European patriotism, where buildings, ancient writings and art played the elemental roles. Centuries of history had given Europeans a sense of belonging and superiority—a lineage to be proud of. In the absence of ruins and antiquity, Americans turned instead to untamed wilderness. Primeval forests, vast plains and imposing waterfalls became invested with patriotism and linked to the national character. The New World's virgin landscape, fertile, imposing and wild, was untainted by history—by contrast, Europe's antiquity became synonymous in the

---

* Despite the success of the expedition, Lewis didn't find much happiness after his return. Jefferson made him governor of the Louisiana Territory, but Lewis failed to make a success and faced financial ruin. In October 1809, only three years after the expedition had arrived back in St. Louis, Lewis was found in a bedroom of a tavern badly injured by several gunshots and died shortly afterward. Though the circumstances of his death remain a mystery, it was most likely that he committed suicide.

American mind with despotism. Why should they admire "the temples which Roman robbers have reared," one American poet wrote, when the native wilderness was untouched by the blood of tyrants? Cathedrals, another writer insisted, were "monuments of a corrupt religion," and castles were emblems for a society "in which every thing was barbarous."

The forest, a magazine article proclaimed in the decades after Lewis's return, was "one of the principal sources of an ardent and deep-felt patriotism." The opening of the West made the United States vast, and "every plant appears to partake of this gigantic character." The wilderness, another writer argued some years later in the mid-nineteenth century, had long confirmed "our destiny as a country."

As commentators began to celebrate the wilderness as the epitome of the national character, adopting the very same arguments that Jefferson had used in the 1780s to combat Buffon's theory of degeneracy, so too did the nation's painters. After the war the most worthy subjects for American art were deemed to have been George Washington and dramatic or historic moments of the revolution. But now painters began to focus on landscapes—Niagara Falls, the Hudson River valley and later the Great Plains. "In no quarter of the globe are the majesty and loveliness of nature more strikingly conspicuous than in America," the artist Joshua Shaw wrote in 1820. Jefferson became a collector of landscape depictions, buying prints of Niagara Falls as well as of the Natural Bridge and the junction of the Potomac and the Shenandoah rivers. The sublime became America's language of national identity, with artists scrambling up mountains to capture the spectacular sights and poets celebrating landscape. As the writer Washington Irving declared in 1820, "never need an American look beyond his own country for the sublime and the beautiful of natural scenery."

As the wilderness became embedded in the American consciousness, tourists began to travel in search of it. Instead of delighting in the pastoral beauty of well-maintained fields, as before, they began to enthuse about the "magnitude" of the rugged mountains and untouched forests. The veneration for the American landscape became so popular that foreigners grumbled that Americans suffered from a "habit of exalting their own things"—to find scenes like this, one Englishman snidely remarked, "it would be needless to go farther than Wales."

By the 1820s, the first tourist shelters were built in the Catskills to accommodate the growing numbers of revelers. "Our lofty mountains and almost boundless prairies, our broad and magnificent rivers, the unexampled magnitude of our cataracts, the wild grandeur of our western forests, and the rich and variegated tints of our autumnal landscapes, are unsurpassed," the painter Joshua Shaw insisted. For those who could not afford to travel to these rugged scenes, portfolios of landscape engravings were also now available, bringing the waterfalls and ancient forests into America's parlors. As the obsession with the American wilderness spread, poets wrote about the prairies and novelists turned to the frontier for inspiration. So-called backwoods novels popularized the wilderness, including James Fenimore Cooper's best-selling Leatherstocking Tales, which included *The Pioneers* (1823) and *The Prairie* (1827). The wide horizons of the vast continent entered the houses of merchants and farmers, giving them a sense of belonging and pride. The boundless land became the embodiment of their future. "Our seventeen states compose a great and growing nation," Jefferson wrote with pride, "their children are as the leaves of the trees, which the winds are spreading over the forest."*

* Vermont had joined the Union in 1791, Kentucky in 1792, Tennessee in 1796 and Ohio in 1803.

8

"THO' AN OLD MAN,
I AM BUT A YOUNG GARDENER"

Thomas Jefferson at Monticello

A LONE RIDER battled through a fierce snowstorm in the foothills of
Virginia's Blue Ridge Mountains. The snow was so deep that the roads
were almost impassable, and for the last seven hours an ice-cold wind
had cut through the rider's heavy coat. It was mid-March 1809, but
instead of the first green flush of spring the forests were hidden under a
stark white blanket, while the layers of mountain ridges had all but disappeared in the hypnotizing dance of light flakes. The traveler was sixty-
five-year-old Thomas Jefferson, who had left Washington four days
earlier after James Madison's inauguration as the fourth president of the
United States. Seventy miles into his journey home he had overtaken his
estate manager, Edmund Bacon, who led two wagons' worth of Jefferson's belongings from the White House and one filled with shrubs from
the capital's nurseries. Jefferson could have traveled the remaining fifty
miles in his carriage but was anxious not to waste any more time—he had
waited for this moment for so long, and a snowstorm was not going to
stop him.

"Never did a prisoner, released from his chains, feel such relief as I
shall on shaking off the shackles of power," claimed the third president of
the United States, who had described his final years in office as "the most

tedious of my life." Desperately lonely in the capital, even his daily rides in the countryside had started to bore him. Like George Washington before him, Jefferson longed to tend to his plantation and garden, and had made the decision to follow Washington's example and not run for a third term. Increasingly his letters to friends and family had mentioned this pining to return to "the enjoyments of rural life." "My views and attentions," he wrote to fellow gardener William Hamilton in Philadelphia, "are all turned homewards." He was so excited about his garden in particular, he said to Hamilton, that "the subject runs away with me whenever I get on it."

His favorite garden correspondents were his eighteen- and twelve-year-old granddaughters, Anne and Ellen. As with his daughters, Martha and Mary, in the early 1790s, Jefferson's love for his family and his garden became intertwined in playful letters—almost as if nature became the stage on which to play out his feelings. While Jefferson was in Washington, Anne would regularly ride the few miles from her parents' farm to Monticello to plant, talk to the gardeners and, most important, report back to her doting grandfather. On the rare occasions when she couldn't go to Monticello, she would always ask the slaves how the flowers were doing. Ellen was too young to be in charge of the garden, but she received potted geraniums from her grandfather and took care of the orange trees. She also mischievously reported any mistakes that Bacon, the estate manager, made—such as covering the entire lawn with charcoal instead of manure.

The letters from Jefferson's granddaughters brought the twin joys of Monticello and his family to the White House. "You have a thousand little things to tell me which I am fond to hear," he told Ellen, adding that he sent kisses by kissing the paper. "I have not much to say, unless I talk about plants," Ellen wrote, but without fail she would write because her meticulous grandfather ran an "account"—every one of her letters would be "credited" and he would owe her one in return. At the end of February 1809, as he prepared at long last to leave office, Jefferson wrote to Ellen that he would be home three weeks later, "and then we shall properly be devoted to the garden." Like Washington, who had relished the years of his retirement at Mount Vernon after his presidency until his death in 1799, or Adams, who had spent the past eight years working his fields and garden at Quincy, it was here that Jefferson would find both solace and inspiration.

Jefferson's longing to retire to Monticello had grown in tandem with the many problems that plagued his last years in office. In his first term he had enjoyed considerable success—he had seen the country grow both geographically and economically in the wake of the Louisiana Purchase, and had managed to reduce the national debt by a third. He had also led the Republicans to unprecedented levels of popularity. The last two years of his presidency, by contrast, had seen dramatic economic decline. Once again the United States of America was suffering from events in Europe, as Britain and France were at war and issuing orders that ships trading with the enemy were to be captured. Britain alone, James Monroe estimated, captured one American ship every other day from 1805 onward. Hoping to avoid war and to pressure Britain and France, Jefferson had introduced the Embargo Act in December 1807, banning all foreign trade. But rather than squeezing Britain and France economically, the ban had been disastrous for America. The thriving merchant communities of New England lost their foreign markets, wheat prices plummeted and Southern plantation owners were unable to sell their tobacco and cotton.

Jefferson found it difficult to stay optimistic in the face of such troublesome conditions—his life, he lamented, had become an "unceasing drudgery," "odious" and "nauseating," and wasn't helped by the fact that his excruciating migraines had returned. And so, during those last years of his presidency, his thoughts increasingly turned to his garden at Monticello. He began to rely more and more on his secretary of state, James Madison, and treasury secretary Albert Gallatin, and spent increasing amounts of time doodling, sketching, scribbling and dreaming up myriad gardens and designs, most of which would never make it from his notebook onto the soil. Not only was he discussing planting schemes with the architect Benjamin Henry Latrobe at the White House in 1807 and sending detailed instructions to the overseer at Poplar Forest, he also decided—once again—to remodel the gardens at Monticello.

A few years earlier, in 1804, at the height of his presidency and after his landslide election victory over the Federalists, his ideas had been grander than anything he had ever planned before, radiating confidence and self-assuredness—he wanted temples, a grove of the highest trees and a labyrinth of flowering shrubs, more vistas across the sea of mountains that stretched to the West, a shady arbor covered with vines and a cascade on Montalto (the mountain opposite Monticello) to be "visible at Monticello." He also planned to build a columned classical temple and four other garden buildings including one "model of the Pantheon" and the "Chinese pavilion of Kew gardens" at Monticello. For these changes he had asked a landscape painter (an Englishman who had immigrated to the United States) to "give me some outlines" but had failed to lure him to Monticello.*

Since then, however, his plans had changed. In the light of the general economic situation and the realization that he had run up a personal debt of more than $10,000 during his time in Washington,† Jefferson abandoned temples and cascades and designed instead a garden that would be an expression of his vision of America—beautiful, sublime, strong, independent and agrarian. Majestic views over the rolling mountains, groves of native trees and shrubs, decorative flowerbeds, experimental vegetable plots, vineyards and crops united into one landscape—an ornamental farm embraced by the American wilderness. The garden that Jefferson designed at Monticello during his last years of the presidency combined his appreciation for beauty and his love for his country with his scientific and agricultural endeavors—it was a celebration of the United States of America and the future.

JEFFERSON REACHED Monticello on 15 March 1809, exhausted from the "very fatiquing journey" but not too tired to inspect his farms and gardens the next morning. "Spring is remarkably backward," he remarked. All the trees were still naked except for the light green veil of the weeping willows and a red flush that tinged the maples. The vegetable plots were unplanted and still covered in snow. In the flowerbeds on the back lawn and at the front of the house the spring bulbs had yet to unfurl their leaves and waxy blossoms. Neither oats nor tobacco had been sown and "little done in the gardens," Jefferson observed, but he could nonetheless feel his "vis vitae"—his energy of life—returning to him.

"I am constantly in my garden," he was soon writing to friends with delight, "as exclusively employed out of doors as I was within doors when at Washington." He talked of droughts, blights, frosts or rains but, as ever, "if the topic changes to politics I meddle little with them." From early morning to dinnertime Jefferson was either on horseback or striding through his property, instructing and overseeing, always humming and

---

* This was the landscape painter George Isham Parkyns and, despite Jefferson's failure to bring him to Monticello, he might have still been influenced by his designs. In his book *Six Designs for Improving and Embellishing Grounds* (1793), Parkyns illustrated one garden that was located in a mountainous area. Many of the design elements that Parkyns presented were also found at Monticello, such as a winding walk around a lawn and a grove of "great forest trees."

† Jefferson had to pay for the entertainment of diplomats and congressmen during his two terms as president from his personal money. With an expensive taste for fine food and exquisite wine, Jefferson had—as so often—lived above his means.

singing. Scribbling into a small ivory notebook he noted ideas, planting and harvest dates, names of species and the amount of seeds planted, all of which could be rubbed off after he had transferred his notes into his Garden Book. He knew every plant in his garden, his estate manager Bacon would later recall, and would instantly spot if a single tree had died or a specimen was missing.

Jefferson's daughter Martha had moved to Monticello as her father's housekeeper, alongside her six youngest children (Ellen and her younger sisters and brothers).* Bacon described how they "delighted to follow him about over the grounds and garden." They clung to him, threw themselves against him, cuddled and kissed him, sat on his lap. When the snow had melted they all eagerly awaited the first greens breaking through the red soil. Every morning the children would check the flowerbeds and then run to Jefferson to announce any new arrivals. He relished their excitement and fostered their love for plants. "Botany here is but an object of amusement," he said, "a great one indeed and in which all our family mingles." It helped that he had a knack for turning play into education, such as giving Ellen pet fowls under the condition that she had to find their proper Latin names in his zoological books or peppering his letters with playful instructions such as "more Latin, madam." When Jefferson's old friend Margaret Bayard Smith arrived from Washington, a few months after his retirement in August 1809, she found him sitting on the back lawn watching the children run along walks that were rimmed with the luscious colors of summer. "It is only with them that a grave man can play the fool," he told her, before getting up to join the race among the flowers.

After his twelve long years as vice president and president, Jefferson was finally home. The building work on the house was finished and had transformed the eight-room villa into a twenty-one-room mansion.† The first thing visitors saw when they entered the hall was the enormous jawbone of a mastodon. Next to it Jefferson had placed the much smaller

---

* The two oldest children did not live at Monticello at the time that Jefferson returned. Anne had married and Thomas Jefferson Randolph was educated in Philadelphia. Martha's husband, Thomas Mann Randolph, remained at their farm in Edgehill, a short ride away from Monticello. Though living apart, Martha had three more children after she moved to Monticello. Martha adored her father more than anybody—so much so that only weeks after her marriage she had pledged never to love anyone more.

† Jefferson had spent so many years building and changing his house that some friends had doubted if he would ever finish it. In September 1802, Anna Thornton remarked that Jefferson "has pulled down & built up again so often, that nothing is compleated, nor do I think ever will be."

jawbone of an elephant—his proof that the New World was indeed superior. Adjacent to his library was his greenhouse, a loggia enclosed with
large sash windows that opened to the garden so that Jefferson could be
close to his plants.

Most exciting of all, however, was Jefferson's reinvention of the
grounds of Monticello itself. In the years leading up to his return he had
created a garden that was a living tapestry of the themes and ideas that
had always inspired him. The plants that Lewis and Clark had brought
back from their expedition were a reminder of the treasures that lay in
the West; small fields near the ornamental part of the garden captured Jefferson's vision of an agrarian republic; large experimental vegetable plots
provided a scientific laboratory, while the grove and woods celebrated
America's magnificent landscape. Monticello had become the nexus of
Jefferson's world.

Over the past few years the changes had involved shifting tons of soil
in order to level parts of the grounds, as well as planting large numbers of
trees, shrubs and flowers. Jefferson had carefully staged these different
elements of his garden, turning the changing landscape along the winding
roads that led up the mountain to the mansion into an orchestrated
approach. In some places roads were cut into the slope, while in others
large areas were raised or flattened; fields were carved out of the forest
and elsewhere trees were planted to create groves. The closer to the
house, the more controlled the landscape became, almost like a journey
from wilderness to civilization. Starting at the bottom at the mountain,
Jefferson presented his visitors with an untamed forest. Halfway up the
mountain, he introduced the first visible agricultural elements and then a
carefully planned eighteen-acre grove that led to an enormous vegetable
terrace, the lawn and the flowerbeds at the house.

Arriving at Monticello after a long journey through the Virginia forest,
visitors first had to ford the Rivanna River in the valley (accidents involv-
ing people and horses slipping into the water were a regular occurrence).
After crossing the river they found themselves once again surrounded by
thick forest. "I looked around everywhere expecting to meet with some
trace of [Jefferson's] superintending care," Margaret Bayard Smith said
when she arrived in summer 1809—but instead of the "labour of man,"
she could see only "untamed woodland."

Where tired visitors expected a straight and manicured driveway, they
were led instead along a winding road known as the North Road. Nestled
along the contours of the steep ridge, this gradually climbed up toward
four interconnected "roundabouts" that slung around the mountain at

different levels. The first, or upper, roundabout was at the top of the mountain and a little over half a mile long. Descending from the top and connected by oblique roads came the second and third roundabouts and then the fourth and lowest, more than two miles long. The first and second roundabouts had been constructed in the 1770s and 1780s, but the third and fourth were later additions—as was the North Road, which had been finished in May 1806 as part of the redesign of Monticello's landscape.

Until the completion of the North Road, visitors had taken the relatively straight Farm Road, which ran along two hundred acres of farmland. The North Road was considerably longer but much more scenic, with spectacular views down to the river. What the irked Bayard Smith did not realize was that she was in fact passing the fields and farmland that were located between the North and the Farm Road. Jefferson had screened them in the forest because he did not want his visitors to see any signs of agriculture—not yet, at least.

The illusion worked, with Bayard Smith complaining that she felt she was penetrating ever deeper into the forest along an "endless" road. She was not the only one who was surprised by the "savage" approach—some visitors worried so much about the state of the rough road that they abandoned their carriages and walked up the mountain. Others compared its slow and steep route to "Satan's ascent to Paradise." Nature ruled in Monticello's forests, and trees decayed naturally. There was white oak, Jefferson's most treasured oak because of its height, and tulip poplar, another giant favorite. They were, Jefferson boasted to his friend Madame de Tessé, "the Jupiter . . . [and] the Juno of our groves." Jefferson claimed never to have felled any trees on this part of the mountain because they were, he said, "majestic" reminders of America's spectacular beauty.

It was almost as if he was continuing what Washington had begun at Mount Vernon after the War of Independence. But instead of creating a manicured shrubbery of native species, Jefferson's garden embraced an entire forest. Bayard Smith might not have been quite ready for this kind of American garden, but in the coming years the wilderness became an elemental part of landscape admiration. McMahon's best-selling *The American Gardener's Calendar* was the first horticultural book published in America that suggested introducing rugged nature into the garden. "Sometimes a blake declivity, rocky ground, or rough vale, is made to exhibit a wild and uncultivated scene," the author advised, adding that native species "so bountifully bestowed upon us by the hand of nature" were great ornaments in the garden.* Jefferson embraced this at Monticello, boasting that "what nature has done for us is sublime & beautiful & unique." Slowly, as America's wilderness became part of the country's national identity and an object of pride, visitors to Monticello began to appreciate Jefferson's approach. What had been dismissed as an uninviting wilderness by Bayard Smith became "a noble forest" and "extremely grand and imposing" to later visitors. It would be a full fourteen years before Bayard Smith embraced these new attitudes—in 1823 she wrote enthusiastically about the "impervious grove of aspens" with "ever quivering leaves" and "aspiring branches" which created a wonderful contrast to the spreading ash and other forest trees at Monticello.

Farther up the mountain, as the visitors climbed closer to the mansion, the forest grew more manicured—this was the "Grove." Jefferson took his inspiration from the landscape gardens he had seen in England as well as his English garden books, yet he adapted these designs to the American landscape (and climate). In England he had admired sprawling lawns on which small clumps of trees grew, but "under the beaming, constant and almost vertical sun of Virginia" he would need more shade. He cut the undergrowth from the existing forest and trimmed off the branches of the tallest trees "as high as the constitution & form of the tree will bear," leaving only the top canopy. The impression created was that of an open ground, as fashionable in England, which at the same time provided the necessary shade.

Instead of shrubberies, Jefferson had decided to introduce thickets of evergreens such as privet and mountain laurel that would thrive in the shade. Sweet-smelling Carolina allspice, with its reddish-black flowers, lilacs, honeysuckle and guelder rose, with its white pompom blossoms, would spread their scent while the white tassels of fringe tree and alabaster blooms of flowering dogwood would light up the scene. Just as Jefferson envisioned when he first sketched his ideas for the Grove, there would be a riot of color under the green roof of ancient oaks, ash and maples—mixing the dark pink blossom of eastern redbud, the flushed white-pinkish rhododendrons and the purple capsules of euonymus.

Closer to the house, on the gentle slope between the Grove and the lawn with the oval flowerbeds, Jefferson created an open area in which the trees were more widely spaced. This linked the densely planted Grove

* McMahon's publication was also the first American garden book that included information on how to propagate and cultivate native trees and shrubs. Like Philip Miller's *Gardeners Dictionary*, McMahon included lists of "Hardy Deciduous Trees and Shrubs," "Hardy Evergreen Trees and Shrubs" and so on that could be used to select species for groves and shrubberies.

below the first roundabout to the wide expanse of the lawn above it. Jefferson had chosen predominantly native species from across the United States for this open area, a select group that one visitor described as Jefferson's "pet trees." He grew southern catalpa for its summer bloom and Kentucky coffee tree, which had been so rare in the early 1790s that William Bartram had asked Jefferson to procure seeds for him through Madison, who had a neighbor who grew them. In spring the pink blossoms of wild crab apple competed with the enormous white flowers of umbrella magnolia, while red buckeye from the southern states paraded upright red blossoms like candles on the branches. Over the years Jefferson had also planted balsam poplar, which he and Madison had admired on their botanical tour in Vermont as well as willow oak, fringe tree and rhododendron. In between these native trees were a few foreign species such as chinaberry, which is today regarded as an invasive.

Riding (or trudging) along the roundabouts toward the house, visitors would then witness the transition from the forest, via the more ornamental Grove, to the flower garden at the front and back of the house—from the wild, rugged and picturesque to the more composed, refined and beautiful. At the same time the useful and practical elements of the landscape also revealed themselves—the scattered fields on the mountain slope. Jefferson had long been planning to implement these, having been inspired during his tour of English gardens with Adams two decades earlier. Yet once again, he would take these ideas and place them in an American context, making them his own.

At The Leasowes and Wooburn Farm in England, Adams and Jefferson had seen how garden owners enclosed grazing sheep, arable land and orchards within their gardens in order to create scenes of rural idylls. These so-called *fermes ornées* celebrated a paternalistic, if unrealistic, image of laborers happily toiling in fields and of a land that yielded enduring stability, prosperity and contentment (as well as income) for all. Jefferson liked the idea of combining utility with beauty but thought that the English had not taken the idea far enough. Wooburn Farm, he complained, was "merely a highly ornamented walk through and round the divisions of the farm and kitchen garden," while The Leasowes was "only a grazing farm with a path round it." Ornamental farms in England emphasized the decorative rather than the agricultural aspects of the landscape.

In the United States, with the embargo banning all trade with Europe, agriculture and home production had become more important than ever before. As if to imprint this onto Monticello's soil, Jefferson had designed a plan for his mountaintop that included small fields nestled on the slope

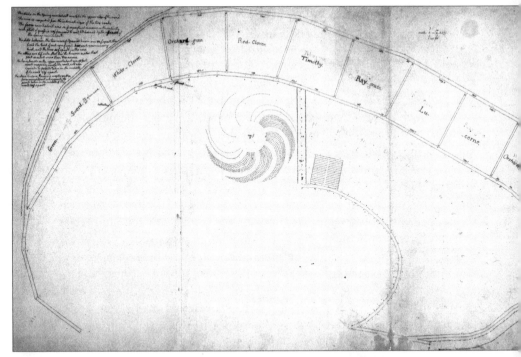

Thomas Jefferson's sketch of fields nestled along the
mountain below the second roundabout

below the lawn and ornamental garden.* After his return from Britain in
1789, he had drawn several sketches with bands of fields weaving along
the contour of the mountain, but had never executed his designs. In the
year before his retirement and in the midst of the embargo crisis, Jefferson informed Bacon that he wanted these agricultural elements disposed
"into a ferme ornée by interspersing occasionally the attributes of a garden." Most certainly he also looked back through his copy of Whately's

---

* The celebration of America's cultivated nature also found an expression in public
buildings. In 1809 Jefferson received from the architect Benjamin Henry Latrobe a
model of the top part (the capital) of the most-loved columns in the Capitol—
composed of ears of maize instead of the traditional acanthus leaves. This American interpretation of a classical design, Latrobe wrote to Jefferson, brought him
"more applause from the Members of Congress" than the magnificent building of
the Capitol itself. They proudly christened it "the Corn Cob Capital." Jefferson
adored this "peculiarly American capital" so much that he turned the model into a
sundial for the garden. Latrobe later designed more "American" capitals for the
Capitol when he included tobacco leaves and flowers as well as magnolias.

Observations on Modern Gardening that he had read during the English tour, the guide that also explained how to lay out gardens and such ornamental farms.

Planted with different grasses that he considered for his crop rotation and as animal fodder, the fields were designed as experimental plots. Some lay like a necklace on the northern side of the mountain and others were scattered halfway up amid the dense forest. Closer to the house, just above the second roundabout, further elements of cultivated nature, such as a large orchard and experimental vineyards, were introduced. Over the years Jefferson grew 125 different varieties of fruit trees, but by the time he retired he concentrated only on a few of his favorites—half of which were peach trees. The most exciting additions to the fruit collection were the gooseberries and currants that Lewis and Clark had found near the Great Falls of the Missouri—McMahon had propagated them prodigiously and given Jefferson cuttings.

Above the orchard and below the first roundabout was Jefferson's 1,000-foot-long vegetable terrace, the experimental hub of the garden. During the last two winters of his presidency, his slaves had moved an amazing 600,000 cubic feet of red clay according to Jefferson's instructions. He had reminded Bacon again and again how important the completion of the building work was—"Consider the garden as your main business, and push it with all your might." The vegetable terrace became Jefferson's favorite retirement project.

Carved out of the southern side of the mountain and buttressed with a massive rock wall that ran up to fifteen feet at its highest point, the terrace was unlike any other kitchen garden in the United States. Not only was it huge, it also offered a spectacular view, a sweeping panorama across the plains of the Virginia Piedmont, stretching south into a seemingly endless horizon. A scientific garden, a laboratory for horticultural experiments, it was a testing ground for potentially useful plants and would allow Jefferson to grow hundreds of varieties of vegetables.

The sheer scale of the vegetable terrace made Jefferson the most extraordinary gardener in the United States. None of his peers collected so many different species and varieties, bringing together vegetables from across the world, uniting horticultural and culinary European and colonial, Native American and slave traditions in the kitchen plots. The geographical labels of the vegetables that Jefferson grew in his first summer of retirement alone proclaimed these merging worlds: "African early pea," "Windsor beans," "solid pumpkin from S. America," "long pumpkin from Malta," "Lettuces Marsailles," "Chinese melon," "Spanish melon," "Broccoli Roman," "Kale. Malta," "Kale. Delaware," "Salsafia.

Columbian," "Eerie corn," "Turnip Swedish," "Peas Prussian blue" and "Lettuce Dutch Brown."

The location of the terrace, on the southern side of the mountain, made it the ideal place for an experimental laboratory, as few Virginia gardens combined heat, humidity and mild winters as successfully as the one at Monticello. While the valley could be freezing, the rising warm air protected the vegetable terrace, which sat safely above the frost line. In fact, the entire terrace was like one gigantic hotbed, with additional beds below the wall, which retained heat. What made Jefferson a truly revolutionary gardener was the way he harnessed this unique microclimate to grow "hot" vegetables. Most Americans were still concentrating mainly on traditional old-world varieties such as cabbages and root vegetables, which were better suited to the colder and wetter climate in England (where they were still fussing over hotbeds and glass frames in an attempt to protect tender plants), but Jefferson also grew species from hotter climates, such as eggplants, peppers and okra. Looking beyond English gardens, he cultivated lima beans, squashes and endless varieties of kidney beans from the Native Americans' gardens as well as gherkins, black-eyed peas, sesame and peanuts from slave garden traditions.

Jefferson's approach to his garden was that of a man of the Enlightenment—observing, experimenting and recording. He categorized and classified his vegetables, dividing his terrace into plots of "Fruits," "Leaves" and "Roots" (vegetables eaten for their fruits, leaves or roots); recorded the dates of sowing, transplanting and harvesting in neat columns in a "Kalendar" that he started in 1809; studied harvest times of vegetables, listing the dates for future reference; and measured the circumference of Lewis's and Clark's gooseberries. To organize his large collection of seeds, Jefferson had a new cupboard built for his study in which he stored seeds in labeled glass vials of different sizes (which his grandson had sent from Philadelphia). Everything, as one visitor noted, was "in the neatest order"—it was this fastidiousness that formed the bedrock of Jefferson's work as an experimental gardener.

Underlying these experiments was Jefferson's search for the best possible varieties. Unlike other plant collectors, he was not trying to assemble the greatest numbers that he could acquire; instead his endeavor was practical and patriotic. He wanted to find the most useful varieties for the American soil and climate, a continuation of his early attempts to introduce useful plants and crops during his time as an American diplomat in Paris. "One service of this kind rendered to a nation," Jefferson said, "is worth more to them than all the victories of the most splendid pages of their history."

Forty sorts of kidney beans were planted over the years before Jefferson finally picked his two favorites. His selection process was so ruthless that even the rare "Ricara bean" that Lewis and Clark had brought back from the Arikara tribe of the northern plains was eventually dismissed from the vegetable plots. One of the reasons for winnowing out the bad from the good and the good from the superior was Jefferson's innovative stance on selective breeding. "I am curious to select only one or two of the <u>best</u> species or variety of every garden vegetable," Jefferson said, "and to reject all others from the garden to avoid the dangers of mixture & degeneracy."

As always he was meticulous, noting the yields but also failures. Doggedly recording the fate of the plants: "killed by bug," "nearly failed," "killed," "a very few plants," "came to nothing," "failed" and "failed" again and again seemingly without much frustration. Because this was an experimental garden, Jefferson never expected that all varieties would do well in his plots—even if only "one species in a hundred is found useful and succeeds," he believed, it was worth the trial. For decades he had exchanged seeds with dozens of people across Europe and the United States, but now in his retirement Jefferson finally had time to test these plants himself. The seeds, he wrote, were "nourishment to my hobby horse."

Having dedicated his huge vegetable terrace to experiments rather than to efficient kitchen gardening, Jefferson regularly fell short of the staples. What he couldn't supply himself he bought from his slaves, who worked on small vegetable plots in the little free time they had on Sundays and in the evenings. Almost one hundred and fifty slaves lived at Monticello during Jefferson's retirement, and many of the families had their own yards. They sold to Jefferson cucumbers, potatoes, cabbages, squashes and lettuces as well as apples and melons. This was nothing unusual—many plantation owners gave their slaves a piece of land to grow their own vegetables or to keep chickens. Often these plots were next to the slave cabins, but they could also be awkwardly shaped slices of lands around the estate—a triangle left between fields, a plot carved out of the forest or a steep slope. Some owners hoped such gardens gave a slave "an interest in his *home*," while others thought that it created "a cheerful, home-like appearance to the quarter." At the same time these small plots also provided an essential supplement to the slaves' diet, as plantation owners, including Jefferson, provided few or no vegetables in their rations.

The lack of basic vegetables in his own garden did not seem to bother Jefferson. The purpose of the huge plots was not to fill Monticello's kitchen larder but to secure America's future—he was experimenting for his country and fellow countrymen. With the increasing hostility between the United States and France and Britain it was imperative that Americans "endeavor to make every thing we want within ourselves," Jefferson believed, "and have as little intercourse as possible with Europe." Consequently he tried but eventually failed to establish an American vineyard and to produce sesame oil (a perfect substitute for olive oil, he reckoned) at Monticello. Even his granddaughters were playfully drawn into the "homespun" production when Jefferson gave eleven-year-old Cornelia, nine-year-old Virginia and seven-year-old Mary some silkworms (soon reduced to a single worm) with the promise that "as soon as they can get III wedding gowns from this spinner they shall be married."

Jefferson was so obsessed with his garden that Bacon never managed to arrive there before his employer, no matter how early he woke up. At dawn the views from the vegetable terrace were particularly spectacular— as the fog clung to the plains below, the entire countryside was transformed into "an ocean." As Jefferson stood above, the billowing fog created miles and miles of white waves, with only the treetops peeping out like "verdant islands." It seemed as if the whole of America stretched out from here. This was Jefferson's favorite place—so much so that the only garden pavilion known to have been built at Monticello was not in the Grove or among the ornamental flowerbeds but in the middle of the vegetable terrace, overlooking the beans, eggplants and tomatoes on the one side and with views across the countryside on the other.

From here it was only a short walk to the lawn at the back of the house, the most manicured area of Jefferson's garden, where Anne had helped him plant oval flowerbeds. They had allocated a single species for each bed, some rarities but most of them common, such as the local cardinal flower with its tall red spikes. Jefferson did not care much for "those of mere curiosity," instead preferring the most "handsome" and "fragrant"—it was almost as if the elderly statesman, freed from the burden of politics, was allowing himself to be a little more whimsical, at least in the ornamental flower garden. There were old-fashioned English favorites such as carnations and sweet William, and from Asia the blackberry lily, which was so successful that its star-shaped orange blossoms can be found everywhere in midsummer at Monticello today. From Europe came the common red field and yellow-horned poppies, and from North America the delicate twinleaf—*Jeffersonia diphylla*—the flower that had been named after Jefferson himself. Some of the beds were planted with hyacinths in three colors as well as tulips. Most exciting of all, two of the oval beds were dedicated to the prizes from the Lewis and

Clark expedition: "the flowering pea of Arkansa" from which Anne had collected fourteen seeds after the first flowering in 1807, and *Fritillaria pudica*, a tiny perennial with a nodding yellow blossom, which Lewis had collected near the Columbia River.

Fearing that the twenty beds were not enough because they "will too much restrain the variety of flowers in which we might wish to indulge," Jefferson—while still in Washington—had sent Anne a sketch of a "winding walk" edged with narrow flower borders, which snaked around the lawn at the back of the house. He had brought "a full collection of roots and plants" from Philadelphia and Washington in order to plant the scented ribbons along the edge. When Anne wasn't there, Jefferson would report to her on the gardening progress, and no other letters reveal his sheer joy in the beauty of flowers so strongly: "the flowers come forth like the belles of the day, have their short reign of beauty and splendor, & retire," he wrote to her, comparing the show on the back lawn to a theatrical production—"the hyacinths and tulips are off the stage, the Irises are giving place to the Belladonnas, as these will to the Tuberoses, Etc." His pleasures ranged from sowing with his granddaughters to his annual competition with his neighbors to harvest the first pea of the season. This was the happiest period in Jefferson's life. "Tho' an old man, I am but a young gardener," he wrote in August 1811, two years after his retirement.

The other great joy of these years was the revival of his friendship with John Adams. Not many signatories of the Declaration of Independence were still alive, and Jefferson described feeling like "a solitary tree from around which the axe of time has felled the companions of it's youth & growth." Their old friend Benjamin Rush, who described Jefferson and Adams "as the North and South Poles of the American Revolution," had been trying to persuade them both to pick up their pens once again. After their acrimonious political battles, Adams and Jefferson had at first been reluctant, but eventually Adams made the opening move with a short letter on 1 January 1812, to which Jefferson immediately replied, writing that he had "given up newspapers" and was "much happier" as a result, before going on to describe the pleasure of being among his grandchildren. Adams was delighted that his old friend had responded so quickly: "You and I ought not to die," he appealed to Jefferson, "before We have explained ourselves to each other."

Like Jefferson, Adams had retired to the tranquillity of rural life after his presidency, and had since become "quite the Farmer," according to Abigail. In the first few months of retirement he had still felt sour about the vicious election campaign, calling himself the "Farmer of Stony Field." But he had quickly begun to enjoy himself, making "a good exchange," he wrote, "of honor & virtues, for manure," and soon bought more land. His life, he summarized, was spent "in the bosom of my family, surrounded by my children and grandchildren; on my farm, in my garden and library." He studied botanical essays and his grandson read Virgil's pastoral verses to him. In 1805 he wrote that he was "happier . . . than I ever was," sentiments that Jefferson would echo in his own retirement.

Compared to Jefferson's and Washington's huge estates of several thousand acres, Adams's farm was but "a Lilliputian Plantation," he wrote modestly, and jokingly referred to it as "Montezillo Alias the little Hill." Adams never attempted anything as ambitious or groundbreaking as, for example, Jefferson's magnificent vegetable terrace, but it didn't seem to bother the aging statesman. In the past there had been times when Adams had resented Jefferson and Washington for their more luxurious lifestyles, envious that they were "riding in gay Coaches and building grand houses." But during his retirement the irritable Adams had mellowed and enjoyed the more simple pleasures of his farm—no less enthusiastic about his new pastime than Jefferson. "I have seen the Queen of France with eighteen millions of Livres of diamonds upon her person," he wrote some years later in 1820, when one winter storm had encased his trees with a coat of ice, but "all the glitter of her jewels, did not make an impression on me equal to that presented by every shrub."

In relation to botany Adams was like "an old Widower, who meets an ancient Widow, who was one of the flames of his Youth," he said, now falling "in love with her a second time." And just as Jefferson was planning his vegetable terrace, Adams embarked on a long study of different species of seaweed that he had collected at the local shores, exploring their relative merits as "manure"—still one of his favorite subjects. Leafing through his botanical books (forever "angry" at himself for not buying enough of them while in Europe) and examining the seaweeds minutely, Adams's conclusions were elaborate and revealed his impeccable botanical knowledge and mastery of the Linnaean classification system.

He had also been involved in the establishment of a botanic garden at Harvard University, and the scientist Benjamin Waterhouse dedicated his collection of botanical essays to Adams "as a token of gratitude for his early recommendation of natural history to his countrymen." Even Madison, who had never particularly liked Adams, admitted that Adams's encouragement of natural history "at so early a day" was proof of his "comprehensive patriotism." Like Jefferson, Adams received exotic vegetable seeds, including "African pumpkin," peppers and corn from

Constantinople as well as scions of fruit trees that he grafted himself and distributed to his friends and neighbors. When he planted the tiny pear saplings, he hoped that "they will be an ornament to this Farm and a Comfort to some good Citizens two hundred years hence."

Over the next fourteen years the two old men exchanged one hundred and fifty letters, slowly rebuilding their friendship and mutual respect. Their correspondence was infused with political discussion but also laced with humor (Adams signed one "J.A. In the 89 year of his age still too fat to last much longer"). They recommended books to each other, wrote about growing older and reminisced about revolutionary times. There was so much to discuss—religion, politics, old friends and enemies, philosophy and natural science—that "I can not see the Wood for Trees," Adams wrote with vigor and delight. "So many Subjects crowd upon me that I know not, with which to begin." They still disagreed about some political issues but their correspondence became a dialogue about what the American Revolution had meant. "Whether you or I were right," Adams reflected, "Posterity must judge."

And though retired from their political careers, both men remained active despite their age. "I walk little," Jefferson wrote to Adams, but "I am on horseback 3. or 4. hours of every day." Adams replied that he preferred walking—three or four miles "every fair day." His hands trembled when writing and reading had become difficult, but he was still a hands-on farmer. "I call for my Leavers and Iron-bars; for my Chissels, drils and wedges to split rocks," he told Rush, "and for my waggon to Cart seaweed for manure upon my farm."

Their time on the political stage might have been over but their passion for their country had not diminished. For them, working the soil, experimenting with new vegetables and examining plants was a patriotic act as well as an assertion of their belief in America's future. Planting trees, Jefferson wrote in June 1812, was a joy even when it was "for a future race." The saplings they nurtured now would shade the next generation of Americans. "I like the dreams of the future better than the history of the past," Jefferson wrote to Adams in the summer of 1816, their friendship now well and truly recovered. "So good night. I will dream on."

9

"BALANCE OF NATURE"

JAMES MADISON AT MONTPELIER

SLAVES DRESSED in smart liveries rushed back and forth across the huge lawn's immaculately scythed grass, dodging scurrying children as they carried food and drinks from table to table. More than one hundred guests and family members sat shaded by tall tulip poplars, chestnut, walnut and other forest trees. Laughter and the mouthwatering smell of roasted animals on the spit drifted across the garden, as did the sweet sound of violin music. The feast was sumptuous, with soups, meats and vegetables from the garden, the best wines available and large bowls of spiced punch. The cooks had even made ice cream from the ice, which was stored in the icehouse that was cleverly hidden under a classical garden temple next to the house.

It was a late summer's day in 1817, and James and Dolley Madison had invited their neighbors and relatives to Montpelier to celebrate the harvest. Some had left their own plantations at dawn, traveling as much as thirty miles to Orange County, Virginia, for the barbeque. Other guests had arrived the night before and spent the day entertaining themselves with Madison's most popular piece of party furniture, a telescope, spying on carriages and riders as they approached. From the large portico at the front of the house they had sweeping views across Montpelier's driveway, clumps of trees, golden wheat fields and the rolling outline of the Blue Ridge Mountains in the distance.

When their guests arrived that day, Madison and his wife had welcomed them in person, as they always did. And, as ever, many would have noticed that their hosts were an odd-looking couple. The voluptuous Dolley seemed to tower over the diminutive Madison, the wife an "Amazon," the husband "like one of the puny knights of Lilliputia," commented one visitor. Another described him, rather uncharitably, as "a withered little apple-John." Dolley looked elegant and vibrant, as always dressed in bright colors with her hair wrapped in a "turban," while Madison still wore black and old-fashioned breeches. Handsome and chatty, Dolley delighted guests with her "overflowing kindness" as she had already done in Washington. But visitors were also surprised to see how much Madison changed in this regard when at Montpelier. In the capital he had often been described as cold and reserved, yet at home he was more relaxed. His "little blue eyes sparkled like stars," one old friend from Washington remarked when she saw Madison at Montpelier, and Dolley agreed that he seemed markedly more leisurely, fun even, always "fond of a frolic and of romping" with the children of relatives and friends. He also enjoyed chasing his wife around the porch—"I do not believe you can out run me," Dolley told the daughter of one guest on another occasion, "Madison and I often run races here."

Having welcomed them, Dolley and Madison would have led their guests into the large drawing room in the center of the house, where three large triple sash windows opened onto the back portico and the vast lawn. Floor-to-ceiling mirrors brought the garden and the surrounding landscape into the room. Stepping out onto the rear portico, they were welcomed by the delicate perfume of the tiny white flowers of climbing jasmine and "ever blooming roses," which snaked around six tall columns. During these summer months greenhouse plants such as elegant gardenias were grown outdoors, their waxy white blossoms adding to the pleasant fragrance. Only one other flower was allowed to grow near the house—sweetbriar, an old-fashioned, sweetly scented plant from Europe.

From the porch more than an acre of velvety green stretched toward the forest. As the only boundary was a ha-ha, the garden appeared to blend seamlessly into the wilderness beyond. In autumn visitors admired the "contrasting shades of color" of the earthy red leaves of oaks, the coppery orange of American beeches and the buttery yellow of the tulip poplars. Wild climbers wove along the tall forest trees, garlanding them with color and scent, "decorating," as one visitor observed, "their crests with a rich tapestry." Whereas at Monticello Jefferson led his guests along a circuitous route through miles of forest which grew gradually more "tamed" toward the house, Madison embraced nature even more by enclosing the lawn with thick forest. It was such an unusual design that most visitors commented on it.

Rather than fashionable shrubberies or colorful flowers, the lawn itself featured only trees, including many fine specimens such as Osage oranges,* grown from the seeds that Meriwether Lewis had sent to Jefferson from St. Louis, and chinaberry, which Madison had almost certainly received from Monticello, where it was planted in the upper Grove. There were "ornamental trees," weeping willows and two enormous tulip poplars so identical that Madison called them his "twins."

Walking across the lawn from the back portico on that hot summer's day, visitors could also see the entrance to a large horseshoe-shaped flower and kitchen garden in the distance. Instead of turning the sloping land into a softly undulating landscape, as had been fashionable in England for many decades, Madison had carved it into a descending series of level semicircular terraces. This was where he cultivated much of the produce that the cooks had used for the feast, such as sweet strawberries, figs and various types of vegetables, including some from Jefferson's experimental plots. Madison also grew flowers in this more formal part of the garden, which one guest enthusiastically described as "a paradise of roses."

There were hotbeds for cucumbers, and probably a hothouse, so that the Madisons could serve pineapples as well as other rare fruits and vegetables that friends occasionally sent him, such as seeds from Algiers and a new giant beetroot species from France. George Divers, one of Jefferson's closest gardening neighbors, swapped his "Hudson bay strawberry" for Madison's "Hautboy strawberry plants" and shared dwarf roses with Dolley. Madison was so knowledgeable about plants that neighbors who were unsure about the precise botanical descriptions, for example, would call upon his expertise to clarify the correct Latin names. He also exchanged seeds with botanists from Europe, such as the director of the Botanic Garden in Madrid, who sent the spoils from his collection in return for North American species.

As he reveled in the music and merriment, the company of friends and the beautiful surroundings that day, Madison was not just celebrating the harvest. He was also enjoying his first summer since his retirement in March 1817, when he had triumphantly left office after two terms. After

---

* Like Jefferson, Madison shared his plants with fellow gardeners and botanists, sending for example seeds of the Osage orange to José Corrèa de Serra, the Portuguese minister in America.

the War of 1812* against Britain, the country had emerged with a revived sense of national unity. Their victory over the Old World was also an assertion of the future of the New World, with the United States emerging as a confident and strong nation.† The country was flourishing, the former secretary of the treasury Albert Gallatin wrote, "more united at home and respected abroad than at any period." The United States that Madison had consigned to his successor, James Monroe, was not only beaming with self-confidence but also boasted a $9 million surplus in the treasury. After the Republicans' sweeping victory at the beginning of Jefferson's second term, the Federalists had continued to dwindle and had all but disappeared as a powerful party, leaving the Republicans to pursue their dream of a nation of farmers unopposed. It was the so-called Era of Good Feeling, and Monroe's Inaugural Address was a celebration of the blessings of the United States. "Never did a government commence under auspices so favorable," proclaimed the new president. Across all other nations of the world, he continued, "we find no example of a growth so rapid, so gigantic, of a people so prosperous and happy."

Even John Adams wrote that Madison's administration "has acquired more glory, and established more Union, than all his three Predecessors, Washington, Adams, and Jefferson, put together." During this time the country had changed: since Washington had taken the oath of office in 1789, the population had more than doubled to almost nine million. Communication had radically improved with an increase in post offices from a mere 75 to almost 3,500, and the cotton gin (a machine that separated cotton fibers from the seeds) had altered the face of the South by mechanizing the process of cleaning cotton.

Transport and travel were also on the cusp of a revolution. During Madison's last year as president, a regular steamboat service had been established on the Mississippi, connecting New Orleans to Louisville,

---

* There had been several reasons for war—Britain had imposed yet more trade restrictions as well as supporting the Native Americans in their fight against western expansion. If the United States wanted to continue to push the Western frontier, they had to oust the British from Canada (from where they supported and supplied the Native Americans). But taking Canada had turned out to be more difficult than many had predicted and by autumn 1814 the Capitol and the White House were nothing more than torched shells. The war had ended in 1815 with the United States winning some decisive battles but no new territories.

† This prosperous time only lasted until the Panic of 1819, the first major financial crisis in the United States, during which banks failed, harvests rotted in barns, farmers were forced to sell their lands and the burgeoning manufacturing industry collapsed.

Kentucky, thereby giving fast access to the largest area of fertile soil in the world. In the same year Baltimore became the first American city to illuminate its streets with gas, and by the time Madison brought in the first harvest of his retirement, construction had begun on the Erie Canal in the state of New York. Mechanization slowly began to transform the United States of America, and Jefferson was hugely excited by all these changes— "schools, roads and canals are every where in operation or contemplation," he wrote excitedly to a friend in Paris in June 1817, and all would aid the United States. "I am not afraid of new inventions or improvements," he explained to another acquaintance, "nor bigotted to the practices of our forefathers." Canals in particular, he believed, would give the republic of farmers access to the interior of the continent and would "render our country the garden which nature has destined it to be."

Madison was equally optimistic, having invested $500 in the Potomac Steam Boat Company two years before his retirement, as well as becoming an early supporter of the inventor John Stevens, the first American to propose the railroad. So much had changed that Madison and his traveling companion James Paulding had been able to take a steamboat down the Potomac for part of the return journey to Montpelier, rather than having to navigate the rugged roads that Jefferson had ridden along eight years previously. Madison had been "playful as a child," Paulding later recalled, as they glided homeward along the river.

Part of this excitement may have been caused by the new mode of transport, but Madison also couldn't wait to arrive back at Montpelier. "If ever man rejoiced sincerely in being freed from the cares of Public Life," Paulding said, "it was him," echoing remarks made by Washington and Jefferson about their own respective retirements years earlier. Madison was particularly looking forward to putting on his old gardening trousers, which were so worn that they were "patched at the knees." He loved working and relaxing in the garden, sometimes picking pears, figs or grapes and other times asking one of his slaves to carry out a chair so that he could sit in the shade reading and writing. Every day he rode across the plantation and when he returned, Dolley would be waiting on the portico with a drink in her hands. The retired Madisons were, as Dolley's close friend Eliza Collins Lee put it, "like Adam and eve in Paradise."

Jefferson congratulated him "on your return to your books & farm, to tranquillity & independence," but Madison also quickly discovered that, like the other founding fathers, he would have to deal with a constant stream of visitors. "He has no particular Business," an old friend wrote apologetically as he introduced one such visitor in June 1817, "but to see those great men of whom he has heard so much." It was as if Madison

ABOVE: This is the earliest depiction—painted in 1798—
of John Adams's house in Quincy.

BELOW: George Washington (second from right) as a farmer
in his fields, with Mount Vernon in the background.

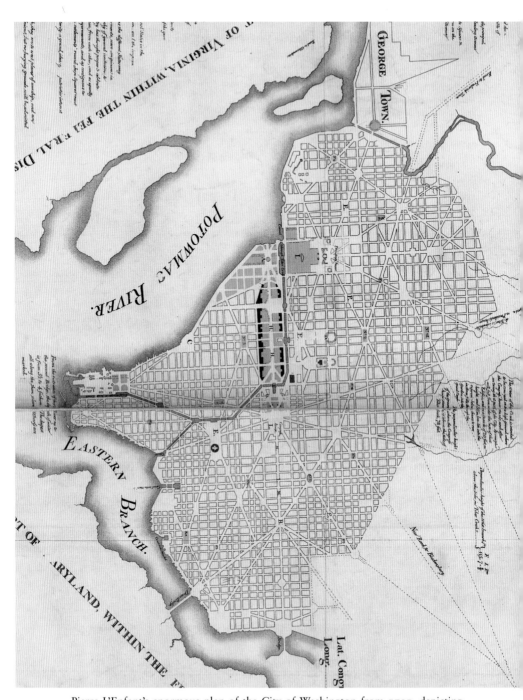

Pierre L'Enfant's enormous plan of the City of Washington from 1791, depicting the President's House and the Capitol connected by an enormous park that was to include an equestrian statue of George Washington (A), a "Grand Cascade" (F), a big "President's park" (I), and a "Grand Avenue" (H).

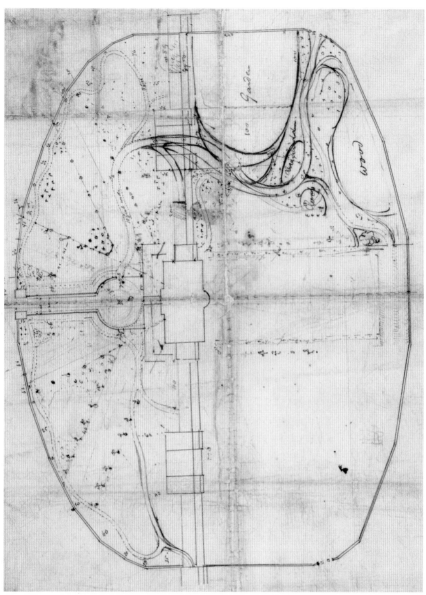

This drawing of the White House garden illustrates Jefferson's ideas. It shows the garden in its reduced size of around five acres. To the north of the house the garden shows a combination of formal and picturesque elements, including radiating avenues and meandering walks. At the back of the house toward the south was a large square rimmed by a narrow flower border. To the right, added probably by Jefferson, was to be a more secluded and screened area planted and laid out in an irregular design that included serpentine paths, groves, and shrubberies. The captions here read "wood" and "clump," as well as "chamaerhodendron" or possibly "chamaedaphne," which were eighteenth-century names for mountain laurel, azalea, and rhododendron. The wings of the house are also drawn with larger square structures midway.

ABOVE: A view of Washington, D.C., just after the federal government moved there.

RIGHT: *Robinia hispida.* The bristly locust was one of the native flowering trees that Jefferson included on his list for the White House garden and that he also planted at Poplar Forest.

N.º 311

Eduard. del. Sansom sc.

Pub. by W. Curtis S.¹ Geo. Crefcent Sept. 1795

LEFT: *Liriodendron tulipifera.*
The stately tulip poplar was
a common tree in all thirteen
states and planted by Washington, Jefferson, and Madison
in their pleasure grounds.

BELOW: John Bartram had
regularly dispatched *Kalmia
angustifolia* to England, where
it was popular in the Georgian
shrubberies. Jefferson ordered it
in January 1786 from Bartram's
son for his friends in Paris, and
Washington also included it in
his large plant order for Mount
Vernon in March 1792.

ABOVE: Harpers Ferry or the Great Falls of the Potomac. Jefferson described the Potomac's passage through the Blue Ridge Mountains as "one of the most stupendous scenes in nature." This painting by George Beck was owned by George Washington.

BELOW: Thomas Jefferson's Natural Bridge in Virginia. Jefferson called the Natural Bridge "the most sublime of Nature's works" in his *Notes on the State of Virginia.*

ABOVE: Monticello's West Lawn, with flowerbeds and trees in the background.
To each side of the house is a service wing with roof terraces.

BELOW: The approach up to the mountain to Monticello, with Charlottesville in the valley.

ABOVE: William Thornton's watercolor of Montpelier in 1802, with suggestions on how to improve the grounds. The landscaping was not executed until around 1810. The mansion is depicted without the two wings that were built only in 1809–10, and the temple to the left (built over the icehouse) was constructed only in 1810–11.

BELOW: A computer rendition of Montpelier at the time of Madison's retirement, showing the house with the two new wings and the new lawn at the back. To the right is a conjectural view of the model slave village, with its six neat buildings, and to the left of the mansion, hidden by the trees and latticework screen, Dolley's detached kitchen. Not included here are the horseshoe-shaped garden and the ha-ha at the back of the lawn.

had become part of the Virginia tourist itinerary—"few visit our country without visiting Monticello and Montpelier," noted Margaret Bayard Smith. Fortunately Dolley, who had earned a reputation during her time as first lady for sociability, was in her element. She loved having visitors, and Montpelier was a great place for a party—the informality of plantation life made the organization of entertainment all the easier. Visitors were greeted with a "cheering smile" and were delighted at the lack of ceremony, many of them repeating over the years that hospitality was the presiding spirit at Montpelier.

Over the past two decades Madison had adapted his father's house to fit his needs. The transformation had begun in 1797 with Madison's first, short-lived, retirement from politics during John Adams's presidency. He had enlarged the house by a third—because with his father and mother still living there, he needed to create a separate space for himself and Dolley. He had also added an enormous two-story portico to the front, displaying his taste for classical architecture. A little more than a decade later, when they moved to the White House at the beginning of his presidency in 1809, Madison had begun the last and most substantial alteration of the mansion. He had added a one-story wing to each side with terraces on the roofs (like the ones Jefferson had designed for the wings of the White House, Monticello and Poplar Forest), enlarged the windows and changed the internal arrangement of rooms, creating the central drawing room through which guests could see the back lawn.

As part of this final redesign of Montpelier, Madison also created a new landscape setting for the mansion, changing his father's much smaller garden, which was surrounded by work yards, to sweeping ornamental grounds. He had spent much time talking to friends and visitors about his vision. William Thornton, the architect of the Capitol and the man who had first tried to create a garden at the White House for John Adams, had visited Montpelier with his wife already in 1802 to discuss the designs in detail. There was clearly much room for improvement, Thornton's wife commented, "and when those he [Madison] contemplates are executed, it will be a very handsome place." Thornton was an amateur painter and had during his visit produced a watercolor depicting the new Montpelier. For years the proposed changes remained just a picture in a frame, a reminder to Madison of what could be done.

It was not until the first year of his presidency, with the alterations to the mansion under way, that Madison turned his attention to the garden and began to implement the new design. First his slaves transformed the rolling land at the back into one large flat expanse, moving hundreds of tons of soil and clay with shovels and picks, draft animals, wheelbarrows and carts. Brick rubble from the building work at the house and huge amounts of red clay that the slaves had excavated from the basement of the new wings was used to fill the dips of the land. With cutting sledges the slaves also removed a ridge behind the house and carted the clay on top of the building rubble. When they had leveled the area, they covered it with topsoil and grass seeds to create the smooth, level lawn.

Given the scale of the alterations, Madison decided it would be a good idea to hire a professional gardener, and so had asked friends and neighbors for recommendations. At the end of July 1810, fellow Virginian James Monroe responded to Madison's pleas and facilitated the services of Charles Bizet, a French gardener who worked in his neighborhood. Bizet was delighted at the prospect of working at Montpelier, though Monroe warned Madison that the Frenchman was no longer quite up-to-date with the latest garden fashions. In addition, Monroe admitted, "his vision is too imperfect to allow him to embrace distant objects"— not an ideal condition for a landscape designer. With his impaired vision and old-fashioned style Bizet was probably not employed to create sweeping vistas or grand landscape schemes, but having been trained in France, he would have been the right man to oversee the terracing, planting and maintenance of the more formal horseshoe-shaped garden.* Madison continued his garden improvements and at the beginning of his retirement hired a second gardener, Archibald Blair, who was originally from Scotland—he had the advantage of having been trained in the English landscape tradition without actually being English. With this background Blair was probably in charge of the creation and maintenance of the more natural-looking aspects of the ornamental landscape, such as the planting of clumps of trees on the lawn and in front of the house.

Assisted by his gardeners, books and friends Madison had created a much-admired garden. Unlike Jefferson, who in the face of the Embargo Act had purposefully combined agricultural utility with America's beauty when he designed Monticello as an ornamental farm, Madison—as the youngest of the founding generation and the one who had led his newly confident, mature country on its "wonderful march of national prosperity and glory"—created grounds that dispensed with any pretense of productivity or practicalities. As if to reflect these new United States, Madison built a classical temple "surmounted by a statue of Liberty"

---

* Bizet must have had some experience with such earthmoving garden schemes because he had injured himself during a previous employment by "blowing a rock."

(which also concealed his icehouse) where his father had run a large blacksmith workshop next to the house. Instead of noisy clatter, smoke and dirt, Madison's design exuded serenity, elegance and tranquillity.

What was also remarkable about Montpelier was that Madison eschewed fashionable shrubberies, instead staging the forest as the main feature. This was an approach that celebrated the American landscape as it was (with a bit of pruning and cutting) rather than creating something entirely new and European. He had certainly discussed this with Thornton, who years later, when making suggestions to Jefferson for the gardens at the University of Virginia, could have been describing Montpelier. "I would advise that the Site be chosen in the woods," he wrote, because this way it would be easier to "clear out whatever is not wanted." By "clumping the most beautiful and thriving of the forest Trees, handsome Groves, and leaving straggling ones occasionally," Thornton continued, "Nature may be so artfully imitated, as to produce a perfect Picture." This was exactly what Madison had done—he had taken elements of the English landscape park and combined them with the American wilderness.

In the midst of this carefully designed space, however, was something that seemed completely incongruous with the Arcadian scene: in the middle of his elegant lawn, less than fifty yards away from the back portico and in full view of the house and roof terraces, Madison had placed the slave quarters. Six small buildings in two rows nestled around a small yard—a kitchen, two smokehouses and three double cottages (for two households each). Unlike the usual flimsy slave cabins with dirt floors and mud-and-stick chimneys, these were sturdy frame buildings with raised wooden floors, brick chimneys and glass windows. Slaves here ate off decorated plates, admittedly cast-offs and chipped items from the Madisons' kitchen, but certainly finer tableware than one would normally expect to find. The yard was neat and clean, animated by chickens pecking for grains and slaves raking the paths or crossing the lawn to disappear into the basement kitchen in Madison's mother's wing of the house. In one cabin lived "Granny Milly," who by 1825 had reached the stately age of 104, retired from her "labors" and, according to one visitor, "living happily."

In order to create this, Madison had razed the old cabins that his father had built farther away from the house behind brick walls. By doing so, he consciously rejected what his father and other plantation owners had done when they separated the slave quarters from the ornamental pleasure grounds with walls, fences, shrubberies or groves. Instead Madison created a model village that was part of the landscape design—a tableau of virtuous industry and paternalistic care. The village was, as Dolley's niece Mary Cutts put it, "an object of interest" for visitors, who would wander across the lawn to the bucolic scene. The children of Madison's friends and family packed luxurious breakfasts to take as gifts for the slaves who lived in the little village—proudly dashing back to the mansion with a potato or fresh egg they had received in return. "None but an eye witness can know of the peace and ease of these sable sons of toil," Cutts said admiringly after her visit.

Madison's immaculate slave village was a radical gesture. Washington, by contrast, had created distinct slave areas around the mansion at Mount Vernon, dividing the space with walls, plantings and buildings. In fact, Washington had instructed his estate manager to reprimand any slave who ventured into the shrubberies and bowling green: "besides bad habit—they too frequently are breaking limbs, or twigs from, or doing other injury to my Shrubs." Similarly, at Monticello the quarters for the house slaves were hidden in the low wings of the mansion, while those along Mulberry Row (located between the vegetable terrace and the lawn at the back of the house) were part of the utilitarian areas of the landscape. Mulberry Row was not pretending to be anything other than a working road with slave cabins, a joinery and a "nailery," but it was screened from the back lawn by trees and shrubs as well as being tucked away due to the lie of the land.

In addition to the highly visible model village, Madison had also built a hidden, detached kitchen that was linked by a large work yard to Dolley's basement kitchen in their wing of the mansion (on the opposite side to the slave village). Madison had concealed it behind a latticework screen and two rows of pine trees that led from the wing to the temple. Dolley's detached kitchen was one of the most intensely used domestic workspaces, unlike the kitchen in the slave village, which was linked by a path to the cellar kitchen in the wing that Madison's mother occupied. Given Madison's mother's age (she was almost ninety when he retired in 1817) it seems certain that the kitchen in the slave village was used far less than the one on the other side of the house.

The rationale behind hiding the busy kitchen from the eyes of visitors while purposefully placing the neat slave cottages in full view lies in the changing attitudes to slavery and the social changes in Virginia. Like Washington and Jefferson, Madison had long struggled to reconcile the idea of slavery with his beliefs in equality and liberty. Throughout his life he called slavery a "stain" and a "blot" on the American nation. Northerners, abolitionists and many foreigners found it difficult to accept that the revolutionaries, who had created this republic, owned fields that were worked by slaves. Madison expected large numbers of visitors to come to Montpelier during his retirement and he also knew that the slave quarters, in particular, would be scrutinized by such travelers (who often published their accounts in America and Europe).

By placing a spotless and well-designed village at the center of his garden, Madison presented himself as a slave owner whose slaves were happy and cared for. They were not "whipped all day," Madison told a visitor, who was astounded to see "his negroes go to church . . . gayly dressed" (even carrying umbrellas). On the contrary, Madison insisted that the conditions at Montpelier were "beyond comparison" with what slaves had experienced during colonial times—his slaves were "better fed, better clad, better lodged, and better treated in every respect."

Over the past decades, many Virginia plantation owners had become increasingly concerned about the living conditions of their slaves. One of the reasons had been the successful slave rebellion in Haiti in the early 1790s, which led to their declaration of independence in 1804, and the fear of similar uprisings in the United States. "It is high time we should foresee the bloody scenes," Jefferson had warned, "which our children certainly, and possibly ourselves (South of Patowmac) have to wade through." These worries were further stoked by changing demographics. In 1790 the white population of Virginia had outnumbered the black, but only a decade later the proportions were reversed. The slave population "increases far faster than the white," Madison said, and the prospect unsettled many Virginians, who dreaded the thought of being "dammed up in a land of slaves." In the first decade of the nineteenth century, just before Madison had built his slave quarters, these anxieties were confirmed when Virginia was rocked by the Gabriel conspiracy, which had to be suppressed by the militia, and the subsequent Easter slave revolt (which also failed).

In some respects the Virginians' worries were similar to those of the large landowners in Britain who had feared that the French Revolution would sweep across the channel. Uvedale Price, a best-selling English garden writer (who had written to Washington about the connection between landscape gardening and politics) had warned in 1797 that the "total revolution of property in France has created very just apprehensions." It was important, Price said, to give an "increased attention" to the laborers who would otherwise be driven to take up arms.*

By the end of the eighteenth century many British landowners, who like Madison and the other founding fathers were involved in innovative

---

* With the accelerated pace of Enclosure Acts during the second half of the eighteenth century, the poor in Britain had become even poorer. As increasing numbers of cottagers had lost the use of the commons, they couldn't keep livestock to subsidize their meager incomes.

agricultural experiments, had become interested in model cottages for their workmen—small sturdy buildings that provided good housing for the families that worked on the estates. Such cottages, British land agent and agricultural writer Nathaniel Kent had written, would be "a real credit to every gentleman's residence" because everybody could see how benevolent the landowner was. By contrast, he warned, "nothing can reflect greater disgrace upon him, than a shattered miserable hovel . . . unfit for human creatures to inhabit."

One of these progressive farmers was Thomas Coke of Holkham in Norfolk, a man whom Madison much admired for his innovative crop rotation and animal breeding and whose "great agricultural merits," he wrote, "have made his name familiar to this Country." In the 1790s Coke had constructed fourteen stone cottages to provide housing for his laborers and their families. As landowners across Britain began to build rows of neat cottages, they advertised their paternalism but also beautified their estates. Old villages were razed or moved and replaced with tidy houses that pleased the eye.

The trend for model villages was spread by a flurry of pattern books that provided floor plans, elevations and information on building materials and construction, often reprinted in agricultural magazines and newspapers—many of which were available in the United States. The first volume of the prestigious *Communications of the Board of Agriculture* (1797), in particular, had sparked interest—a book that John Sinclair, the director of the Board of Agriculture, had sent to Washington, Jefferson, Adams and probably to Madison. Even if Madison did not receive it directly from Sinclair, he would have read it, because Washington had previously lent him the publications of the Board of Agriculture and Jefferson's library was always open to him.

The similarities between the slave village at Montpelier and the advice in the *Communications* are striking: double cottages, laid out in regular rows, with raised floors, comfortable, quality building materials and a small garden.* It was as if Madison ticked off all the suggestions made. By placing his neat slave quarters on his lawn, Madison took an idea that had been discussed for more than two decades in Britain and applied it, for the very first time, to an American context.

---

* Plantation owners in the West Indies were also improving slave villages by following British agricultural books. In the West Indies, one of the reasons was an increased concern about slave health—with the end of the slave trade, slaves had become a more valuable commodity. There was also a greater worry about security, exacerbated by a slave revolt in the 1820s.

Double cottage in the *Communications*
of the Board of Agriculture, 1797

Much of the discussion in Britain had happened under the pretext of paternalistic care, but model cottages were also a form of social control. Gardens next to the cottages would keep laborers "sober, industrious, and healthy," one contributor to the *Communications* insisted, since those without a garden were "often drunken, lazy, vicious, and frequently diseased." At Montpelier the location of the village, squarely in the middle of the huge lawn, deprived the slaves of the little privacy they traditionally had. Madison placed his slaves on a stage, a living scene of a bucolic idyll. Instead of being able to withdraw to their own separated community spaces after their long days of arduous work, these slaves were in constant view of the house, the family and their guests.

The cottages, then, were not a real attempt to improve the lives of the slaves. When Madison retired he owned more than one hundred slaves, and most lived not near the house in the little village but in cabins by the fields of the 3,000-acre plantation. These cabins, attached to the farm operation and stables beyond the boundaries of the landscape garden, were the usual rickety structures with dirt floors. Madison also had no intention of freeing his slaves. Quite the contrary—in the second summer of their retirement, Dolley was so annoyed with her maid Sucky (whom she caught stealing) that she considered buying a new one, writing to her sister, "I would buy a maid but good ones are rare & as high as 8 & 900$—I should like to know what you gave for yours." Madison might have abhorred the idea of slavery but never went as far as his former secretary Edward Coles, who moved to Illinois, where he freed his slaves and gave each one some land.*

Madison congratulated Coles for following the "true course," how-

---

* Throughout his retirement, Madison gradually sold off his slaves to pay back some debts, reducing their number by nearly two-thirds by the time he died in 1836, but he didn't free a single one in his will.

ever, writing that he wished things could be different and that his "philanthropy would compleat its object, by changing their colour as well as their legal condition." For he believed that emancipation would only work if the freed slaves were repatriated elsewhere, away from the white citizens of the United States. In fact he was a member of the American Colonization Society, which proposed that free slaves be resettled in a newly created African country. Freed blacks were "regarded every where as a nuisance"—not because they were inferior, Madison hastened to add, but because of the prejudices white people had against them.* This was a common view among Virginia plantation owners—Jefferson, for example, had also talked about his fear of mixing slave blood with that of white Americans. Emancipation, Jefferson told a visitor to Monticello, was only viable if the slaves were colonized somewhere far away "all at once."†

Virginians also insisted that slaves had a better quality of life than the freed black population. Fanny Wright, a passionate abolitionist from Britain, was encouraged by a Virginia landowner to have a "Look into the cabins of our free negroes," in order to judge for herself just how bad their living conditions were. Madison's orderly slave quarters seemed to confirm this argument. Wright later visited Montpelier and together with Lafayette inspected Madison's little village. Even Lafayette, who never stopped arguing with Madison and Jefferson about the question of slavery, thought that the visit to Granny Milly's cabin was "one of the most interesting sights . . . in America," with the immaculate quarters and yard providing "a pleasant walk." Seemingly Madison's slave quarters fulfilled his intentions—"the slaves here wore a very different aspect, from those we had before seen," one visitor remarked during a visit some years later, while another declared Madison to be "a model of kindness to his slaves."

AS IN BRITAIN, where model villages were often built by landowners who were engaged in innovative agricultural methods, Madison also

---

* Another side to this argument was the "diffusion" theory, in which Madison and Jefferson argued that newly admitted states to the Union should be slave states. As slavery was spreading across the expanding United States, they said, the ratio of black to white people would decline (because the slave trade had been abolished). This "diffusion" would therefore ease the tensions between the two races and, Jefferson said, would "dilute the evil."
† Earlier in his life Jefferson had been a fierce opponent of slavery. In the 1770s he had drafted a Virginia law that abolished the importation of slaves from Africa, and in the 1780s he suggested banning slavery in the new Northwest territories. He regarded slavery as a stain on the American nation, but at the same time he wrote in his *Notes on the State of Virginia* that Africans were an inferior race.

ran other aspects of his plantation as a model farm, applying the lessons he had learned from the latest publications. "There is no form in which Agricultural instruction can be so successfully conveyed," he said. He always found time to take visitors on tours of his plantation because he believed that agricultural knowledge needed to be shared. Riding on his horse Liberty, he would open the gates with a crooked stick ("without dismounting," recalled one admiring visitor who failed to learn the trick), and explain different aspects of the farm operations, talking "sometimes didactic, sometimes scientific" about Montpelier's agricultural methods.

Madison's passion for agricultural innovation and education was well known, and within four weeks of his return from Washington, he had been unanimously elected as the first president of the newly founded Agricultural Society of Albemarle. In May 1817, a group of progressive Virginia farmers met and established the society in order to improve agricultural practices and the Virginia soil. Though on first sight this might seem like a parochial endeavor, it was as much a political act as an agricultural one because the goal was to stop Virginia's economic downfall. For although the rest of the United States was thriving, Virginia—once the wealthiest and most powerful of the former colonies—was facing ruin.

Already in 1800, William Strickland, an Englishman who traveled on behalf of the British Board of Agriculture, had been struck by Virginia's "rapid decline." Small and large landowners across the state were feeling the effects—Jefferson was so broke that he sold his library to Congress to pay off some of his debts, and Madison would later admit that he had lived the first years of his retirement "on borrowed means." One of the problems was that two centuries of tobacco cultivation had ravaged the once fertile soils; another was that the Hessian fly, which Jefferson and Madison had investigated during their northern tour in 1791, had traveled south, where it attacked Virginia wheat fields. After Madison brought in the first harvest of his retirement, he was left with only one third of the yield that he had expected. Nine years later, he wrote to Jefferson that "since my return to private life . . . I have made but one tolerable crop of Tobacco, and but one of Wheat," adding that both had failed to sell well because of the declining markets.

In stark contrast to Virginia's plight, the southwestern frontier had become the new Eden. After the Louisiana Purchase, the War of 1812 and the victories over the Native Americans in the South, huge swaths of land had opened for white settlements. As cotton prices rose from 1815 onward, increasing numbers of farmers left Virginia in search of new lands in the South and across the Appalachian Mountains to plant cotton.

One agricultural writer counted the acres of farms listed for sale in Virginia newspapers and calculated in 1818 that almost 500,000 acres were advertised. The exhausted fields, another agricultural writer warned, would lead to an "exhausted country." In the years to come, Madison would see this within his own circle: his sister and husband moved to Alabama, his nephew went to New Orleans, a cousin moved to Kentucky and his former secretary Edward Coles had left for Illinois. If nothing changed, Virginia would be drained of its independent yeomen. Jefferson's and Madison's foot soldiers of the republic were fleeing.

The members of the Albemarle society had not hesitated to elect Madison as their president. Known as a man who believed that agriculture was "the surest basis of our national happiness, dignity, and independence" and who declared "I am a farmer," he was an obvious choice. Fourteen years previously he had held the same position for the short-lived national Board of Agriculture in Washington, D.C., which he had been involved in founding. He had always kept abreast of the latest agricultural methods, swapping seeds for new crops, discussing experiments and testing inventions. One friend commended him for "sweetening the evening of life with agricultural theory, experiment, and practice," the improvement of which held the key to solving Virginia's current crisis. Now Madison had been chosen as the "directing light" for the "agricultural fellow citizens to follow."

Madison had long discussed the importance of an agricultural society with his friends and neighbors and Jefferson had already drafted a "Constitution" for this very purpose six years earlier. Most of Jefferson's suggestions were incorporated into the rules and regulations of the new society. Members should answer questionnaires about crop rotation, average yields of fields, how much land they had cleared, the proportion of "worn out Land" on their farms, how much and what type of manure (if any) they applied to their fields and so on. It was also decided that the society should found a nursery in the vicinity of Charlottesville and encourage a manufacturer for "Implements of Husbandry." These "Patriotic Societies," as Madison called them, were the best agents in changing the state of agriculture.*

In May 1818, exactly a year after the foundation of the society, Madison rode from Montpelier to Charlottesville to one of their meetings. He was going to give a speech that would make him one of the most respected

---

* Seven years after the foundation of the Agricultural Society of Albemarle, Madison thought that it did have "a valuable effect in exciting attention"—methods of manuring and "cultivating the soil" had improved.

farmers in America and would place him at the vanguard of forest and soil conservation, decades before a concerted effort was made to preserve America's nature.

Madison's speech was the sum of all that he had learned from reading the most progressive agricultural publications over the past decades and his own observations and experiments at Montpelier, as well as a life's worth of conversations with farmers and scientists. The speech was a lament of all that was wrong with American agriculture as well as a catalogue of measures that could rectify the problems. Most important, it was a call for change and an explanation of what Madison called the "symmetry of nature"—the interrelationship between earth and mankind.

More than thirty wealthy landowners and progressive farmers listened when Madison stood up to talk about soil erosion and the devastating effect of ploughing "up and down hilly land." This method was fatally flawed because rain turned the furrows into channels that washed away the soil and seeds. Instead, Madison advised, farmers should plough along the lie of the land, following the contours of the hills—the horizontal ridges created by the plough would act as mini-dams, keeping the soil and seeds where they belonged. Madison acknowledged Thomas Mann Randolph—Jefferson's son-in-law, who was also in the audience—as the inventor of this method, although he had already used a similar technique at Montpelier almost three decades earlier. He also underlined the importance of irrigation, and highlighted the need to restore the depleted soils using manure and plaster of Paris.

But Madison's speech was more than just a list of practical advice about ploughing and manure. He wanted to change his fellow Americans' perception of nature by putting an end to the destruction of once fertile soil and the increasing exploitation of timber resources. He knew that man's reckless use of his environment would change only if Americans understood the broader context of agriculture, its pivotal place within the delicate balance between man and nature. When Madison began to explain what he meant, it became clear just how radical his ideas were.

Taken individually, no single argument or proposition of his speech was an entirely original one, but Madison was the first to weave together a myriad of theories from different areas, combining political ideology, soil chemistry, ecology and plant physiology into one comprehensive idea. He brought together Thomas Malthus's theories on population growth (and decline through disease and famine), Humphry Davy's recent writings on agricultural chemistry, Joseph Priestley's discovery of oxygen and Jan Ingenhousz's understanding of plant respiration, as well as practical experiments recorded by the British Board of Agriculture. Just as he had digested two hundred books on modern and ancient republics into one succinct paper in preparation for the Constitutional Convention three decades previously, he now fused the latest theories into one voice, rallying Americans to safeguard their environment.

In a world where many still believed that God had created plants and animals entirely for human benefit, Madison told the members of the Agricultural Society of Albemarle that nature was not "subservient" to the use of man. Not everything could be appropriated, Madison said, for the "increase of the human part of the creation"—if it was, nature's balance would collapse.

Plants gained their nutrition from their environment—from the atmosphere, soil and water—but they could also return it. This reciprocity, Madison pointed out, "is sufficiently seen in our forests; where the annual exuviae of the trees and plants, replace the fertility of which they deprive the earth." Instead of exploiting nature ruthlessly as most farmers did, Madison's conclusion was that man had to return what he took from the soil. The more those parts of the crops (digested by cattle as manure or as stalks, straw and chaff) were ploughed back into the soil, the more fully the exhausted fields would be restored—"Vegetable matter which springs from the earth," he said, must "retur[n] to the earth."

Madison's theory of nature was complex and innovative. Soil chemistry, for example, was still in its infancy and scientists had yet to grasp the full implications of ecological systems such as the nitrogen and carbon cycle.* But at least since the early 1790s Madison had been struck by the symmetry of nature, writing that the different species of flora and fauna "have a relation & proportion" to one another.

In preparation for his address, Madison had also read Diderot's groundbreaking *Encyclopédie,* which had hinted at this interrelationship. If man were to eradicate the weasel (which was regarded as a pest), one entry in the *Encyclopédie* read, a chain of destruction would be set in motion. With no weasels, their natural prey—field mice—would multiply excessively. In turn the increased population of field mice would devour the chestnuts, acorns and beech masts that were needed for the natural

---

* Madison probably not only read Humphry Davy's revolutionary *Elements of Agricultural Chemistry* (1813), which he had received only a few months previously, but also Erasmus Darwin's *Phytologia* (1800), which explained the importance of nitrogen, carbon and phosphorus in plant nutrition. Madison had procured it for a friend and had also, he admitted, "a very unfashionable admiration of Darwin's poetry," a publication in which Darwin had turned Linnaeus's plant classification system into a charming poem.

regeneration of the forest. If the balance of nature is broken, the entry concluded, "we can no longer trust nature" to restore herself.

Animals, plants and their environment were in an equilibrium, Madison realized, and brilliantly linked these ideas to Priestley's and Ingenhousz's theories of plant respiration. Animals respired air that was "unfitted for their further uses," he explained, but plants reversed the process. If the "whole class of vegetables were extinguished," Madison concluded, animals would not survive, as they were dependent upon each other. The "economy of nature," Madison told the members of the Agricultural Society, was an "admirable arrangement" and a "beautiful feature." Never before had an American so vividly explained how to learn from nature.

Having established the principle of the balance of nature, Madison now added a Malthusian flavor. Having just read Malthus's three volumes on the limits of the growth of populations—which included his famously gloomy prediction that human populations would grow faster than their food supply—Madison asserted that, left alone, nature guarded against "excessive multiplication" of one species over another. Overcrowding of one species always resulted in its eventual reduction through epidemics and the demise of its food supply and habitat. Enter man, Madison said, and the equation changed dramatically. Man had increased certain plants and animals—crops and livestock—"beyond their natural amount," thereby tipping the scales toward his own advantage. The danger was that it could also swing the other way.

Today, Madison's thoughts on nature's balance and ecology are all but forgotten, but at the time his approach was radically new. Decades before Transcendentalists such as Henry David Thoreau called for the protection of America's nature, Madison warned about man's destructive force. The preservation of the environment was essential for the survival of mankind, Madison believed, not so much in order to live in romantic harmony with nature but to live off it without destroying it. The reasons were economic rather than idealistic, but the goal was the same.

Madison ended his speech by discussing what he believed to be man's most calamitous error: "the excessive destruction of timber." What was left of the woodlands had to be preserved, he insisted, and what was destroyed had to be replanted. Early colonists had regarded trees with "antipathy" and had seen the forest as "the great obstacle to their settlement," but this attitude needed to change, Madison explained—it was essential to deal with it now. He was not the first to worry about the destruction of trees and to articulate ideas about forest conservation, but he was the first politician (albeit a retired one) to make a public speech about it, and it was this aspect of his address more than any other that seems to have had the most impact. Until this point there had been isolated voices in America, but the discussion had never strayed beyond the realm of private letters and conversations. Madison lifted it onto the public stage, bringing together opinions of friends, acquaintances and writers into one concerted plea, arguing his case with the best possible evidence.

Although there were only some thirty people in the audience that day, Madison's visionary call for change was published as a pamphlet and in major newspapers across the country, as well as in the journals of other agricultural societies. Over the next year every enlightened farmer in the United States of America read Madison's *Address to the Agricultural Society of Albemarle,* and dozens of letters arrived at Montpelier from across the United States and Europe.

"I see, after a long night of darkness & obscurity, the Dawn of agricultural Light & Prosperity," the Pennsylvania farmer and agricultural writer Richard Peters wrote after reading Madison's *Address.* A London bookseller inquired if he could publish a British edition of it and the Portuguese minister in America, José Corrèa de Serra—a talented naturalist and friend of Madison and Jefferson—was sure that Madison's words would "produce the same sensation" in Europe as Jefferson's innovative and award-winning moldboard had done. Richard Rush, the American minister in London, forwarded the pamphlet to John Sinclair, the former president of the British Board of Agriculture, and it was also deposited at the library of the American Philosophical Society in Philadelphia.

Madison did not see nature through a romantic lens of transcendent beauty but as a fragile ecological system that could be easily destroyed by mankind. As such the origin of the notion of conservation arguably lies not, as generally assumed, in the mid-nineteenth century with Henry David Thoreau or George Perkins Marsh's *Man and Nature* (1864)—a publication that has been hailed as the beginning of the environmental movement—but in the previous century with men like John Bartram and the founding fathers. Already in 1737 Bartram had written about the "wonderfull order and balance that is maintain'd between ye vegetable and Animal Oeconomy,"* and a decade later lamented that "timber will soon be very much destroyed." By the early 1760s, he mourned the disappearance of animals and increasing scarcity of trees "as most of ye land is cleared." Benjamin Franklin expressed the same sentiment when he

---

* Bartram's English correspondent Peter Collinson was astounded by the theory, writing that he had never heard anything like it before and that "it Deserved to be read before the Royal Society."

talked of the "loss for wood"—and as always he tried to tackle the problem with a practical solution, designing the fuel-efficient Pennsylvania fireplace in order to reduce timber consumption. Similarly, Washington had complained that "the waste which has been committed on my timber and Wood hitherto, has really been shameful" while Jefferson had written to his overseer that "we must use a good deal of economy in our wood."

Within their own lifetime attitudes to woodlands had been slowly changing, reflecting the progress the country had made from being mere colonies that served Britain to becoming a strong independent nation. As the colonies became the United States, and as settlers became patriots, trees that had been regarded as obstacles were now imbued with patriotic pride. In the 1750s, the twenty-year-old John Adams had still hoped that the forests would be removed and boasted that the country had been transformed from "dismall Wilderness" to cornfields and laden fruit trees. Three decades later, as he negotiated with Britain and France after the victorious War of Independence, he wrote to Abigail, with palpable concern, "Pray dont let a Single Tree be cutt" when she had purchased a grove that he admired—"I would not part with it, for Gold." A decade later, in the summer of 1796, Adams recorded in his diary that the villagers who had stripped an ancient walnut tree of its bark to use as dye had "murdered" it. Similarly, Madison complained to a visitor that in his forests "Great depredations are committed" by neighboring tanners who left his trees naked when they scoured the forest for bark, which they needed for the manufacturing of leather, while Jefferson had been shocked about the felling of trees in Washington, D.C.*

These isolated concerns about American trees became stronger with increasing deforestation. People had initially believed that axing America's wilderness into fields had improved its climate, as summers apparently became cooler and winters less harsh. Hugh Williamson, for example—one of the delegates who had visited Bartram's garden during the Constitutional Convention—had, in 1770, told the members of the American Philosophical Society that forests created an air "charged with a gross putrescent fluid," creating a desperately unhealthy atmosphere

---

* When Jefferson received, however, an essay on forest management that called for "some regulations for the conservation" of timber, he didn't show any interest—possibly because he disdained a central government that could meddle with local issues of forestry. He was not being honest when he claimed that Virginia had not seen any decline in forests, because only a few months previously he had told Bernard McMahon that the Gloucester hickory nut had almost disappeared from Virginia since the areas where they had grown were "now almost entirely cleared."

for mankind. As the new century dawned, however, opinions were slowly changing. Where Williamson had believed that "Every friend to humanity must rejoice" in the advantages gained from cultivation, Jefferson's and Adams's old revolutionary friend Benjamin Rush traced the increasing number of sick people in Philadelphia to "the cutting down of wood." He advised that more trees should be planted for they "absorb unhealthy air, and discharge a highly purified air."*

Three decades later, some Americans had become so worried about the destruction of the native flora that they felt the need to collect and preserve them. Madison had called for "plantations of the trees" in his *Address* and four years previously, in 1814, William Thornton had written to Madison that he feared that "by clearing Lands, whole Families of plants are likely to be lost." To safeguard them, America needed a national botanic garden, he insisted, knowing that Madison had long supported the idea. Yet the country had not been ready for such drastic measures—all four founding fathers had tried, but failed, to establish a botanic garden in Washington, D.C., during their presidencies. In a twist of irony, it was only in the year after Madison retired that Congress gave the charter to the Columbian Institute for the Promotion of Arts and Sciences to create a five-acre garden at the foot of Capitol Hill.

"Our stately forests are a national treasure," a lone voice had declared after the War of Independence, "deserving the solicitous care of the patriotic philosopher and politician"—but nothing had been done. It would take until the 1870s for the first national park to be created. But in terms of conservation Madison made the first step by preserving some of his own forest. Proud of his very own piece of conservation propaganda, which proved that he "had been at great pains to preserve some fine trees," as one visitor enthused, he always ensured that tours of Montpelier featured this part of the estate. At the same time Madison remained a plantation owner who had to turn a profit, and to do so he continued to fell trees to bring new fields into cultivation. But today the James Madison Landmark Forest—a stately, 200-acre deciduous forest of soaring tulip poplars, hickories and several species of oak—still stands as a testimony to his vision.

Madison's *Address* that day in May 1818 didn't turn Americans into innovative farmers and environmentalists overnight. Many Americans, as

---

* Underlying this were Joseph Priestley's experiments with plants and their release of oxygen. Almost prophetically, Franklin remarked on the restorative power of plants in 1772, "I hope this will give some check to the rage of destroying trees that grow near houses, which has accompanied our late improvements in gardening, from an opinion of their being unwholesome."

one English traveler observed in 1820, continued to regard every acre wrestled from the wilderness as "a conquest of civilized man over uncivilized nature." But attitudes did gradually change. Ten years after Madison's *Address*, the members of the new Horticultural Society in New York were asked to ensure "the preservation and the culture of plants indigenous to our soil." Native American plants were now under the "guardianship" of the people. In the same year the naturalist John James Audubon yearned for the time when Ohio's forests had been "unmolested by the axe of settlers." By 1832 the *North American Review* reported that "a better taste is growing among us" since increasing numbers of Americans had begun to agree that their forests were worthy of protection and celebration. "Our forests offer us treasures, such as few lands can rival," the article continued.

By the 1830s Madison's rallying call was reverberating across the country, and writers were calling for the "necessity of economizing" and protecting what was left. "Wherever they [trees] perish, the earth suffers," the *North American Review* declared. In the same year the *New York Daily Commercial Advertiser* published a letter from the painter George Catlin, calling for "A nation's Park, containing man and beast, in all the wild and freshness of their nature's beauty."

By this time, of course, the revolutionary generation had gone but they had left a legacy that continues to this day. Not only did they create the United States in a political sense, they had also understood the importance of nature for their country. The American landscape, forests, soil and plants made the nation. Nature was the backbone to her economy, feeding, clothing and sheltering the people. The United States was a republic of farmers, and the opening of the West extended the vision of an agrarian people across a whole continent. At the same time the vast landscapes and stately forests became monuments of the country's national identity.

With the maturing of the country from thirteen colonies to a strong and confident United States, the perception of the landscape changed dramatically, from an aversion to the wilderness to a patriotic celebration of it and concern for its preservation. Where once productivity had been the only measure, now nature was also appreciated for its sublime magnificence. At the same time, all over America, farmers were mixing manure and using the same methods of crop rotation that the founding fathers had pioneered, and those in the new states of Tennessee and Ohio were breaking the fertile earth with improved ploughs. As new cities were founded in the West, the gardens of Memphis, Indianapolis and Cincinnati abounded with ornamental and edible plants, plucked from the riches of American soil. Andrew Jackson Downing, the most influential American garden writer of the nineteenth century, advocated native flora and suburban "country" living for city dwellers, as well as suggesting that the Washington Monument on the Mall in the capital be surrounded by a grove of "American trees, of large growth"—an appropriately arboreal symbol to celebrate their greatest hero.

Hundreds of thousands of visitors have seen and continue to see the founding fathers' gardens today. As they walk through the groves and shrubberies that are planted with native species and see ornamental landscapes that incorporate experimental vegetable plots, agricultural elements and the forest, they can still experience the revolutionary ideas of Washington, Adams, Jefferson and Madison. The founding fathers' vision is indelibly imprinted onto their estates. In no other country, one magazine reported in 1819, would heads of state return to their private lives to promote agriculture, botany and other useful sciences that add "to the welfare of their country and of mankind in general." Only in America "we have witnessed, and still witness, such examples in the retired lives of Washington, Adams, Jefferson and Madison."

EPILOGUE

In april 1826, Thomas Jefferson received the seeds of a "mammoth cucumber." During the previous winter he had read in a newspaper that a gardener in Ohio had grown the four-foot giants and was so excited that he had immediately written to the former governor there with the request that he "spare a few to a beggar." Though almost eighty-three, Jefferson's fascination with American plants—in particular those that were bigger and larger than their European relatives—had never diminished. He still went outside, riding across the plantation to inspect his crops every day, even though he had almost drowned a year earlier when his horse had slipped while fording a river. He felt that his death was long overdue and once again used nature as a metaphor to make his point. "Man, like the fruit he eats, has his period of ripeness," he said. "Like that, too, if he continues longer hanging to the stem, it is but an useless and unsightly appendage."

Botany and plants were, as ever, always on his mind. Two weeks after he received the seeds of the giant cucumber, Jefferson wrote a long letter to John Patton Emmet, the professor of natural history at the University of Virginia, urging him to consider the establishment of a "school of Botany" as well as of a botanic garden. Jefferson had been involved in every detail of the University of Virginia in Charlottesville, from its foundation to the design of the buildings and gardens.* "I have diligently examined all our grounds," the octogenarian wrote on 27 April, and promptly suggested a site for the botanic garden near the academic village of the university, sending information on the lie of the land, instructions on "serpentine" garden walls, and details about plants that should be grown. Jefferson also engaged Madison in the project and over the next weeks letters crisscrossed between Monticello, Charlottesville and Montpelier, discussing the creation of the botanic garden and the procurement of seeds. At the beginning of May, Jefferson met Emmet to finalize the site and by the end of the month an enthusiastic Jefferson wrote that the "work should be begun immediately," instructing the

* The university had opened in March 1825.

proctor of the university a few days later that the botanical garden should be made a priority. There was an almost breathless energy to these letters. Knowing that his life was coming to an end, Jefferson was determined to leave a botanical legacy at the university that he had founded. The success of the university, a visitor to Monticello observed, "would make a *beau finale* indeed to his life."

Yet Jefferson would not be able to bring this final project to completion. During the night of 2 July 1826, two days before the fiftieth anniversary of the Declaration of Independence, he fell into a fitful coma in his bedroom at Monticello. He had been ill for several days and his family was keeping watch day and night. On 3 July he briefly woke at seven o'clock in the evening, speaking his last discernible words—"Is it the 4th?"—and when assured by his doctor that "It soon will be," he lapsed into semiconsciousness. As the evening turned into night, the family stared at the slow-moving hands of the clock, praying that Jefferson would last until after midnight.

As the sun rose on the Fourth of July at Quincy, John Adams also lay in bed, battling to breathe and with his eyes closed, surrounded by his children, grandchildren and great-grandchildren. The ninety-year-old had spent the previous two days restless and in much pain, but had tenaciously clung to life with this iconic day in mind. As he woke his family told him that it was the Fourth, to which he replied, with great effort, "It is a great day it is a *good* day."

At noon, as the chimes of the bells of Charlottesville rose to Monticello's mountaintop, Jefferson died. Only a few hours later, as the firing of the celebratory cannons grew louder in Quincy, Adams whispered the words, "Thomas Jefferson survives," and then passed away shortly afterward. As he took his last breath, a thunder shook the house and then a rainbow arched across the horizon, "a sublime sight," Adams's granddaughter said. The rain stopped and the sun broke through the clouds that had shrouded the sky in darkness all day—for a moment the light was "beautiful and grand beyond description."

EXACTLY FIVE YEARS LATER, again on 4 July, America's fifth president, James Monroe, died. James Madison was now the last of the founding fathers. By the end of June 1836 he was so weak that he knew his time had arrived. His doctors offered stimulants to extend his life to the Fourth of July, but Madison refused—on 28 June, aged eighty-five, he "ceased breathing as quietly as the snuff of a candle goes out."

Appendix:
Maps of Mount Vernon, Peacefield, Monticello and Montpelier

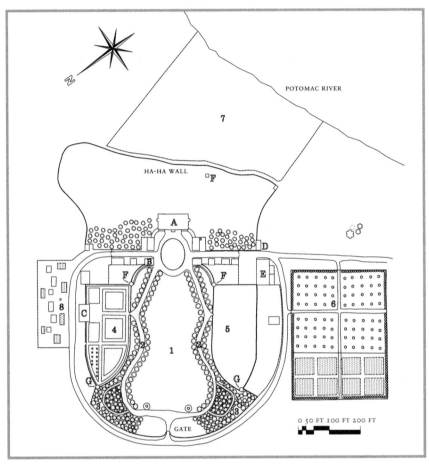

POTOMAC RIVER

7

HA-HA WALL

GATE

0 50 FT 100 FT 200 FT

Mount Vernon, c. 1786. Historic landscape plan
of the pleasure grounds and walled gardens

A. Mansion
B. Gardener's house
C. Greenhouse
D. Dung depository
E. Stable
F. Necessaries
G. Garden houses

1. Bowling Green
2. Serpentine walks
3. Wildernesses
4. Upper Garden
5. Lower Garden
6. Vineyard Enclosure
   (orchard and experi-
   mental nursery)

7. Deer park
8. Slave cabins and
   gardens

*Please note that the trees are
stylized and don't indicate the
irregular planting of the
shrubberies nor the labyrinths
of the wildernesses.*

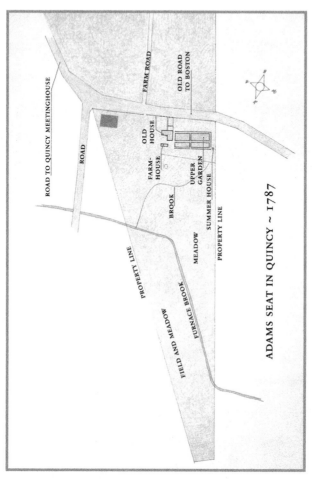

Peacefield, 1787, historic landscape plan of Adams's farm
in Quincy. The "upper garden" is the flower garden.

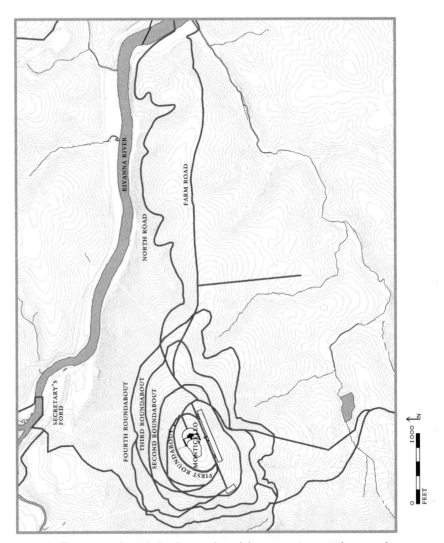

Monticello, c. 1809, historic landscape plan of the mountaintop and approach, including the scenic North Road, the Farm Road and the four roundabouts.

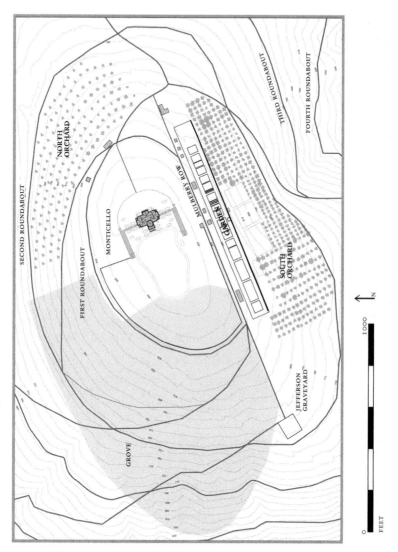

Monticello, c. 1809, historic landscape plan of the pleasure grounds, including the Grove, orchards, and the vegetable terrace (here labeled as "Garden"). The Grove is shaded in gray.

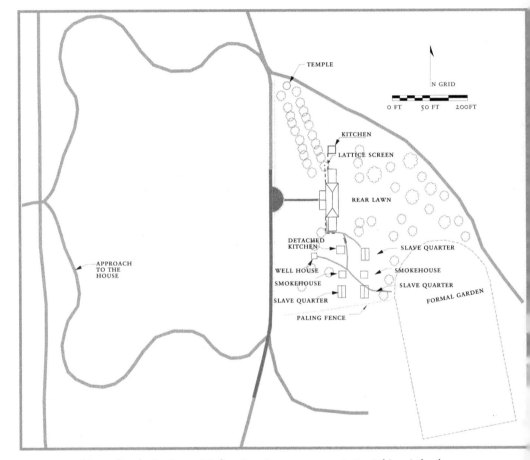

Montpelier during James Madison's retirement years, 1818–48, historic landscape
plan of the pleasure grounds. While most of the finds shown on this map have been
confirmed through archaeological excavations, the curvilinear approach to the mansion
and the horseshoe shape of the formal garden are conjectural based on a combination
of archaeological finds and historic accounts.

Notes

ABBREVIATIONS: PEOPLE

AA	Abigail Adams
AA2	Abigail Adams Smith
BF	Benjamin Franklin
DF	Deborah Franklin
GW	George Washington
JA	John Adams
JB	John Bartram
JM	James Madison
JQA	John Quincy Adams
TJ	Thomas Jefferson

ABBREVIATIONS: ARCHIVES AND SOURCES

MHS	Massachusetts Historical Society, Boston.
MHS online	Adams Family Papers. An Electronic Archive at MHS.
AFC	Butterfield, L. H., Richard A. Ryerson, and Margaret A. Hogan (eds.). Adams Family Correspondence. Cambridge: Harvard University Press, 1963–2009, vols. 1–9.
AP	Adams Papers.
JA Diary	John Adams's Diary at MHS online.
JA Papers	Taylor, Robert J. (ed.), et al. Papers of John Adams. Cambridge: Belknap Press of Harvard University Press, 1977–2008, vols. 1–14.
JA Autobiography	Butterfield, L. H. (ed). Diary and Autobiography of John Adams. Cambridge: Belknap Press of Harvard University Press, 1961, vols. 1–4.
TJ Papers	Boyd, Julian P. (ed.), et al. The Papers of Thomas Jefferson. Princeton and Oxford: Princeton University Press, 1950–2009, vols. 1–35.
TJ Papers RS	Looney, Jeff (ed.), et al. The Papers of Thomas Jefferson: Retirement Series. Princeton and Oxford: Princeton University Press, 2004–2009, vols. 1–5.
TJ Memorandum Book	Bear, James A., and Lucia C. Stanton (eds.). Jefferson's Memorandum Books: Accounts, with Legal Records and Miscellany, 1767–1826. Princeton: Princeton University Press, 1997, vols. 1–2.

MHS TJ EA   Thomas Jefferson Papers. An Electronic Archive at MHS.

JM Papers   Hutchinson, William T., and William M. E. Rachal (eds.). The Papers of James Madison. Chicago: University of Chicago Press, 1962–91, vols. 1–17.

JM Papers SS   Brugger, Robert J., Mary A. Hackett, and David B. Mattern. The Papers of James Madison: Secretary of State Series. Charlottesville: University Press of Virginia, 1986–2007, vols. 1–8.

JM Papers PS   Rutland, Robert A. and J. C. A. Stagg. The Papers of James Madison: Presidential Series. Charlottesville: University of Virginia Press, 1984–2004, vols. 1–5.

JM Papers RS   Mattern, David B., J. C. A. Stagg, Parke Johnson, Mary and Anne Mandeville (eds.). The Papers of James Madison: Retirement Series. Charlottesville: University of Virginia Press, 2009, vol 1.

DMDE   Dolley Madison Digital Edition. University of Virginia Press (access by subscription only).

GW Papers Colonial   Abbot, W. W., Dorothy Twohig, and Philander D. Chase (eds.). The Papers of George Washington: Colonial Series. Charlottesville: University of Virginia Press, 1983–95, vols. 1–10.

GW Papers RWS   Chase, Philander D., and Dorothy Twohig (eds.). The Papers of George Washington: Revolutionary War Series. Charlottesville: University of Virginia Press, 1985–2008, vols. 1–18.

GW Papers CS   Abbot, W. W., and Dorothy Twohig (eds.). The Papers of George Washington: Confederation Series. Charlottesville: University of Virginia Press, 1992–97, vols. 1–6.

GW Papers PS   Abbot, W. W., and Dorothy Twohig (eds.). The Papers of George Washington: Presidential Series. Charlottesville: University of Virginia Press, 1987–2008, vols. 1–14.

GW Papers RS   Chase, Philander D., and Dorothy Twohig (eds.). The Papers of George Washington: Retirement Series. Charlottesville: University of Virginia Press, 1998–99, vols. 1–4.

GW Diaries   Jackson, Donald, and Dorothy Twohig (eds.). The Diaries of George Washington. Charlottesville: University of Virginia Press, 1976–79, vols. 1–6.

GWW   Fitzpatrick, John C. Writings of George Washington, 1745–1799. Washington: U.S. Government Printing Office, 1931–44, vols. 1–39.

BF Papers   Labaree, Leonard, W. (ed.), et al. The Papers of Benjamin Franklin. New Haven and London: Yale University Press, 1956–2008, vols. 1–39.

BF online   Papers of Benjamin Franklin online.

AH Papers   Syrett, Harold C., and Jacob E. Cooke (eds.). The Papers of Alexander Hamilton. New York: Columbia University Press, 1961–87, vols. 1–27.

Journals Lewis and Clark	Journals of the Lewis and Clark Expedition online.
Bicentennial Daybook	Bicentennial of the Constitution of the United States. Research Project Working Files, 1983–87, in the collections of Independence National Historical Park.
DLC	Library of Congress.
NA	National Archives, Washington, D.C.
APS	American Philosophical Society, Philadelphia.
Cutts 1817	Mary Cutts, c. 1817, Mary Cutts's Memoir, Cutts Collection, DLC.
ViU	University of Virginia Library, Charlottesville.
MV	Mount Vernon Library.

PROLOGUE

5 "The first is by *War*": BF, "Positions to be examined concerning National Wealth," 4 April 1769, BF Papers, vol. 16, p. 109.

5 Stamp Act: The House of Commons passed the Bill on 27 February, the House of Lords on 8 March and the Royal Assent was given on 22 March 1765.

5 house raids: Burk 2007, p. 122.

5 Stamp Act protest in Boston: Schlesinger 1952, pp. 437–38; Burk 2007, p. 121; JA Autobiography, vol. 1, pp. 259–61.

5 "proprietors" and BF: The proprietors, who practically owned Pennsylvania, had the right to overturn laws and decisions made by the Assembly, which, according to Franklin and other Pennsylvanians, was a "tyrannical and inhuman" state of affairs. Franklin had come to London to plead for a royal instead of the proprietary government because, he believed, nothing should come between "Crown and the People." (Pennsylvania Assembly: "Resolves upon the Present Circumstances," 24 March 1764, BF Papers, vol. 11, pp. 127, 130.)

6 BF's interest in plants: BF to Jared Eliot, 16 July 1747, BF Papers, vol. 3, pp. 147–48; Peter Collinson to BF, 27 January 1753, BF Papers, vol. 4, pp. 412–15; BF to Jane Mecom, 21 February 1757, BF Papers, vol. 7, p. 134; BF to Samuel Ward, 24 March 1757, BF Papers, vol. 7, pp. 154–55; BF to Charles Norris, 16 September 1758 and 5 August 1762, BF Papers, vol. 8, p. 155 and vol. 10, p. 139; BF to Sir Alexander Dick, 21 January 1762 and 11 December 1763, BF Papers, vol. 10, pp. 16, 385; BF to DF, 24 March 1762, BF Papers, vol. 10, p. 70; John Mills to BF, 12 July 1764, BF Papers, vol. 11, pp. 357–58; BF to Rudolph Erich Raspe, 9 September 1766, BF Papers, vol. 13, p. 407; JA Diary, 26 May 1760, 5:1–2, MHS online; JB to BF, 10 April 1769, Berkeley and Smith Berkeley 1992, p. 709; see also BF's agricultural and horticultural books in Hayes 2006 and Library Thing: Benjamin Franklin's Library (online).

6 BF's own experiments: BF to Jared Eliot, 16 July 1747; BF to Jared Eliot, 3 May 1753, BF Papers.

6 offered the entire produce: Anthony Todd to BF, 31 October 1768, BF Papers, vol. 15, p. 248.

6 seeds sent by BF from London: BF to DF, 21 December 1768–26 January 1769, BF Papers, vol. 15, p. 292; BF to Joseph Chew, 12 December 1769, BF Papers, vol. 16, p. 261; BF to JB, 9 July 1769 and 11 January 1770, Berkeley and Smith Berkeley 1992, pp. 714, 727; BF had already sent some rhubarb seeds to Joshua Babock on 10 December 1761, BF Papers, vol. 9, p. 398.

7 "besotted": BF to Joseph Galloway, 11 October 1766, BF Papers, vol. 13, p. 449; see also BF to David Hall, 14 February 1765, BF Papers, vol. 12, pp. 65–66; the meeting with Grenville was on 2 February 1765.

7 BF and independence: BF remained wedded to the idea of the empire. His vision was one of separate states which were led by one sovereign. Each would have their own representative assemblies so that the British Parliament would have no control over America. (BF to Samuel Cooper, 8 June 1770, BF Papers, vol. 17, p. 163; Morgan 2003, p. 160.)

7 "faithful Adherence": BF to John Hughes, 9 August 1765, BF Papers, vol. 12, p. 235.

7 threats to destroy BF's house: John Hughes to BF, 8–17 September 1765, BF Papers, vol. 12, p. 264; Isaacson 2004, p. 224.

7 British exports to colonies: Langford 1989, pp. 168–71.

7 manufacturing in colonies: North 1974, pp. 50ff.

7 colonists and agriculture: BF to Lord Kames, 25 February 1767, BF Papers, vol. 14, pp. 69–70.

7 boycott: wheat, oats and rice could feed America, Franklin wrote. They had barley to make ale, and—hailing an all-American beverage—"the buds of our pine [are] infinitely preferable to any tea from the Indies." (BF, " 'Homespun': Second Reply to 'Vindex Patriae,' " *The Gazetteer and New Daily Advertiser*, 2 January 1766, BF Papers, vol. 13, p. 8.

7 "I do not know": Examination of Dr Benjamin Franklin in the House of Commons, 13 February 1766, *The Parliamentary History of England* 1813, vol. 16, p. 144.

7 BF and repeal of Stamp Act: William Strahan to David Hall, 7 April 1766, BF Papers, vol. 13, p. 125.

8 more duties imposed: These were the so-called Townshend Acts, starting in 1767.

8 boycott of British goods: BF to Joseph Galloway, 29 January 1769, BF Papers, vol. 16, p. 31.

8 "I wish it may": BF to Humphry Marshall, 22 April 1771, BF Papers, vol. 18, p. 82.

8 tofu and chickpeas: BF to JB, 11 January 1770, Berkeley and Smith Berkeley 1992, p. 727.

8 BF sent seeds: Upland rice, tallow tree, Indian plants, kohlrabi and Scottish kale, BF to Noble Wimberly Jones, March or April 1771 and 7 October 1772; BF to William Franklin, 3, 14 February, 3 March 1773; BF to JB, 10 February 1773; BF to David Colden, 5 March 1773; BF to DF, 1 September 1773, BF Papers, vol. 18, p. 65; vol. 19, p. 324; vol. 20, pp. 39, 62, 90, 95–7, 384; Berkeley and Smith Berkeley 1992, p. 756.

8 BF and chickpeas: BF to JB, 11 January 1770, Berkeley and Smith Berkeley, 1992, p. 727.
8 "chairman of British Colonies": Allan 2000, p. 255; the Society for the Encouragement of Arts Manufactures and Commerce was British and had been founded in London 1754.
8 premiums and awards: William Shipley to BF, 1 September 1756, BF Papers, vol. 6, pp. 499–500.
8 "true Spirit of all": BF notes, 1770, in margins of Josiah Tucker's "A Letter from a Merchant in London to His Nephew in North America," London, 1766, BF online.
9 "one shilling worth": Humphrey Ploughjogger to Boston Gazette, 14 October 1765, JA Papers, vol. 1, p. 147.
9 "the seeds [are] sown": BF to the Massachusetts House of Representatives Committee of Correspondence, 15 May 1771, BF Papers, vol. 18, p. 102.
9 "this catastrophe": Ibid., p. 103.
9 BF attacked in Privy Council: Alexander Wedderburn, 29 January 1774, "The Final Hearing before the Privy Council Committee," BF Papers, vol. 21, p. 47; BF to Thomas Cushing, 15–19 February 1774, BF Papers, vol. 21, p. 90; Edward Bancroft on BF, Isaacson 2004, pp. 277–78.
9 "my Office of Deputy-Postmaster": BF to William Franklin, 2 February 1774, BF Papers, vol. 21, p. 75.
9 "I wish you were": BF to William Franklin, 2 February 1774, BF Papers, vol. 21, p. 75; William Franklin had been royal governor of New Jersey since 1762 but had also purchased a farm near Burlington, New Jersey.
9 "this old rotten State": BF to Joseph Galloway, 25 February 1775, BF Papers, vol. 21, p. 509.
9 BF made delegate: BF to David Hartley, 8 May 1775, BF Papers, vol. 22, p. 34.
9 "We should be prepared": BF to Humphry Marshall, 23 May 1775, BF Papers, vol. 22, p. 51.
10 "all Ranks of": BF to David Hartley, 8 May 1775, BF Papers, vol. 22, p. 34.
10 America's ability to survive: BF to Lord Kames, 25 February 1767, BF Papers, vol. 14, pp. 69–70.
10 "it will itself": BF to Jonathan Shipley, 13 September 1775, BF Papers, vol. 22, p. 199.
10 "food movements": Pollan 2010.
11 "made subservient to": JM, "Address to the Agricultural Society of Albemarle," 12 May 1818, JM RS, vol. 1, p. 263.
11 "symmetry of nature": Ibid., pp. 269 and 263–70.

1 "THE CINCINNATUS OF THE WEST":
GEORGE WASHINGTON'S AMERICAN GARDEN AT MOUNT VERNON

13 Manhattan in summer 1776: McCullough 2006, pp. 134–35.
13 "in commotion": Ewald Shewkirk, quoted in McCullough 2006, p. 135.
13 size of British fleet: McCullough 2006, p. 148.

14 "Freemen, fighting for": GW, General Orders, 23 August 1776, GW Papers RWS, vol. 6, p. 110.

14 "clever kind[s] of Trees" and following references to plants: GW to Lund Washington, 19 August 1776, GW Papers RWS, vol. 6, p. 86.

14 "I tremble for": GW to Lund Washington, 10 December 1776, GW Papers RWS, vol. 7, p. 289.

14 "it runs in my": Ibid.

14 "infinitely amusing": GW to Lund Washington, 28 March 1781, GWW, vol. 21, p. 386.

14 Lund's horticultural reports: For example, Lund Washington to GW, 30 December 1775; 22 April 1778, GW Papers RWS, vol. 2, p. 621; vol. 14, p. 589.

14 "principal objects": GW to Lund Washington, 28 February 1778, GW Papers RWS, vol. 13, pp. 699–700.

14 "the Buds of": GW, 16 April 1785, GW Diaries, vol. 4, p. 121.

15 "regimental Gardens": General Orders, 24 March 1783, GWW, vol. 26, p. 257.

15 "matter of amusement": Ibid., p. 258.

15 "exceeded anything of": GW to Lafayette, 18 March 1780, GWW, vol. 18, p. 125.

15 "Trees and Earth being glazed": GW, 25 March 1780, GW Diaries, vol. 3, p. 349.

15 Liberty Tree as temple: Thomas Paine's "Liberty Tree. A new Song" was published widely across the colonial press in 1775. Schlesinger 1952, p. 436.

15 "Ax at the Tree": GW to Robert Morris, 31 December 1776, GW Papers RWS, vol. 7, p. 497.

15 "their heads adorned": Lafayette, "Memoir of 1776," Idzerda 1977–1983, vol. 1, p. 92.

16 "quit the walks": GW to Chastellux, 12 October 1783, GWW, vol. 27, p. 189.

16 war officially over: GW to Luzerne, 17 November 1783, GWW, vol. 27, p. 243.

16 "our Swords and": GW to Lafayette, 30 September 1779, GWW, vol. 16, p. 370.

16 "The life of a Husbandman": GW to Alexander Spotswood, 13 February 1788, GW Papers CS, vol. 6, p. 111.

16 vine and fig tree: GW to Lafayette, 1 February 1784; GW to Marquis de Chastellux, 1 February 1784, GW to Madame de Lafayette, 4 April 1784, GW Papers CS, vol. 1, pp. 85, 87–88, 258.

16 "with dictatorial power": Unlike some others, Rush only wanted to give GW dictatorial powers for a few months. (Benjamin Rush to Richard Henry Lee, 30 December 1776, Butterfield 1951, vol. 1, p. 123.)

16 "sole Dictator": Ezekial Cornell to William Greene, 1 August 1780, Smith 1976–2000, vol. 15, p. 527; see also JM to TJ, 2 June 1780, TJ Papers, vol. 3, p. 412.

16 "the title of king": Lewis Nicola to GW, 22 May 1782, GWW, vol. 24, p. 273.

16 "such ideas exist": GW to Lewis Nicola, 22 May 1782, GWW, vol. 24, p. 272.

16 "whole world in peace": GW to Armand, 7 October 1785, GW Papers CS, vol. 3, p. 296.

17 "I can truly say": GW to David Stuart, 15 June 1790, GW Papers PS, vol. 5, p. 526.

17 "wading to the conquest": Elkanah Watson, 23 January 1785, Lee 2006, p. 22.

17 "perfectly straight": Robert Hunter, November 1785, Lee 2006, p. 27; see also Captain George Mercer's description of GW in 1760, Brookhiser 1997, pp. 107–8.

17 "something uncommonly majestic": Latrobe, 1796, Lee 2006, p. 65.

17 "most beautiful Groves": GW, 13 March 1748, GW Diaries, vol. 1, p. 7.

17 "a goodly field before us": GW to Elias Boudinot, 18 February 1784, GW Papers CS, vol. 1, p. 127.

18 "hardly a member of Congress": James McHenry to Margaret Caldwell, 23 December 1783, Smith 1976–2000, vol. 21, p. 221.

18 "get a touch": James Tilton to Gunning Bedford, 25 December 1783, Seymour Adelman Letters and Documents Collection, Special Collections Department, Bryn Mawr College Library.

18 "intent upon eating": Ibid.

18 "philosophical retreat": GW to APS, 13 December 1783, *The Freeman's Journal: or The North-American Intelligencer,* 17 December 1783.

18 Martha Custis Washington: When Martha's first husband, Daniel Parke Custis, died, she inherited one third of his estate, including several plantations and £30,000 in personal property and slaves. (Dalzell and Dalzell 1998, p. 43.)

18 changes to Mount Vernon, late 1750s: Dalzell and Dalzell 1998, pp. 48–49, 58–60. By 1762 three walls of the garden had been built.

18 Changing Mount Vernon's entrance: Dalzell and Dalzell 1998, pp. 52–53, 250–51.

18 half-mile vista: GW, 9 January 1769, GW Diaries, vol. 2, pp. 120, 125.

18 "Land of promise": GW to Lafayette, 25 July 1785, GW Papers CS, vol. 3, p. 152.

19 ordered building materials: GW to Robert Cary & Co, 26 July 1773, GW Papers Colonial, vol. 9, p. 289.

19 cupola: The cupola had also a practical use because it ventilated the top floor of the house during the hot and humid Virginia summers.

19 GW's early landscape: Dalzell and Dalzell 1998; Griswold 1999; Pogue 1996.

19 "without any order": GW to Lund Washington, 19 August 1776, GW Papers RWS, vol. 6, p. 86.

19 "barren": Claude Blanchard, July 1782, MV Folder "Early Descriptions ante 1800," Mount Vernon Library.

20 "I am become a private citizen": GW to Lafayette, 1 February 1784, GW Papers CS, vol. 1, p. 88.

20 "Free from the": Ibid.

20 "The tranquil walks": GW to Rochambeau, 1 February 1784, GW Papers CS, vol. 1, p. 102; see also GW to Lauzun, 1 February 1784; GW to Adrienne de Noailles de Lafayette, 4 April 1784, GW Papers CS, vol. 1, pp. 91, 258.

20 "wearied Traveller": GW to Henry Knox, 20 February 1784, GW Papers CS, vol. 1, p. 138.

20 "dress and manners": Benjamin Rush to Granville Sharp, 27 April 1784, Butterfield 1951, vol. 1, p. 330; old grey coat: Luzerne to Rayneval, 12 April 1784, MV Folder, "Early Descriptions ante 1800," Mount Vernon Library.

20 "His simplicity is": Lafayette to Adrienne de Noailles de Lafayette, 20 August 1784, Idzerda 1977–1983, vol. 5, p. 237.

20 GW's daily life: Winthrop Sargent, 13 October 1793, MV Folder, "Early Descriptions ante 1800," Mount Vernon Library.

20 GW's death: Tobias Lear, "The Last Illness and Death of General Washington," 14 December 1799, GW Papers RS, vol. 4, pp. 547ff.

20 "completely involved with": Lafayette to Adrienne de Noailles de Lafayette, 20 August 1784, Idzerda 1977–1983, vol. 5, p. 237.

20 GW's mud-splattered boots: Joshua Brookes, 4 February 1799, MV Folder, "Early Descriptions ante 1800," Mount Vernon Library; Robert Hunter, November 1785, Lee 2006, p. 28.

21 "out of the way": GW to Thomas Lewis, 1 February 1784, GW Papers CS, vol. 1, p. 95.

21 GW's paperwork: GW to Benjamin Walker, 24 March 1784, GW Papers CS, vol. 1, pp. 233–34; GW owned almost 60,000 acres in the West, Brookhiser 1997, p. 49.

21 "the state of the Lands": GW to Thomas Lewis, 1 February 1784; see also GW to Samuel Lewis, 1 February 1784, GW Papers CS, vol. 1, pp. 95, 91–92, and GW to Gilbert Simpson, 13 February 1784, GW Papers CS, vol. 1, pp. 117–18.

21 "a tour of business": GW to James Craik, 10 July 1784, GW Papers CS, vol. 1, p. 492.

21 "fertile plains of the Ohio" and following quotes: GW to Lafayette, 25 July 1785, GW Papers CS, vol. 3, p. 152.

21 "diversify the scene": GW to William Grayson, 22 January 1785, GW Papers CS, vol. 2, p. 282.

21 "I shall hope to receive": GW to George Clinton, 25 November 1784, GW Papers CS, vol. 2, p. 146.

21 white pine and eastern hemlock: GW to George Clinton, 8 December 1784, GW Papers CS, vol. 2, p. 74.

22 live oak: GW to George Augustine Washington, 6 January 1785, GW Papers CS, vol. 2, p. 258.

22 *Magnolia grandiflora* and umbrella magnolia and quote: GW to George Augustine Washington, 6 January 1785, GW Papers CS, vol. 2, p. 258. On 21 May 1785 Washington received the first delivery from his nephew. GW, 21 May 1785, GW Diaries, vol. 4, p. 143.

22 "become my amusement": GW to William Grayson, 22 January 1785, GW Papers CS, vol. 2, p. 282.

22 "Road [*sic*] to my Mill Swamp": GW, 12 January 1785, GW Diaries, vol. 4, p. 75.

22 John Custis's plants: Peter Collinson to John Custis, 15 December 1735, Armstrong 2002, pp. 36–39; John Custis to Peter Collinson, 1738, Swem 1948, p. 69.

23 GW and native species in gardens: More than two decades later Bernard McMahon, author of the first American garden book, still bemoaned that Americans cultivated "foreign trifles" instead of native species. (McMahon 1806, p. 72.)

23 Miller's *Gardeners Dictionary:* Wulf 2009, pp. 34–36.

23 John Bartram: Wulf 2009, pp. 34–47.

23 Miller's American plants: JB to Peter Collinson, 14 August 1761, Berkeley and Smith Berkeley 1992, p. 534.

23 "In looking into": GW to George Clinton, 8 December 1784; see also GW to George Augustine Washington, 6 January 1785, GW Papers CS, vol. 2, pp. 174, 258.

23 GW's books: GW's Inventory Library, Prussing 1927, p. 429.

23 "agriculture and English history": TJ to Walter Jones, 2 January 1814, DLC.

23 GW's agricultural book order in NY: Custis 1861, p. 297.

23 "a great abundance of" and following quotes and plant references: GW, 12 January 1785, GW Diaries, vol. 4, p. 75.

25 "Employed until dinner": GW, 19 January 1785, GW Diaries, vol. 4, p. 78.

25 "exceeding miry & bad": GW, 8 and 11 February 1785, GW Diaries, vol. 4, pp. 86, 88.

25 "serpentine road": Washington called his new driveway either "Serpentine Road" or "Serpentine Walk"—in order to avoid confusion it will be "Serpentine Walk" throughout this chapter.

25 "promiscuously without Order": Miller 1731, entry "Wilderness."

25 GW's trees and shrubs in Serpentine Walk: GW, 12 January, 16, 18, 22, 23, 28 February; 3, 6 March 1785, GW Diaries, vol. 4, pp. 75, 91, 92, 94, 96, 97, 99.

26 "Miller . . . seems to": GW to George Clinton, 20 April 1785, GW Papers CS, vol. 2, p. 511.

26 GW and Batty Langley's book: Invoice from Robert Cary & Co, 6 August 1759, GW Papers Colonial, vol. 6, p. 333.

26 "after Nature's own Manner": Langley 1728, p. vii.

26 "shrubberies": For the development of shrubberies in the eighteenth century see Laird 1999.

26 "The Trees should": Miller, 1731, entry "Wilderness"; for Langley's advice on graduating plantations, Langley 1728, p. 182.

26 "forwarder upon the lawn": Miller 1768 entry "Garden": for GW's planting see GW, 26 February 1785, GW Diaries, vol. 4, p. 96.

26 "drudgery of the pen": GW to George William Fairfax, 27 February 1785, GW Papers CS, vol. 2, p. 390.

26 "raising of shrubberies": Ibid.

26 "Dick, Tom, and Harry": GW to David Humphreys, 7 February 1785, GW Papers CS, vol. 3, pp. 487–88.

26 "references of a": Ibid.

27 "may be compared": GW to Mary Ball Washington, 15 February 1787, GW Papers CS, vol. 5, p. 35.

27 Jean-Antoine Houdon: GW, 2 October 1785, GW Diaries, vol. 4, p. 200.

27 tea for ill guests: Elkanah Watson, 23 January 1785, Lee 2006, p. 23.

27 "dined with only": GW, 30 June 1785, GW Diaries, vol. 4, p. 157.

27 "No pilgrim ever": Elkanah Watson, 23 January 1785, Lee 2006, p. 21.

27 "from all parts": Robert Hunter, November 1785, Lee 2006, p. 27. The numbers of visitors who had stayed overnight and for dinner were becoming so unmanageable that on 18 August 1785 Washington advertised in the *Virginia Journal* for a "House-Keeper, or Household Steward, who is competent to the charge of a large family, and attending on a good deal of company."

27 "first by the coming": GW, 25 February 1785, GW Diaries, vol. 4, p. 95.

27 "hard froze": GW, 26 February 1785, GW Diaries, vol. 4, p. 96.

27 "like a common man": Robert Hunter, November 1785, Lee 2006, p. 31.

27 "which my hands": GW to Chastellux, 2 June 1784, GW Papers CS, vol. 1, p. 413.

27 clumps of native trees: GW, 2 March 1785, GW Diaries, vol. 4, p. 97.

27 design of "public walks": and following quotes, GW to Henry Knox, 28 February 1785, GW Papers CS, vol. 2, p. 400.

27 "pruning and shaping": GW, 3 March 1785, GW Diaries, vol. 4, p. 97.

27 "tubes of Ice": GW, 9 March 1785, GW Diaries, vol. 4, p. 99; for the damage to the shrubberies see the following days, GW Diaries, vol. 4, pp. 101ff.

28 British garden writers: Langley 1728, p. x.

28 typical American: Washington's gardening friend Samuel Vaughan followed his lead and also placed a necessary in the shrubberies of the State House garden in Philadelphia. Coxe Toogood 2004, vol. 1, pp. 94–97.

28 plants near the necessaries: GW, 22 February, 31 March 1785, GW Diaries, vol. 4, pp. 94, 111. George Mason had sent Washington the guelder rose and the Persian lilac after the Mount Vernon conference. GW, 29 March 1785, GW Diaries, vol. 4, p. 109.

28 "a Plant of Liberty": Langley 1728, p. 173.

28 GW's wilderness: GW, 15, 17 March 1785, GW Diaries, vol. 4, p. 103.

29 "Pine labyrinths": GW to Anthony Whitting, 14 October 1792, GW Papers PS, vol. 11, p. 223.

29 "Miniature Labyrinth": Winthrop Sargent, 13 October 1793, MV Folder "Early Descriptions ante 1800," Mount Vernon Library.

29 Langley and Miller's wilderness: Langley 1728, plate VII and Miller 1768, entry "Wilderness." Years later, in 1806, Bernard McMahon in *The American Gardener's Calendar* also asserted that a "Wilderness" consisted of "winding mazes or labyrinths." (McMahon 1806, p. 58.)

29 three wagonloads of pines: GW, 18 March 1785, GW Diaries, vol. 4, p. 104.

29 "yielded to the Wind": GW, 19 March 1785, GW Diaries, vol. 4, p. 104.

29 GW called back to public duty: GW, 20–28 March 1785, GW Diaries, vol. 4, pp. 105–9.

29 Mason brought plants: GW, 22, 29 March 1785, GW Diaries, vol. 4, pp. 107, 109.

29 "rather too thin": GW, 24 March 1785, GW Diaries, vol. 4, p. 107.

30 plants from Mason and Daniel of St. Thomas Jenifer: GW, 29 March, 12 November 1785, GW Diaries, vol. 4, pp. 107, 222; Daniel of St.Thomas Jenifer to GW, 28 February 1785, GW Papers CS, vol. 2, p. 397.

30 "All nature seemed alive": GW, 25 April 1785, GW Diaries, vol. 4, p. 127.

30 "The tender leaves" and "the Dogwood": GW, 16 April 1785, GW Diaries, vol. 4, p. 121.

30 "shedding its fragrant perfume": GW, 9 May 1785, GW Diaries, vol. 4, p. 136.

30 "some being of a deep scarlet": GW, 16 April 1785, GW Diaries, vol. 4, p. 121.

30 "would look very pretty": GW, 26 April 1785, GW Diaries, vol. 4, p. 128.

30 "deserves a place": GW, 14 May 1785, GW Diaries, vol. 4, p. 138.

30 "Most of my transplanted" and following quotes: GW, 7 May 1785, GW Diaries, vol. 4, p. 135.

30 "In a word nature": GW, 11 August 1785, GW Diaries, vol. 4, p. 181.

31 "the work of ones own hands": GW to Edward Newenham, 20 April 1787, GW Papers CS, vol. 5, p. 152.

31 "Once he has begun": Robert Hunter, November 1785, Lee 2006, pp. 28–29.

31 replanting of shrubberies: for example GW, 4, 7, 8, 10, 18 November 1785, GW Diaries, vol. 4, pp. 218, 220–21, 232.

31 sowing bowling green: GW, 11 October 1785, GW Diaries, vol. 4, p. 205.

31 deer park: GW, 18 August, 30 September 1785, GW Diaries, vol. 4, pp. 184, 199.

31 walls of enclosed gardens: GW, 12 July 1785, 4 February 1786, GW Diaries, vol. 4, pp. 164, 271.

31 greenhouse drawing: GW Diaries, vol. 4, p. 87.

31 "in dry sand as soon": GW to George Augustine Washington, 6 January 1785, GW Papers CS, vol. 2, p. 259.

31 "Salt is pernicious": GW to William Gordon, 8 March 1785; *Virginia Journal and Alexandria Advertiser,* 17 March 1785, GW Papers CS, vol. 2, pp. 413–14.

31 Botanical Garden: GW, 13 June and 8 July 1785, GW Diaries, vol. 4, pp. 151, 161.

31 code for seed labels: GW, 1 July 1786, GW Diaries, vol. 5, p. 1.

31 GW's horticultural records: GW to George Augustine Washington, 31 March 1789, GW Papers PS, vol. 1, p. 474.

31 "Not a day's": William Maclay, 1 May 1790, Maclay 1890, p. 253.

31 "experiments by intelligent": GW to Charles Carter, 20 January 1788, GW Papers CS, vol. 6, p. 48.

32 "(if not forgot) they": GW to Anthony Whitting, 3 February 1793, GW Papers PS, vol. 12, p. 96.

32 old vineyard: GW, 6 April 1785, GW Diaries, vol. 4, p. 114.

32 GW's non-native species and following plant references: GW, 13 and 24

April, 20 May, 23 July, 2 November 1785, GW Diaries, vol. 4, pp. 118, 127, 142, 167, 217.

32 fruit trees in walled gardens: GW, 12 February 1785, GW Diaries, vol. 4, p. 89; GW to John Marsden Pintard, 2 August 1786, GW Papers CS, vol. 4, p. 188. For varieties and species available to American gardeners, see also Prince 1790.

32 GW and tobacco: GW to Stewart & Campbell, 4 September 1766, GW Papers Colonial, vol. 7, p. 462; GW to Charles Carter, 20 January 1788, GW Papers CS, vol. 6, pp. 48–49; see also Dalzell and Dalzell 1998, p. 62.

32 "ruinous" agricultural methods: GW to George William Fairfax, 10 November 1785, GW Papers CS, vol. 3, p. 349; see also GW to Arthur Young, 6 August 1786, GW Papers CS, vol. 4, p. 196.

32 "Nothing in my opinion": GW to William Drayton, 25 March 1786, GW Papers CS, vol. 3, p. 606.

33 "every experiment is": GW to Charles Carter, 20 January 1788, GW Papers CS, vol. 6, p. 49.

33 "Plaister of Paris": GW, 25 April 1785, GW Diaries, vol. 4, pp. 127–28. Only two weeks later an impatient Washington noted that "I cannot discover that the grass ground on which the Powdered plaister of Paris was strewed, in different quantities, is benefitted in the smallest degree by it." (GW, 7 May 1785, GW Diaries, vol. 4, p. 135.)

33 "Mr. Donaldson's Hippopotamus": GW to Levi Hollingsworth, 20 September 1785, GW Papers CS, vol. 3, p. 268.

33 "to make a full experiment": Arthur Donaldson to GW, 1 October 1785; see also GW to Arthur Donaldson, 16 October 1785, GW to George Gilpin, 29 October 1785, GW Papers CS, vol. 3, pp. 286–88, 307, 324; GW, 3 November 1785, GW Diaries, vol. 4, pp. 217–18.

33 GW's experiments with fertilizers: GW, 30 January 1786, GW Diaries, vol. 4, p. 269; GW, 1 March 1787, GW Diaries, vol. 5, p. 111; GW, 9 May 1787 but entered in GW, 21 September 1787, GW Diaries, vol. 5, p. 187; GW to George Augustine Washington, 24 July 1787, GW Papers CS, vol. 5, p. 270.

33 "no Country has carried": GW to George William Fairfax, 30 June 1785, GW Papers CS, vol. 3, p. 89; for agricultural books see Custis 1861, p. 297, and LibraryThing: George Washington's Library (online).

33 "Midas-like": GW to George William Fairfax, 30 June 1785, GW Papers CS, vol. 3, p. 90.

33 James Bloxham: GW, 21 April 1786, GW Diaries, vol. 4, p. 315.

33 "the first farmer": Robert Hunter, November 1785, Lee 2006, p. 31.

33 "quite in keeping": Stephen Duponceau, quoted in Berg 2008, p. 96.

34 "a rural village": Jedidiah Morse, 26 March 1786, MV Folder "Early Descriptions ante 1800," Mount Vernon Library.

34 "trim, handsome & thriving": GW to William Pearce, 6 October 1793, GW Papers PS, vol. 14, p. 173.

34 "brother farmers": Arthur Young to GW, 7 January 1786, GW Papers CS, vol. 3, p. 499.

34 "I wish most devoutly": GW to Arthur Young, 4 December 1788, GW Papers PS, vol. 1, p. 162.

2 "GARDENS, PECULIARLY WORTH THE ATTENTION
OF AN AMERICAN": THOMAS JEFFERSON'S AND
JOHN ADAMS'S ENGLISH GARDEN TOUR

35 TJ's garden tour: unless otherwise referenced all descriptions are based on TJ's Notes of a Tour of English Gardens," March and April 1786, TJ Papers, vol. 9, pp. 369–75; TJ Memorandum Book, vol. 1, pp. 614–21.

36 "Come here without": JA to TJ, 21 February 1786, TJ Papers, vol. 9, p. 295.

36 "I dare not communicate": JA to TJ, 21 February 1786, see also TJ to John Jay, 12 March 1786, TJ Papers, vol. 9, pp. 295, 325.

37 "There is a strong propensity": JA to Richard Henry Lee, 26 August 1785, MHS AP reel 111.

37 "Sufficiently insane": JA to John Jay, 21 October 1785, MHS AP reel 111.

37 Summary of negotiations: Butterfield 1961, vol. 3, pp. 181–83.

37 Jefferson's hating idleness: Edmund Bacon's Memoir and Isaac Jefferson's Memoir, Bear 1967, pp. 18, 72–73; Martin 1952, pp. 20–21.

37 "Ennui": TJ to Martha Jefferson, 21 May 1787, Betts and Bear 1986, p. 41.

37 "doubtless is the best": Daniel Solander to Carl Linnaeus, 14 August 1761, Duyker and Tingbrand 1995, p. 169.

37 "visit all the notable gardens": Catherine the Great to Vasily and Pyotr Neyelov, December 1770, Hayden 2005, p. 84.

37 Franklin's garden visits: BF to DF, 6 September 1758, BF Papers, vol. 8, p. 145; BF to William Franklin, 3 August 1773, BF Papers, vol. 20, p. 339.

37 "combining public service": TJ to Lafayette, 4 August 1781, TJ Papers, vol. 6, p. 112.

37 "affection in every bud": TJ to JM, 9 June 1793, TJ Papers, vol. 26, p. 240.

37 "pair of slippers": TJ to David Humphreys, 5 January 178[6], TJ Papers, vol. 9, p. 152.

37 TJ on English gardens: TJ to John Page, 4 May 1786, TJ Papers, vol. 9, p. 445.

38 TJ's garden books: TJ to John Page, 17 May 1776, TJ Papers, vol. 1, p. 294. This was Thomas Whately's *Observations on Modern Gardening* (1770). It seems that Page did not manage to procure the book because TJ bought it eventually in 1785 from Samuel Henley together with George Mason's *Essay on Gardening* (1768). (TJ to Samuel Henley, 3 March 1785, TJ Papers, vol. 8, pp. 12–13.)

38 TJ's garden ideas: TJ's plans for Monticello, 1771, Betts 1944, pp. 25–27.

38 British gardener for TJ: Alexander McCaul to TJ, 8 July 1772, TJ Papers, vol. 1, p. 92.

38 TJ travel to Wooburn: TJ, 2 and 3 April 1786, TJ Memorandum Book, vol. 1, p. 617.

38 "But I am not" and following quote: AA2 to JQA, 27 July 1786, AFC, vol. 7, p. 297.

38 vandalism in gardens: Horace Walpole to William Cole, 16 June 1781, Lewis 1937–61, vol. 2, p. 275; Wulf and Gieben-Gamal 2005, p. 152.

38 "the savages": Horace Walpole to William Cole, 16 June 1781, Lewis 1937–61, vol. 2, p. 275.

39 "spotted cows": John Parnell's account of Wooburn Farm, 22 August 1763, transcribed in Sambrook 1979, p. 83.

39 "simple delights" and the following quotes: Whately 1770, pp. 177, 181.

39 plants at Wooburn: Laird 1999, pp. 102–3.

39 GW's building walls: GW, 10 April 1786, GW Diaries, vol. 4, p. 307.

40 "With what majesty": and the following quotes, TJ to Maria Cosway, 12 October 1786, TJ Papers, vol. 10, pp. 447–48.

40 TJ's inheritance: Jefferson inherited 2,650 acres on the Rivanna river and around the same elsewhere from his father. In 1774, after his father-in-law's death, he inherited about 10,000 acres but had to sell half of it to pay off the debts that came with the inheritance. (Malone 1948–81, vol. 1, pp. 439–41.)

41 TJ and slaves: Randall 1858, vol. 1, p. 11; Malone 1948–81, vol. 1, pp. 439–41; Elkins and McKitrick 1993, p. 202.

41 TJ's ornamental farm: See Chapter 8 and TJ's drawing of fields planted with grasses along the roundabout; TJ's sketch of ornamental fields (ViU 9090-a); TJ's sketch of timber zone, N129 K94d, MHS TJ EA.

41 Carmarthen requested new draft: Mr Fraser to JA, 3 April 1786; JA and TJ to Lord Carmarthen, 4 April 1786, TJ Papers, vol. 9, p. 375.

41 Summary of negotiations: Butterfield 1961, vol. 3, pp. 181–83; see also JA to John Jay, 21 October 1785, MHS AP reel 111.

42 "in aweful Pomp": JA to TJ, 17 February 1786, TJ Papers, vol. 9, p. 286 (unless otherwise referenced, all quotes are from this letter).

42 $80,000 granted by Congress: JA to John Jay, 16 February 1786, MHS AP reel 112.

42 "a universal and horrible War": JA to TJ, 21 February 1786, TJ Papers, vol. 9, p. 295.

42 "written in their Koran": JA and TJ to John Jay, 28 March 1786, TJ Papers, vol. 9, p. 358.

42 "An ambassador from": *London Public Advertiser,* quoted in McCullough 2001, p. 333.

42 "This People cannot": JA Diary, 30 March 1786, 44:2, MHS online.

42 British government united in opposition to America: TJ to Richard Henry Lee, 22 April 1786, TJ Papers, vol. 9, p. 398.

42 "the quantity of animal food": TJ to AA, 25 September 1785, TJ Papers, vol. 8, pp. 548–49.

42 "To pay that debt at": TJ to Alexander McCaul, 17 April 1786, TJ Papers, vol. 9, pp. 388, 390.

42 "nobility, wealth, and": TJ to George Wythe, 13 August 1786, TJ Papers, vol. 10, p. 245.

42 new draft of treaty: JA and TJ to Lord Carmarthen, 4 April 1786; JA and TJ to John Jay, 25 April 1786, TJ Papers, vol. 9, pp. 375, 406.

43 "lost a great deal of time": TJ to William Short, 28 March 1786, TJ Papers, vol. 9, p. 362.

43 JA willing companion: AA to Mary Smith Cranch, 6 April 1786, AFC, vol. 7, p. 134.

43 William Hamilton: JA Diary, 30 March 1786, 44:1, MHS online; William Hamilton to George Smith, 30 September 1785, Betts 1979, p. 225.

43 "the only rival": TJ to William Hamilton, July 1806, Betts 1944, p. 323.

43 William Hamilton tried for treason: Jacobs 2006, p. 186.

43 "tranquil Walks": JA to Richard Cranch, 27 April 1785, AFC, vol. 6, p. 111.

43 "putrid Streets": JA Diary, 17 August 1784, 43:5, MHS online.

43 "zeal at my Heart": JA to AA, 9 July 1774, MHS online.

43 "Such Excursions are": JA to AA, 17 July 1775, MHS online.

44 JA and garden visits: JA Diary, 16 January 1766, 12:23; 12 September 1774, 22:9; JA to AA, 17 July 1775; JA Diary 18 September 1775, 24:6, MHS online.

44 "how the Trees flourish": AA to Mary Smith Cranch, 24 April 1786, AFC 7, p. 148.

44 "old swamp . . . digging": JA Diary, 24 October 1762, 8:10-11, MHS online.

44 "an insipid round": JA to AA2, 14 April 1783, AFC, vol. 5, p. 123.

44 "to Farming": JA to AA, 17 July 1783, MHS online.

44 TJ and JA set off to Wooburn: TJ, 4 April 1786, TJ Memorandum Book, vol. 1, p. 618.

44 traveling in England: Johanna Schopenhauer in 1803-05, Michaelis-Jena and Merson 1988, p. 1; Carl Philip Moritz in 1782, Nettel 1965, p. 24.

44 "beautifull": JA Diary, "Notes on a Tour of English Country Seats & c., with Thomas Jefferson," April 1786, 44:5, MHS online.

44 TJ's and JA's garden tour: Unless otherwise referenced, descriptions are based on TJ "Notes of a Tour of English Gardens," March and April 1786, TJ Papers, vol. 9, pp. 369-75; TJ Memorandum Book, vol. 1, pp. 614-21; JA Diary, "Notes on a Tour of English Country Seats & c., with Thomas Jefferson," April 1786, 44:3-6, MHS online.

44 "load the memory": TJ, "Jefferson's Hints to Americans Travelling in Europe," 19 June 1788, TJ Papers, vol. 13, p. 268.

44 "waste my time": TJ to Philip Mazzei, 4 April 1787, TJ Papers, vol. 11, p. 266.

45 "remarkeable for their": TJ "Notes of a Tour of English Gardens," March and April 1786, TJ Papers, vol. 9, p. 369.

45 appearance of TJ and JA: Edmund Bacon's Memoir, Bear 1967, p. 71; JA to Skelton Jones, 11 March 1809, Adams 1850-56, vol. 9, p. 612; see also AA to Mary Smith Cranch, 24 April 1786, AFC, vol. 7, p. 147; Mather Brown's portrait of TJ, 1786-88, National Portrait Gallery, Smithsonian; see also Wilson and Chew 2002, pp. 21-22; Mather Brown's portrait of JA, 1788, the Boston Athenaeum.

45 candlestick and cannonball: Ellis 1998, p. 76.

45 TJ to hairdresser: TJ, 7 April 1786, TJ Memorandum Book, vol. 1, p. 619.

45 "but what is American": JA Diary, 3 May 1785, 43:13, MHS online.

45 "always an honest Man": BF to Robert Livingston, 22 July 1783, BF online.

45 "vain" and "irritable": TJ to JM, 30 January 1787, TJ Papers, vol. 11, p. 94.

45 "abhorrence of dispute": TJ to GW, 8 May 1791, TJ Papers, vol. 20, p. 292.

45 "the man must be of rock": TJ to AA, 25 September 1785, TJ Papers, vol. 8, p. 548.

45 "I keep what I feel": McCullough 2001, p. 312.

45 "confined himself from the world": 27 January 1785, Smith 1841–42, vol. 1, p. 45.

46 never "ruffled": Edmund Bacon's Memoir, Bear 1967, p. 71.

46 JA envied GW, BF, TJ: JA Diary, June–July 1776, Butterfield 1961, vol. 3, p. 336.

46 "Fool! Fool!": McCullough 2001, pp. 619–20.

46 "Nothing was too small": Edmund Bacon's Memoir, Bear 1967, p. 78.

46 "The departure of": TJ to JA, 25 May 1785, TJ Papers, vol. 8, p. 164.

46 gardens at Stowe and Whig politics: Wulf and Gieben-Gamal 2005, pp. 87–130.

46 Whigs and the influence in America: Wood 1987, pp. 14ff.

47 "opposes . . . systematic despotism": Uvedale Price to GW, 31 March 1798, GW Papers RS, vol. 2, p. 165. Price sent GW a copy of his *Essay on the Picturesque*.

47 "Freedom was given": Walpole, Horace, 1780, Charlesworth 1993, vol. 2, p. 403.

47 "still too much of art": TJ "Notes of a Tour of English Gardens," March and April 1786, TJ Papers, vol. 9, pp. 369, 370, 372.

47 Stowe guidebook: Seeley's Description of Stowe, 1783; TJ, 6 April 1786, TJ Memorandum Book, vol. 1, p. 618; TJ, 1789 Catalog of Books, MHS.

47 paths of vice and virtue: Wulf and Gieben-Gamal 2005, pp. 96ff; Wheeler, Richard, "Icons and Emblems," unpublished conference paper, Stowe Estate Office (n.d.). Adams had proposed a depiction of the "Choice of Hercules" for a seal that commemorated the British defeat in Boston. (Wood 1987, p. 49.)

47 "Mysterious Orgies": West 1732, l. 168.

47 "quite unnecessary as": JA Diary, "Notes on a Tour of English Country Seats & c., with Thomas Jefferson," April 1786, 44:5, MHS online.

48 TJ and JA reading Addison: JA Diary, 9 February 1761, MHS online; TJ, 1783 Book Catalogue, MHS; TJ to Robert Skipwith, 3 August 1771, TJ Papers, vol. 1, p. 79. Joseph Addison's essay was published in *Tatler*, no.123, 21 January 1710.

48 "the good of their country": Addison, Joseph, *Tatler*, no. 123, 21 January 1710; for Stowe and Addison, see Wulf and Gieben-Gamal 2005, pp. 105–13; Clarke 1970, pp. 113–21.

48 "most corrupt and unprincipled government": TJ to William Duane, 13 November 1810, TJ Papers RS, vol. 3, p. 208.

48 "My dear Country men": JA to AA, 3 June 1778, MHS online.

49 "a great deal of ill": TJ to Henry Skipwith, 6 May 1786, TJ Papers, vol. 9, p. 465.

49 "bewitching Charms": JA to AA, 3 June 1778, MHS online.

49 "the only Foundation": JA to Mercy Warren, 16 April 1776, Adams 1917, vol. 1, p. 222.

50 TJ's pantheon of heroes: Already on 8 February 1786 Jefferson had suggested to Madison to commission several busts for the new Capitol of Virginia, but it was in Stowe that he first saw "worthies" in a private context. (TJ to JM, 8 February 1786, TJ Papers, vol. 9, pp. 266–67.)

50 "my trinity": TJ to Benjamin Rush, 16 January 1811, TJ Papers RS, vol. 3, p. 305. TJ was recalling a conversation he had with Alexander Hamilton in April 1791 in Philadelphia; for Shakespeare and John Hampden see John Trumbull to TJ, 5 February 1789, TJ Papers, vol. 14, p. 525; for Raleigh see TJ to William Stephens Smith, 22 October 1786, TJ Papers, vol. 10, p. 479.

50 "our country should not be without": TJ to Joseph Delaplaine, 3 May 1814, DLC.

50 "to add it to": TJ to William Stephens Smith, 22 October 1786, TJ Papers, vol. 10, p. 479; TJ's Instructions to Adrien Petit, circa 2 July 1787, TJ Papers, vol. 11, p. 531.

50 portraits and busts of BF, GW, JM and Thomas Paine: TJ, 10 September 1786, TJ Memorandum Book, vol. 1, p. 638; Dickson 1976, pp. 111, 116; Stein 1993, pp. 73–74.

50 "my American worthies": TJ to William Short, 6 April 1790, TJ Papers, vol. 16, p. 318; TJ to Joseph Delaplaine, 3 May 1814, DLC.

51 ha-ha: For a more detailed discussion on the ha-ha, see Wulf and Gieben-Gamal 2005, pp. 93–94; and Dézallier d'Argenville 1709.

51 GW's ha-ha: GW to Lund Washington, 10–17 December 1776, GW Papers RWS, vol. 7, p. 291; GW, 3 April 1787, GW Diaries, vol. 5, p. 127.

51 Stowe was "superb": JA Diary, "Notes on a Tour of English Country Seats & c., with Thomas Jefferson," April 1786, 44:5, MHS online.

51 "We have Seen": JA to AA, 5 April 1786, AFC, vol. 7, pp. 132–33.

51 food in taverns: TJ, Tavern Bills, April 1786, ViU.

51 "to estimate the expence": TJ "Notes of a Tour of English Gardens," March and April 1786, TJ Papers, vol. 9, p. 369.

51 "the highest Entertainment": JA Diary, "Notes on a Tour of English Country Seats & c., with Thomas Jefferson," April 1786, 44:5, MHS online.

51 TJ and Shenstone: TJ purchased the book on 11 October 1765, *Virginia Gazette* Daybooks, 1764–66, ViU.

52 "I had lords and ladies": Matthew Boulton to J. L. Baumgarten, August 1767, Uglow 2002, p. 211.

52 "manufactory of Paintings": JA Diary, "Notes on a Tour of English Country Seats & c., with Thomas Jefferson," April 1786, 44:5, MHS online.

52 "it would be a waste": TJ, "Jefferson's Hints to Americans Travelling in Europe," 19 June 1788, TJ Papers, vol. 13, p. 269.

52 "I make a job of it": TJ to Lafayette, 11 April 1787, TJ Papers, vol. 11, p. 283.

52 TJ and JA reading Pope: LibraryThing: John Adams's Library (online); LibraryThing: Thomas Jefferson's Library (online); TJ, 1783 Book Catalogue, MHS. Both Adams and Jefferson also read Virgil and Homer in the original.

52 TJ and Shenstone: LibraryThing: Thomas Jefferson's Library (online); TJ, 1783 Book Catalogue, MHS; Beiswanger 1983, p. 173.

52 TJ's books at The Leasowes: TJ, 7 April 1786, TJ Memorandum Book, vol. 1, p. 619.

53 "blue distant mountains": Dodsley's *Description of The Leasowes,* in Shenstone 1764, p. 349.

53 "landscape at No. 18": TJ "Notes of a Tour of English Gardens," March and April 1786, TJ Papers, vol. 9, p. 371.

53 "not even an ornamented farm": Ibid.

53 "Variety of Beauties": JA Diary, "Notes on a Tour of English Country Seats & c., with Thomas Jefferson," April 1786, 44:6, MHS online.

53 American species in English gardens: See Wulf 2009, in particular pp. 247–65. One of the gardens that was famous for its large amount of American species was Painshill in Surrey, but Adams and Jefferson visited it separately on another occasion. (TJ, 2 April 1786, TJ Memorandum Book, vol. 1, p. 617; TJ "Notes of a Tour of English Gardens," March and April 1786, TJ Papers, vol. 9, p. 370; JA Diary, 26 June 1786, 44:12, MHS online.)

53 John Bartram: Wulf 2009; Berkeley and Smith Berkeley 1992.

53 American species at Stowe: Wulf and Gieben-Gamal 2005, p. 109; Laird 1999, p. 152.

54 "We have only to": TJ, "Jefferson's Hints to Americans Travelling in Europe," 19 June 1788, TJ Papers, vol. 13, p. 269.

54 "rare Shrubbs and Trees": JA Diary, 24 July 1786, 45:2, MHS online.

54 American species at The Leasowes: James Woodhouse's poem "The Leasowes" (1763), quoted in Laird 1999, p. 114.

54 Hagley and Blenheim: TJ "Notes of a Tour of English Gardens," March and April 1786, TJ Papers, vol. 9, p. 372.

54 "the greatest Curiosities": JA to Thomas Boylston Adams, 29 June 1795, Albany Institute of History and Art.

54 "far beyond my ideas": TJ to John Page, 4 May 1786, TJ Papers, vol. 9, p. 445.

54 "charmd with the beauties": AA to Elizabeth Smith Shaw, 24 April 1786, APC, vol. 7, p. 149.

54 "absolutely fruitless": TJ to Nicholas Lewis, 22 April 1786, TJ Papers, vol. 9, p. 399.

54 TJ's shopping in London: TJ Memorandum Book, vol. 1, pp. 614–17, 620–23.

55 Osterley House and Syon House: TJ, 20 April 1786, TJ Memorandum Book, vol. 1, p. 622.

55 "All the Evergreens": JA Diary, 20 April 1786, 44:9, MHS online; for plants in the shrubberies see Laird 1999, p. 142.

55 "6 weeks have elapsed": TJ to John Jay, 23 April 1786, TJ Papers, vol. 9, p. 402.

55 "We are young": TJ to C.W.F. Dumas, 6 May 1786, TJ Papers, vol. 9, p. 463; TJ on mission being futile see TJ to William Carmichael, 5 May 1786, TJ Papers, vol. 9, pp. 448–49.

55 "tedious and expensive": JA and TJ to John Jay, 25 April 1786, TJ Papers, vol. 9, p. 407; for treaty with Portugal see "Negotiations for a Treaty of Amity and Commerce with Portugal," March–April 1786, TJ Papers, vol. 9, pp. 410ff.

55 "drop in the bucket": TJ to William Carmichael, 5 May 1786, TJ Papers, vol. 9, p. 448.

55 United States and Barbary States: Brandt 2006, p. 75.

55 Vineyard nursery: Willson 1982, pp. 35ff.

55 exotics at The Vineyard nursery: Nelson 1983, p. 350; Lady Mary Coke, 26 August 1771, Coke 1970, vol. 3, p. 443; *Catalogue of Plants and Seeds, sold by Kennedy and Lee, Nursery and Seedsmen at the Vineyard*, 1774.

56 TJ and American species: TJ, 26 April 1785, TJ Memorandum Book, vol. 1, p. 623; for English nurseries and their specialization in American plants, see Wulf 2009, pp. 135–37.

56 TJ and Vineyard nursery: Seed catalogue in LibraryThing: Thomas Jefferson's Library (online); TJ, 1783 Book Catalogue, MHS; Invoice James Lee & Co, 24 April 1786, Betts 1944, p. 115.

56 plant transport to U.S: TJ to Andrew Limozin, 11 February 1787, TJ Papers, vol. 11, p. 138.

56 "It is now a fashion": Münchhausen 1770, vol. 5, p. 224.

56 JA garden visits in UK: JA to TJ, 25 June 1786, TJ Papers, vol. 10, p. 86; JA Diary, 26 June and 24 July 1786, 44:12 and 45:1-2, MHS online; AA to Elizabeth Cranch, 18 July 1786, AFC, vol. 7, pp. 256–58; AA to Lucy Cranch, 3 October 1787, AFC, vol. 8, pp. 177–80.

56 JA and Whately's *Observations*: AA to Elizabeth Cranch, 18 July 1786, AFC, vol. 7, p. 257; LibraryThing: John Adams's Library (online).

56 "We wished for your Company": JA to TJ, 25 June 1786, TJ Papers, vol. 10, p. 86.

56 JA at Thorndon: JA Diary, 24 July 1786, 45:1, MHS online.

56 "Living Pencils": Peter Collinson to Philip Southcote, 9 October 1752, Armstrong 2002, p. 159; Miller 1739, entry "Wilderness"; and Petre at Thorndon: Philip Southcote on Petre, after 1751, Osborn 1966, vol. 1, point 603; Wulf 2009, pp. 85ff.

56 "when I walk amongst": Peter Collinson to JB, 1 September 1741, Berkeley and Smith Berkeley 1992, p. 167.

56 "a List of these Trees": JA Diary, 24 July 1786, 45:2, MHS online.

57 "indifferent to their Beauties": Ibid.

57 "beauty, Convenience, and": JA Diary, 20 April 1786, 44:10, MHS online.

57 JA garden visits in UK: JA saw for example Painshill, Thorndon, The Hyde, Blenheim: JA to TJ, 25 June 1786, TJ Papers, vol. 10, p. 68; JA Diary, 26 June and 24 July 1786, 44:12 and 45:1-2, MHS online; AA to Elizabeth Cranch, 18 July 1786, AFC, vol. 7, pp. 256–58; AA to Lucy Cranch, 3 October 1787 AFC, vol. 8, pp. 177–80.

57 TJ's daily rambles in Bois: TJ to Madame de Corny, 30 June 1787, TJ Papers, vol. 11, p. 509; TJ saw the English gardens at La Chartreuse, Folie de Saint James, Louveciennes, Desert, Bagatelle, TJ Memorandum Book, vol. 1, pp. 573, 628, 638, 639, 712.

57 JA and seeds; lists to U.S.: AA to Thomas Brand Hollis, 5 April 1788; Thomas Brand Hollis to AA, 7 April 1788, AFC, vol. 8, pp. 252–53.

57 "many places": and following quotes, AA to Elizabeth Cranch, 18 July 1786, AFC, vol. 7, p. 257.

57 "improveing my Garden": AA to TJ, 26 February 1788, AFC, vol. 8, p. 238.

57 gardens important for Americans: TJ, "Jefferson's Hints to Americans Travelling in Europe," 19 June 1788, TJ Papers, vol. 13, p. 269.

57 "surpasses all the": TJ to John Page, 4 May 1786, TJ Papers, vol. 9, p. 445.

3 "A NURSERY OF AMERICAN STATESMEN": THE CONSTITUTIONAL CONVENTION IN 1787 AND A GARDEN VISIT

58 GW's arrival: 13 May 1787, Bicentennial Daybook; 13 May 1787, GW Diaries, vol. 5.

58 GW's journey: GW's diary from 9–13 May 1787, GW Diaries, vol. 5.

58 Constitutional Convention: Farrand 1911; Bicentennial Daybook; Bowen 1986; Berkin 2002.

59 "every minute you run the risk": Baron de Montlezun, 13 September 1816, Moffat and Carrière 1945, vol. 42, no. 2, p. 114.

59 "our downfal as a Nation": GW to Benjamin Harrison, 18 January 1784, GW Papers CS, vol. 1, p. 56.

59 "diplomatic assembly": JA *Defence*, Adams 1850–56, vol. 4, p. 579.

60 "threaten to blast": John Jay to GW, 16 March 1786, GW Papers CS, vol. 3, p. 601.

60 "no bigger than half a piece": Bowen 1986, p. 13; see also for JM's appearance and voice Ketcham 1990, pp. 89, 471. Madison's voice was so quiet that he was often asked to speak up when he gave a speech.

60 "so much mind in so little matter": *Richmond Enquirer*, July 1836, in McCoy 1989, p. xiii.

60 "great little Madison": Dolley Madison, May 1794, in Ketcham 1990, p. 376.

60 "dangerous defects in": JM to TJ, 4 December 1786, TJ Papers, vol. 10, p. 574.

60 JM ordered books from TJ: JM to TJ, 16 March 1784, TJ Papers, vol. 7, p. 37.

60 JM's two essays: Morton Smith 1995, vol. 1, pp. 440–41.

60 "a patient bleeding": JM, Preface to Debates in the Convention of 1787, Farrand 1911, vol. 3, p. 542.

60 "disinterested & dispassionate": and JM's preference for strong federal government, JM to GW, 16 April 1787, GW Papers CS, vol. 5, p. 146.

60 JM luring GW away from Mount Vernon: JM to GW, 8 November 1786, 7 December 1786, 21 February 1787, GW Papers CS, vol. 4, pp. 344–45, 448–49; vol. 5, pp. 92–94; JM also visited Mount Vernon several times, for example on 23–25 October 1786 and 25–26 January 1787. (GW, 23 October 1786 and 25 January 1787, GW Diaries, vol. 5, pp. 56, 98; GW to Edmund Randolph, 28 March 1787, GW Papers CS, vol. 5, p. 113; JM to TJ, 23 April 1787, TJ Papers, vol. 11, p. 310.)

61 "National character": GW to JM, 5 November 1786, GW Papers CS, vol. 4, p. 331.

61 "We are either": GW to JM, 30 November 1785, GW Papers CS, vol. 3, p. 420.

61 biographical information for the delegates: Berkin 2002, pp. 211–26; Bicentennial Daybook.

61 Husbandmen "the best basis": JM, "Republican Distribution of Citizens," *National Gazette*, 2 March 1792.

62 "degeneracy of America": Jefferson 1982; Cohen 1995, pp. 72–79; Thomson 2008a, pp. 54–72; Pauly 2007, pp. 20–32; Martin 1952, pp. 162–87.

62 French scientists: These were Comte de Buffon, Abbé Raynal and Cornélius de Pauw.

62 "shrink and diminish": Buffon, quoted in Martin 1952, p. 157.

62 TJ consulted books: Jefferson 1982, p. 53; TJ to Francis Hopkinson, 14 August 1786, TJ Papers, vol. 10, p. 250; Humphry Marshall was John Bartram's cousin. Jefferson and Washington both owned a copy of the book and it was dedicated to Franklin, who proudly dispatched it to his friends in France. Botany, Marshall wrote in the introduction, was a subject that demanded "the attention and encouragement of every patriotic and liberal mind." (Marshall 1785, p. v; BF to Jean-Baptiste Le Roy, 27 March 1786; Duc de La Rochefoucauld to BF, 14 February 1787, BF online.) TJ's copy: LibraryThing: Thomas Jefferson's Library (online); TJ, 1783 Book Catalogue, MHS (although dated 1783, TJ continued to add book titles to this catalogue); GW's copy: LibraryThing: George Washington's Library (online); BF's copy: LibraryThing: Benjamin Franklin's Library (online).

62 "the heaviest weights": TJ to Thomas Walker, 25 September 1783, TJ Papers, vol. 6, p. 340.

63 "Let both parties rise" and following quotes: TJ to Robert Walsh, 4 December 1818, with Anecdotes about Benjamin Franklin, DLC.

63 "uncommonly large panther skin": TJ in conversation with Daniel Webster, December 1824, Webster 1903, vol. 1, p. 371.

63 moose from Vermont: TJ's correspondence with John Sullivan, 12 March 1784; 7 January 1786; 26 January 1787; 16 April 1787; 5 October 1787; and also TJ to William Stephens Smith, 31 August and 28 September 1787; TJ to Buffon, 1 October 1787, TJ Papers, vol. 12, pp. 71–72, 193–95. The skin and bones of the moose arrived in September 1787 in Paris: TJ Memorandum Book, vol. 1, p. 677.

63 "length of nails": JM to TJ, 19 June 1786, TJ Papers, vol. 9, p. 663.

63 Notes on the State of Virginia: Jefferson began to compile the Notes in 1781 (as a response to a questionnaire by François de Barbé-Marbois) but quickly turned it into something much larger. He took the manuscript with him to France and printed it in Paris (1785). The first English edition was published during the summer of the Constitutional Convention by the London bookseller John Stockdale. For the English publication: TJ to William Short, 27 March, TJ Papers, vol. 11, p. 246; TJ to John Stockdale, 1 July 1787, TJ Papers, vol. 11, pp. 521–22.

63 "nothing so charming" and following quotes: TJ to Angelica Schuyler Church, 17 February 1788, TJ Papers, vol. 12, p. 601.

63 "despicable dreams" and following quote: JA Defence, Adams 1850–56, vol. 4, p. 293.

63 "larger in America" and list of measurements: Jefferson 1982, pp. 50–52, 53.

64 "could walk under the belly": TJ in conversation with Daniel Webster, December 1824, Webster 1903, vol. 1, p. 372.

64 mammoth/mastodon in the West: Jefferson 1982, p. 54. The mastodon was in fact extinct. For TJ and the mastodon, see Thomson 2008b, pp. 30–31.

64 plant lists in the *Notes:* Jefferson 1982, pp. 38–43.

64 wildflowers: The only wildflowers he listed were in the category of medicinal plants.

64 pecan tree: Jefferson 1982, p. 39.

64 "procure and send": TJ to JM, 8 February 1786, TJ Papers, vol. 9, p. 267.

64 JM sent pecan nuts: JM to TJ, 19 March and 15 May 1787, TJ Papers, vol. 11, pp. 219, 363.

65 "plant as soon": GW to George Augustine Washington, 27 May 1787, GW Papers CS, vol. 5, p. 197.

65 *"une assemblée des notables"*: BF to Thomas Jordan, 18 May 1786, BF online.

65 "purely patriotic": Richard Peters quoted in Fletcher 1976, p. 9.

65 "every State in the Union": GW to James Warren, 7 October 1785, GW Papers CS, vol. 3, p. 300; see also GW to William Drayton, 25 March 1786, GW Papers CS, vol. 3, p. 605; TJ to William Drayton, 6 May 1785, TJ Papers, vol. 9, p. 461.

65 delegates and agricultural society in Philadelphia: The other two were Robert Morris and James Wilson—all founding members of the society, Baatz 1985, p. 7.

65 delegates and agricultural society in South Carolina: Charles Cotesworth Pinckney and John Rutledge, TJ to Charles Cotesworth Pinckney, 8 October 1792, TJ Papers, vol. 24, p. 451; Haw 1997, p. 180.

65 Caleb Strong: The Foundation of the Massachusetts Professorship of Natural History, 1805, p. 17.

65 George Mason and Daniel of St. Thomas Jenifer: GW, 29 March and 12 November 1785, GW Diaries, vol. 4, pp. 109, 222; Daniel of St. Thomas Jenifer to GW, 28 February 1785, GW Papers CS, vol. 2, p. 397.

65 George Wythe: George Wythe to TJ, 9 March 1770, TJ Papers, vol. 1, p. 38; TJ to George Wythe, 13 June 1790, TJ Papers, vol. 16, p. 495.

65 "fine Gardens": JA Diary, 12 September 1774, 22:9, MHS online.

65 Robert Morris: TJ to John Bartram Jr., 27 January 1786, TJ Papers, vol. 9, pp. 228–30; Manasseh Cutler, 13 July 1787, Cutler 1888, vol. 1, p. 257.

65 Mason quizzed Williamson: George Mason to GW, 7 October 1787, GW Papers CS, vol. 5, p. 356.

66 "as far as I": JM to JM Sr., 28 July 1787, JM Papers, vol. 10, p. 119.

66 Morris asked GW for plough: GW to George Augustine Washington, 26 August 1787, GW Papers CS, vol. 5, p. 304.

66 GW voted president of Convention: GW, 25 May 1787, GW Diaries, vol. 5, p. 162.

66 JM at Convention: James Madison, Debates in the Federal Convention, 1830–36, Peterson 1974, p. 131.

66 "almost killed": JM quoted in Ketcham 1990, p. 207.

66 Madison "the best informed": William Pierce, Character Sketches of Delegates to the Federal Convention, Farrand 1911, vol. 3, p. 94.

66 guards and sealed windows: GW, 28 May 1787, GW Diaries, vol. 5, p. 163; George Wythe, 29 May 1787, Bicentennial Daybook.

66 "show that we have not Wisdom": BF to TJ, 19 April 1787, TJ Papers, vol. 11, p. 302.

66 JA's *Defence* in Philadelphia: JM to TJ, 6 June 1787, TJ Papers, vol. 11, pp. 401–02; Richard Cranch to JA, 24 May 1787, AFC, vol. 8, pp. 59–60; *Pennsylvania Gazette* advertised the publication on 6 June 1787; William Samuel Johnson purchased the book 27 June 1787, Bicentennial Daybook; Jefferson also praised it, TJ to JA, 23 February 1787, TJ Papers, vol. 11, p. 177; Benjamin Rush said it provided "excellent principles" to the delegates, Benjamin Rush to Richard Price, 2 June 1787, Farrand 1911, vol. 3, p. 33.

66 "All Nature's difference": JA *Defence*, Adams 1850–56, vol. 4, p. 271.

67 "checking one power": Ibid., p. 391.

67 three branches of government: 30 May 1787, Farrand 1911, vol. 1, p. 30.

67 two houses of legislature: 31 May 1787, Farrand 1911, vol. 1, pp. 45–47.

67 slaves as three-fifths of a person: 11 June 1787, Farrand 1911, vol. 1, p. 201; voting on three-fifths clause: 11 June and 13 July 1787, Farrand 1911, vol. 1, pp. 195, 600.

67 long speeches: Alexander Hamilton's speech, 18 June 1787, and Luther Martin's speech, 27 June 1787.

67 "We move slowly": William Richardson Davie to Governor Caswell, 17 June 1787, Bicentennial Daybook.

67 "still in such a stage": John Lansing to Phillip Schuyler, 26 June 1787, Bicentennial Daybook.

68 gravel on street: 22 June 1787, Bicentennial Daybook.

68 "on almost every Question": BF, Dr. Franklin's Motion for Prayers in the Convention, 28 June 1787, BF online.

68 delegates at BF's garden: Manasseh Cutler, 13 July 1787, Cutler 1888, vol. 1, pp. 267–68.

68 BF's garden: BF to Mary Stevenson Hewson, 6 May 1786, BF online; Carr 1868, p. 59.

68 "private Amusements": BF to Mary Stevenson Hewson, 6 May 1786, BF online.

68 BF and botany and botanical books: Manasseh Cutler, 13 July 1787, Cutler 1888, vol. 1, pp. 269–70.

68 BF's gardener: This was William Rees. BF Wastebook, 1785–87, 8 May 1786, APS. For Rees's work in the State House garden, see Coxe Toogood 2004, vol. 1, pp. 74, 76, 90.

68 work in BF's garden and seeds from Bartram: BF Wastebook, 1785–87, 8 May, 15 June, and 9 December 1786, APS.

68 GW and excursions outside Philadelphia: GW, 20 May, 17 June, 26 August, 31 August 1787, GW Diaries, vol. 5, pp. 159, 170, 182; and Jacob Hiltzheimer, 3 July 1787, Hiltzheimer 1892, p. 173.

68 "see the effect": GW, 10 June 1787, GW Diaries, vol. 5, p. 167; GW testing plaster of Paris at Mount Vernon, GW, 9 March, 8, 26 April, 7 May 1785, GW Diaries, vol. 4, pp. 100, 115, 135.

68 GW at vineyard: GW, 22 July 1787, GW Diaries, vol. 5, p. 177.

68 "sturdy farmer": Henry Woodmann, 31 July 1787, Bicentennial Daybook.

68 deadlock over one-state-one-vote: On 2 July the state delegations voted on the one-state-one-vote issue with five "ayes" and five "nos." Georgia's vote

didn't count because the delegation was divided. (2 July 1787, Farrand 1911, vol. 1, p. 510.)

68 GW at Agricultural Society: GW, 3 July 1787, GW Diaries, vol. 5, p. 173; for a description of the display in Carpenter's Hall see Manasseh Cutler, 14 July 1787, Cutler 1888, vol. 1, pp. 281–82.

68 GW's notes on harvest: GW to George Augustine Washington, 3 June 1787, GW Papers CS, vol. 5, p. 217.

68 GW's Sunday farm letters: See correspondence between GW and George Augustine Washington during the Constitutional Convention.

69 dining room at Mount Vernon: GW to George Augustine Washington, 1 July 1787, GW Papers CS, vol. 5, p. 243.

69 agricultural motifs in dining room: GW to John Rawlins, 13 April 1787; GW to George Augustine Washington, 1 July 1787, GW Papers CS, vol. 5, pp. 141, 243.

69 mantelpiece with agricultural ornaments: Samuel Vaughan had given Washington the marble mantelpiece as a present. (GW to Samuel Vaughan, 6 April 1784 and 5 February 1785, GW Papers CS, vol. 1, p. 273; vol. 2, p. 326.)

69 Philadelphia and garden estates: O'Malley 1991, p. 268; McLean 1983, pp. 136–47.

69 visits to Gray's Ferry tavern: Jacob Hiltzheimer, 17 July 1787, Hiltzheimer 1892, p. 173; for other visits see GW, 18 May 1787, 26 June, 17 July 1787, 2 September 1787, GW Diaries, vol. 5, pp. 158, 171, 176, 183; Manasseh Cutler, 14 July 1787, Cutler 1888, vol. 1, pp. 274–78.

69 garden at Gray's Ferry tavern: Manasseh Cutler, 14 July 1787, Cutler 1888, vol. 1, pp. 274–78.

69 Vaughan and the State House garden: Manasseh Cutler, 13 July 1787, Cutler 1888, vol. 1, pp. 262–63; Coxe Toogood 2004, vol. 1, pp. 72–89; Stetson 1949, pp. 465–66.

69 "pensive wandering": John Swanwick, "On a Walk in the State House Yard," June 30, 1787, quoted in Coxe Toogood 2004, vol. 1, p. 112; for other visitors: GW, 2 July 1787, GW Diaries, vol. 5, p. 173; James McHenry to Peggy McHenry, 26 August 1787, Bicentennial Daybook.

69 "compose their thoughts": Wansey 1798, p. 118.

69 State House garden: *Columbian Magazine,* vol. 1, July 1787, p. 513; Manasseh Cutler, 13 July 1787, Cutler 1888, vol. 1, pp. 262–63; many of the native species in the State House Garden had been supplied by Bartram: Bartram's plant bills 7 April 1786 and 15 April 1786, Coxe Toogood 2004, vol. 1, pp. 85–86; John Bartram House and Garden, HALS No. PA-1, pp. 50–51.

69 excursions to The Woodlands: GW, 23 May 1787, GW Diaries, vol. 5, p. 160; and for descriptions of The Woodlands: Betts 1979, pp. 224–26; McLean 1983, pp. 142–43.

69 correspondence with Peters: See GW to Richard Peters, 4 March 1788; Richard Peters to GW, 12 March 1788, GW Papers CS, vol. 6, pp. 142–43, 154–55; Richard Peters to JM, 30 July and 24 August 1818; JM to Richard Peters, 15 August 1818, 22 February and 4 November 1819, JM Papers RS, vol. 1, pp. 320–21, 345–47, 349–51, 422–23, 543–44.

69 AH and his gardens at The Grange: AH to Charles Cotesworth Pinckney, 29 December 1802; AH to Richard Peters, 29 December 1802; Richard Peters to AH, 8 January 1803, AH Papers, vol. 26, pp. 70–71, 75, 182–83.

70 TJ's tour in Europe: TJ to JA, 1 July 1787, TJ Papers, vol. 11, pp. 516ff.

70 TJ's broken wrist: TJ to JM, 30 January 1787, TJ Papers, vol. 11, p. 96; Morton Smith 1995, vol. 1, p. 400.

70 "Objects of Attention": TJ, "Jefferson's Hints to Americans Travelling in Europe," 19 June 1788, TJ Papers, vol. 13, p. 269.

70 "courted the society of gardeners": TJ to Chastellux, 4 April 1787, TJ Papers, vol. 11, p. 261.

70 "examining the culture": TJ to Lafayette, 11 April 1787, TJ Papers, vol. 11, p. 283.

70 "as much as my coat": TJ to Edward Rutledge, 14 July 1787, TJ Papers, vol. 11, p. 587; for death penalty, see TJ to John Jay, 4 May 1787, TJ Papers, vol. 11, p. 339.

70 "Agriculture . . . the surest road": TJ to John Blair, 13 Aug 1787, TJ Papers, vol. 12, p. 28.

70 "continued feast": TJ to William Short, 7 April 1787, TJ Papers, vol. 11, pp. 280–81.

71 almonds too "precarious": TJ to William Drayton, 30 July 1787, TJ Papers, vol. 11, p. 647.

71 "Of all the gifts of heaven": Ibid., p. 648.

71 "this is the object for the patriots": TJ to Edward Rutledge, 18 September 1789, TJ Papers, vol. 15, p. 452.

71 "I must press on you": TJ to John Rutledge Jr., 19 June 1788, TJ Papers, vol. 13, p. 263.

71 TJ growing sulla: TJ to William Drayton, 6 February 1788, TJ Papers, vol. 12, p. 567. Jefferson also cultivated Indian corn in his garden in Paris (TJ to Nicholas Lewis, 17 September 1787, TJ Papers, vol. 12, p. 153); for JM receiving sulla, see JM to GW, 5 November 1788 (n. 1, JM to Crèvecoeur, 30 November 1788); GW to JM, 17 November 1788, GW Papers PS, vol. 1, pp. 94–96, 114.

71 "It is impossible to": William Paterson to Euphemia White Paterson, 2 July 1787, Bicentennial Daybook.

71 Connecticut Plan: 11 June and 5 July 1787, Farrand 1911, vol. 1, pp. 193–95, 524; 5 July 1787, Bicentennial Daybook.

71 "I wish you were back": GW to Alexander Hamilton, 10 July 1787, GW Papers CS, vol. 5, p. 257.

71 BF and two-headed snake: Manasseh Cutler, 13 July 1787, Cutler 1888, vol. 1, pp. 268–69.

72 Cutler and delegates to Bartram's Garden: Manasseh Cutler, 13 July 1787, Cutler 1888, vol. 1, p. 271.

72 "first work of American literature": Crèvecoeur 1998, p. viii.

72 visit to Bartram's Garden: Descriptions are based on Cutler's journal entry, Manasseh Cutler, 14 July 1787, Cutler 1888, vol. 1, pp. 271–74. Extensive archival research has failed to find any other accounts of this visit. My thanks go to all the archivists, librarians and scholars who assisted in the search.

72 61°F: The temperature was recorded by diarist Christopher Marshall, 14 July 1787, Bicentennial Daybook.

72 Bartram's house: Fry 1998.

72 "a library within himself": Henry Muhlenberg to Zaccheus Collins, 22 November 1813, APS, Botanical Correspondence of Zaccheus Collins, 1805–1827.

72 "instil republican principles": This was Charles Thomson, one of the American revolutionaries (who then became the secretary of the Continental Congress). Robert Carr about WB: Harper 1953, p. 573.

72 BF and Bartram: There are many letters in BF's correspondence related to the Bartrams; see for example BF to JB, 27 May 1771, Berkeley and Smith Berkeley 1992, p. 771; BF to Luzerne, 5 March 1780, BF Papers, vol. 32, pp. 54–55; William Temple Franklin to Richard Bache, 24 February 1781; BF to Richard and Sarah Bache, 27 July 1783, Franklin to Ingenhousz, 29 April 1785 (all BF online). There are also some plant lists that WB sent to France in the Bartram Papers at the Historical Society of Pennsylvania dating from 3 March, July, 20 August and 16 October 1779. Franklin also recommended that the grandson of his former London landlady should board with the Bartrams to learn farming and gardening. (Mary Stevenson Hewson to Barbara Hewson, 21 October 1788, BF online.)

72 BF and Bartram's French catalogue: Fry 1996, p. 9.

73 GW's visit to Bartram's before delegates: GW, 10 June 1787, GW Diaries, vol. 5, pp. 166–67.

73 GW's plant order from Bartram's: Tobias Lear to Clement Biddle, 2 October 1789, GW Papers PS, vol. 4, pp. 124–25; George Augustine Washington to GW, 8 April 1792, GW Papers PS, vol. 10, pp. 230–31; List of Plants from John Bartram's Garden, March 1792, GW Papers PS, vol. 10, pp. 175–83.

73 TJ and Bartram: TJ, 20 May 1776, 20 January 1783, TJ Memorandum Book, vol. 1, pp. 418, 526; "Catalogue of Seeds of American Forest Trees, Shrubs and Herbacious Plants," William Bartram to TJ, circa 1786–1790, MHS, copy at Bartram's Garden, Philadelphia; see also TJ's correspondence with Madame de Tessé, for whom he organized many seeds and plants from America; TJ, 9 April 1791, TJ Memorandum Book, vol. 2, p. 815; TJ to John Bartram, 27 January 1786; TJ to Francis Hopkinson, 3 January 1786; for books to Bartram, see TJ to John Bartram Jr., 27 January 1786, TJ Papers, vol. 9, pp. 149, 228–30; John Bartram Jr. to TJ, 14 December 1786, TJ Papers, vol. 10, p. 593. Darwin had translated Linnaeus's *Systema Vegetabilium* as *System of Vegetables*.

73 "He at first stared": Manasseh Cutler, 14 July 1787, Cutler 1888, vol. 1, p. 273.

73 Bartram's leg fracture: WB to Benjamin Smith Barton, 1786, Ewan and Ewan 2007, p. 110; William Bartram to Lachlan McIntosh, 31 May 1796, Hallock and Hoffmann 2010, p. 182.

75 "Pug Puggy": William Bartram to Lachlan McIntosh, 31 May 1796, Hallock and Hoffmann 2010, p. 183; my thanks to Kathryn Braund for her help and translations.

75 Bartram's nature descriptions: "Proposals for Printing by Subscription,

Travels by William Bartram," June 1790, DLC; William Bartram quoted in Magee 2007, p. 139.

75 Bartram and subscriptions in 1786: Enoch Story Jr. to BF, 1786, BF Papers BF online; for the subscription of the *Travels* see Ewan and Ewan, 2007, pp. 105ff.

75 reception Bartram's *Travels* in Europe and America: Harper 1958, p. xxvii and Magee 2007, pp. 133ff.

75 Bartram and subscriptions in 1790: for GW: Samuel Powell to GW, 11 June 1790; GW to Samuel Powell, 20 June 1790, GW Papers PS, vol. 5, pp. 512–14; for Adams: Robert Parrish to William Bartram, 20 June 1790, Hallock and Hoffmann 2010, pp. 156–57; for TJ: TJ, 23 June 1790, TJ Memorandum Book, vol. 1, p. 759. Franklin had died by then but his grandson added his name; "Proposals for Printing by Subscription, Travels by William Bartram," June 1790, DLC.

75 Bartram's portrait at Montpelier: Inventory of Effects at Montpelier, 1 July 1836, DMDE.

76 plants at Bartram's Garden: Unless otherwise referenced, plants are based on *Bartram's Broadside*, 1783, in Fry 1996, pp. 3–66; "A List of Seeds, circa 1769, probably in William Bartram's hand and probably sent to Benjamin Franklin in London," Stanford University Library, Department of Special Collections (copy at Bartram's Garden, Philadelphia); "Catalogue of Seeds of American Forest Trees, Shrubs and Herbacious Plants," William Bartram to TJ, circa 1786–1790, MHS (copy at Bartram's Garden, Philadelphia); "A List of Seeds of Forest Trees and flowering Shrubs, gather'd in Pensilvania, the Jerseys and New York, by John and William Bartram, and sent over the last Year to their Correspondents, being the largest Collection that has ever been imported into this Kingdom," *The Gentleman's Magazine*, vol. 24 (February 1754). For Bartram's Garden in general, see Wulf 2009, pp. 72–76, 158–61.

76 Bartram's balsam firs: JB to Peter Bayard, c. June 1741; JB to Peter Collinson, 22 July 1741, Berkeley and Smith Berkeley 1992, pp. 155, 163.

76 "species of which": Schöpf 1911, vol. 1, p. 91.

76 GW and Vaughan: GW to Samuel Vaughan, 14 January 1784, GW Papers CS, vol. 1, p. 45; GW, 30 May 1787, GW Diaries, vol. 5, p. 164: GW to Samuel Vaughan, 12 November 1787, GW Papers CS, vol. 5, pp. 432–33; Coxe Toogood 2004, vol. 1, p. 75.

77 "a specimen of every sort": Samuel Vaughan to Humphry Marshall, 14 May 1785, Darlington 1849, p. 557; plants in State House Yard: John Bartram House and Garden, HALS, p. 50; Bartram's bills, 7 and 15 April 1786, Coxe Toogood 2004, vol. 1, pp. 85–86. List of trees "Planted in the Statehouse square," from Samuel Vaughan , c. 1785, Humphry Marshall Papers, USDA History Collection, Special Collections, National Agricultural Library (online).

77 plants in tubs: Wulf 2009, p. 72.

77 "covered over w^t weeds": Alexander Garden to Cadwallader Colden, 4 November 1754, Colden 1918–37, p. 472.

77 "was not laid off": GW, 10 June 1787, GW Diaries, vol. 5, p. 167.

77 "curious plts, Shrubs": GW, 10 June 1787, GW Diaries, vol. 5, p. 166.

77 "jumbled together": Manasseh Cutler, 14 July 1787, Cutler 1888, vol. 1, p. 273.

77 *Franklinia alatamaha*: Manasseh Cutler, 14 July 1787, Cutler 1888, vol. 1, p. 273; see also Wulf 2008, pp. 406–7; JB Diary, 1 October 1765, Harper 1942, pp. 31, 66; Thomson 1993, pp. 15–21.

77 botanists to see Franklinia: André Michaux to unidentified, 11 June 1786; transcript of letter at Bartram's Garden, Philadelphia.

77 *Gordonia pubescens*: The name was first published by Lamarck in the *Encyclopédie Méthodique: Botanique*, vol. 2, 1788. The name *Franklinia alatamaha* was only internationally legitimized in 1925.

78 "very free and sociable": Manasseh Cutler, 14 July 1787, Cutler 1888, vol. 1, p. 273.

78 Hugh Williamson: Craige 1987, pp. 131–33; Williamson 1769–71, pp. 272–80; Smith 1996, p. 50.

78 "nobody thinks it worth while": Hugh Williamson to James Iredell, 8 July 1787, Kelly and Baradell 2003, vol. 3, p. 286.

78 "a scale of more magnificence": Hosack 1821, p. 164.

78 thirteen sweetgums at The Grange: Chernow 2004, p. 643.

78 final vote on the Connecticut Plan and the following description: 16 July 1787, Farrand 1911, vol. 2, pp. 13–20.

79 Massachusetts's previous votes: 11 June, 2 July 1787, Farrand 1911, vol. 1, pp. 195, 510.

79 slave-owning states voted with Virginia: For example, 11 June 1787, Farrand 1911, p. 195.

79 JM on Great Compromise: JM, *Federalist Papers* no. 39, Wills 1982, p. 193.

80 "If no Accommodation": 14 July 1787, Farrand 1911, vol. 2, p. 7.

80 "as a security": William Richardson Davie, quoted in Craige 1987, p. 43.

80 Strong, Williamson and Martin in previous votes: On 11 June MA and NC voted for proportional representation in the first branch and against each state having one vote in the second branch. On 2 July, MA and NC voted against each state having one vote in the second branch. (11 June 1787 and 2 July 1787, Farrand 1911, vol. 1, pp. 195, 510.)

80 "Union is the vital sap": Fisher Amers, 5 February 1788, Allen 1983, vol. 1, p. 556.

4 "PARTIES AND POLITICKS":
JAMES MADISON'S AND THOMAS JEFFERSON'S
TOUR OF NEW ENGLAND

81 TJ's correspondence with daughters: For example, TJ to Mary Jefferson, 9 March 1791; TJ to Martha Jefferson Randolph, 6 April 1792, Betts and Bear 1986, pp. 74, 97.

81 "I suppose you are": TJ to Martha Jefferson Randolph, 24 March 1791, Betts and Bear 1986, p. 76.

81 "Have you noted the first appearance": TJ to Mary Jefferson, 9 March 1791, Betts and Bear 1986, p. 74.

81 "indicates the approach": Ibid.

81 TJ sent dates of leafing and blossom: TJ to Mary Jefferson, 31 March, 8 May 1791, Betts and Bear 1986, pp. 77, 82.

81 "I shall envy your occupations": TJ to Martha Jefferson Randolph, 26 February 1792, Betts and Bear 1986, p. 95.

82 too "lazy": TJ to Mary Jefferson, 9 March 1791, Betts and Bear 1986, p. 74.

82 "counted too much on you": TJ to Mary Jefferson, 24 April 1791, Betts and Bear 1986, p. 79.

82 "fruit was not killed": Mary Jefferson to TJ, 29 May 1791, Betts and Bear 1986, p. 83.

82 "the seeds of amendment": GW to JM, 20 May 1792, GW Papers PS, vol. 10, p. 401.

82 "well-cultivated fields" and following quote: Luigi Castiglioni, 1785–1787, Pace 1983, pp. 87, 249.

82 "the most insignificant Office": JA to AA, 19 December 1793, MHS online.

83 description of Alexander Hamilton: Chernow 2004, pp. 17, 30, 41, 51, 169, 187, 251, 333.

83 first fissures between JM, TJ and AH: Elkins and McKitrick 1993, pp. 88–153; Ellis 2002, pp. 55–65; McCoy 1980, pp. 136–165.

84 "The spirit of enterprise": AH, Reports on Manufacturers, 5 December 1791, AH Papers, vol. 10, p. 256.

84 Madison denounced Hamilton's Assumption Plan: Elkins and McKitrick 1993, pp. 88–153; Ellis 2002, pp. 55–65.

84 "nothing which I dread So much": JA to Jonathan Jackson, 2 October 1780, JA Papers, vol. 10, p. 192; JM on political parties, McDonald 1994, p. 233.

84 "in commercial manacles": JM in Congress on Tonnage Duties, 4 May 1789, JM Papers, vol. 12, p. 126.

85 "stock-jobbers": TJ to George Mason, 4 February 1791, TJ Papers, vol. 9, p. 242.

85 "Wealth acquired by": TJ to GW, 15 August 1787, TJ Papers, vol. 12, p. 38.

85 "I have no hesitation: TJ to William Crawford, 20 June 1816, Ford 1892–99, vol. 10, p. 35.

85 "Experiments for introducing": JM to Peter S. Chazotte, 30 January 1821, DLC.

85 "greatest service": TJ, Summary of Public Service, after 2 September 1800, TJ Papers, vol. 32, p. 124.

85 "the most valuable sciences": TJ to Thomas Cooper, 7 October 1814, Betts 1944, p. 534.

85 TJ and European agriculture: There are many letters during TJ's time in Europe that reveal his systematic investigation, for example, TJ's "Notes of a Tour into the Southern Parts of France," 3 March–8 June 1787, TJ Papers, vol. 11, pp. 415–62; TJ to William Drayton, 20 July 1787, TJ Papers, vol. 11, pp. 644–50; TJ to Edward Rutledge, 18 September 1789, TJ Papers, vol. 15, pp. 451–53.

85 TJ and upland rice: TJ to William Drayton, 13 January 1788, TJ Papers, vol. 12, pp. 507–8; TJ to Malesherbes, 11 March 1789, Benjamin Vaughan

to TJ, 17 and 26 March 1789, TJ Papers, vol. 14, pp. 636, 673–74, 707–8; Benjamin Vaughan to TJ, 27 March 1790; TJ to Benjamin Vaughan, 27 June 1790, TJ Papers, vol. 16, pp. 274, 578; TJ to Benjamin Waterhouse, 1 December 1808, Betts 1944, pp. 380–81.

85 TJ planting rice in pots: TJ to George Wythe, 13 June 1790; TJ to Benjamin Vaughan, 27 June 1790, TJ Papers, vol. 16, pp. 495, 578.

85 TJ supplying rice to JM and Bartram: JM to JM senior, 13 June 1791, JM Papers, vol. 13, pp. 241–42; TJ to Benjamin Waterhouse, 1 December 1808, Betts 1944, p. 381.

86 "Botany is the school": TJ to Madame de Tessé, 25 April 1788, TJ Papers, vol. 13, p. 108.

86 "the ninety nine": TJ to Samuel Vaughan, 27 November 1790, TJ Papers, vol. 18, p. 98; in 1799 the Spanish Minister to America told the Portuguese naturalist Hipólito José da Costa Pereira Furtado de Mendonça that Jefferson had introduced around twenty varieties of rice to Virginia alone. (Smith 1954, p. 92.)

86 TJ rice distribution: TJ to Nathaniel Cutting, 26 November 1790, TJ Papers, vol. 18, p. 79; TJ to George Wythe, 13 June 1790, TJ Papers, vol. 16, p. 495.

86 TJ and rice: TJ to John Milledge, 10 October 1809, TJ Papers RS, vol. 1, p. 596; TJ to James Ronaldson, 12 January 1813, TJ Papers RS, vol. 5, p. 560.

86 TJ judging his own services: TJ, Summary of Public Service, after 2 September 1800, TJ Papers, vol. 32, pp. 122–24.

86 gardening as refuge from politics: TJ to Martha Jefferson Randolph, 9 February 1791, Betts and Bear 1986, pp. 71–72; TJ to GW, 15 May 1791, TJ Papers, vol. 20, p. 417.

86 "against my love of silence": TJ to GW, 8 May 1791, TJ Papers, vol. 20, p. 292.

86 "I feel with redoubled": TJ to Thomas Mann Randolph, 1 January 1792, TJ Papers, vol. 23, p. 8.

86 TJ's house in Philadelphia: TJ to William Temple Franklin, 16 July 1790, TJ Papers, vol. 17, p. 211.

86 "labouring without pleasure": TJ to Thomas Mann Randolph, 1 May 1791, TJ Papers, vol. 20, p. 341.

87 creation of federal bank: Elkins and McKitrick 1993, pp. 223ff.

87 "corruption" . . . "rotten": TJ to Philip Mazzei, 24 April 1796, TJ Papers, vol. 29, p. 82.

87 botanical ramble: JM to Ambrose Madison, 2 March 1791, JM Papers, vol. 13, p. 402.

87 TJ's headaches: TJ to GW, 15 May 1791, TJ Papers, vol. 20, p. 417.

87 "a long journey": JM to Horatio Gates, 23 February 1794, JM Papers, vol. 15, pp. 264–65.

87 Paine's *Rights of Man*: TJ to GW, 8 May 1791; TJ to JM, 9 May 1791; TJ to JA, 17 July 1791; TJ Papers, vol. 20, pp. 291–94, 302–3; for the scandal in general, pp. 268–90.

87 TJ on *Rights of Man* and JA: TJ to Jonathan B. Smith, 26 April 1791, TJ Papers, vol. 20, p. 290; Benjamin Rush to JA, 13 April 1790, Butterfield 1951, vol. 1, p. 546.

87 "the most stupendous": JA *Defence,* Adams 1850–56, vol. 4, p. 358.
87 JA and British constitution: TJ to Benjamin Rush, 16 January 1811, TJ Papers RS, vol. 3, p. 305; AA to JQA, 20 March 1787, AFC, vol. 8, p. 12.
88 "We are not to expect": TJ to Lafayette, 2 April 1790, TJ Papers, vol. 16, p. 293.
88 "shambles": JA to AA, 10 February 1794, MHS online.
88 JA's essays: JA's "Discourses on Davila" were published in the *Gazette of the United States* from April 1790.
88 "flushed with recent pay": JA to TJ, 15 July 1813, Cappon 1987, p. 358.
88 "His Highness the President": JM to TJ, 23 May 1789, TJ Papers, vol. 15, p. 148.
88 "most superlatively ridiculous": TJ to JM, 29 July 1789, TJ Papers, vol. 15, pp. 315–16.
88 "creature of French puffs": JA to John Trumbull, 25 April 1790, MHS AP reel 115.
88 TJ accusing JA as monarchist: Benjamin Rush to JA, 13 April 1790, Butterfield 1951, vol. 1, p. 546.
88 "political heresies": TJ to Jonathan B. Smith, 26 April 1791, TJ Papers, vol. 20, p. 290.
89 AH "open mouthed against": TJ to JM, 9 May 1791, TJ Papers, vol. 20, p. 293.
89 TJ in opposition to JA: Tobias Lear to GW, 8 May 1791, GW Papers PS, vol. 8, p. 168.
89 "mortified": TJ to GW, 8 May 1791, TJ Papers, vol. 20, p. 292.
89 "thunderstruck": TJ to JA, 17 July 1791, TJ Papers, vol. 20, p. 302.
89 TJ explaining situation to GW: TJ to GW, 8 May 1791, TJ Papers, vol. 20, pp. 291–93.
89 JA would be "displeased": TJ to JM, 9 May 1791, TJ Papers, vol. 20, p. 293.
89 change of itinerary: Ibid.
89 TJ and JM meeting political allies in NY: Axelrod 1967, pp. 201ff; JM to TJ, 1 May 1791; TJ to Thomas Mann Randolph, 15 May 1791, TJ Papers, vol. 20, pp. 336, 416.
89 "brother agriculturalist": TJ to Robert Livingston, 20 April 1812, TJ Papers RS, vol. 4, p. 638.
90 "upstart attorney": Chernow 2004, p. 237.
90 "a pasionate courtship": Robert Troup to AH, 15 June 1791, AH Papers, vol. 8, p. 478. According to Robert Troup, Jefferson and Madison met Livingston and Burr. (Robert Troup to AH, 15 June 1791, AH Papers, vol. 8, p. 478.) Clinton may or may have not been in New York at that time. (Young 1967, p. 198.)
90 Livingston and AH's fiscal policies: Robert Livingston to TJ, 20 February 1791, TJ Papers, vol. 19, p. 296.
90 "twistings, combinations, and": Robert Troup to AH, 19 January 1791, AH Papers, vol. 7, p. 445, and 15 June 1791, AH Papers, vol. 8, p. 478.
90 "Ghost of Antifederalism": James Tillary to AH, January 1791, AH Papers, vol. 7, p. 615.

90 TJ and JM leave NY: TJ, 21 May 1791, TJ Memorandum, vol. 2, p. 819.

90 list of taverns: JM, "Notes on Hudson Valley Lodgings," after 24 April 1791, JM Papers, vol. 14, p. 14.

90 descriptions of tour: Unless otherwise referenced TJ, "Journal of the Tour," 29 May 1791; TJ to Thomas Mann Randolph, 5 June 1791, TJ Papers, vol. 20, pp. 454–55, 465; TJ to Martha Jefferson Randolph, 31 May 1791, Betts and Bear 1986, p. 84.

90 "you should . . . not permit": TJ to Peter Carr, 19 August 1785, TJ Papers, vol. 8, p. 407.

90 satisfy JM's botanical curiosity: JM to Ambrose Madison, 2 March 1791, JM Papers, vol. 13, p. 402.

90 "either unknown or rare": TJ to Thomas Mann Randolph, 5 June 1791, TJ Papers, vol. 20, p. 465.

90 TJ and list of inns: TJ, "Table of Distances and Ratings of Inns," 17 May–19 June 1791, TJ Papers, vol. 20, pp. 471–73.

90 "loaded richly with large flowers": TJ, "Journal of the Tour," 24 May 1791, TJ Papers, vol. 20, p. 453.

91 "the richest shrub": TJ to Thomas Mann Randolph, 5 June 1791, TJ Papers, vol. 20, p. 465; *Rhododendron periclymenoides* was then called *Azalea nudiflora.*

91 "I am sorry we did": TJ to JM, 21 June 1791, TJ Papers, vol. 20, p. 560.

91 "the most beautiful water": TJ to Martha Jefferson Randolph, 31 May 1791, Betts and Bear 1986, p. 84.

91 "honey suckle of the gardens": TJ to Thomas Mann Randolph, 5 June 1791, TJ Papers, vol. 20, p. 465.

91 letters on birch bark paper: TJ to Maria Jefferson, 30 May 1791; TJ to Martha Jefferson Randolph, 31 May 1791, Betts and Bear 1986, pp. 83–84.

91 TJ's horticultural instructions: TJ to Thomas Mann Randolph, 5 June 1791, TJ Papers, vol. 20, p. 465.

91 "the botanical objects": Ibid.

91 "the drudgery of business": TJ to Martha Jefferson Randolph, 23 June 1791, Betts and Bear 1986, p. 85.

92 JM and TJ seed exchange: JM to TJ, 15 May 1787 and 6 June 1787, TJ Papers, vol. 11, pp. 363, 402; JM to TJ, 24 October 1787, TJ Papers, vol. 12, p. 270; TJ to JM, 17 September 1787, JM to TJ, 9 December 1787 and 6 February 1788, TJ Papers, vol. 12, pp. 137, 408–9, 412, 568–69; on 27 January 1788 TJ pays for two boxes of seeds that had been sent by JM, Betts 1944, p. 133.

92 inhabitants NY and Philadelphia: North 1974, p. 68.

92 "Each man . . . owns": Weld 1807, vol. 1, p. 233.

92 "meadows, newly snatched": Brissot de Warville, 9 August 1788, Brissot de Warville 1970, vol. 1, p. 125.

92 "mixture of romantic wilderness": Rochefoucauld-Liancourt 1799, vol. 1, p. 4.

93 TJ, notes on the Hessian fly: 24 May–18 June 1791, TJ Papers, vol. 20, pp. 456–61.

93 Hessian fly at Mount Vernon: GW, 22 July 1786, GW Diaries, vol. 5, p. 13.

93 "whole continent will be over-run": American Museum 1787, quoted in Pauly 2007, p. 38.

93 questionnaire on Hessian fly: TJ to Benjamin Smith Barton and Others, 12 May 1791, TJ Papers, vol. 20, p. 395; about the committee at the APS: TJ to Thomas Mann Randolph, 1 May 1791, TJ Papers, vol. 20, p. 341.

93 Hessian fly and Britain: Joseph Banks to Lord Carmarthen, 4 June 1788; Joseph Banks to Charles Jenkinson, 23 February 1789, Chambers 2007, vol. 3, pp. 406–7; 462–66.

93 "only a political manoeuvre": Thomas Paine to TJ, 16 February 1789, TJ Papers, vol. 14, p. 567.

93 "to do us injury": TJ to Benjamin Vaughan, 17 May 1789, TJ Papers, vol. 15, p. 134.

93 "obloquy": Joseph Banks, quoted in Pauly 2007, p. 46.

93 "scourge of Heaven": Duke of Grafton, quoted in Pauly 2007, p. 46.

93 "to proselyte . . . a commercial war": Sir John Temple to Duke of Leeds, 23 May 1791, TJ Papers, vol. 20, p. 435.

93 "favorite objects in behalf of France": George Beckwith to Grenville, 14 June 1791, TJ Papers, vol. 20, p. 439.

94 TJ and distillery owner: TJ to Seth Jenkins, 21 June 1791. TJ had met Jenkins on 25 May 1791: TJ Papers, vol. 20, p. 559.

94 sugar maples: TJ to Benjamin Vaughan, 27 June 1790, TJ Papers, vol. 16, pp. 578–80.

94 "supply themselves sugar": TJ to Thomas Mann Randolph, 1 May 1791, TJ Papers, vol. 20, p. 341.

94 facts and figures: TJ to Benjamin Vaughan, 27 June 1790; TJ to GW, 1 May 1791, TJ Papers, vol. 16, pp. 578–80; vol. 20, p. 343.

94 sugar samples: TJ to GW, 1 May 1791, TJ Papers, vol. 20, p. 343; GW to Edward Newenham, 5 September 1791, GW Papers PS, vol. 8, p. 496; GW sent sugar maple seeds to his estate manager at Mount Vernon: GW to Anthony Whitting, 4 November 1792, GW Papers PS, vol. 11, p. 331.

94 Rush on sugar maple: Benjamin Rush to TJ, "An Account of the Sugar Maple Tree," 10 July 1791, Butterfield 1951, vol. 1, pp. 587–97. Jefferson must have also known about Tench Coxe's 1790 report on sugar imports and the calculations of sugar maple yields. (Coxe 1965, pp. 78–80.)

94 Bennington: William Loughton Smith, August 1790, Smith Loughton 1917, p. 51.

95 balsam poplar: TJ to JM, 21 June 1791, TJ Papers, vol. 20, p. 560.

95 "young groves": Joseph Fay to TJ, 9 August 1791, TJ Papers, vol. 22, p. 18.

95 "attention to our sugar": The Vermont Gazette, 13 June 1791.

95 "feel the pulse of the country": George Beckwith to Grenville, 14 June 1791, TJ Papers, vol. 20, p. 439.

95 "Charles Fox of America": The Pennsylvania Mercury, 9 June 1791, but also reprinted in New York Daily Advertiser, 6 June 1791, Federal Gazette, 8 June 1791, and the Gazette of the United States, 8 June 1791.

95 "entered . . . itinerary conversations": JM to Margaret Bayard Smith, September 1830, Madison 1865, vol. 4, p. 112.

95 "party Jugglings": James Tillary to Alexander Hamilton, January 1791, AH Papers, vol. 7, p. 614.

95 "disseminating the doctrines": TJ to Thomas Mann Randolph, 15 May 1791, TJ Papers, vol. 20, p. 416; sending *Gazette* during tour: TJ to Henry Remsen, 16 and 28 May 1791, TJ Papers, vol. 20, pp. 419, 462.

95 "defects of British Government" and changing his opinion: Joseph Fay to TJ, 20 September 1791, TJ Papers, vol. 22, p. 150.

96 "secured to themselves": *The Vermont Gazette,* 13 June 1791.

96 "soil good but" and following quotes: JM Journal, 31 May, 2, 3, 4 June 1791, JM Papers, vol. 14, pp. 26–28.

96 "ridiculed, J___n & M__n's Tour": Nathaniel Hazard to AH, 25 November 1791, AH Papers, vol. 9, p. 534.

96 "dwindled . . . to the insignificant leader": John Trumbull to JA, 5 February 1791, MHS AP reel 374.

96 Trumbull's satire: Nathaniel Hazard to AH, 25 November 1791, AH Papers, vol. 9, p. 534. Trumbull called TJ and JM the "Southern Smoke" and the force of the Federalists a "North-East Gale."

96 Prince's nursery: TJ, 15 June 1791, TJ Memorandum Book, vol. 2, p. 822; see also Prince 1790.

96 JM, GW and JA at Prince's nursery: JM to TJ, 9 December 1787, TJ Papers, vol. 12, p. 408; GW, 10 October 1789, GW Diaries, vol. 5, p. 458; Abigail Adams to Mary Smith Cranch, 11 October 1789, AFC, vol. 8, p. 421.

96 "shrubs were trifling": GW, 10 October 1789, GW Diaries, vol. 5, p. 458.

96 "all you have": TJ to William Prince, 6 July 1791. The first part of this letter refers to the note that Jefferson had left with Prince on 15 June 1791; see also Prince's delivery invoice, 8 November 1791, TJ Papers, vol. 20, pp. 603–4; vol. 22, pp. 268–69.

97 AH's industrial city: Cooke 1975, pp. 370–92; Chernow 2004, pp. 372–74.

97 AH and manufacturing: AH, Report on Manufactures, 5 December 1791, AH Papers, vol. 10, p. 253; Chernow 2004, p. 376; JA to Tench Coxe, May 1792, MHS, Misc. Bound Coll.

97 "one of the finest situations": William Hall to AH, 29 August 1791, quoted in Cooke 1975, p. 386.

97 Niagara Falls "worth a voiage": TJ to Maria Cosway, 12 October 1786, TJ Papers, vol. 10, p. 447.

97 no sugar in US: TJ to William Short, 25 November 1791, TJ Papers, vol. 22, p. 334.

97 TJ and Prince's nursery: TJ to JM, 6 July 1791; JM to TJ, 10 July 1791, TJ Papers, vol. 20, pp. 603, 616.

97 failure of sugar maple at Monticello: Thomas Mann Randolph to TJ, 27 March 1792, TJ Papers, vol. 23, p. 347.

97 "too hopeful an object": TJ to Thomas Mann Randolph, 19 April 1792, TJ Papers, vol. 23, p. 435.

98 "Mr. Madison's health": TJ to GW, 20 June 1791, TJ Papers, vol. 20, pp. 558–59.

98 TJ's headache had disappeared: TJ to Martha Jefferson Randolph, 23 June 1791, Betts and Bear 1986, p. 85.

98 essays by "Publicola": Over the next two months, eleven essays were published in the *Columbian Centinel*.

98 "eternal buzz": JM to TJ, 10 July 1791, TJ Papers, vol. 20, p. 617.

98 fortunes and morals: TJ to John Taylor, 28 May 1816, DLC.

98 JA refusing to invest in national bank: AA to Mary Smith Cranch, 10 October 1790, AFC, vol. 9, pp. 130–31.

98 "I regret—deeply regret": GW to TJ, 18 October 1792, TJ Papers, vol. 24, p. 499.

98 "the hint of which": Philip Freneau to TJ, 4 August 1791, TJ Papers vol. 20, p. 754.

99 "the pretext of": Hamilton 1859, vol. 4, p. 506.

99 "made us immediate companions" and following quote: JM to Margaret Bayard Smith, September 1830, Madison 1865, vol. 4, p. 111.

5 "POLITICAL PLANTS GROW IN THE SHADE":
   THE SUMMER OF 1796

100 "I will not sit here": JA to AA, 1 April 1796, MHS online.

100 "I long for rural sceanes": JA to AA, 16 March 1777, MHS online.

100 "I want to take a Walk with you": JA to AA, 22 May 1776; see also JA to AA, May 1772, 17 May 1777, 21 May 1777, 1 May 1789, 27 January 1793, 7 March 1796, 1 April 1796, 16 April 1796, MHS online; JA to TJ, 11 May 1794, TJ Papers, vol. 28, p. 71.

100 JA complained: JA to AA, 29 January 1796, MHS online.

100 AA's letters: AA to JA throughout spring 1796, MHS online.

100 "No Letter for The Vice President": JA to AA, 26 January 1796, MHS online.

101 JA's nature rambles: See for example JA Diary, January 1759, 10 June 1760, 25 June 1760, 23 October 1762, 19 August 1770, 1 May 1771, 28 February 1774, 16 March 1777, MHS online.

101 JA's dreams about farm and garden: See for example JA Diary, 24 October 1762, 23 August 1773, 12 September 1774, 18 September 1775; JA to AA, 1 May 1771, 29 June 1774, 17 August 1774, 17 July 1774, 17 July 1783, 22 January 1794, 23 June 1795; 13 March 1796, MHS online.

101 JA's excursion outside Philadelphia: JA to AA, 24 June 1795, MHS online; see also Thomas Boylston Adams to JA, 14 May 1794, MHS AP reel 377.

101 "Oh my farm": JA to AA, 12 May 1794, and JA to AA, 27 February 1793, MHS online.

101 Jay Treaty: Elkins and McKitrick 1993, pp. 431ff.

101 Jay's quip about burning effigies: Stahr 2005, p. 337.

101 "occasions some smoke": JA to Oliver Wolcott, 16 September 1795, Wolcott Papers, Connecticut Historical Society.

101 "in the Mire": JA to Charles Adams, 24 April 1796, MHS, Seymour Coll., Adams Papers; JA to AA, 24 April 1796, MHS online.

101 "the Ultimate Object": JA to AA, 3 December 1778, MHS online.

101 JA requested leave of absence: JA to AA, 3 May 1796, MHS online.

102 "the most worrying": JM to TJ, 1 May 1796, TJ Papers, vol. 29, p. 94.

102 "fortify the Republican cause": JM to TJ, 22 May 1796, TJ Papers, vol. 29, p. 29.

102 "absolutely deceased": William Cobbett writing as "Peter Porcupine," May 1796, quoted in Ketcham 1990, p. 365.

102 JM leaves Philadelphia defeated: JA to AA, 28 April 1796, MHS online; see also Ketcham 1990, p. 365.

102 GW exhausted: GW to John Jay, 8 May 1796; GW to David Humphreys, 12 June 1796, GWW, vol. 35, pp. 37, 91–92; GW attacked by opposition, see Ellis 2002, pp. 126–27; Freeman 1948–57, vol. 7, p. 398.

102 "North and South will hang together": TJ to GW, 23 May 1792, TJ Papers, vol. 23, p. 539.

102 "their heads shorn by": TJ to Philip Mazzei, 24 April 1796, TJ Papers, vol. 29, p. 82.

102 "Be upon your guard": Anonymous to GW, 3 January 1792, GW Papers PS, vol. 9, p. 369.

102 "Old Hero looks very grave": JA to AA, MHS, 9 April 1796, MHS online.

103 "turpitude of their attacks": JA to AA, 1 March 1796, MHS online.

103 GW wants to retire: GW to John Jay, 8 May 1796; GW to David Humphreys, 12 June 1796, GWW, vol. 35, pp. 37, 91–92.

103 "like an Antediluvian patriarch": TJ to Edward Rutledge, 30 November 1795, TJ Papers, vol. 28, p. 541.

103 "politics, a subject I never loved": TJ to JA, 28 February 1796, TJ Papers, vol. 28, p. 618.

103 TJ conversing only about agriculture: TJ to William Branch Giles, 27 April 1795, TJ Papers, vol. 28, p. 337.

103 "execrable" treaty and "against the legislature": TJ to Edward Rutledge, 30 November 1795, TJ Papers, vol. 28, p. 542.

103 JA working next to his laborers: JA Diary, 15 July 1796, 46:33, MHS online.

103 "never saved any thing": AA to Mary Smith Cranch, 10 October 1790, AFC, vol. 9, p. 131.

103 TJ and harvest: TJ, Diary of Harvest, June and July 1796, Betts 1944, p. 246.

104 GW as successful businessman: Fusonie and Fusonie 1998, pp. 37–49.

104 GW discussing pineapples: Carlos Martinez de Yrujo to GW, 31 July 1796, DLC.

104 GW and merits of ploughs: Benjamin Henry Latrobe, 16–17 July 1796; Lee 2006, p. 64.

104 JA and manure: JA Diary, entries throughout July and August 1796, MHS online; AA to Thomas Boylston Adams, 16 August 1796, MHS AP reel 382.

104 JM and mill: JM to JM Sr., 10 August 1796, JM Papers, vol. 16, p. 390.

104 JA in his fields: JA Diary, entries August 1796, MHS online.

104 TJ and agricultural inventions: TJ to Thomas Mann Randolph, 19 August 1796, TJ Papers, vol. 29, p. 170.

104 agricultural correspondence in 1796: For example, JA to TJ, 31 January 1796, TJ Papers, vol. 28, p. 800; TJ to GW, 19 June 1796 and GW to TJ, 6 July 1796, TJ Papers, vol. 29, pp. 12, 144.

104 "I have Spent my Summer": JA to TJ, 21 November 1794, TJ Papers, vol. 28, p. 208.

104 "This has been the most quiet": JA to Thomas Boylston Adams, 8 August 1796; see also AA to Thomas Boylston Adams, 16 August 1796, MHS AP reel 382.

105 plants in JA's garden: Mary Smith Cranch to AA, 27 June 1797, MHS AP reel 384; AA to Catherine Nuth Johnson, 8 May 1801, MHS AP reel 400; AA to JA, 31 May 1789, MHS online; Lacy 1997, p. 8.

105 "humble citizen": AA to Catherine Nuth Johnson, 8 May 1801, MHS AP reel 400.

105 fruit trees and vegetables in JA's garden: AA to JA, 31 May 1789, MHS online; JA Diary, 27 July 1796, 46:43, MHS online; AA to Catherine Nuth Johnson, 8 May 1801, MHS AP reel 400; AA to Mary Smith Cranch, 10 October 1790 and 18 April 1791, AFC, vol. 9, pp. 131, 211; Mary Smith Cranch to AA, 27 June 1797, MHS AP reel 384.

105 JA only happy when working the soil: JA to AA 15 May 1777, 15 March 1796, MHS online; JA to John Trumbull, 18 March 1793, deCoppett Collection, Princeton University; JA to Francis Adriaan van der Kemp, 30 December 1794, Historical Society of Pennsylvania.

105 "I should prefer the Delights of a Garden": JA to AA, 16 March 1777, MHS online.

105 "I had rather build stone Wall": JA to AA, 18 August 1776, MHS online.

105 "unpleasant Moments": JA to JQA, 19 May 1796, MHS AP reel 381.

105 "no Paris advocate": Rochefoucauld-Liancourt 1799, vol. 1, p. 408.

105 JA's land: In late 1788 or early 1789 Cotton Tufts calculated that the Adamses' real estate was 446 acres. In 1790 Adams added another 30 acres (bordering their land to the north) and in 1791 20 acres of woodland to the west of their land. In addition, Abigail purchased 1,650 acres in Vermont in 1782 and a year later inherited from her father a half share in an 86-acre farm in Medford, Massachusetts. MHS, "Schedule of Adamses' Real Estate in Braintree and Milton," post 1787; Adams Papers, Topical Supplements: Wills and Deeds, folder 3; AFC, vol. 7, p. 459, n. 1; AFC, vol. 5, p. 249, n. 3.

105 house in Quincy: Mary Cranch Smith to AA, 22 April 1787; Cotton Tufts to JA, 13 June 1787; AA to Cotton Tufts, 1 July 1787; Mary Cranch Smith to AA, 23 September 1787; AA to Cotton Tufts, 6 November 1787, AFC, vol. 8, pp. 20, 89, 104, 170–71, 201.

106 "it feels like a wren's house": AA to AA2, 7 July 1788, AFC, vol. 8, p. 278.

106 garden a "wilderness": AA to AA2, 6 August 1788, AFC, vol. 8, p. 284.

106 best orchard: AA to JA, 27 December 1783, MHS online.

106 "two or three spots": JA to Thomas Brand-Hollis, 3 December 1788, MHS AP reel 371.

106 JA and improving his land: JA Diary, 28 February 1774, 20:2, MHS online.

106 "My Farm gallops": JA to JQA, 26 March 1795, MHS AP reel 379.

106 work on the new house and farm: AA to Cotton Tufts, 6 November 1787; AA to AA2, 6 June 1788, AFC, vol. 8, pp. 202, 284; AA to JA, 26 April 1789, MHS online; Lacy 1997, p. 10.

107 flowers from England: Elizabeth Cranch to AA, 23 September 1787; AA to

Thomas Brand Hollis, 5 April 1788; Thomas Brand Hollis, 7 April 1788, AFC, vol. 8, pp. 170, 252–53.

107 flowers in the garden: AA to Mary Smith Cranch, 24–26 April 1800, American Antiquarian Society; AA to Catherine Nuth Johnson, 8 May 1801 MHS AP reel 400.

107 Thomas Boylston Adams brings seeds: AA to JA, 20 February 1799, MHS online.

107 JA worrying he would not have garden: JA to Richard Cranch, 27 April 1785, AFC, vol. 6, p. 111.

107 "I shall mourn my garden": AA to Elizabeth Cranch, 8 May 1785, AFC, vol. 6, pp. 131–32.

107 "in as good an Air": JA to Richard Cranch, 22 August 1785, AFC, vol. 6, p. 294.

107 "one of the pleasantest squares": AA to Mary Smith Cranch, c. July or August 1785, AFC, vol. 6, p. 242.

107 "a folly": JA Diary, MHS, 26 July 1786, 45:5, MHS online.

107 JA's ha-ha: JA Diary, MHS, 21 and 27 July 1796, 46:38, 42, MHS online.

107 "ornamented Farm . . . an Innocent": AA to Elizabeth Cranch, 18 July 1786, AFC, vol. 7, p. 256. AA wrote "half a Million of Money."

107 ornamental farms cost a fortune in England: AA to Elizabeth Cranch, 18 July 1786, AFC, vol. 7, p. 257.

107 JA and Addison's essay: This was Addison's "On the Pleasures of the Imagination," LibraryThing: John Adams's Library (online).

107 JA and Whately's Observations: LibraryThing: John Adams's Library (online); giving Whately as present, see AA to Elizabeth Cranch, 18 July 1786, AFC, vol. 7, p. 257.

108 "To blend the useful": Whately 1770, p. 161.

108 "We have opened the Prospect" and fifty cedars: JA Diary, 15 July 1796, 46:33, MHS online.

108 "opening the garden": Whately 1770, p. 161.

108 "mere Ostentations of Vanity": JA Diary, 20 April 1786, 44:10, MHS online.

108 "the farm of a Patriot": JA to Thomas Brand-Hollis, 3 December 1788, MHS AP reel 371.

108 naming Peacefield: JA Diary, 8 September 1796, 46:61–62, MHS online.

108 JA and GW's retirement: and JA's internal battles see JA to AA, 5, 12, 20, 21 January; 2, 20 February; 1 March 1796, MHS online.

109 "Think of it and say nothing": JA to AA, 12 January 1796, MHS online.

109 "I hate to live in Philadelphia": JA to AA, 1 March 1796, MHS; see also JA to AA, 2 and 20 February 1796, MHS online.

109 "I sighed, sobbed": JA to Harrison Gray Otis, 29 March 1823, MHS AP reel 124.

109 JA releasing tension: JA to AA, 3 August 1777, MHS online. See also JA Diary, 24 October 1762, 8:10 MHS online; JA to Cotton Tufts, 26 December 1800, MHS, Misc. Bound Coll.

109 "My Time . . . might have been improved": JA to AA, 1 July 1774, MHS online.

109 "keeps his Spirits in action" and following quote: AA to Thomas Boylston Adams, 16 August 1796, MHS AP reel 382.

109 "pale, withered, haggard": JA to AA, 28 April 1796, MHS online.

110 "the little spice of ambition": TJ to JM, 27 April 1795, TJ Papers, vol. 28, p. 339.

110 "I have not seen Jefferson": JM to James Monroe, 29 September 1796, JM Papers, vol. 16, p. 404.

110 GW plans retirement: GW to JM, 20 May 1792, GW Papers PS, vol. 10, pp. 400–1; GW to James Anderson, 7 April 1797, GW Papers RS, vol. 1, p. 79; GW to Oliver Wolcott, 15 May 1797, GW Papers RS, vol. 1, pp. 142–43; GW to Thomas Pinckney, 28 May 1797, GW Papers RS, vol. 1, p. 157.

110 "untrodden ground": GW to Catharine Sawbridge Macaulay Graham, 9 January 1790, GW Papers PS, vol. 4, p. 552; see also GW to JM, 5 May 1789, GW Papers PS, vol. 2, pp. 216–17.

110 instructions for garden to be in "prime order": GW to William Pearce, 15, 29 May; 5, 26 June 1796, Conway 1889, pp. 248, 252–53, 256.

110 plants in Mount Vernon: The description of plants is based on visitor accounts, Bartram's list of plants and GW's diary entries; see for example List of Plants from John Bartram's Garden, March 1792, GW Papers PS, vol. 10, pp. 175–83; Julian Ursin Niemcewicz, 2 June 1798, Lee 2006, pp. 70–71, 74–75.

111 "A thousand other bushes": Julian Ursin Niemcewicz, 2 June 1798, Lee 2006, p. 75.

111 oval beds and Bartram's plants: Tobias Lear to Clement Biddle, 2 October 1789, GW Papers PS, vol. 4, pp. 124–25; List of Plants from John Bartram's Nursery, March 1792, GW Papers PS, vol. 10, pp. 175–83; George Augustine Washington to GW, 8–9 April 1792, GW Papers PS, vol. 10, p. 231; George Augustine Washington to GW, 15–16 April 1792, GW Papers PS, vol. 10, p. 272; GW's Directive to John Christian Ehlers, 7 November 1792, GW Papers PS, vol. 11, pp. 354–55. For GW's visits to Bartram's Garden, GW, 10 June and 2 September 1787, GW Diaries, vol. 5, pp. 166–67, 183.

111 "rising clumps": Miller 1752, entry "Wilderness."

111 birds in Mount Vernon: Julian Ursin Niemcewicz, 2 June 1798, Lee 2006, pp. 74, 85; Winthrop Sargent, 13 October 1793, MV Folder "Early Descriptions ante 1800," Mount Vernon Library.

111 AH's draft for GW's Farewell Address: AH to GW, 5 and 30 July 1796, AH Papers, vol. 20, p. 170.

111 "considerable changes": GW to AH, 15 May 1796, AH Papers, vol. 20, p. 169.

111 "honest; unaffected": Ibid., p. 175.

111 GW wants radical change of management: GW, "Terms on which the Farms at Mount Vernon may be obtained," 1 February 1796, Conway 1889, p. 286.

112 GW and slaves: 316 slaves were living on the plantation in 1799, of whom 201 were regarded as fit for work. (Pogue 2002, p. 5.)

112 GW's proposals: GW, "Terms on which the Farms at Mount Vernon may be obtained," 1 February 1796, Conway 1889, p. 286.

112 farm "for amusement": GW to John Sinclair, 20 February 1796, GWW, vol. 34, p. 469.

112 "separate the Negroes from the Land": GW to William Pearce, 20 March 1796, GWW, vol. 34, p. 501.

112 "the Neighbouring Negros": GW to William Pearce, 27 January and 7 February 1796, GWW, vol. 34, pp. 427, 448; GW wanted to avoid splitting slave families, GW to Robert Lewis, 17 August 1799, GW Papers RS, vol. 4, p. 256 ; see also GW to David Stuart, 7 February 1796, GWW, vol. 34, p. 452.

112 "liberate a certain species of property": GW to Tobias Lear, 6 May 1794, GWW, vol. 33, p. 358.

112 GW's advertisements: GW to David Stuart, 7 February 1796; GW to William Pearce, 7 February 1796; GW to Jeremiah Wadsworth, 11 February 1796; Western lands: GW to Isaac Craig, 13 February 1796; GW to Thomas Lewis, 13 February 1796; GW to Rufus Putnam, 13 February 1796, GWW, vol. 34, pp. 451–52, 456–57, 459–60, 462.

112 "I shall be able to": GW to David Stuart, 7 February 1796, GWW, vol. 34, pp. 433–47, 453.

112 "slovenly farmers of this country": GW to William Strickland, 20 February 1796, GWW, vol. 34, p. 468.

112 seed drills "violently opposed": Willich 1802, vol. 2, p. 166.

112 "a lazy, ignorant sett": JA to AA, 25 May 1777, MHS online.

112 "abuse" of the land: GW to Arthur Young, 1 November 1787, GW Papers CS, vol. 5, p. 404.

113 "green manure": However, no one had yet discovered the chemical principle behind the effect of green manure whereby plants such as clover and vetch fix atmospheric nitrogen, which can then be used by crops that require high amounts of nitrogen, such as wheat.

113 GW and Arthur Young: GW Papers; the correspondence between GW and Arthur Young began in 1786.

113 crop rotation and no tobacco: Plan for Crop Rotation annexed to GW "Terms on which the Farms at Mount Vernon may be obtained," 1 February 1796, Conway 1889, pp. 285, 287–88.

113 "particularly from Great Britain": GW to Earl of Buchan, 20 February 1796, GWW, vol. 34, p. 471.

113 GW and English estate managers: GW, 21 April 1786, GW Diaries, vol. 4, p. 315; GW to George William Fairfax, 30 June 1785; Articles of Agreement with James Bloxham, 31 May 1786, GW Papers CS, vol. 4, pp. 86–87.

113 "His favourite subject": Julian Ursyn Niemcewicz, 1798, Lee 2006, p. 81.

113 "very minute account of the Hessian fly": Benjamin Henry Latrobe, 16–17 July 1796, Lee 2006, p. 63.

113 GW's observation during the Whiskey Rebellion: GW to William Pearce, 1 October 1794, GWW, vol. 33, pp. 517–18.

113 "Our welfare and prosperity depend": GW to Samuel Chamberline, 3 April 1788, GW Papers CS, vol. 6, p. 190.

113 "common farmer will not depart": GW to John Beale Bordley, 17 August 1788, GW Papers CS, vol. 6, p. 450.

113 "making Experiments": "U" to the *Boston Gazette,* 18 July 1763, JA Papers, vol. 1, p. 68.

113 JA growing clover, grasses and hemp: JA Diary, 24 October 1762, 8:11, MHS online; JA to Henry Guest, 5 September 1809, Rutgers, New Brunswick, N.J.

113 "the few who can afford it": TJ to JM, 13 May 1810, TJ RS, vol. 2, p. 388; and TJ to Joseph Dougherty, 27 June 1810, TJ Papers RS, vol. 2, pp. 490–91.

113 TJ, crop rotation and fodder crops: TJ to GW, 28 June 1793; TJ to JM, 29 June 1793; TJ to Thomas Mann Randolph, 28 July 1793; TJ to GW, 14 May 1794; John Taylor to TJ, 5 March 1795, TJ to JM, 5 March 1795; TJ to GW, 12 September 1795, TJ Papers, vol. 26, pp. 396–97, 401–3, 576–78; vol. 28, pp. 74–75, 291–301, 464–65; TJ, Questions on the Cow Pea, with Answers by Philip Tabb, 1796, TJ Papers, vol. 29, p. 179.

114 "the best farmers of all": TJ to Thomas Mann Randolph, 28 July 1793; see also TJ to JM, 29 June 1793; TJ to GW, 28 June 1793, TJ Papers, vol. 26, pp. 396–97, 402–3, 576–78.

114 founding fathers advising one another on crop rotation: JM to TJ, 23 March 1795, TJ Papers, vol. 28, p. 315. The pamphlet was J. Beale Bordley's "Sketches on Rotations of Crops" (1791); TJ to Thomas Mann Randolph, 11 August 1793, TJ Papers, vol. 26, p. 658 ; TJ to John Taylor, 29 December 1794, TJ Papers, vol. 28, pp. 232–33; GW to Arthur Young, 1 November 1787, GW Papers CS, vol. 5, pp. 403–4 ; GW to Arthur Young, 4 December 1788, GW Papers PS, vol. 1, pp. 159–62 ; GW to John Beale Bordley, 17 August 1788, GW Papers CS, vol. 6, pp. 450ff ; GW to William Pearce, 18 December 1793, 26 January 1794, Conway 1889, pp. 11, 34.

114 TJ's ravaged fields: TJ to GW, 14 May 1794; see also TJ to Madame de Tessé, 6 September 1795, TJ Papers, vol. 28, pp. 75, 451.

114 "best Farmer in the State": Samuel Powell, October 1787, Lee 2006, p. 53; for other praise see Edward Thornton to James Bland Burges, 3 October 1792, MV Folder, "Early Descriptions ante 1800," Mount Vernon Library; Robert Hunter, November 1785; Lee 2006, p. 31.

114 TJ too theoretical: Rochefoucauld-Liancourt, 1796, Peterson 1993, p. 23; Sir Augustus Foster, 1805–7, Davis 1954, p. 147.

114 "I am but a learner": TJ to William Branch Giles, 27 April 1795, TJ Papers, vol. 28, p. 337.

114 TJ on horseback all day: TJ to JA, 25 April 1794; TJ to JA, 6 February 1795; TJ to JM, 27 April 1795; TJ to Philip Mazzei, 30 May 1795; TJ to Henry Knox, 1 June 1795; TJ to Thomas Pinckney, 8 September 1795, TJ Papers, vol. 28, pp. 57, 261–62, 339–40, 370, 374, 458; Rochefoucauld-Liancourt, June 1796, Peterson 1993, p. 28.

114 "I have made researches": TJ to Jonathan Williams, 3 July 1796, TJ Papers, vol. 29, p. 140.

114 "I am entirely a farmer": TJ to Thomas Pinckney, 8 September 1795, TJ Papers, vol. 28, p. 458.

114 JM searching for a vocation: Madison had studied law but did not want to practice. He also tried his luck in land speculation. (Ketcham 1990, p. 144.)

114 JM's two farms: Madison acquired the Swaney's Tract (sometimes called

Edmondson Tract) from his father for a nominal $1 and bought Black Meadows in 1792. (Miller 1985, pp. 19–20, 22–23.)

114 JM's letters and instructions: JM to JM Sr., 17 January, 21 February, 6 March, 13 March, 10 August 1796, JM Papers, vol. 16, pp. 192, 228, 248–49, 265–67, 390. For JM enjoying physical work, see Jennings 1983, p. 51.

115 "now immersed in farming": TJ to JM, 29 June 1793, TJ Papers, vol. 26, p. 402.

115 ploughs and Jethro Tull: JM to TJ, 12 April 1793, TJ Papers, vol. 25, p. 534; TJ to JM, 9 June 1793; JM to TJ, 17 June 1793; JM to TJ, 30 July 1793, TJ Papers, vol. 26, pp. 241, 303, 586.

115 *"patent plow"*: JM to TJ, 30 July 1793, TJ Papers, vol. 26, p. 586.

115 "an Agrarian people is the best": Aristotle 1992, p. 368.

115 "of all the occupations": Cicero, *De Officiis*, Book 1:42.

115 French republican calendar: Schama 1989, pp. 768–74.

115 Republics and virtue: Wood 1987, pp. 65–70; McCoy 1980, pp. 69–75.

115 "Only a virtuous people": BF to the Abbés Chalut and Arnoux, 17 April 1787, BF online.

115 "whether there is public Virtue enough": JA to Mercy Warren, 8 January 1776, Adams 1917, vol. 1, p. 202.

116 public virtue and private virtue: JA to Mercy Warren, 16 April 1776. JA wrote that "Public Virtue cannot exist in a Nation without Private." (Adams 1917, vol. 1, p. 222.)

116 "Cultivators of the earth": TJ to John Jay, 23 August 1785, TJ Papers, vol. 8, p. 426.

116 BF and independent farmers: BF, "The Interest of Great Britain Considered, With Regard to her Colonies, And the Acquisitions of Canada and Guadaloupe," 1760, BF online.

116 "are less tied": JM to Richard Peters, 22 February 1819, JM Papers RS, vol. 1, p. 423; JA to AA, December 1796, MHS online.

116 farmers "the true representatives": TJ to Arthur Campbell, 1 September 1797, TJ Papers, vol. 29, p. 522.

116 merchants who "have no country": TJ to Horatio Gates Spafford, 17 March 1814, DLC; TJ on ownership of land and morals, see Jefferson 1982, p. 165.

116 "The small landholders": TJ to Madison, 28 October 1785, TJ Papers, vol. 8, p. 682.

116 fifty acres for each free man: TJ's draft for the Virginia Constitution, before 13 June 1776 (all three drafts include this provision), TJ Papers, vol. 1, pp. 337ff.

116 "the more free": JM, "Republican Distribution of Citizens," *National Gazette*, 2 March 1792.

116 Legal base for elevation of agriculture: Constitution of Massachusetts, Chapter V, Section II, 1779.

117 duty "To promote the Progress": Constitution of the United States, Article 1, Section 8; today "Useful Arts" is often interpreted as relating to crafts and manufacture but in the eighteenth century, agriculture was regarded as the most important; see for example JM to John S. Skinner, 14 April 1829,

Mattern 1997, p. 12; BF draft reply written on Marquis de Ponçins to BF, 12 February 1785, BF online.

117 TJ and slavery: TJ to Edward Bancroft, 26 January 1789, TJ Papers, vol. 14, p. 492; TJ to William Short, 9 April 1788, TJ Papers, vol. 13, p. 48; GW Will, 9 July 1799, GW Papers RS, vol. 4, p. 480.

117 "as simple as those of a common farmer": TJ to JM, 6 March 1796, TJ Papers, vol. 29, p. 6.

117 "Earth is grateful": JA to TJ, 21 November 1794, TJ Papers, vol. 28, p. 208.

117 "slow and sure": TJ to GW, 14 May 1794, TJ Papers, vol. 28, p. 75.

117 "patriotic individuals": JM to George William Featherstonhaugh, June 1820, DLC.

117 "worshippers of Ceres": JM to James Monroe, 29 October 1793, JM Papers, vol. 15, p. 132.

117 founding fathers and agricultural exchanges: GW to TJ, 13 May 1793; JM to TJ, 19 June 1793; JM to TJ, 23 March 1795; TJ to JA, 27 May 1795, TJ Papers, vol. 26, pp. 28, 323–24; vol. 28, pp. 315–18, 363; GW to JM, 8 February 1794, JM Papers, vol. 15, p. 253; Timothy Pinckney to JA, 6 August 1796, MHS AP reel 382; JM and wheat and beans: JM recalls this in 1824: JM to David Gelston, 11 September 1824, DLC; JA and wheat to Academy, Manasseh Cutler to JA, 5 February 1794, MHS AP reel 377. Adams had been elected president of the American Academy of Arts and Sciences in 1791. (AFC, vol. 9, p. 390.) JA and GW and vineyard: Peter Legaux to JA, 15 May 1794, NA Record Group 46. Washington had visited Legaux during the Constitutional Convention: Peter Legaux to GW, 26 January 1791, GW Papers PS, vol. 7, p. 288. TJ "delighted" by Indian corn: JM to James Monroe, 29 October 1793, JM Papers, vol. 15, p. 132. TJ as GW's courier: GW to William Pearce, 6 January 1794, Conway 1889, p. 30.

118 "where it forms a": JM to TJ, 1 July 1791, TJ Papers, vol. 20, p. 593.

118 "as one of the greatest": TJ to GW, 12 September 1795, TJ Papers, vol. 28, p. 464; TJ to David Bailie Warden, 8 July 1811, TJ Papers RS, vol. 4, p. 33.

118 agricultural books: LibraryThing: Thomas Jefferson's Library (online), John Adams's Library (online); George Washington's Library (online); James Madison's Library (online).

118 TJ and Miller's *Dictionary*: William Strickland to TJ, 20 May 1796, TJ Papers, vol. 29, p. 103; TJ to JM, 5 February 1795, TJ Papers, vol. 28, p. 259.

118 GW and agricultural books: Prussing 1927, p. 429.

118 founding fathers and Bordley's *Sketches on Rotations of Crops*: JM's copy: JM to TJ, 23 March 1795, TJ Papers, vol. 28, p. 315. TJ's copy: TJ, 1783 Book Catalogue, MHS, LibraryThing: Thomas Jefferson's Library (online). GW's copy: LibraryThing: George Washington's Library (online). JA's copy: JA owned a later publication by Bordley called *Essays and Notes on Husbandry and Rural Affairs*, LibraryThing: John Adams's Library (online).

118 GW's sixteen-sided barn: Fusonie and Fusonie 1998, pp. 19–24.

118 GW and TJ inspected threshing machine: GW to TJ, 21 August 1791, TJ Papers, vol. 22, p. 57.

118 "I expect every day": TJ to JM, 19 May 1793, TJ Papers, vol. 26, p. 62. Following quotes: TJ to JM, 9 June 1793, TJ Papers, vol. 26, p. 241; TJ to JM, 1 September 1793, TJ Papers, vol. 27, p. 7.

118 "great success": TJ to William Booker, 4 October 1796; see also TJ to Thomas Mann Randolph, 19 August 1796, TJ Papers, vol. 29, pp. 170, 187.

119 "mould-board of least resistance": TJ to John Sinclair, 23 March 1798, TJ Papers, vol. 30, p. 202; TJ started using his moldboard in 1794.

119 plough "what the wand is to the sorcerer": TJ to Charles Willson Peale, 17 April 1813, Betts 1944, p. 509.

119 TJ and gold medal: TJ to M. Silvestre, 29 May 1807; TJ to Charles Willson Peale, 13 June 1815, Betts 1944, pp. 332, 545.

119 TJ drawing plough: TJ to John Sinclair, 23 March 1798, TJ Papers, vol. 30, p. 199.

119 "report on manures": JA Diary, 3 August 1796, 46:48, MHS online. This was Robert Somerville's *Outlines of the Fifteenth Chapter of the Proposed General Report from the Board of Agriculture, on the Subject of Manures, 1795.* John Sinclair to TJ, 15 July 1795 (TJ received it in May 1796), TJ Papers, vol. 28, p. 409; John Sinclair to JA, 18 July 1795, MHS AP reel 380; John Sinclair to GW, 18 July 1795, DLC; GW to JM, 6 December 1795, JM Papers, vol. 16, p. 140.

119 JA and manures: JA, "Recipe to make Manure," JA Diary, 25 June 1771, 18:9; 8 August 1771, 16:55–56 MHS online. JA and manure in 1796: see JA Diary for summer 1796, which is filled with comments on manure. JA's letters to Abigail also often included instructions regarding manuring the fields: JA to AA, 3 April 1794, 2 December 1794, 20 January 1796, 9 March 1796, MHS online; see also JA to Benjamin Waterhouse, 4 September 1805, MHS, Adams-Waterhouse Collection.

119 "carefully examined" and following quote: JA Diary, 8 July 1786, 44:15, MHS online.

119 JM calculating manure: JM to JM Sr., 17 January, 13 March 1796, JM Papers, vol. 16, pp. 192, 266.

120 GW's stercorary: GW to George Augustine Washington, 24 July 1787, GW Papers CS, vol. 5, p. 270.

120 "Nothing, is more wanting": GW to TJ, 24 April 1794, TJ Papers, vol. 28, p. 56.

120 "charming treatise": TJ to William Strickland, 23 March 1798, TJ Papers, vol. 30, p. 211.

120 Sinclair and pamphlet: John Sinclair to TJ, 15 July 1795 (TJ received it in May 1796), TJ Papers, vol. 28, p. 409; John Sinclair to JA, 18 July 1795, MHS AP reel 380; GW to JM, 6 December 1795, JM Papers, vol. 16, p. 140; John Sinclair to TJ, 28 May 1796, TJ Papers, vol. 29, p. 114; GW to John Sinclair, 12 June 1796, GWW, vol. 35, pp. 92–93; John Sinclair to TJ, 10 September 1796, TJ Papers, vol. 29, p. 183; John Sinclair to GW, 10 September 1796, DLC; John Sinclair to JA, 10 September 1796, MHS AP reel 382.

120 JA, TJ and European scientific societies: JA to Timothy Pickering, 4 September 1797, AP reel 114; John Sinclair to TJ, 21 June 1797, TJ Papers, vol.

29, pp. 449–50; TJ to John Sinclair, 23 March 1798, TJ Papers, vol. 30, pp. 197–98.

120 "the profit of every Farm": GW to George Augustine Washington, 31 March 1789, GW Papers PS, vol. 1, p. 472.

120 "in each and every Colony": JA Autobiography, pt. 1, 21 March 1776, MHS online; see also JA to Benjamin Waterhouse, 7 August 1805, Ford 1927, pp. 24–25.

121 "the last I shall ever address" and following quote: GW to AH, 2 November 1796, AH Papers, vol. 20, p. 364.

121 "Agriculture is of primary importance": GW, Eighth Annual Address to Congress, December 7, 1796, GWW, vol. 35, p. 315. For GW on importance of agriculture for the American nation, see also GW to Samuel Chamberline, 3 April 1788, GW Papers CS, vol. 6, p. 190.

121 "I am sorry to": GW to John Sinclair, 6 March 1797, GW Papers RS, vol. 1, p. 14.

121 JM and Board of Agriculture: Isaac Briggs to JM, 1 January 1803; Samuel Latham Mitchill to JM, 10 January 1803, JM to Isaac Briggs, 11 January 1803, JM Papers SS, vol. 4, pp. 232–33, 247–49; *National Intelligencer,* 25 February 1803; Isaac Briggs, *Journal of the American Board of Agriculture,* 22 February 1803, DLC; True 1969, p. 24.

121 "Of all the Summers in my Life": JA Diary, 4 August 1796, 46:48, MHS online.

121 GW's Farewell Address published: Freeman 1948–57, vol. 7, pp. 402–3; and following quotes, Claypoole's *American Daily Advertiser,* 19 September 1796.

121 "a signal, like dropping a hat": Fisher Ames to Oliver Wolcott, 26 September 1796, Allen 1983, vol. 2, p. 1192.

121 "mutually accuse each other": Rochefoulcauld-Liancourt, June 1796, Peterson 1993, p. 31.

122 "advocate for hereditary": AA to Thomas Boylston Adams, 8 November 1796, MHS AP reel 382.

122 "enemity . . . to Banks": JM to TJ, 5 December 1796, TJ Papers, vol. 29, p. 214.

122 JM informs TJ on elections: JM to TJ, 5, 10 December 1796, TJ Papers, vol. 29, pp. 214, 218. For TJ's reply, see TJ to JM, 17 December 1796, TJ Papers, vol. 29, p. 223.

122 "then for Frugality": JA to AA, 7 December 1796, MHS online.

122 election results: Morton Smith 1995, vol. 2, p. 944.

122 JA announced result: Smith 1962, vol. 2, p. 914.

122 "no ambition to" and following quote: TJ to Edward Rutledge, 27 December 1796, TJ Papers, vol. 29, p. 232. The correct quote would have been "flumina amem silvasque inglorius" ("may I love the rivers and the woods, though fame be lost") from Virgil, *Georgics,* 2.486.

122 "the most flattering incident": TJ to APS, 28 January 1797, TJ Papers, vol. 29, p. 279. For TJ's apparent reluctance to become president of the United States, see for example TJ to Edward Rutledge, 27 December 1796, TJ Papers, vol. 29, p. 232: "My name however was again brought forward, without concert or expectation on my part."

123 "Seemed to . . . enjoy a Tryumph": JA to AA, 5 March 1797, MHS online.
123 JM's retirement: Smith Morton 1995, vol. 2, p. 947.
123 "the Mode of becoming great": JA to AA, 14 January 1797, MHS online.

6 "CITY OF MAGNIFICENT INTENTIONS":
THE CREATION OF WASHINGTON, D.C.,
AND THE WHITE HOUSE

124 description of Washington, D.C.: John Davis, 1798–1802; John Cotton
     Smith 1800; William Janson 1804; Busey 1898, pp. 131, 230, 235; Com-
     missioners to Mrs. Fenwick, 30 October 1800, NA Record Group 42;
     Christian Hines, 1800, Hines 1981, pp. 20, 43; Young 1966, p. 42. On 15
     May 1800 there were 109 brick houses and 263 wooden houses. By
     November 1801, one year after JA's arrival, only another 82 brick houses
     and 145 wooden houses had been built. (Commissioners to TJ, November
     1801, Padover 1946, pp. 245ff.)
124 "small miserable huts": Oliver Wolcott, 4 July 1800, Wolcott 1846, vol. 2,
     p. 377.
124 "We have the name": James A. Bayard to Andrew Bayard, 8 January 1801,
     Donnan 1913, p. 119.
125 "deep morass": John Cotton Smith, 1800, Busey 1898, p. 230.
125 "is as much a wilderness": William Janson, 1804, Busey 1898, p. 235.
125 crops on Pennsylvania Avenue: David Carroll to Commissioners, 12
     November 1800, NA Record Group 42.
125 "City of Magnificent Distances": Charles Dickens, *American Notes,* quoted
     in Berg 2008, p. 251.
125 naming of White House: Bryan 1932, p. 306.
125 White House at JA's arrival: Latrobe, Drawing of White House. Principal
     story, 1803, DLC; AA to AA2, 21, 27 November 1800, Adams 1848,
     pp. 383–84; see also Seale 1992, p. 34, Seale 1986, Seale 1992, Seale 2000.
125 "our Presidents as very unfortunate men": Oliver Wolcott, 4 July 1800,
     Wolcott 1846, vol. 2, p. 377.
126 "May none but honest": JA to AA, 2 November 1800, MHS online.
126 "Yours, Yours, Yours": JA to AA, 12 February 1780, MHS online.
126 "I am with tenderness": JA to AA, 28 November 1798, MHS online.
126 "He is made of the oak": AA to Mary Smith Cranch, 8 June 1798, Mitchell
     1947, p. 190.
126 "habitable": JA to AA, 2 November 1800, MHS online. For Abigail's wor-
     ries about the White House, see AA to William Cranch, 3 February 1800,
     MHS AP reel 397; AA to Anna Greenleaf Cranch, 17 April 1800, DLC.
126 grounds of White House: Oliver Wolcott, 4 July 1800, Wolcott 1846, vol.
     2, p. 377; Latrobe, Report on the Public Buildings, 11 December 1809, Van
     Horne 1984–88, vol. 2, pp. 797–98; AA to AA2, 21 November 1800,
     Adams 1848, p. 383.
126 carpenters' sheds at White House: Petition of Carpenters to Commission-
     ers, 21 October 1800; Proceedings of Commissioners, 29 October 1800,
     NA Record Group 42.

126 "This place . . . known" and AA's impressions: AA to Mary Smith Cranch, 21 November 1800, Mitchell 1947, p. 257.

126 "mere swamp": Sir Augustus John Foster, 1805–07, Davis 1954, p. 7.

127 accommodation in Washington: James A. Bayard, 3 January 1801, Donnan 1913, p. 117; Brown 1975, p. 198; Oliver Wolcott, 4 July 1800, Wolcott 1846, vol. 2, p. 377; Everly and Wehman 2005, pp. 66–67; Abraham Bradley to Robert Patten, 2 June 1800, Busey 1898, p. 66.

127 problems with public buildings: Scott 2000, p. 72; Commissioners to John Marshall, 13 January 1801; Commissioners to Speaker of House of Representatives, 20 January 1801, NA Record Group 42.

127 "might be difficult to reach": Thomas Claxton to Commissioners, 8 November 1800, NA Record Group 42.

127 "two of the most irritating questions": TJ to James Monroe, 20 June 1790, TJ Papers, vol. 16, p. 536.

127 JM and location of capital: JM, Debate of Location of the Capital, 4 September 1789, JM Papers, vol. 12, pp. 377–81.

127 "We pity the poor congress-men": *New York Advertiser*, 27 January 1791, Young 1966, p. 13.

128 "more in danger": GW to de la Luzerne, 10 August 1790, GW Papers PS, vol. 6, p. 229.

128 Assumption Plan exacerbated divide: See Ellis 2002, pp. 57ff; Elkins and McKitrick 1993, pp. 114–23.

128 "Big Knife": Richard Peters to TJ, 20 June 1790, TJ Papers, vol. 16, p. 539.

128 "a mutual sacrifice": TJ to Thomas Mann Randolph, 20 June 1790, TJ Papers, vol. 16, p. 540.

128 "the pill would be" and description of dinner: TJ, c. 1792, Jefferson's Account of the Bargain on the Assumption and Residence Bills, TJ Papers, vol. 17, p. 207.

128 Dinner Table Bargain: Ellis, 2002, pp. 48–50.

128 TJ and JM on assessment mission: They were in Georgetown from 13 to 14 September 1790, and then went to Mount Vernon to discuss the federal city with Washington. (TJ Memorandum to GW, 14 September 1790; TJ to GW, 17 September 1790, GW Papers PS, vol. 6, pp. 434–37, 463.)

129 TJ's and JM's memorandums: TJ Memorandum to GW, 29 August 1790; JM Memorandum to GW, 29 August 1790, GW Papers PS, vol. 6, pp. 368–72.

129 TJ's and JM on cities and merchants: TJ said that merchants were "the least virtuous and possess the least of the amor patriae [patriotism]." JM agreed and argued that "most of our political evils may be traced up to our commercial ones" and talked of the "vice of overgrown cities." Great cities bred the worst in people, TJ believed; "the mobs of great cities add just as much to the support of pure government as sores do to the strength of the human body." (TJ to Jean Nicolas Démeunier, 24 January 1786, TJ Papers, vol. 10, p. 16; JM to TJ, 18 March 1786, TJ Papers, vol. 9, p. 334; JM, "Republican Distribution of Citizens," *National Gazette*, 2 March 1792; TJ to JM, 20 December 1787, TJ Papers, vol. 12, p. 442; Jefferson 1982, p. 165.)

129 Federalists "all live in cities": TJ's Notes on the Letter of Christoph Daniel Ebeling, after October 1795, TJ Papers, vol. 28, p. 509.

129 TJ's ideas for the capital: TJ, Draft of Agenda for the Seat of Government, TJ Papers, vol. 17, pp. 460–66; TJ Memorandum to GW, 29 August 1790, GW Papers PS, vol. 6, pp. 368–69; TJ Memorandum to GW, 14 September 1790 (with sketch), GW Papers PS, vol. 6, pp. 434–37; TJ, Plan of the Federal District, 1791, DLC.

129 "public walks": TJ, Draft of Agenda for the Seat of Government, TJ Papers, vol. 17, pp. 460–61.

131 "A government continually at a distance": AH, *The Federalist Papers,* no. 27, Wills 1982, p. 132.

131 L'Enfant and capital: Harris 1999, pp. 529ff.; Berg 2008.

131 "tiresome and insipide": Memorandum of L'Enfant, 26 March 1791, GW Papers PS, vol. 8, p. 9.

131 "enlarged plan": GW to TJ, 31 March 1791, TJ Papers, vol. 20, p. 82.

131 L'Enfant's 5,000 acres: GW to TJ, 31 March 1791, TJ Papers, vol. 20, p. 82.

131 L'Enfant's unwieldy plan of the capital: TJ to JM, 26 August 1791, TJ Papers, vol. 22, p. 77.

131 "Hobby-horsical federal City": Nathanial Hazard to JA, 29–31 January 1792, MHS AP reel 375.

131 "too large a scale": David Stuart to GW, 26 February 1792, GW Papers PS, vol. 9, p. 600.

131 "shou'd look beyond": GW to David Stuart, 8 March 1792, GW Papers PS, vol. 10, p. 63.

131 "the trans-Alleghenians with the Atlantic states": JA recalling a conversation with GW, JA to Benjamin Rush, 28 December 1807, Schutz and Adair 2001, p. 109.

131 L'Enfant's plan infused with political ideology: Scott 1991, pp. 37ff.

132 "grand fountains" and following references: L'Enfant, Plan of the City of Washington in the Territory of Columbia, 1791, Observations Explanatory of the Plan, DLC; L'Enfant to GW, 22 June 1791, GW Papers PS, vol. 8, p. 291.

132 "a pedestal waiting" and following quote: L'Enfant to GW, 22 June 1791, GW Papers PS, vol. 8, p. 290.

132 "the most advantageous": L'Enfant, Plan of the City of Washington in the Territory of Columbia, 1791, Observations Explanatory of the Plan, DLC.

132 L'Enfant and the picturesque: Dougherty 1974.

133 "waves of a tempestuous": L'Enfant to TJ, 11 March 1791, TJ Papers, vol. 20, p. 77.

133 "nature had done": William Loughton Smith, 22 April 1791, quoting L'Enfant after a visit to the site of the federal city (Smith Loughton, 1917, p. 62).

133 "sumptuousness of a palace": L'Enfant to GW, 22 June 1791, GW Papers PS, vol. 8, p. 290.

133 L'Enfant's plans for President's House: Seale 1986, vol. 1, p. 18; Seale 1992, p. 2.

133 "upon a scale far superior": TJ and GW, Agenda for Commissioners of the Federal District, c. 5 March 1792. The part about the size of the Capitol and the White House was written by GW, TJ Papers, vol. 23, p. 195.

133 TJ admiring Palladio: Palladio's architectural books were Jefferson's "bible," a friend said. (Isaac Coles to John Hartwell Cocke, 1816, quoted in Howard 2003, p. 85.)

133 TJ trying to steer GW to smaller design: Harris 1999, p. 529; TJ, Draft of Agenda for the Seat of Government, TJ Papers, vol. 17, pp. 460–61; TJ Memorandum to GW, 29 August 1790, GW Papers PS, vol. 6, pp. 368–69; TJ Memorandum to GW, 14 September 1790 (with sketch), GW Papers PS, vol. 6, pp. 434–37; TJ, Plan of the Federal District, 1791, DLC.

133 "I do not conceive": GW to L'Enfant, 4 April 1791, GW Papers PS, vol. 8, p. 62.

133 L'Enfant and Carroll's house: Commissioners to GW, 25 November 1791; Commissioners to L'Enfant, 25 November 1791, NA Record Group 42; for L'Enfant's downfall and Carroll's house see Berg 2008, pp. 139–60.

134 "there is as yet no such thing": TJ to GW, 11 December 1791, Enclosure: Observations on L'Enfant's Letter to GW, 7 December 1791, TJ Papers, vol. 22, p. 391.

134 TJ and L'Enfant's end of services: TJ to L'Enfant, 27 February 1792, TJ Papers, vol. 23, p. 161.

134 "astonishes me beyond measure": GW to TJ, 18 January 1792, TJ Papers, vol. 23, p. 51.

134 L'Enfant and Paterson: Berg 2008, pp. 198–99, 208–9.

134 TJ and architectural competition for President's House: Adams 1976, pp. 238–39; Seale 1992, p. 5; Howard 2006, pp. 82–87. The drawing is held at the Maryland Historical Society (reproduced in Seale 1992, p. 5).

134 TJ's scheming at the Capitol: Harris 2005, pp. 82–83; Harris 1999, pp. 553–56; Harris 2005, pp. 82–83.

134 GW and tomb space: Harris, 1999, p. 556.

135 "of all the errors": TJ to GW, 9 September 1792, TJ Papers, vol. 24, p. 352.

135 "President has much at heart": Alexander White to JM, 26 September 1796, JM Papers, vol. 16, p. 401.

135 visitors' conversations with GW: Latrobe, 16 July 1796, Lee 2006, p. 64.

135 "when friendships are formed" and following quote: GW to AH, 1 September 1796, AH Papers, vol. 20, pp. 311–12.

135 "forrest of the different trees": William Thornton, 1795–97, MS on National Education, Harris 1995, vol. 1, p. 365.

136 "serve as parent-trees": William Thornton to GW, 1 October 1796, Harris 1995, vol. 1, p. 401.

136 flurry of letters: GW to AH, 1 September 1796, AH Papers, vol. 20, p. 311; White to JM, 26 September 1796, JM Papers, vol. 16, pp. 401–2; William Thornton to GW, 1 October 1796, Harris 1995, vol. 1, p. 398; Gustavus Scott and Alexander White to GW, 1 October 1796, NA Record Group 42; GW to Commissioners, 21 October 1796, GWW, vol. 35, pp. 248–50; Alexander White to JM, 2 December 1796, JM Papers, vol. 16, pp. 421–22.

136 "last request of a departing Friend": Alexander White to JM, 26 September 1796, JM Papers, vol. 16, p. 402; for AH's response see AH to GW, 4 September 1796, AH Papers, vol. 20, p. 316.

136 "extremely well calculated": Alexander White to JM, 26 September 1796,

JM Papers, vol. 16, p. 402. Botanic garden a premature idea: see Gustavus Scott and Alexander White to GW, 1 October 1796, NA Record Group 42.

136 "a good appendage": GW to Commissioners, 21 October 1796, GWW, vol. 35, p. 248.

136 botanic garden in Washington: Latrobe, Proposed National University, 1816, DLC; Scott 1991, p. 46; Fallen 2006, pp. 16ff.

136 "I was strenuously opposed": JA to Benjamin Rush, 14 November 1812, Schutz and Adair 2001, p. 275.

136 "Charge as much Ignorance": JA to Benjamin Rush, 25 February 1808, MHS AP reel 118.

136 "you will probably be dragged": Benjamin Rush to JA, 19 March 1789, Butterfield 1951, vol. 1, p. 508.

137 JA on seat of capital: William Maclay, 24 September 1789, Maclay 1890, p. 165; for Congress and JA's salary: JA to Abigail, 28 January 1797, MHS online.

137 "the whole of this Business": JA to Commissioners, 17 April 1797, DLC.

137 "The Importance of the City to the Union": JA to Tristram Dalton, 1 July 1797, MHS AP reel 117.

137 "Beds of Roses": JA to AA, 27 March 1797, MHS online.

137 JA looking at the map of Washington: Alexander White to William Thornton and Gustavus Scott, 11 February 1798; William Thornton to JA, 19 February 1798, Harris 1995, vol. 1, p. 437.

137 "Situation of the United States": JA to Tristram Dalton, 1 July 1797, MHS AP reel 117.

137 unfinished White House in 1797: Seale 1986, vol. 1, p. 73.

138 "wherever you can find it": JA to Commissioners, 5 December 1797, MHS AP reel 117; shortage of funds, see Commissioners to JA, 10 October, 3 and 25 November 1797, NA Record Group 42.

138 "make himself a Slave": White about JA, Alexander White to GW, 20 February 1798, GW Papers RS, vol. 2, p. 96.

138 "clashing interests": Alexander White to Commissioners, 3 March 1798, Harris 1995, vol. 1, p. 440.

138 JA about renting a simple house: Ibid.

138 White complains to GW: Alexander White to GW, 10 March 1798, GW Papers RS, vol. 2, pp. 134ff.

138 rumors about JA and capital: TJ to JM, 29 March 1798, TJ Papers, vol. 30, p. 228.

139 "the late President always": Commissioners to JA, 18 April 1798, NA Record Group 42.

139 "nothing short of insanity": GW to Alexander White, 25 March 1798, GW Papers RS, vol. 2, p. 159. For JA being overruled by Commissioners, see Alexander White to Commissioners, 11 March 1798, Harris 1995, vol. 1, p. 443; Commissioners to JA, 18 April 1798, NA Record Group 42.

139 "I may have been inclined to an opinion": JA to Commissioners, 10 May 1798, MHS AP reel 117; see also Commissioners to JA, 7 May 1798, NA Record Group 42.

139 problems in Washington and agricultural squatters: Commissioners to Mrs.

Young, 24 July 1799; Commissioners to Mrs. Burnes, 24 July 1799, NA Record Group 42.

139 "to be cut down" and description of GW's death: Tobias Lear, *The Last Illness and Death of General Washington,* 14 December 1799, GW Papers RS, vol. 4, pp. 547–49.

139 "Have me decently buried": Ibid., p. 551.

139 GW's last correspondence: GW to Alexander White, 8 December 1799; GW to William Thornton, 7, 8 December 1799; GW to James Anderson, 13 December 1799; "Washington's Plans for His River, Union and Muddy Hole Farms," 10 December 1799, GW Papers RS, vol. 4, pp. 445–46, 449–51, 455–77.

140 JA's attention to capital and garden at White House: Benjamin Stoddert to Commissioners, 2 January 1800, NA Record Group 42.

140 "make it an agreeable place" Benjamin Stoddert to William Thornton, 20 January 1800, Harris 1995, vol. 1, p. 532 (Stoddert recalled a conversation with JA).

140 Thornton as gardener: Thornton and Washington had often shared their adoration for gardens and exchanged seeds and plants. Thornton did often collect plants on his rides across the district and grafted his own trees, GW to Thornton, 7 October 1797, GW Papers RS, vol. 1, p. 387; GW to Thornton, 14 March 1799, GW Papers RS, vol. 3, p. 419; Anna Thornton, 2 May 1800, Thornton 1907, p. 137.

140 "large, naked, ugly" and Bingham garden: Benjamin Stoddert to William Thornton, 20 January 1800, Harris 1995, vol. 1, p. 532.

140 JA's rooms opposite the Bingham house: Samuel A. Otis to JA, 28 October 1794, MHS AP reel 378. Adams quickly decided that he did not like the rooms and moved again, JA to AA, 9 November 1794, MHS online.

140 Bingham garden: Simpson 1859, p. 88; see also Julian Ursin Niemcewicz, 22 January 1797, Budka 1965, p. 37; Henry Wansey, 8 June 1794, Wansey 1798, p. 123.

140 AA sent greenhouse: AA to JA, 12 January 1799, MHS online.

140 gardening as "Medicine" : JA to AA, 13 March 1797, MHS online.

140 Thornton and garden at the White House: William Thornton to Benjamin Stoddert, 30 January 1800, Harris 1995, vol. 1, p. 533; see William Thornton, sketch of President's House and executive offices, DLC.

140 "in great confusion": Anna Thornton, 20 March 1800, Thornton 1907, pp. 119–20.

140 funds very low: Anna Thornton, 30 January 1800, Thornton 1907, p. 101.

141 "it will not be done": Anna Thornton, 20 March 1800, Thornton 1907, p. 120.

141 "much more difficulty and expense" and following quote: William Thornton and Gustavus Scott to Benjamin Stoddert, 19 April 1800, NA Record Group 42. For Thornton's persistence, see Anna Thornton, 25 April 1800, Thornton 1907, p. 134.

141 "too extravagant a scale": William Thornton to Benjamin Stoddert, 30 January 1800, Harris 1995, vol. 1, p. 533.

141 continuous problems at the White House: Commissioners to Benjamin

Stoddert, 9 April 1800, Commissioners to Denis Littleton, 15 April 1800, Commissioners to Harbaugh, Lennox & Bryan, 9 May 1800, NA Record Group 42; Seale 1986, vol. 1, p. 76.

141 AA was "discouraged": AA to William Cranch, 3 February 1800, MHS AP reel 397; see also AA to Anna Greenleaf Cranch, 17 April 1800, DLC.

141 JA liked the capital "very well": JA to AA, 13 June 1800, MHS online.

141 AA's reluctance: AA to Catherine Johnson, 20 August 1800, MHS AP reel 398.

142 "Huge Castle": AA to Thomas Boylston Adams, 25 December 1800, MHS AP reel 399.

142 White House bell hanger: Commissioners to William Smith Shaw, 7 November 1800, NA Record Group 42.

142 East Room to dry laundry: AA to AA2, 21 November 1800, Adams 1848, p. 383.

142 "because people cannot be found": AA to AA2, 21 November 1800, Adams 1848, p. 382.

142 "disgusting egotism" and following quotes: Hamilton 1800, pp. 12, 9, 38.

142 "would prefer Mr. J.": JA to AA, 15 November 1800, MHS online.

142 "that I am disgusted": AA to Mary Smith Cranch, 26 May 1800, Mitchell 1947, p. 253.

142 "hideous hermaphroditical character": James Thomson Callendar in *The Prospect Before Us*, Bordewich 2008, p. 249; see also McCullough 2001, pp. 536–37, 544.

143 "An infant city grows apace": Freneau, Philip, *On the Federal City*, 1797, Pattee 1907, vol. 3, pp. 184–85.

143 election results: Larson 2007, pp. 241–44.

143 "The only Question": JA to Cotton Tufts, 26 December 1800, MHS AP reel 120.

143 "farmer John": JA to William Tudor, 20 January 1801, MHS, Tudor Papers.

143 "potter in my garden": JA to Cotton Tufts, 26 December 1800, MHS AP reel 120.

143 "blackest calumny" and following quote: AA to TJ, 1 July 1804, Cappon 1987, pp. 272–73.

143 "plain citizen": Editorial note to TJ's Inaugural Address, 4 March 1801, TJ Papers, vol. 33, p. 134.

144 "the original simplicity": TJ to Volney, 20 April 1802, DLC.

144 "republican principles": TJ to Maria Jefferson Eppes, 15 February 1801, TJ Papers, vol. 32, p. 593.

144 Inaugural Address: TJ, Inaugural Address, 4 March 1801, TJ Papers, vol. 33, pp. 148–52; Ellis 1998, pp. 214–21.

144 TJ intended to slice expenditures: TJ to Nathaniel Macon, 14 May 1801, TJ Papers, vol. 34, p. 110.

144 "a plan much too magnificent": John Williams, quoted in Morales-Vasquez 2004, p. 42.

144 "fall into a pit": Young 1966, p. 46.

144 "numerous dead carcasses": Albert Gallatin, quoted in Young 1966, p. 42.

144 fence around the WH and TJ's laundry: Latrobe, Drawing of White House. Principal Story, 1803, DLC; Walter Muir Whitehill, 1803, Froncek 1977, p. 85.

144 TJ and lists: TJ Memorandum Book; Betts 1944, p. 4; Cullen 2005, p. 313; TJ, A Statement of the Vegetable market of Washington, during a period of 8. years, wherein the earliest & latest appearance of each article within the whole 8. Years is noted, reproduced in Randall 1858, vol. 1, plate facing p. 44.

145 "there is not a sprig": TJ to Martha Jefferson Randolph, 23 December 1790, Betts and Bear 1986, p. 67.

145 "added wonderfully to": TJ to John Barnes, 27 April 1809, TJ Papers RS, vol. 1, p. 166.

145 "but a corner of the mansion": Moore, Thomas, 1804, quoted in Norton 1976, p. 211; see also TJ to Martha Jefferson Randolph, 28 May 1801, Betts and Bear 1986, p. 202.

145 "under the tent of heaven": TJ to Benjamin Hawkins, 22 March 1796, TJ Papers, vol. 29, p. 43.

145 TJ and invisible government: Margaret Bayard Smith, in Hunt 1906, p. 397.

145 "Avoid palaces": William Thornton, 1795–97, MS on National Education, Harris 1995, vol. 1, p. 366.

145 reduction of WH grounds: Sketch Plan for Landscaping the Grounds of the President's House, c. 1807, DLC; Seale 1992, p. 40.

145 GW and TJ as presidents: For a comparison of Washington's and Jefferson's presidencies see McDonald 1994, pp. 252–53.

145 GW's formality: Ellis 2002, p. 127; Seale 1986, vol. 1, p. 8.

146 "Levees are done away": TJ to Nathaniel Macon, 14 May 1801, TJ Papers, vol. 34, p. 110.

146 TJ's dinner parties: Cullen 2005; Margaret Bayard Smith, in Hunt 1906, pp. 50, 387–88; Manasseh Cutler to Dr. Torrey, 4 January 1802, Cutler 1888, vol. 2, pp. 65–66; JQA, 3 November 1807, Adams 1874–77, vol. 1, p. 473.

146 JA's Levee Room became TJ's study: Latrobe, Drawing of White House. Principal story, 1803, DLC; Inventory of the White House 1801, reprinted in Seale 2000, pp. 30–31.

146 "When brought together in society": TJ, "Rules of Etiquette," November, 1803, Ford 1892–99, vol. 8, p. 276.

146 "show . . . that the civil is superior": Margaret Bayard Smith, in Hunt 1906, p. 397.

146 "without any tincture": Samuel Latham Mitchell, 10 January 1802, Mitchell 1879, p. 743.

146 portraits of TJ and GW: Rembrandt Peale's portrait of Thomas Jefferson, 1805, and Gilbert Stuart's portrait of George Washington, 1797.

146 TJ's "neglected" hair: Sir Augustus John Foster, 1805–07, Davis 1954, p. 10.

146 TJ's "dissheiveled" hair: William Plumer, 29 July 1805, Brown 1923, p. 333.

146 "down at the heel": Sir Augustus John Foster, 1805–07, Davis 1954, p. 10.

146 "with his toes out" and following quotes: William Plumer, 29 July 1805, 10 November 1804, Brown 1923, pp. 193, 333.

146 "a tall large-boned farmer": Sir Augustus John Foster, 1805–07, Davis 1954, p. 10.

146 Washington as a rural retreat and following descriptions: TJ to St. George Tucker, 3 June 1801, TJ Papers, vol. 34, pp. 245–46; William Janson, 1804, Busey 1898, p. 235.

147 "Excellent snipe shooting" and following quote: Sir Augustus John Foster, 1805–07, Davis 1954, pp. 8, 20.

147 Mall, wetlands and fishing: William Gunton, 1807, Busey 1898, p. 237.

147 TJ's study at the White House: Margaret Bayard Smith, in Hunt 1906, p. 385.

147 "delight to attend" and following quotes: Margaret Bayard Smith, in Hunt 1906, p. 385; see also TJ to Martha Jefferson Randolph, 23 November 1807, TJ to Ellen Wayles Randolph, 23 February 1808, Betts and Bear 1986, pp. 315, 329.

147 TJ's correspondence: Ellis 1998, p. 228.

147 TJ's rides in the countryside: Christian Hines, 1801–09, Hines 1981, p. 13; also Margaret Bayard Smith, in Hunt 1906, p. 393; Daniel Brent to TJ, 26 June 1802, Padover 1946, p. 275.

147 "rural improvements": Margaret Bayard Smith, in Hunt 1906, p. 395.

147 "Not a plant from the lowliest weed": Ibid., p. 393.

148 trees for ornamental purposes: TJ, 12 October 1803, recollecting the chronology of the building of the capital, Padover 1946, p. 323.

148 TJ's suggestion to plant trees: TJ to Thomas Johnson, 8 March 1792, TJ Papers, vol. 23, p. 237.

148 "cutting wood of any description": Commissioners to Theophilus Holt, 30 October 1798, NA Record Group 42; for felling of trees see also Christian Hines, 1796–97, Hines 1981, p. 11; Warden 1816, Busey 1898, p. 132. In May 1802, a year after Jefferson's inauguration, the commissioners sent someone to mark the trees that "as yet are left" on the President's Square— "2 wild cherry Trees, 2 Walnut Trees, 2 Buttonwood Trees & some black Gum Tree" was the meager spoil. (Commissioners to Mrs. Burnes, 19 and 20 May 1802, NA Record Group 42.)

148 "ornamented Trees": Commissioners to Daniel Carroll, 21 June 1793, NA Record Group 42.

148 trees continued to disappear: Augustus John Foster to Lady Elizabeth Foster, 8/15 February 1805, Parr 2000, p. 82; Commissioners to Leonard Harbaugh, 31 July 1800; Commissioners to Mrs. Burnes, 19 May 1802; Commissioners to Mrs. Burnes, 20 May 1802, NA Record Group 42.

148 tulip poplars "girdled": Margaret Bayard Smith, in Hunt 1906, p. 11.

148 Thornton and trees: William Thornton to GW, 1 October 1796, Harris 1995, vol. 1, p. 401.

148 "spite to them who cherished": Lord Francis Jeffrey, Journal from his Visit to the United States, 1813, copies at the Office of the Curator, White House (original in the National Library of Scotland).

148 "a crime little short of murder" and following quote: Margaret Bayard Smith, in Hunt 1906, pp. 11–12.

148 TJ's work on the roads: Commissioners to TJ, 24 August 1801; TJ to Commissioners, 29 August 1801; Commissioners to TJ, 15 October 1801, TJ Papers, vol. 35, pp. 131, 167–68, 450.

148 trees at Pennsylvania Avenue: Thomas Munroe to TJ, 14 March 1803; TJ to Thomas Munroe, 21 March 1803, Padover 1946, pp. 297–300; Christian Hines, 1803, Hines 1981, p. 21; Margaret Bayard Smith, in Hunt 1906, p. 394; TJ to Thomas Munroe, 21 March 1803; Padover 1946, p. 300.

148 Lombardy poplars: Scott 2006, p. 22; Hunt 1906, p. 394; TJ to Thomas Munroe, 17 June 1807, Padover 1946, p. 393.

149 vegetable market in Washington: TJ Proclamation, 1802, Padover 1946, p. 283.

149 TJ and seeds in Washington and following references: Margaret Bayard Smith, in Hunt 1906, p. 394; see also Nicholas King to TJ, 11 September 1806, Betts 1944, p. 325; TJ to Robert Bailey, 10 October 1803; TJ to Bernard McMahon, 8 January 1809, Betts 1944, pp. 287, 401; TJ to William Johnson, 17 March 1810, TJ Papers RS, vol. 2, pp. 301–2.

149 "This . . . was the means" and following quote: Margaret Bayard Smith, in Hunt 1906, p. 394.

149 plants for Monticello: TJ to Robert Bailey, 19 October 1803; John Threlkeld to TJ, 25 March 1807, Betts 1944, pp. 287, 353; TJ, 11 February 1794; TJ to Mrs Bailey, 7 March 1805; TJ, 2 March 1808; TJ Memorandum Book, vol. 2, pp. 913, 1147, 1220; TJ to Martha Jefferson Randolph, 23 November 1807, Betts and Bear 1986, p. 315.

149 funds for roads and Capitol: Latrobe to TJ, 20 February 1804, Padover 1946, p. 338.

149 building work on White House: Latrobe to TJ, 1 December 1804, Padover 1946, pp. 347–50; Latrobe, Report on the Public Buildings, 11 December 1809, Latrobe to Stephen Row Bradley, c. 13–21 December 1808, Van Horne 1984–88, vol. 2, pp. 686–87, 797–98. The wings were built between 1805 and 1811 but never connected to the Treasury and War Department. (Seale 1992, p. 47; Seale 1986, vol. 1, pp. 109ff.)

150 "often threaten[ing] your": Charles Janson, 1806, Reps 1991, p. 64.

150 travelers at the center of D.C.: John Melish, 3 October 1806, Busey 1898, p. 235.

150 "like glue": Young 1966, p. 44.

150 "either los[ing] one's shoes": Sir Augustus John Foster, 1805–07, Davis 1954, p. 86.

150 congressmen getting lost in Washington: Margaret Bayard Smith, in Hunt 1906, pp. 9–10.

150 "out of sight or hearing": Young 1966, p. 75.

150 TJ and Latrobe discussing the garden: Latrobe to Mary Elizabeth Latrobe, 18 March 1807, Van Horne 1984–88, vol. 2, p. 396.

150 "dressed in black": Sir Augustus John Foster, 1805–07, Davis 1954, p. 15.

150 election results: McDougall 2005, p. 396.

150 TJ decided to retire: TJ to William Hamilton, July 1806, Betts 1944, p. 323.

150 "require but a moderate sum": TJ to Latrobe, 22 May 1807, Van Horne 1984–88, vol. 2, p. 432.

150 enclose grounds at White House: Latrobe to TJ, 17 March 1807, 29 April 1807 (sent on 21 May 1807), 13 August 1807; TJ to Latrobe, 22 May 1807, Van Horne 1984–88, vol. 2, pp. 394–95, 432–33, 461–62; Latrobe to TJ, 2 September 1807, DLC.

151 "for the use of the Pts House": Joseph Elgar to JQA, 30 July 1825, NA Record Group 42.

151 "exclusively with Trees . . . indigenous" and following quote: Margaret Bayard Smith, in Hunt 1906, p. 393.

151 "Large trees for Single trees": List of Trees & Shrubs for the Presidents Garden, 31 March 1809, JM Papers PS, vol. 1. pp. 93–94.

151 levelling and walls: TJ to Latrobe, 22 May 1807, 25 April 1808, Van Horne 1984–88, vol. 2, pp. 432, 612. There are many letters between TJ and Latrobe regarding the walls. The wall was completed (except the coping) at the end of 1808. (Latrobe to TJ, 18 November 1808.) For work done during TJ's presidency: Latrobe to Stephen Row Bradley, c. 13–21 December 1808; Latrobe, Report on the Public Buildings, 11 December 1809, Van Horne 1984–88, vol. 2, pp. 672, 686–87, 797–98.

151 White House garden and JM: Latrobe to JM, 14 March 1809; List of Trees & Shrubs for the Presidents Garden, 31 March 1809, JM Papers PS, vol. 1, pp. 48, 93–94; Joseph Dougherty to TJ, 15 May 1809, TJ Papers RS, vol. 1, p. 199; Latrobe, Report on Public Buildings, 28 December 1810, Van Horne 1984–88, vol. 2, p. 946.

151 "scarcely fit for": William Thornton to Samuel Harrison Smith, 20 April 1808, *Washington Federalist*, 30 April 1808, Van Horne 1984–88, vol. 2, p. 605. See also the drawing of the arch by Baroness Hyde de Neuville from circa 1820 reprinted in Seale 1992, p. 47. Thornton felt no reason to be nice to Latrobe as the two architects were involved in a vicious public row about their architectural merits.

151 TJ's plans for White House garden: Sketch Plan for Landscaping the Grounds of the President's House, c. 1807, DLC; see also matching plan for topography of the grounds Survey Map of the White House Grounds, c. 1807, DLC; Latrobe, View of the East front of the President's House, 1807, and Latrobe, Elevation of the South Front of the President's House, 1807, DLC; Fazio and Snadon 2000, p. 40.

152 Poplar Forest: Work started with brick making in 1805. Brown 1990; McDonald 2006.

152 digging sunken parterre: TJ to Hugh Chisholm, 5 June 1807, Brown 1990, p. 126.

152 planting Poplar Forest: TJ, Notes on Poplar Forest Plantings and Geography, 1811–1816, TJ Papers RS, vol. 3, pp. 353–54; for planned planting at White House see List of Trees & Shrubs for the Presidents Garden, 31 March 1809, JM Papers PS, vol. 1, pp. 93–94.

153 "vermin of all filths": JQA, 12 August 1819, Adams 1874–77, vol. 4, p. 409.

153 carriages stuck in mud: JQA, 4 April 1818, Adams 1874–77, vol. 4, p. 74.

153 "a very agreeable country residence": TJ to Thomas Mann Randolph, 28 May 1801, TJ Papers, vol. 34, p. 257.

7 "EMPIRE OF LIBERTY":
JEFFERSON'S WESTERN EXPANSION

154 Descriptions of the celebrations of Independence Day 1803: Hunt 1906, pp. 38–39; 398–99.

154 "the only birthday": Hunt 1906, p. 398.

154 trees on Pennsylvania Avenue: Thomas Munroe to TJ, 14 March 1803, TJ to Thomas Munroe, 15 March 1803; Padover 1946, pp. 297–300.

155 news of Louisiana Purchase: TJ to Thomas Mann Randolph, 5 July 1803, DLC; for Louisiana Purchase, see McCoy 1989, pp. 196–208.

155 "the most important . . . transaction": Caspar Wistar to TJ, 13 July 1803, Jackson 1978, vol. 1, pp. 108–9.

155 make TJ "immortal": Bayard Smith in Hunt 1906, p. 38.

155 Spain ceded Louisiana territory: The news reached the White House in 1802, Ellis 1998, p. 244.

155 "we must marry ourselves": Jefferson to Robert Livingston, 18 April 1802, Ford 1892–99, vol. 8, p. 145.

155 Monroe as seed courier: TJ to Madame de Tessé, 30 January 1803, Betts 1944, p. 285.

155 Lewis's departure: Lewis to Lucy Marks, 2 July 1803, Jackson 1978, vol. 1, p. 100.

156 "increased infinitely the interest": TJ to Paul Allen, 18 August 1813, Jackson 1978, vol. 2, p. 591.

156 "man of letters" and following quote: Edward Thornton to Lord Hawkesbury, 9 March 1803, Jackson 1978, vol. 1, p. 26.

156 credit note for Lewis: TJ to Lewis, 4 July 1803, Jackson 1978, vol. 1, pp. 105–6.

156 cipher and instructions for Lewis: Cipher for Correspondence with Jefferson, 1803, Jefferson's Instructions to Lewis, 1803, Jackson 1978, vol. 1, pp. 9–10, 61–66.

156 "signs of the soil": Albert Gallatin to TJ, 13 April 1803; see also James Madison's Notes to TJ, 14 April 1803, Jackson 1978, vol. 1, pp. 33–34.

156 "The object of your mission" and the following quotes are from Jefferson's Instructions to Lewis, 1803, Jackson 1978, vol. 1, pp. 61–66.

156 paper birch in 1791: TJ to Maria Jefferson, 30 May 1791, Betts and Bear 1986, p. 83.

157 TJ's hopes for the expedition: TJ to Bernard Lacépède, 24 February 1803, Jackson 1978, vol. 1, pp. 15–16.

157 "like two mice": TJ to Martha Jefferson Randolph, 28 May 1801, Betts and Bear 1986, p. 202.

158 "remarkable store of accurate" and following quote: TJ to Benjamin Smith Barton, 27 February 1803, Jackson 1978, vol. 1, p. 17; for TJ and botanical excursions in Washington, see Christian Hines, 1801–09, Hines 1981, p. 13; Hunt 1906, p. 393; Daniel Brent to TJ, 26 June 1802, Padover 1946, p. 275.

158 "no regular botanist": TJ to Benjamin Smith Barton, 27 February 1803, Jackson 1978, vol. 1, p. 17.

158 "adapted to the woods": TJ to Caspar Wistar, 28 February 1803; TJ to Benjamin Rush, 28 February 1803, Jackson 1978, vol. 1, pp. 18–19.

158 "three kingdoms": TJ to Benjamin Barton Smith, 28 February 1803, Jackson 1978, vol. 1, p. 17.

158 "portable horizon": Andrew Ellicott to TJ, 6 March 1803; see also Lewis to TJ, 20 April 1803, Jackson 1978, vol. 1, pp. 24, 37–40.

158 TJ and *Megalonyx:* Thomson 2008b, p. 35; TJ to Caspar Wistar, 28 February 1803, Jackson 1978, vol. 1, p. 18; Ambrose 2005, p. 91; TJ to David Rittenhouse, 3 July 1796; TJ's Memoir on the Megalonyx for the APS, 10 February 1797, TJ Papers, vol. 29, pp. 138–39, 291–304; Thomson 2008a, pp. 80–85; Thomson 2008b, pp. 34–37.

158 Benjamin Rush: TJ to Benjamin Rush, 28 February 1803, Jackson 1978, vol. 1, pp. 18–19.

158 "Thunderclappers": Ambrose 2005, p. 89.

158 "Rules of Health": "Benjamin Rush's Rules of Health," 11 June 1803, Jackson 1978, vol. 1, pp. 54–55.

158 "Is Suicide common": Benjamin Rush to Lewis, 17 May 1803, "Questions to Merryweather Lewis," Jackson 1978, vol. 1, p. 50.

158 Lewis with Barton: TJ to Benjamin Smith Barton, 27 February 1803, Jackson 1978, vol. 1, pp. 16–17; Ambrose 2005, p. 91.

159 Native Americans to adopt agriculture: Ambrose 2005, p. 124; Ellis 2007, pp. 232ff.; see also Thomas Law to JM, 18 July 1804, JM Paper SS, vol. 7, pp. 478–79.

159 "cultivate corn, beans": Clark, winter 1804–5, Estimate of the Eastern Indians, Journals Lewis and Clark.

159 BF and western boundaries: BF to TJ, 8 April 1790, TJ Papers, vol. 16, p. 326.

159 TJ and exploration to the West: TJ to George Rogers Clark, 4 December 1783, TJ Papers, vol. 6, p. 371; Hindle 1956, pp. 325–26.

159 subscription Michaux: American Philosophical Society's Subscription Agreement for André Michaux's Western Expedition, c. 22 January 1793 and Editorial Note to Jefferson and André Michaux's Proposed Western Expedition, 1793, TJ Papers, vol. 25, pp. 75–83.

159 founding fathers and West: Friedenberg 1992, p. 325; Chaplin 2006, pp. 184–85; Brookhiser 1997, pp. 49–50.

159 BF and West: Ross 1929, pp. 67–68; McCoy 1980, pp. 62ff.; BF, "Observations concerning the Increase of Mankind, Peopling of Countries, &c.," 1755.

159 "placed in the most enviable": GW, Circular to the States, 8 June 1783, GWW, vol. 26, p. 484.

160 "a storehouse and granary": GW to Lafayette, 19 June 1788, GW Papers CS, vol. 6, p. 338.

160 "By enlarging the empire" and following quotes: TJ to Representatives of the Territory of Indiana, 28 December 1805, DLC.

160 "a vast wilderness": William Plumer, 20 October 1803, Brown 1923, p. 13.

160 "prove worse than useless": Ibid.

160 "like a comet": Fisher Ames to Christopher Gore, 3 October 1803, Allen 1983, vol. 2, p. 1462.

160 "we already have too much": Ambrose 2005, p. 101.

161 "the less will it be shaken": TJ, Second Inaugural Address, 4 March 1805, Ford 1892–99, vol. 8, p. 344.

161 TJ pretended expedition was for commerce: Carlos Martinez de Yrujo to Pedro Cevallos, 2 December 1802; Jefferson's Confidential Message to Congress, 18 January 1803; Louis André Pichon to the Minister of Foreign Affairs, 4 March 1803; Edward Thornton to Lord Hawkesbury, 9 March 1803, Jackson 1978, vol. 1, pp. 4, 10–13, 22, 26.

161 "The Feds. . . . treat it": TJ to Lewis, 13 January 1804, Jackson 1978, vol. 1, p. 163; see also Ambrose 2005, pp. 78, 410.

161 JA and Louisiana Purchase: JA to Josiah Quincy, 9 February 1811, Adams 1850–56, vol. 9, p. 631.

161 "Travellers in our Wilderness": JA to Francis Adriaan van der Kemp, 5 November 1804, MHS AP reel 118.

161 JA and Michaux subscription: American Philosophical Society's Subscription Agreement for André Michaux's Western Expedition, c. 22 January 1793 and Editorial Note to Jefferson and André Michaux's Proposed Western Expedition, 1793, TJ Papers, vol. 25, pp. 75–83.

161 "Country is explored and thinly planted": JA to Francis Adriaan van der Kemp, 5 November 1804 MHS AP reel 118.

161 "I care not a farthing": JA to Francis Adriaan van der Kemp, 8 January 1806, MHS AP reel 118.

161 "The spirit of party": JA to Francis Adriaan van der Kemp, 26 January 1802, MHS AP reel 118.

161 "pitiful Bagatelles": JA to Francis Adriaan van der Kemp, 5 November 1804, MHS AP reel 118.

162 members of expedition: Coues 1970, vol. 1, pp. 2–3.

162 provisions of expedition: Lewis's List of Requirements & Summary of Purchases, Jackson 1978, vol. 1, pp. 69–74, 93–99; Clark to Lewis, April 1804, Jackson 1978, vol. 1, p. 176.

162 "cheap looking Glasses": Lewis's List of Requirements & Summary of Purchases, Jackson 1978, vol. 1, p. 72.

162 botanical books: Benjamin Smith Barton's *Elements of Botany* (1803); John Miller's *An Illustration of the Sexual System of Linnaeus* (1779) and John Miller's *An Illustration of the Termini Botanici of Linnaeus* (1789).

162 botanical correspondence at WH: TJ to John Bartram Jr., 11 June 1801, TJ Papers, vol. 34, p. 306; Julian Ursyn Niemcewicz to TJ, 16 June 1801; William Maclure to Jefferson, 20 November 1801, TJ Papers, vol. 35, pp. 361, 706–7; TJ Garden Book, 11, 26 May 1802, Betts 1944, p. 277; TJ to John Bartram Jr., 5 April 1802; TJ to John Bartram Jr., 2 December 1802, Betts 1944, pp. 279–80.

162 fruit trees from St. Louis: John Armstrong to TJ, 20 February 1804, Betts 1944, pp. 294–95.

162 "some slips of the": Lewis to TJ, 26 March 1804, Jackson 1978, vol. 1, p. 170.

163 "flavor and size": This was *Amelanchier alnifolia*, Lewis, 2 August 1805, Journals Lewis and Clark; Cutright 1989, p. 289. For roots against snakebite, see Lewis to TJ, 5 March 1805, Jackson 1978, vol. 1, p. 220.

163 "vastly preferable to": Lewis, 17 July 1805, Journals Lewis and Clark; Cutright 1989, p. 172.

163 beatifull bowlinggreen" and following quotes: Lewis, 17 September 1804 and 12 April 1805, Journals Lewis and Clark.

163 "sweetest" hay: and following quotes, Clark, 4 July 1804, Journals Lewis and Clark.

163 "fertile in the extreem": Lewis to Lucy Marks, 31 March 1805, Jackson 1978, vol. 1, p. 223.

163 Lewis struck by landscape: Lewis, 22 April 1805 and 30 May 1805, Journals Lewis and Clark.

163 plants and botanical specimens of the expedition: Journals Lewis and Clark; Munger 2003; Cutright 1989 (in particular pp. 357–75 and Appendix A); Hatch 2003.

163 "virtues and properties": Lewis to TJ, 7 April 1805, Jackson 1978, vol. 1, p. 231.

163 Lewis sent collection to St. Louis: Lewis to TJ, 7 April 1805, Jackson 1978, vol. 1, pp. 231–42.

164 black-tailed prairie dog: Clark, 7 September 1804, and John Ordway, 7 September 1804, Journals Lewis and Clark.

164 Mandan corn at Monticello: TJ to Lewis, 16 August 1809, TJ Papers RS, vol. 1, pp. 436–37; Jackson 1978, vol. 1, p. 239.

164 winter at Mandan village: Ambrose 2005, pp. 182, 200; Hatch 2003; Lavender 2001, p. 168.

164 Lewis collection arrives at White House: The cargo arrived in St. Louis in May 1805 and in Washington in August 1805 while Jefferson was still in Monticello. Pierre Chouteau to William Henry Harrison, 22 May 1805; Etienne Lemaire to TJ, 12 August 1805. For Jefferson's "examinations," see for example TJ to Charles Willson Peale, 9 October 1805, Jackson 1978, vol. 1, pp. 242, 253–54, 263.

164 prairie dog and magpie at White House: Etienne Lemaire to TJ, 20 August 1805; TJ to Charles Willson Peale, 6 October 1807, Jackson 1978, vol. 1, pp. 256, 260.

164 botanical specimens to American Philosophical Society: Jackson 1978, vol. 1, pp. 239–40; Minutes of APS, 15 November 1805 in Cutright 1989, p. 358.

164 "for an Indian Hall": TJ to Charles Willson Peale, 6 October 1806, Jackson 1978, vol. 1, p. 260.

164 William Hamilton and seeds: TJ to William Hamilton, 6 November 1805, Betts 1944, p. 307 ; Minutes of APS, 15 November 1805 in Cutright 1989, p. 358.

164 favorite dinner subjects at White House: Cullen 2005, p. 325; Margaret Bayard Smith, Hunt 1906, p. 50; JQA, 3 November 1807, Adams 1874–77, vol. 1, p. 473.

164 TJ's interests and experiments: Isaac Briggs to TJ, 11 June 1804, DLC; John P. van Ness to TJ, 5 July 1806, Betts 1944, p. 320; TJ to Thomas Mann Randolph, 1 January 1802, DLC.

164 fossils in East Room: TJ to Caspar Wistar, 20 March 1808, Rice 1951, p. 608; Thomson 2008b, p. 40.

165 grizzly bears: TJ to Charles Willson Peale, 5 November 1807; Charles Willson Peale to TJ, 7 November 1807, Miller 1983–2000, vol. 2, pt. 2, pp. 1041–44; Margaret Bayard Smith in Hunt 1906, p. 393.

165 "a Philosopher at our Head": William Thornton to JM, 16 March 1801, JM Papers SS, vol. 1, p. 24.

165 "the enlightened philosopher": Alexander Wilson to William Bartram, 4 March 1805, Hunter 1983, p. 232.

165 Sacagawea and her husband hired as translators: Lewis, 7 April 1805, Journals Lewis and Clark.

165 "country is as yesterday beatifull": Lewis, 5 May 1805, Journals Lewis and Clark.

165 "So perfect indeed are those walls": Lewis, 31 May 1805, Journals Lewis and Clark.

165 2,500 miles: Journals Lewis and Clark, Part 3: Miscellany. This is in Clark's hand, giving mileages for the expedition.

165 "wide expance" and following quotes: Lewis, 8 June 1805, Journals Lewis and Clark.

166 "disgusted" and following quote: Lewis, 13 June 1805, Journals Lewis and Clark.

166 "the most sublime of Nature's works" and following quote: Jefferson 1982, pp. 24, 19.

166 "sublime" in American context: Furtwanger 1999, pp. 23–51; Nygren 1986; for the sublime in England see Burke 1998, Manwaring 1965; for the sublime in gardens see Wulf and Gieben-Gamal 2005, pp. 131–73.

166 "a sort of delightful horror": Burke 1998, p. 67.

166 "prince of rivers": Philip Freneau, quoted in Nash 1982, p. 68.

166 "but a rivulet": JA to Thomas Brand-Hollis, 1 June 1790, MHS AP reel 115.

166 "greater magnificence": AA to Elizabeth Cranch, 18 July 1786, AFC, vol. 7, p. 257.

166 "the most sublime": JA to AA, 22 March 1782, MHS online.

166 "this singular landscape": TJ to John Trumbull, 20 February 1791, TJ Papers, vol. 19, p. 298.

167 "grand objects": GW to Commissioners of DC, 5 September 1793, GWW, vol. 33, p. 83.

167 "with the intention of": Samuel Latham Mitchell, 10 January 1802, Mitchell 1879, p. 744.

167 "For these last forty years": Uvedale Price to GW, 31 March 1798, GW Papers RS, vol. 2, p. 166.

167 "made the satellite larger" and Paine and the American landscape: Thomas Paine, quoted in Marx 1974, pp. 8–10.

167 "Men are like plants": Crèvecoeur 1998, p. 45.

167 "national character often": Silliman 1824, p. 18.

167 expedition at Great Falls: Whitehouse, 29 June 1805, and Lewis, 4 June 1805, Journals Lewis and Clark; Ambrose 2005, p. 244.

168 source of Missouri: Lewis, 12 August 1805, Journals Lewis and Clark.

168 "I shudder with the": Clark, 14 June 1806; see also Lewis, 2 August 1805, Journals Lewis and Clark.

168 plants in the snow: Lewis, 16 June 1806, Journals Lewis and Clark.

168 "So complete is this deseption": Lewis, 12 June 1806, Journals Lewis and Clark.

168 "I recieved, my dear Sir": TJ to Lewis, 26 October 1806, Jackson 1978, vol. 1, p. 350.

168 "a pretty extensive collection": Lewis to TJ, 23 September 1806, Jackson 1978, vol. 1, p. 323.

168 Frederick Pursh: Cutright 1989, pp. 359–63.

169 "small portion of every kind": McMahon to TJ, 26 December 1806, Jackson 1978, vol. 1, p. 354.

169 TJ sharing seeds: TJ to McMahon, 6 January 1807, Jackson 1978, vol. 1, p. 356; 20 March 1807, 22 March 1807, TJ to William Hamilton, 22 March 1807, Betts 1944, pp. 343–44.

169 couldn't do "justice": TJ to McMahon, 20 March 1807, Betts 1944, p. 343.

169 "public treasures": TJ to McMahon, 22 March 1807, Betts 1944, p. 344.

169 first precious seedlings: McMahon to TJ, 2 April 1807, 5 April 1807, Jackson 1978, vol. 2, p. 398.

169 "state of preservation": McMahon to TJ, 27 March 1807, Betts 1944, p. 345.

169 "Some of them are curious": TJ to Madame de Tessé, 8 December 1813, Betts 1944, p. 520.

169 McMahon's report on the seedlings: McMahon to TJ, 27 March, 2, 5, 10 April 1807, Betts 1944, pp. 345–47.

170 "plants of *every kind*": McMahon to TJ, 27 March 1807; thirty new species, McMahon to TJ, 28 June 1808, Betts 1944, pp. 345, 373.

170 seeds planted in 1807: Betts 1944, pp. 334–35.

170 Lewis's seeds at Monticello: TJ, 18 April 1807, Betts 1944, pp. 334–35; "Missouri great Salsafia" was *Tragopon* sp.; "flowering pea of Arkansa" was probably *Vicia americana;* "Lilly, the yellow of the Columbia" was probably *Fritillaria pudica,* Cutright 1989, pp. 373–74.

170 "one of the most excellent": TJ to Benjamin Smith Barton, 6 October 1810, TJ Papers RS, vol. 3, p. 150.

170 "some of the most beautiful berries": TJ to McMahon, 11 October 1812, TJ Papers RS, vol. 5, p. 382.

170 "addition to our knowledge": TJ to Bernard Lacépède, 14 July 1808, Betts 1944, p. 373.

170 Lewis's death: TJ Papers RS, vol. 1, pp. 607–8.

170 "hideous and desolate": William Bradford, 1620, Morison 1952, p. 62.

171 "temples which Roman robbers": Charles Fenno Hoffman, 1833, quoted in Nash 1982, p. 73.

171 "monuments of a corrupt religion" and following quote: Browne 1832, p. 403.

171 "one of the principal sources": Browne 1837, p. 360.

171 "every plant appears to partake": Browne 1837, p. 338.

171 "our destiny as": Magoon 1852, p. 3.

171 "In no quarter of the globe": Shaw, Joshua, *Picturesque Views of American Scenery, 1820–21,* quoted in Nygren 1986, p. 46.

171 TJ collecting landscape prints: Stein 1993, pp. 188–92.

171 "never need an American look beyond": Washington Irving, 1820; see also Wilson, Alexander, *The Forester*, 1804, quoted in Nygren 1986, p. 38.

171 "magnitude" of mountains and forests: James Kirke Paulding, 1816, *Letters from the South*, Letter 13, reprinted in Branch and Philippon 1998, p. 139; see also Kelly and Rasmussen 2000, p. 13.

171 "habit of exalting their own": Count Carlo Vidua, quoted in Kelly and Rasmussen 2000, p. 14.

171 "needless to go farther than Wales": Weld 1807, vol. 1, 1807, p. 244.

171 tourist shelters in Catskills: Nygren 1986, p. 38.

171 "Our lofty mountains": Joshua Shaw's *Picturesque Views of American Scenery, 1820–21,* quoted in Nygren 1986, p. 46.

172 landscape engravings: Joshua Shaw's *Picturesque Views of American Scenery, 1820–21* and William Guy Wall's *Hudson River Portfolio* (1821–25).

172 backwoods novels: Nash 1982, p. 76.

172 "Our seventeen states": TJ to Choctaw Nation, 17 December 1803, DLC.

8 "THO' AN OLD MAN, I AM BUT A YOUNG GARDENER":
THOMAS JEFFERSON AT MONTICELLO

173 TJ's journey to Monticello: TJ to JM, 17 March 1809, TJ Papers RS, vol. 1, p. 61; Edmund Bacon's Memoir, Bear 1967, pp. 106–7.

173 "Never did a prisoner": TJ to Pierre-Samuel Dupont de Nemours, 2 March 1809, Betts 1944, p. 394.

173 "the most tedious of my life": TJ to Martha Jefferson Randolph, 20 October 1806, Betts and Bear 1986, p. 289.

174 TJ's daily rides: Ibid.

174 "the enjoyments of rural life": TJ to Monsieur le Comte Diodati, 29 March 1807, Betts 1944, p. 346.

174 "My views and attentions" and following quotes: TJ to William Hamilton, July 1806, Betts 1944, pp. 323–24.

174 TJ's correspondence with Anne and Ellen: TJ to Anne Cary Randolph, 8 December 1806, 7 June 1807, 1 November 1807, 24 November 1807, 22 March 1808; Ellen Wayles Randolph to TJ, 11 March 1808; Anne Cary Randolph to TJ, 9 November 1807, 19 February 1808, 18 March 1808, 15 April 1808; TJ to Martha Jefferson Randolph, 18 October 1808; Ellen Wayles Randolph to TJ, 15 December 1808; TJ to Ellen Wayles Randolph, 6 February 1809; Ellen Wayles Randolph to TJ, 1 April 1808, Betts and Bear 1986, pp. 292, 307–8, 312, 314, 316, 328, 337, 332, 334, 339, 342, 351, 371, 380.

174 Anne getting reports from slaves: Anne Cary Randolph to TJ, 18 March 1808, Betts and Bear 1986, p. 334.

174 Ellen and gardening: TJ to Ellen Wayles Randolph, 23 February 1808; Ellen Wayles Randolph to TJ, 1, 14 April 1808, Betts and Bear 1986, pp. 329, 339, 341.

174 "a thousand little things to tell me": TJ to Ellen Wayles Randolph, 8 February 1807, Betts and Bear 1986, p. 295. For TJ sending kisses, see TJ to Ellen

Wayles Randolph, 30 November 1806; 29 March 1808, Betts and Bear 1986, pp. 291, 338.

174 "I have not much to say": Ellen Wayles Randolph to TJ, 26 January 1809, Betts and Bear 1986, p. 379.

174 TJ's "account" of letters: TJ to Martha Jefferson Randolph, 1 June 1807; TJ to Ellen Wayles Randolph, 8 December 1807, Betts and Bear 1986, pp. 307, 316.

174 "be devoted to the garden": TJ to Ellen Wayles Randolph, 20 February 1809, Betts and Bear 1986, p. 383.

175 Britain capturing American vessels: Burk 2007, p. 217.

175 "unceasing drudgery": TJ to John Dickinson, 13 January 1807, Betts 1944, p. 330. For following quotes, see TJ to Timothy Matlack, 19 October 1807, Betts 1944, p. 352; TJ to Martha Jefferson Randolph, 10 January 1809, Betts and Bear 1986, p. 377.

175 TJ decided to remodel Monticello's garden: TJ to William Hamilton, July 1806, Betts 1944, p. 324.

175 TJ garden plans and following quotes: TJ, General Ideas for the Improvement of Monticello, in TJ, Monticello: Notebook of Improvements, 1804–1807, pp. 1–2, K161 and K162, MHS TJ EA; see also Beiswanger 1983, p. 183.

176 asked Parkyns "give me some outlines": TJ to William Hamilton, July 1806, Betts 1944, p. 323.

176 Parkyns's book: Parkyns 1793, p. 8 and plate 1.

176 TJ's debt of $10,000: TJ to Martha Jefferson Randolph, 5 January 1808, 27 February 1809, Betts and Bear 1986, pp. 319, 386; TJ Memorandum Book, vol. 2, p. 1238.

176 "very fatiquing journey" and following quotes: TJ to JM, 17 March 1809, TJ Papers RS, vol. 1, p. 61.

176 "I am constantly": TJ to Etienne Lemaire, 25 April 1809, TJ Papers RS, vol. 1, p. 162.

176 "if the topic changes to politics": TJ to Benjamin Rush, 22 September 1809, TJ Papers RS S, vol. 1, p. 559; TJ repeated this sentiment many times; see also TJ to Robert Livingston, 20 April 1812, TJ Papers RS, vol. 4, p. 637.

176 TJ humming and singing: Edmund Bacon's Memoir, Bear 1967, p. 83.

177 TJ knew every plant in his garden: Ibid., p. 47.

177 Martha and her husband: Wayson 2008, pp. 201–2, 318–44.

177 "delighted to follow him about": Edmund Bacon's Memoir, Bear 1967, p. 85; TJ and his grandchildren, see Margaret Bayard Smith, August 1809, Peterson 1993, p. 53; Margaret Bayard Smith to Mrs. Kirkpatrick, 4 May 1806, Hunt 1906, pp. 50, 405; Margaret Bayard Smith, "Recollections of a Visit to Monticello," *Richmond Enquirer*, 18 January 1823; Sir Augustus John Foster, August 1807, Peterson 1993, p. 39.

177 grandchildren checked flowers: Ellen Wayles Randolph to Henry S. Randall, no date, Betts 1944, p. 636.

177 "Botany here is": TJ to Benjamin Smith Barton, 22 October 1810, TJ Papers RS, vol. 3, p. 181.

177 Ellen must find Latin names for pet fowls: TJ to Ellen Wayles Randolph, 30 November 1806, Betts and Bear 1986, p. 291.

177 "more Latin, madam": TJ to Ellen Wayles Randolph, 8 February 1807, Betts and Bear 1986, p. 295.

177 "It is only with them": Margaret Bayard Smith, August 1809, Peterson 1993, p. 53.

177 "has pulled down": Anna Thornton, September 1802, Peterson 1993, p. 35.

177 bones at Monticello: Stein 1993, p. 66.

178 first visible agricultural elements: Bayard Smith mentioned a cornfield after about a mile. Margaret Bayard Smith, August 1809, Peterson 1993, p. 46.

178 accidents at Rivanna River: Sir Augustus John Foster, 1807; Francis Hall, 1817, Peterson 1993, pp. 37, 79.

178 "I looked around" and following quotes: Margaret Bayard Smith, August 1809, Peterson 1993, pp. 45–46.

178 North Road and roundabouts: TJ, Garden Book, 14 March 1806, Betts 1944, p. 310. TJ also advised Madison to take the new North Road when he visited in September 1806. TJ to JM, 2 September 1806, Morton Smith 1995, vol. 3, p. 1438; TJ drawing, estate lands, recto, 1806, N209; K168, MHS TJ EA; Betts 1944, pp. 34, 94.

179 TJ screening fields in the forest: TJ drawing, Monticello, east fields, probably from 1793, N195; K167c, MHS TJ EA. This sketch, though done before the North Road was begun, clearly shows how Jefferson nestled his fields into the forest.

179 "endless" road: Margaret Bayard Smith, August 1809, Peterson 1993, p. 46.

179 "savage" approach: George Ticknor, 1815, Peterson 1993, p. 61.

179 visitors abandoned carriages: Anna Thornton, 18 September 1802, Peterson 1993, p. 33.

179 "Satan's ascent to Paradise": George Ticknor, 1815, Peterson 1993, p. 61.

179 "the Jupiter . . . [and] the Juno": TJ to Madame de Tessé, 26 October 1805, Betts 1944, p. 306; for TJ's forest see Francis Calley Gray, February 1815, Peterson 1993, p. 57; TJ to William Hamilton, July 1806, Betts 1944, p. 323.

179 "majestic" reminders: TJ to William Hamilton, July 1806, Betts 1944, p. 323.

179 "Sometimes a blake declivity": McMahon 1806, p. 59.

179 "so bountifully bestowed": McMahon 1806, p. 72.

180 McMahon's book: McMahon 1806, pp. 261–70, 589ff.

180 "what nature has done": TJ to Latrobe, 10 October 1809, TJ Papers RS, vol. 1, p. 595.

180 "a noble forest": Francis Calley Gray, February 1815, Peterson 1993, p. 57.

180 "extremely grand and": Francis Calley Gray, February 1815, Peterson 1993, p. 57.

180 "impervious grove of" and following quotes: Margaret Bayard Smith, "Recollections of a Visit to Monticello," *Richmond Enquirer*, 18 January 1823.

180 "under the beaming": TJ to William Hamilton, July 1806, Betts 1944, pp. 323–24.

180 "as high as the": TJ to William Hamilton, July 1806, Betts 1944, p. 324.

180 plants in the Grove: TJ, General Ideas for the Improvement of Monticello, in TJ, Monticello: Notebook of Improvements, 1804–1807, pp. 1–2, K161 and K162, MHS TJ EA; TJ to William Hamilton, July 1806, Betts 1944, p. 324.

180 trees planted in the slope behind the lawn: TJ Garden Book, 5 November 1778, 3 October 1778, 16 April 1807, Betts 1944, pp. 79, 334; William Prince to TJ, 8 November 1791, TJ's instructions on how to plant the trees and shrubs from Prince, footnote, TJ Papers, vol. 22, pp. 268–69; TJ to Thomas Mann Randolph, 22 March 1798, TJ Papers, vol. 30, p. 193; TJ drawing: plan of Monticello, N61, K34, MHS TJ EA.

181 "pet trees": Francis Hall, 1816–17, Peterson 1993, p. 75.

181 JM, TJ, Bartram and Kentucky coffee tree: TJ to JM, 2 June 1793, JM to TJ, 13 June 1793, TJ Papers, vol. 26, pp. 168, 274.

181 *fermes ornées* at Monticello: There are several plans and sketches in TJ's hand that illustrate his ideas. Most are reproduced in Betts 1944 but probably dated wrongly. See also Monticello mountaintop, 1809, N225, K169, MHS TJ EA and Monticello, timberzone, recto N129, K94d, MHS TJ EA.

181 "merely a highly ornamented walk": TJ "Notes of a Tour of English Gardens," March and April 1786, TJ Papers, vol. 9, p. 370.

181 "only a grazing farm": TJ "Notes of a Tour of English Gardens," March and April 1786, TJ Papers, vol. 9, p. 371.

182 Corn Cob Capital: Latrobe to TJ, 28 August 1809, Van Horne 1984–88, vol. 2, pp. 749–50; TJ to Latrobe, 27 August 1816; Latrobe to TJ, 5 November 1816, Van Horne 1984–88, vol. 3, pp. 808, 823; Brownell and Cohen 1994, vol. 2, pt. 2, p. 391.

182 "into a ferme ornée": TJ's Instruction for Bacon, 1 February 1808, Betts 1944, p. 360.

182 instructions in Whately's *Observations:* Whately 1770, pp. 161–82.

183 fields in forest: TJ's drawing of Monticello, east fields, probably 1793, N195, K167c, MHS TJ EA. This sketch shows how Jefferson nestled his fields into the forest.

183 TJ's orchard and vineyard: Hatch 1998a, pp. 39, 52–53, 175; TJ Garden Book, 1810 and TJ to Bernard McMahon, 13 January 1810, TJ Plan for the Orchard 1811, Betts 1944, pp. 420–425, 431, 468; TJ's drawing: Monticello: orchard and vineyard, undated, N234, K169i, MHS TJ EA.

183 Lewis's gooseberries and currants: McMahon to TJ, 28 June 1808 (McMahon sent gooseberries to taste first), 28 February 1812; TJ to McMahon, 6 July 1808, 8 February 1809, TJ Garden Book, 12 March 1812, Betts 1944, pp. 373, 406, 474–75, 481; Lewis, 17 July and 2 August 1805, Journals Lewis and Clark.

183 TJ's vegetable garden: In addition to TJ's own notes, much of the information on the local climate and Jefferson's vegetable garden in Monticello is based on Peter Hatch's (Director of Gardens and Grounds at Monticello) extraordinary expertise, knowledge and his forthcoming book, *Thomas Jefferson's Revolutionary Garden.*

183 work on vegetable terrace: Beiswanger 1978; TJ to Edmund Bacon, 28 December 1806, 13 May 1807, 24 November 1807, 23 February 1808, 7

June 1808, Betts 1944, pp. 319, 347, 355, 364, 371; Hatch, Peter, manuscript for *Thomas Jefferson's Revolutionary Garden* (forthcoming).

183 "Consider the garden": TJ to Bacon, 7 June 1808, Betts 1944, p. 371.

183 geographical labels of the vegetables: TJ Garden Book, 1809, Betts 1944, pp. 386–93; Peter Hatch identified eighty geographic adjectives (representing six continents) attached to the vegetables listed in Jefferson's Garden Book. Hatch, Peter, manuscript for *Thomas Jefferson's Revolutionary Garden* (forthcoming).

184 "hot" vegetable varieties: TJ Garden Book and Kalendar for the early retirement years, Betts 1944; Hatch, Peter, manuscript for *Thomas Jefferson's Revolutionary Garden* (forthcoming).

184 "Fruits," "Leaves" and "Roots": TJ, Arrangement of the Garden, 1812, Betts 1944, p. 469.

184 list of harvest times: TJ Garden Book, 1813 "Dates of Artichokes coming to table," Betts 1944, p. 497.

184 measured gooseberries: TJ to George Divers, 18 March 1812, TJ Papers RS, vol. 4, p. 561.

184 vials for seeds: TJ to Thomas Jefferson Randolph, 6 May 1809; Thomas Jefferson Randolph to TJ, 29 May 1809, TJ Papers RS, vol. 1, pp. 190, 245.

184 "in the neatest order": and seed cupboard, Margaret Bayard Smith, August 1809, Peterson 1993, p. 50.

184 "One service of this kind": TJ to Alexandre Giroud, 22 May 1797, TJ Papers, vol. 29, p. 387; Nicholas King, who worked at the Office of Surveyor of the City in Washington, wrote that "no person has been more zealous to enrich the United States by the introduction of new and useful vegetables." (Nicholas King to TJ, 11 September 1806, Betts 1944, p. 325.)

185 TJ abandons Ricara bean: TJ to Benjamin Smith Barton, 6 October 1810, TJ Papers RS, vol. 3, p. 150; TJ, 1 July 1809, Garden Kalendar, Betts 1944, p. 389.

185 "I am curious to select": TJ to Bernard McMahon, 13 January 1810, TJ Papers RS, vol. 2, p. 140.

185 "killed by bug" and following quotes: TJ, 1809, Garden Kalendar, Betts 1944, pp. 388–93.

185 "one species in a hundred": TJ to Samuel Vaughan, 27 November 1790, TJ Papers, vol. 18, p. 98; see also TJ to Charles Willson Peale, 20 August 1811, TJ Papers RS, vol. 4, p. 93.

185 plant exchange: throughout this time of his retirement TJ was extensively exchanging and receiving plants and seeds from his horticultural correspondents—too many to list here. For details see Betts 1944 and TJ's Retirement Papers.

185 "nourishment to my hobby horse": TJ to William Johnson, 17 March 1810, TJ Papers RS, vol. 2, p. 302.

185 slave gardens at Monticello: Anne Cary Randolph Household Account, 1805–08, Gawalt 1994; Martha Wayles Jefferson Account Book, 1772–82, DLC; Stanton 2000, pp. 28–30; Hatch 2001; for the number of slaves see TJ, Census of Inhabitants and Supplies at Monticello, 8 November 1810, TJ Papers RS, vol. 3, p. 202.

185 slave gardens in general: Delle 1998, p. 146; Higman 2001, pp. 261–62. George Washington's slaves also had their own garden plots and sold their vegetables on the market in Alexandria. (Julian Ursin Niemcewicz, June 1798, Lee 2006, p. 79; GW to Arthur Young, 18 June 1792, GW Papers PS, vol. 10, p. 461.)

185 "an interest in his *home*": Breeden 1980, p. 270.

185 "cheerful, home-like": Ibid., p. 272.

185 food rations at Monticello: The weekly ration for one adult slave at Monticello included a peck of cornmeal, one half pound of pork or pickled beef, and four dried fish—similar to other Virginia plantations, though the ration for meat was less than usual. (Stanton 2000, p. 29.)

186 "every thing we want within ourselves": TJ to John Dortic, 1 October 1811, TJ Papers RS, vol. 4, p. 176.

186 TJ's vineyard: In March 1807, just months before the Embargo Act in 1807, TJ planted more than twenty varieties of European grapes. When the European cultivars perished, he tried to procure American varieties and in April 1810 Jefferson planted 165 cuttings of native fox grape (*Vitis labrusca*)— though once again he was unsuccessful and probably never produced a single bottle of wine. TJ Weather Memorandum Book, 25 March 1807, Betts 1944, p. 333; TJ to John Dortic, 1 October 1811, TJ Papers RS, vol. 4, p. 176; TJ to John Adlum, 7 October 1809, TJ Papers RS, vol. 1, p. 586; TJ, Garden Book, 20 April 1810, Betts 1944, p. 423.

186 TJ and sesame oil: TJ to William Few, 3 January 1808; TJ to Robert Livingston, 3 January 1808, Betts 1944, p. 361; TJ to Anne Cary Randolph, 22 March 1808, Betts and Bear 1986, p. 337; TJ to Bernard McMahon, 8 April 1811, TJ Papers RS, vol. 3, p. 545.

186 "as soon as . . . shall be married": TJ to Cornelia Jefferson Randolph, 11 June 1811, Betts and Bear 1986, p. 401.

186 TJ in the garden first thing in the morning: Edmund Bacon's Memoir, Bear 1967, p. 72.

186 "an ocean": Margaret Bayard Smith, "Recollections of a Visit to Monticello," *Richmond Enquirer,* 18 January 1823.

186 "verdant islands": Ibid.

186 TJ's garden pavilion: The pavilion was built in 1812 and visitors recalled that it was Jefferson's favorite place to read and sit. Beiswanger 1983, p. 184; Beiswanger 1984. See also TJ's drawings of garden pavilions in different styles in Monticello: Farm Book Notes, 1807–09, N182, K164, MHS TJ EA; Henry D. Gilpin, 1827, Peterson 1993, p. 112.

186 planting of oval beds: Unless otherwise referenced, from TJ's planting list of 18 April 1807, Betts 1944, p. 335.

186 "those of mere curiosity" and following quotes: TJ to Bernard McMahon, 8 April 1811, TJ Papers RS, vol. 3, p. 545.

187 "the flowering pea of Arkansa": TJ Garden Book, 18 April 1807, Betts 1944, p. 335. This was probably *Vicia americana,* Cutright 1989, p. 374; Anne Cary Randolph to TJ, 9 November 1807, Betts and Bear 1986, p. 314.

187 "Lilly, the yellow of the Columbia": TJ Garden Book, 18 April 1807, Betts 1944, p. 335. Jefferson's seeds didn't germinate, which is unsurprising

because *Fritillaria pudica* persistently fails in central Virginia. (Cornett 2001.)

187 "too much restrain the variety": TJ to Anne Cary Randolph, 7 June 1807, Betts and Bear 1986, p. 307.

187 "winding walk": TJ to Anne Cary Randolph, 7 June 1807, Betts and Bear 1986, p. 308; TJ might have been inspired by McMahon's *American Gardener's Calendar,* which suggested a similar design, McMahon 1806, p. 55ff.; McMahon had sent a copy to Jefferson in April 1806, Betts 1944, p. 313.

187 "a full collection": TJ to Anne Cary Randolph, 16 February 1808, Betts and Bear 1986, p. 328; see also TJ to McMahon, 6 July 1808, Betts 1944, p. 373.

187 "the flowers come forth": TJ to Anne Cary Randolph, 26 May 1811, TJ Papers RS, vol. 3, p. 633.

187 pea-growing competition: George Divers to TJ, 30 April 1815, Betts 1944, p. 544.

187 "Tho' an old man": TJ to Charles Willson Peale, 20 August 1811, TJ Papers RS, vol. 4, p. 93.

187 "a solitary tree": TJ to William Duane, 28 March 1811, TJ Papers RS, vol. 3, p. 507.

187 "as the North and South Poles": Rush to JA, 17 February 1812, Butterfield 1951, vol. 2, p. 1127; for their renewed correspondence see also Cappon 1987, pp. 283–89, and Ellis 1998, pp. 296–300.

187 "given up newspapers": TJ to JA, 21 January 1812; see also JA to TJ, 1 January 1812, TJ Papers RS, vol. 4, pp. 390, 428–30.

187 "You and I ought not to die": JA to TJ, 15 July 1813, Cappon 1987, p. 358.

187 "quite the Farmer": AA to JQA, 30 May 1801, MHS AP reel 400.

187 "Farmer of Stony Field": JA to Thomas Boylston Adams, 27 January, 30 January, 11 July 1801, MHS AP reels 400, 401; JA to William Stephens Smith, 24 March 1801; JA to William Cranch, 23 May, 29 June 1801, MHS AP reel 118. JA mentioned "Stony Field" for the first time in January 1801 but used it for only a few months.

187 "a good exchange": JA to Samuel Dexter, 23 March 1801, MHS AP reel 118.

188 "in the bosom of": JA to Skelton Jones, 11 March 1809, Adams 1850–56, vol. 9, p. 612.

188 botanical essays and Virgil: JA to Benjamin Waterhouse, 27 February 1811, MHS, Adams-Waterhouse Coll.; AA to JQA, 30 September 1809, MHS AP reel 408.

188 "happier . . . than I ever was": JA to Francis Adriaan van der Kemp, 5 February 1805, MHS AP reel 118.

188 "a Lilliputian Plantation": JA to JQA, 23 December 1805, MHS AP reel 404.

188 "Montezillo Alias the little Hill": JA started using "Montezillo" instead of "Quincy" in his letters to Jefferson in 1819. JA to TJ, 23 November 1819, Cappon 1987, p. 547.

188 "riding in gay Coaches": JA to Charles Adams, 9 February 1796, MHS, Seymour Coll., Adams Papers.

188 "I have seen the Queen": JA to John Peter de Windt, 15 March 1820, MHS AP reel 124.

188 "in love with her a second time": JA to Benjamin Waterhouse, 9 August 1805, MHS, Adams-Waterhouse Coll.

188 JA's study of seaweed: JA to Benjamin Waterhouse, 9 August, 4 September, 13 September, 19 September, 26 December 1805; MHS, Adams-Waterhouse Coll.; JA to Francis Adriaan van der Kemp, 8 January 1806, MHS AP reel 118.

188 "angry" at himself: JA to Benjamin Waterhouse, 9 August 1805, MHS, Adams-Waterhouse Coll.

188 JA and botanic garden at Harvard University: The Foundation of the Massachusetts Professorship of Natural History at Harvard College 1805, pp. 3–21; JA to Benjamin Waterhouse, 7 August 1805, Ford 1927, pp. 26–28.

188 "as a token of gratitude": Waterhouse 1811; Benjamin Waterhouse to JA, 12 March 1811, Ford 1927, pp. 54–55.

188 "at so early a day": JM to Benjamin Waterhouse, 27 December 1822, DLC.

188 JA and seed exchange: William Cunningham to JA Adams, 27 March 1804, MHS AP reel 403; JA to William Bentley, 8 October 1809, private owner; William Bentley to JA, 1 November 1809, MHS, Misc. Bound Coll., and 11 April 1810, MHS AP reel 409.

189 "they will be an ornament": JA to William Bentley, 10 November 1811, Sabetta private collection.

189 "J.A. In the 89 year": JA to TJ, 10 November 1823, Cappon 1987, p. 602.

189 "I can not see the Wood": JA to TJ, 9 July 1813, Ibid., p. 350.

189 "Whether you or I were right": JA to TJ, 1 May 1812, Ibid., p. 301.

189 "I walk little": TJ to JA, 21 January 1812, TJ Papers RS, vol. 4, p. 429.

189 "every fair day": JA to TJ, 3 February 1812, TJ Papers RS, vol. 4, p. 475.

189 JA's difficulties writing and reading: JA to Francis Adriaan van der Kemp, 15 December 1809, MHS AP reel 118.

189 "I call for my Leavers": JA to Benjamin Rush, 27 February 1805, MHS AP reel 118.

189 "for a future race": TJ to Andrew Ellicott, 24 June 1812, TJ Papers RS, vol. 5, p. 166.

189 "So good night": TJ to JA, 1 August 1816, Cappon 1987, p. 485.

9 "BALANCE OF NATURE":
JAMES MADISON AT MONTPELIER

190 party at Montpelier: The following description is based on Mary Cutts's account of a party in summer 1817, to which I have added other visitors' accounts from different years—nothing is invented, but the party is a composite of several parties that happened over the years in Montpelier. (Cutts 1817; DM to Anna Payne Cutts, 5 July 1816, DMDE; Margaret Bayard Smith, Hunt 1906, pp. 81–83, 233–37.)

191 DM an "Amazon" and JM a "puny" knight: Abraham Joseph Hasbrouck to Severyn Bruyn, 29 January 1814, DMDE.

191 "a withered little apple-John": Washington Irving to Henry Brevoort, 13 January 1811, Hellman 1915, p. 24.

191 DM's "turban": Anne Mercer Slaughter, 1825, Slaughter 1937, p. 35.

191 JM old-fashioned clothes: Henry D. Gilpin to Joshua Gilpin, 16 September 1827, Gray 1968, p. 470; Paul Jennings, Jennings 1983, p. 51.

191 "overflowing kindness": Margaret Bayard Smith, Hunt 1906, p. 233.

191 JM reserved and relaxed: Baron de Montlezun, 16 September 1816, Moffatt and Carriere 1945, p. 199; James K. Paulding, Ketcham 1959, p. 432.

191 "little blue eyes sparkled": Margaret Bayard Smith to Mrs Boyd, 17 August 1828, Hunt 1906, p. 236.

191 "fond of a frolic" and following quotes: Margaret Bayard Smith to Mrs. Boyd, 17 August 1828, Hunt 1906, p. 236; see also Cutts 1817.

191 "I do not": Anne Mercer Slaughter, 1825, Slaughter 1937, p. 35; John H. B. Latrobe to Charles Carrol Harper, August 1832, Semmes 1917, p. 240.

191 "ever blooming roses": Cutts 1817; for other plants see also Anne Mercer Slaughter, 1825, Slaughter 1937, p. 35; DM to Mary Estelle Elizabeth Cutts, 16 September 1831, DMDE.

191 "contrasting shades of color" and following quote: Baron de Montlezun, 16 September 1816, Moffatt and Carriere 1945, p. 198.

192 visitors commenting on forest: Baron de Montlezun, 16 September 1816, Moffatt and Carriere 1945, p. 198; Judith Page Walker Rives, 1820s, *Autobiography of Mrs. William Cabell Rives*, 1861, DLC; Henry D. Gilpin to Joshua Gilpin, 16 September 1827, Gray 1968, p. 469; Margaret Bayard Smith, Hunt 1906, pp. 233–37; George Shattuck to Dr. G. C. Shattuck, 24 January 1835, MHS George Shattuck Papers; *Letters of a Convalescent*, October 1839, Peter Force Scrapbook, ViU.

192 trees at Montpelier: Cutts 1817; Margaret Bayard Smith, Hunt 1906, p. 233.

192 JM and Corrèa de Serra: José Corrèa de Serra to JM, 12 February 1819, JM Papers RS, vol. 1, p. 414.

192 "ornamental trees": Margaret Bayard Smith, Hunt 1906, p. 233.

192 tulip poplar "twins": Cutts 1817.

192 vegetables and fruits in horseshoe-shaped garden: in general, Cutts 1817; Scott 1907; Judith Page Walker Rives, 1820s, *Autobiography of Mrs. William Cabell Rives*, 1861, DLC; for cucumber 7 April 1791, JM, Meteorological Journal of James Madison at his plantation 1789–1793, APS; for pineapples, Margaret Bayard Smith, Hunt 1906, p. 81; for seeds from Algiers, James Leander Cathcart to JM, 25 June 1804, JM Papers SS, vol. 7, p. 371; for giant beetroot, Joel Barlow to DM, 21 December 1811, DMDE.

192 "a paradise of roses": Cutts 1817.

192 "Hudson bay strawberry": George Divers to JM, 11 October 1819, JM Papers RS, vol. 1, p. 531.

192 JM and Latin names: Peter Minor to JM, 12 January 1822, DLC.

192 JM and Botanic Garden in Madrid: Mariano la-Gasco y Segura to JM, in Richard S. Hackley to JM, 23 May 1819, JM Papers RS, vol. 1, p. 462. Later JM would also receive seeds from the Jardin du Roi in Paris. (Eyrien Frères & Cie to JM, 2 April 1821, DLC; see also José Corrèa de Serra to JM, 12 February 1819, JM Papers RS, vol. 1, p. 414.)

193 "more united at home": Albert Gallatin, 17 July 1817, JM Papers RS, vol. 1, p. 91.

193 $9 million surplus: JM, Eighth Annual Address, 3 December 1816.

193 "Never did a government commence": James Monroe, First Inaugural Address, 4 March 1817.

193 "has acquired more glory": JA to TJ, 2 February 1817, Cappon 1987, p. 508.

193 population more than doubled: North 1966, p. 75.

193 number of post offices: Cunningham 1996, p. 24.

194 "schools, roads and canals": TJ to Alexander von Humboldt, 13 June 1817, de Terra 1959, p. 795.

194 "I am not afraid": TJ to Robert Fulton, 17 March 1810, TJ Papers RS, vol. 2, p. 301.

194 "render our country the garden": TJ to Joshua Gilpin, 15 March 1810, TJ Papers RS, vol. 2, p. 296.

194 JM invested $500: Robert Patton to JM, 17 March 1818, JM Papers RS, vol. 1, p. 238. JM had bought five shares worth $500 in March 1815.

194 JM supports John Stevens: JM to John Stevens, 17 November 1818, JM Papers RS, vol. 1, p. 380.

194 "playful as a child": James K. Paulding, Ketcham 1959, p. 435.

194 "If ever man rejoiced": Ibid.

194 "patched at the knees": D. N. Logan, 22 November 1824, quoted in Ketcham 1990, p. 621.

194 JM at Montpelier: Cutts 1817; "Madison's Servant. Uncle Ben Stewart talks about his Master and Mistress," in *Decatur Republican,* 14 June 1888.

194 "like Adam and eve": Eliza Collins Lee to DM, 30 March 1819, DMDE.

194 "on your return to your books": TJ to JM, 15 April 1817, JM Papers RS, vol. 1, p. 28.

194 "He has no particular Business": William Thornton to JM, 18 June 1817, JM Papers RS, vol. 1, p. 67.

195 "few visit our country without": Margaret Bayard Smith, Hunt 1906, p. 235; another visitor noted that Madison was "keeping tavern here." (Richard Rush to Charles J. Ingersoll, 9 October 1816, Ketcham 1990, p. 608.)

195 Montpelier a great place for parties: DM to Anna Payne Cutts, 5 July 1816, DMDE.

195 "cheering smile": Margaret Bayard Smith, Hunt 1906, p. 81; see also Cutts 1817.

195 alterations to house: Mark and Maul 2008 (unpublished manuscript, Archaeology Department, Montpelier); Hyland 2007; Ketcham 2009, pp. 4–9; Green and Miller 2007; see also TJ to JM, 19 April 1809, TJ Papers RS, vol. 1, p. 155; Dinsmore to JM throughout 1809, JM Papers PS, vol. 1.

195 new garden at Montpelier: Reeves 2009 (online report), Reeves 2008 (unpublished manuscript, Archaeology Department, Montpelier). Archaeologists used the examination of stratigraphy, ceramics, nails, mortar, brick rubble, as well as other artifacts to date different elements in the garden.

195 "and when those he contemplates": Anna Thornton, September 1802,

quoted in Green and Miller 2007, p. 8. Thornton presented the watercolor to Madison in February 1803. (Green and Miller 2007, p. 37.)

195 work on the rear lawn: In spring 1809, Hugh Chisolm began the underpinning of the mansion and replaced several layers of brick—archaeological evidence shows that this brick rubble was used to level the lawn at the back. The clay used to fill the dips was from the basement excavations and from the hill. The work was finished by 1810. (Reeves 2009 [online report], pp. 9–10, 14–16; Reeves, Tinkham and Marshall 2009 [online report], chaps. 2, 4, 6.)

196 "his vision is too imperfect": James Monroe to JM, 25 July 1810, JM Papers PS, vol. 2, p. 437.

196 Bizet at Montpelier: Bizet remained for several years at Montpelier, but there might have been some problems. In 1813 a friend from Richmond apologized to Madison for talking to Bizet about possible employment. "I understood that his Service with you would soon expire," he wrote to Madison, "I shall not receive him until he brings me a certificate, that you have no further claims upon him." At the end of October 1817, Madison wrote that "Bizet has indicated a disposition to remain with us," but by 1822 Bizet was listed in the Washington Directory as "gardener to president." He remained James Monroe's gardener at the White House until 1825 when John Quincy Adams became president. (James Monroe to JM, 25 July 1810, JM Papers PS, vol. 2, p. 437; Cutts 1817; George Hay to JM, 28 September 1813, DLC; JM to Richard Cutts, 12 October 1817, JM Papers RS, vol. 1, pp. 139–40; Delano 1822, p. 18; Joseph Elgar to JQA, 30 July 1825, NA Record Group 42.)

196 "blowing a rock": James Monroe to JM, 25 July 1810, JM Papers PS, vol. 2, p. 437; JM's letter to Monroe asking about Bizet is privately owned, dated 16 July 1810.

196 Archibald Blair: He had worked for John Hartwell Cooke in 1817; Archibald Blair to John Hartwell Cooke, 20 August 1825, ViU; JM to James Maury, 24 March 1823, DLC. For Scottish gardeners: even Joseph Banks, the nominal director of Kew Gardens in London, preferred Scottish gardeners and plant hunters for their "habits of industry attention & Frugality." (Banks to George Harrison, 1 September 1814, Chambers 2007, vol. 6, pp. 141–42.)

196 "wonderful march of national prosperity": James Preston to JM, 28 February 1817, Brant 1941–61, vol. 6, p. 419.

196 "a statue of Liberty": Cutts 1817. The temple was part of the new landscape design and built in 1810–11; see Dinsmore and Nielson's account with JM, 28 September 1811, JM Papers PS, vol. 3, p. 472.

197 blacksmith workshop: Reeves 2009 (online report), p. 5. Next to the temple archaeologists found slag, iron artifacts, nails and horseshoes, spreading out across an area of two acres.

197 lack of shrubberies: None of the visitor accounts mentions flowering shrubs but only trees.

197 "I would advise that": and following quotes, William Thornton to TJ, 27 May 1817, DLC.

197 slave village: An 1837 insurance policy (taken out by Dolley Madison) included a map that depicted the exact location of the slave quarters. We know that the floors were raised because of the brick foundation of the chimney as well as the lack of burned soil in the chimney area (which indicates that the hearth was in a crib); the amount and type of nails used suggest a substantial frame building, and the large amount of window glass found in the ground indicates that the windows were glazed. Archaeologists also discovered door hardware and the insurance policy of 1837 described the dwellings as "of wood covered with shingles." At the same time, the existence of an insurance indicates that the dwellings were regarded as being valuable enough to be insured. Large amounts of the Madisons' Davenport china was found around the location of the slave village—by contrast, so far not a single shard was discovered near the field cabins. Archaeologists found a surprisingly small amount of trash in the slave village. Matthew Reeves (Director of Archaeology at Montpelier) concludes that this indicates constant sweeping of the yard. Final analysis of this village will only be possible by mid-2014, when the slave quarter excavations at Montpelier and their comparative study will be completed. Reeves 2008 (unpublished manuscript, Archaeology Department, Montpelier); Reeves 2010 (conference paper); Trickett 2009a (online report). The 1924 copy of the 1837 Montpelier Insurance Map is reprinted in Trickett 2009a (online report), p. 12.

197 "Granny Milly" and following quote: Cutts 1817.

197 "an object of interest" and following quote: Ibid.

198 "besides bad habit": GW to William Pearce, December 1793, Conway 1889, p. 23.

198 detached kitchen: Archaeological digs have revealed the exact location of the kitchen (corresponding with the map in the 1837 insurance policy), the position of the lattice screen (also to be seen on an 1818 watercolor by Baroness Hyde de Neuville) and the exact line of the pine allée. Marshall 2009 (online report). The rows of trees were also described in visitor accounts: Cutts 1817; John H. B. Latrobe to Charles Carrol Harper, August 1832, Semmes 1917, p. 239.

198 JM and slavery: McCoy 1989, pp. 260–86.

198 "stain" and "blot": JM to Lafayette, 1821, DLC.

198 visitors writing about slave cabins: For example, Louis-Philippe 1797, pp. 31–32; Julian Ursin Niemcewicz 1798 in Lee 2006, pp. 77–79; Sir Augustus John Foster, 1807, Davis 1954, pp. 141–42.

199 "whipped all day": JM on his slaves as recounted by Harriet Martineau, Martineau 1838, vol. 1, p. 193.

199 "beyond comparison": JM to Robert Walsh Jr., 2 March 1819, JM Papers RS, vol. 1, p. 428; JM told Harriet Martineau the same in 1835, Martineau 1838, vol. 1, p. 192.

199 slave rebellion in Haiti: Matthewson 1995, p. 238; Matthewson 1996, p. 23.

199 "It is high time we": TJ to James Monroe, 14 July 1793, TJ Papers, vol. 26, p. 503.

199 changing demographics in Virginia: McCoy 1989, p. 272.

199 "increases far faster": JM on slave population as recounted by Harriet Martineau, Martineau 1838, vol. 1, p. 191.

199 "dammed up in a land of slaves": Spencer Roane to James Monroe, 16 February 1820, quoted in McCoy 1989, p. 273.

199 revolts in Virginia: Matthewson 1995, p. 238; Matthewson 1996, pp. 22–25.

199 "total revolution of property": Price 1797, p. 3.

200 "a real credit" and following quote: Kent 1775, p. 238.

200 "great agricultural merits": JM to Isaac Coffin, 1 October 1819, JM Papers RS, vol. 1, p. 519. Madison sent wild turkeys from Montpelier to Thomas Coke and enjoyed reading the pamphlet *Holkham: Its Agriculture* (1819). (Richard Rush to JM, 8 September 1819, JM Papers RS, vol. 1, p. 519; JM to Richard Rush, 12 August 1820, DLC.)

200 Coke's model cottages: Wade Martins 1980, p. 212.

200 British model villages: Some model villages were created for paternalistic reasons; others on purely aesthetic grounds. Whole villages were razed and rebuilt elsewhere to make space for landscape gardens. Early model villages in Britain were Nuneham Courtenay for the Earl of Harcourt in Oxfordshire, Harewood for the Earl of Harewood in Yorkshire, Milton Abbas for Lord Milton in Dorset and Lowther in Westmorland for Sir James Lowther in the 1760s, as well as the picturesque village of Blaise Hamlet in Somerset for the Quaker banker John Scandrett Harford in 1809. Not only landowners built model villages—in 1770 potter Josiah Wedgwood built the village Etruria for his workmen in Staffordshire.

200 pattern for model cottages: Kent 1775; Gandy 1805; Wood 1781; Soane 1793; Pocock 1807; Middleton 1795; Dickson 1805, vol. 1.; Plaw 1800; Miller 1787; *Communications of the Board of Agriculture*, vol. 1, 1797; Arthur Young's *Annals of Agriculture*.

200 *Communications of the Board of Agriculture*: For GW: Griffin 1897, p. 91; for TJ: John Sinclair to TJ, 15 July 1797, TJ Papers, vol. 29, p. 480, John Sinclair to TJ, 6 June 1800 (in this letter Sinclair also mentions that he sent the publication to JA, TJ Papers, vol. 32, p. 14); for JM: in 1819 after Richard Rush, the American Minister in London had given Sinclair a copy of Madison's Address to the Agricultural Society of Albemarle, Madison wrote to Rush "I owe perhaps an apology for not doing it myself; having being favored with several marks of that sort of an attention from him"— he also referred to other pamphlets that Sinclair had sent in his Address, JM, Notes on Agriculture, ante 12 May 1818; JM to Richard Rush, 10 May 1819, JM Papers RS, vol. 1, pp. 256, 453. Several other publications refer to the *Communications* as the reason to publish patterns of cottages such as Gandy 1805, p. 3; Dickson 1805, vol. 1, p. 77; Plaw 1800.

200 JM receiving books: GW to JM, 10 January 1794, JM Papers, vol. 15, p. 175; GW to JM, 6 December 1795, JM Papers, vol. 16, p. 140.

200 suggested design of cottages: *Communications of the Board of Agriculture*, vol. 1, 1797, pp. 115–16. The only aspect that JM changed was to make his cottages bigger. For construction details of the slave village at Montpelier, see Reeves 2008 (unpublished manuscript, Archaeology Department, Montpelier).

200 slave housing West Indies: Chapman 1991; Higman 2001, p. 244.

201 "sober, industrious, and healthy" and following quote: John Townsend in *Communications of the Board of Agriculture*, vol. 1, 1797, p. 106.

201 size of Montpelier: Not much work has been done on the exact acreage of Madison's plantation. Thomas C. Chapman, research coordinator at Montpelier, estimates the size of the plantation at the beginning of Madison's retirement around 3,000 acres or a little more. See also Miller 1985 (unpublished manuscript held at Montpelier Foundation).

201 field cabins at Montpelier: Reeves and Barton 2009 (online report).

201 "I would buy a maid": DM to Anna Payne Cutts, 23 July 1818, DMDE.

201 JM and slaves at Montpelier: Ketcham 2009, p. 45.

201 "true course' ": JM to Edward Coles, 3 September 1819, JM Papers RS, vol. 1, p. 505.

202 slaves to be settled in a New African country:" Madison wrote extensively about this; see for example JM to Robert Evans, 15 June 1819, JM Papers RS, vol. 1, p. 469, and also JM's letters to Robert Walsh Jr. in JM Papers RS, vol. 1; McCoy 1989, p. 281.

202 "regarded every where as a nuisance": JM to Lafayette, 1821, DLC.

202 "dilute the evil": TJ to Lafayette, 26 December 1820, McCoy 1989, p. 270.

202 TJ and mixing slave blood: TJ to John Lynch, 21 January 1811, TJ Papers RS, vol. 3, p. 318; Rochefoucauld-Liancourt, June 1796, Stanton 1993, p. 174. This was somehow hypocritical, since Jefferson was most certainly the father of his slave Sally Hemings's six children. DNA tests in the late twentieth century, together with oral history of the Hemings family and Jefferson's presence at Monticello at time of conception of all children, confirmed that he was most likely the father. All slaves he freed were members of the Hemings family. (Stanton 2009, pp. 91–92; Gordon-Reed 1997, pp. 59ff. and 210ff.)

202 "all at once": Rochefoucauld-Liancourt, June 1796, Stanton 1993, p. 174.

202 "Look into the": Wright 1821, p. 382.

202 Lafayette and Wright at slave village: Levasseur 1829, pp. 220–24; Cutts 1817; Roberts 1919, p. 212.

202 "one of the most interesting" and following quote: Cutts 1817.

202 "the slaves here wore": Richard Harlan to George William Featherstonhaugh, 28 May 1831, Harlan 1831, p. 60.

202 "a model of kindness": Richard Rush to Charles J. Ingersoll, 9 October 1816, quoted in Ketcham 1990, p. 608.

203 "There is no form": This was in relation to running a model farm at the University of Virginia, 7 October 1822, Minutes Albemarle Agricultural Society, True 1921, pp. 298–99; see also JM in *The American Farmer*, 22 November 1822; JM to Richard Peters, 22 February 1819, JM Papers RS, vol. 1, p. 422.

203 JM's agricultural tours: George Ticknor to William Prescott, 16 December 1824, Hillard 1876, vol. 1, p. 347; James K. Paulding, Ketcham 1959, p. 436.

203 "without dismounting": James K. Paulding, Ketcham 1959, p. 436.

203 "sometimes didactic, sometimes scientific": James K. Paulding, Ketcham

1959, p. 436; see also Richard Harlan to George William Featherston-haugh, 28 May 1831, Harlan 1831, p. 60.

203 JM and Agricultural Society of Albemarle: 5 May 1817, 7 October 1817, Minutes Albemarle Agricultural Society, True 1921, pp. 263, 270.

203 Virginia's "rapid decline": Strickland 1800, pp. 128ff. For an account on Virginia's decline see Dunn 2007, pp. 3–14.

203 TJ selling his library: After the British burned the Capitol, including the Library of Congress, Jefferson sold his library to Congress. (Malone 1948–91, vol. 6, pp. 169ff.)

203 "on borrowed means": JM to TJ, 24 February 1826, Morton Smith 1995, vol. 3, p. 1967.

203 Hessian fly in Virginia: JM to Richard Cutts, 27 May 1817, JM Papers RS, vol. 1, p. 51.

203 "since my return": JM to TJ, 24 February 1826, Morton Smith 1995, vol. 3, p. 1967.

204 Virginia farms for sale: Stoll 2002, p. 46.

204 "exhausted country": Taylor 1977, p. 160.

204 JM's family and friends leaving Virginia: Ketcham 2009, p. 36.

204 "the surest basis of": Isaac Briggs to JM, 1 January 1803, JM Papers SS, vol. 4, p. 232.

204 "I am a farmer": JM to Horatio Gates Spafford, 10 March 1802, JM Papers SS, vol. 3, p. 19.

204 JM and national Board of Agriculture: Madison organized members of Congress to form a national Board of Agriculture in 1803 and convinced the editor of the *National Gazette* to publish an invitation for the inaugural meeting. He was elected as its president on 22 February 1803. (Isaac Briggs to JM, 1 January 1803; Samuel Latham Mitchill to JM, 10 January 1803, JM to Isaac Briggs, 11 January 1803, JM Papers SS, vol. 4, pp. 232–33, 247–49; *National Intelligencer,* 25 February 1803; Isaac Briggs, *Journal of the American Board of Agriculture,* 22 February 1803, DLC.)

204 JM's agricultural correspondence: See letters between TJ and JM through-out their friendship, as well as James Monroe to JM, 13 July 1799, JM Papers, vol. 17, p. 253; Thomas Moore to JM, 2 May 1802 and 12 August 1802, JM Papers SS, vol. 3, pp. 94, 474; JM to Isaac Briggs, post 8 October 1802, JM Papers SS, vol. 4, p. 1; Edward Coles to JM, 20 March 1817; William Crawford to JM, 18 April 1817; JM to Richard Rush, 23 April 1817; JM to William Crawford, 24 April 1817; JM to Richard Cutts, 22 May 1817; Michael Hutton to JM, 25 June 1817; John Love to JM, 15 July 1817, JM Papers RS, vol. 1, pp. 15, 32, 38, 39, 51, 73, 88–89.

204 "sweetening the evening": Tench Coxe to JM, 2 February 1819, JM Papers RS, vol. 1, p. 406.

204 "directing light": Thomas Mann Randolph to JM, 14 October 1817, JM Papers RS, vol. 1, p. 142.

204 TJ's "Constitution": TJ, Constitution for Proposed Agricultural Society of Albemarle, c. 1 February 1811, TJ Papers RS, vol. 3, pp. 347–51.

204 "worn out Land" and other references: 4 November 1817, Minutes Albemarle Agricultural Society, True 1921, pp. 273–75.

204 nursery near Charlottesville: On 12 May 1818 it was reported that a gardener had been found to establish the nursery. (4 November 1817, 12 May 1818, Minutes Albemarle Agricultural Society, True 1921, pp. 275, 279–80.)

204 "Implements of Husbandry": 2 March 1818, Minutes Albemarle Agricultural Society, True 1921, p. 277.

204 "Patriotic Societies": JM, Address to the Agricultural Society of Albemarle, 12 May 1818, JM Papers RS, vol. 1, p. 270.

204 "a valuable effect in": JM to Le Ray de Chaumont, 14 September 1824, DLC.

204 JM's speech: JM, Address to the Agricultural Society of Albemarle, 12 May 1818 and editorial note, JM Papers RS, vol. 1, pp. 257–59; Nelson 2007, pp. 69–73; Stoll 2002, pp. 37–41.

205 "symmetry of nature": JM, Address to the Agricultural Society of Albemarle, 12 May 1818, JM Papers RS, vol. 1, p. 269.

205 "up and down hilly land": Ibid., p. 271.

205 JM and contour ploughing: JM, Instructions for the Montpelier Overseers and Laborers, c. 8 November 1790, JM Papers, vol. 13, p. 302.

205 publications that informed JM's Address: JM, Notes on Agriculture, ante 12 May 1818. Malthus: Richard Rush sent the fifth edition of Malthus's *Principle of Population* (1817) from London. (Richard Rush to JM, 14 January 1818; JM to Richard Rush, 24 July 1818.) Humphry Davy: JM received *Elements of Agricultural Chemistry* (published 1813) a few months before giving the Address. (Charles Stuart Waugh to JM, 8 September 1817; Joseph Priestley and Jan Ingenhousz: JM Papers RS, vol. 1, pp. 127, 203–4, 253–56, 314, 257.)

206 "subservient": JM, Address to the Agricultural Society of Albemarle, 12 May 1818, JM Papers RS, vol. 1, p. 263.

206 "increase of the human part": Ibid.

206 "sufficiently seen in our forests": Ibid., p. 272.

206 "Vegetable matter which springs": Ibid., p. 273.

206 JM and Erasmus Darwin: Edmund Randolph to JM, 8 June 1801, JM Papers SS, vol. 1, p. 268; JM as recounted by Harriet Martineau, Martineau 1838, vol. 1, p. 197; Charles Stuart Waugh to JM, 8 September 1817, JM Papers RS, vol. 1, p. 127; Uglow 2002, pp. 486–88.

206 "have a relation": JM, Preliminary Draft of an Essay on Natural Order, "Symmetry of Nature," c. 10 November 1791, JM Papers, vol. 14, p. 101. JM used this draft as the basis for his article on population and emigration published in the *National Gazette* on 19 November 1791.

206 JM and *Encyclopédie*: Madison scribbled a reference to the *Encyclopédie* in the margin of his draft for the Address, JM Papers RS, vol. 1, p. 284.

207 "we can no longer trust nature": "On ne peut plus s'en fier à la nature," Diderot's and d'Alembert's *Encyclopédie, 1751–1772*, entry "Forêts," (Botan. & Econom.), ARTFL Encyclopédie Project online.

207 "unfitted for their further uses": JM, Address to the Agricultural Society of Albemarle, 12 May 1818, JM Papers RS, vol. 1, p. 265.

207 "whole class of vegetables": Ibid., p. 266.

207 "economy of nature" and following quotes: Ibid., p. 265.

207 "excessive multiplication": Ibid., p. 266.

207 "beyond their natural": Ibid., p. 268.

207 "excessive destruction of timber": Ibid., p. 282.

207 trees regarded with "antipathy" and following quote: Ibid. For JM's rallying call to deal with deforestation, he had again perused Diderot's *Encyclopédie,* which had underlined the duty to plant new trees. (Diderot's and d'Alembert's *Encyclopédie, 1751–1772,* entry "Forêts" [Botan. & Econom.], ARTFL Encyclopédie Project online.)

208 JM's Address in newspapers and pamphlets: 12 May 1818, Minutes Albemarle Agricultural Society, True 1921, p. 280; *Niles' Weekly Register,* 18 July 1818; *Franklin Gazette,* 15 August 1818; *American Advocate* and *Kennebec Advertiser,* 5 September 1818; *Massachusetts Spy,* 19 August 1818; *Village Record,* or *Chester and Delaware Federalist,* 26 August 1818; *New Hampshire Patriot,* 15 September 1818; *Rochester Telegraph,* 29 September 1818; *American Farmer,* 27 August 1819; *Plough Boy,* 5 June 1819.

208 enlightened farmers read JM's Address: Latrobe to JM, 8 July 1818; Asher Robbins to JM, 17 July 1818; Horatio Gates Spafford, 9 August 1818; Francis Corbin to JM, 24 September 1818; Robert Walsh to JM, 15 February 1819; Isaac Davis to JM, 16 February 1819; JM Papers RS, vol. 1, pp. 298ff., 306ff., 343ff., 357ff., 417, 419; Samuel Wyllys Pomeroy to JM, 7 February 1820, DLC.

208 "I see, after a long night": Richard Peters to JM, 30 July 1818, JM Papers RS, vol. 1, p. 320.

208 London bookseller and JM's Address: Mordecai M. Noah to JM, 1 September 1818 (the bookseller was John Miller), JM Papers RS, vol. 1, pp. 352–53.

208 "produce the same": José Corrèa de Serra to JM, 5 September 1818, JM Papers RS, vol. 1, p. 353.

208 JM's Address to Sinclair and APS: Richard Rush to JM, 13 December 1818; Robert Walsh to JM, 17 March 1819, JM Papers RS, vol. 1, pp. 392, 439.

208 "wonderfull order and balance": JB to Peter Collinson, 26 April 1737, Berkeley and Smith Berkeley 1992, p. 45.

208 "it Deserved to be": Peter Collinson to JB, 10 December 1737, Berkeley and Smith Berkeley 1992, p. 68.

208 "timber will soon": JB, "An Essay for the Improvements of Estates, by Raising a Durable Timber for Fencing, and Other Uses," *Poor Richard Improved,* ed. by BF, 1749, Berkeley and Smith Berkeley 1992, p. 294.

208 "as most of ye land is cleared": JB to Peter Collinson, 6 January 1763, Berkeley and Smith Berkeley 1992, p. 582.

209 "loss for wood": BF to Jared Eliot, 25 October 1750, BF Papers, vol. 4, p. 70. For BF's Pennsylvania fireplace: BF wrote "any new Proposal for Saving the Wood . . . may at least be thought worth Consideration." (BF, An Account of the New Invented Pennsylvanian Fire-Places, 1744, BF Papers, vol. 2, p. 422.)

209 "the waste . . . on my timber": GW to William Pearce, 9 February 1794, Conway 1889, p. 38.

209 "use a good deal of economy": TJ to Edmund Bacon, 8 December 1806; TJ to Edmund Bacon, 13 May 1807, Betts 1944, pp. 327, 347.

209 "dismall Wilderness": JA Diary, 15 June 1756, 1:21, MHS online.

209 "Pray dont let a": JA to AA, 14 August 1783, MHS online.

209 villagers "murdered" tree: JA Diary, 25 July 1796, 46:41, MHS online.

209 "Great depredations": Sir Augustus John Foster, 1807, Davis 1954, p. 140; for TJ and trees in Washington, see Margaret Bayard Smith, Hunt 1906, pp. 11–12.

209 "some regulations for": Louis Philippe Gallot de Lormerie to TJ, 14 April 1809; TJ to Louis Philippe Gallot de Lormerie, 22 July 1809, TJ Papers RS, vol. 1, pp. 133–34, 354; Louis Philippe Gallot de Lormerie to TJ, 16 August 1810, TJ Papers RS, vol. 3, pp. 34–35; TJ to McMahon, 3 January 1809, Betts 1944, p. 401.

209 "a gross putrescent fluid": Williamson 1769–71, p. 280.

210 "Every friend to humanity": Ibid., p. 279.

210 "the cutting down of wood" and following quote: Benjamin Rush, 15 December 1785, quoted in Chinard 1945, p. 454.

210 "I hope this will give": BF to Joseph Priestley, July 1772, BF Papers, vol. 19, p. 216.

210 "plantations of the trees": JM, Address to the Agricultural Society of Albemarle, 12 May 1818, JM Papers RS, vol. 1, p. 283.

210 "by clearing Lands": William Thornton to JM, 28 January 1814, DLC.

210 botanic garden in Washington and founding fathers: Alexander White to JM, 26 September 1796, JM Papers, vol. 16, p. 402; William Thornton to GW, 1 October 1796; Commissioners of DC to GW, 1 October 1796, Thornton Papers, vol. 1, pp. 398, 400; GW to Commissioners of DC, 21 October 1796, DLC; Isaac Briggs to JM, 1 January 1803, JM Papers SS, vol. 4, p. 233; JA to Benjamin Waterhouse, 7 August 1805, Ford 1927, pp. 26–28; William Thornton to TJ, 20 January 1812, TJ Papers RS, vol. 4, p. 426; William Thornton to JM, 28 January 1814, DLC. The charter was granted on 20 April 1818 and the bill was signed by President James Monroe in May 1820; however, the garden ran into financial difficulties. (Fallen 2006, pp. 16ff.)

210 "Our stately forests": Nicholas Collin, 3 April 1789, quoted in Chinard 1945, p. 461.

210 "had been at great pains": John Finch, 1824, Finch 1833, p. 247.

211 "a conquest of civilized man": Adam Hodgson, 1820, quoted in Chinard 1945, Appendix 7, p. 483.

211 "the preservation and the culture" and "guardianship": John Frederick Schroeder, 1829, quoted in Otis 2002, p. 109.

211 "unmolested by the axe": Audubon 1970, p. 4.

211 "a better taste is growing" and following quote: Browne 1832, p. 401.

211 "necessity of economizing": Browne 1837, p. 357.

211 "Wherever they [trees]": Browne 1832, p. 416.

211 "A nation's Park,": George Catlin, 1832, quoted in Huth 1950, p. 120.

212 "American trees, of large growth": A. J. Downing to Millard Fillmore, 3 May 1851, quoted in Pauly 2007, p. 85.

212 "to the welfare of their country" and following quote: Editorial, "Mr Madison's Address," 5 June 1819, *The Plough Boy*, vol. 1.

EPILOGUE

213 "mammoth cucumber": TJ to Thomas Worthington, 29 November 1825; Thomas Worthington to TJ, 7 January 1826; TJ to Leonard Case, 8 April 1826, Betts 1944, pp. 616–18.

213 "spare a few to a beggar": TJ to Thomas Worthington, 29 November 1825, Betts 1944, p. 616.

213 TJ almost drowned: Henry D. Gilpin to Joshua Gilpin, 16 September 1827, Gray 1968, p. 468; Daniel Webster, December 1824, Ticknor Curtis 1872, vol. 1, p. 225.

213 "Man, like the fruit": TJ to Henry Dearborn, 17 August 1821, Ford 1892–99, vol. 10, p. 191.

213 "school of Botany": TJ to John Patton Emmet, 27 April 1826, DLC.

213 "I have diligently examined": and suggestions for botanic garden, TJ to John Patton Emmet, 27 April 1826, DLC.

213 letters about botanic garden at UVA: TJ to John Patton Emmet, 27 April 1826, DLC; TJ to John Patton Emmet, 2 May 1826, DLC; TJ to John Patton Emmet, 12 May 1826, DLC; John Patton Emmet to TJ, 28 April 1826, Huntington Library; John Patton Emmet to TJ, 13 May 1826, Huntington Library; TJ to JM, 3 May 1826, Morton Smith 1995, vol. 3, p. 1970; John Patton Emmet to Arthur Brockenbrough, probably 9 May 1826, ViU; TJ to Arthur Brockenbrough, May 1826, ViU; TJ to John Hartwell Cooke, 20 May 1826, ViU.

213 "work should be begun": TJ to John Hartwell Cooke, 20 May 1826, ViU; meeting with Emmet, John Patton Emmet to TJ, 13 May 1826, DLC; botanic garden as priority, TJ to Arthur Brockenbrough, May 1826, ViU.

214 "would make a *beau finale*": George Ticknor to William Prescott, 16 December 1824, Hillard 1876, vol. 1, p. 348.

214 botanic garden not completed: For more information on the proposed botanic garden, see Lily Fox Bruguiere's research and transcriptions of the letters (online).

214 TJ's last illness: Randolph 1976, pp. 422ff; Malone 1948–1981, vol. 6, pp. 497–99; Radbill 1963, pp. 32–33.

214 "Is it the 4th?" and following quote: Radbill 1963, p. 32.

214 JA's last illness: Susan Boylston Adams Clark to Abigail Louisa Smith Adams Johnson, 9 July 1826, MHS, Alexander B. Johnson Letters; Diary of Rev. George Whitney, 6 April–7 July 1826, MHS AP reel 475; John Marston to JQA, 8 July 1826, MHS AP reel 476.

214 "It is a great day": Susan Boylston Adams Clark to Abigail Louisa Smith Adams Johnson, 9 July 1826, MHS, Alexander B. Johnson Letters.

214 "Thomas Jefferson survives": Susan Boylston Adams Clark to Abigail Louisa Smith Adams Johnson, 9 July 1826, MHS, Alexander B. Johnson Letters.

214 "a sublime sight": Susan Boylston Adams Clark to Abigail Louisa Smith
      Adams Johnson, 9 July 1826, MHS, Alexander B. Johnson Letters.

214 "beautiful and grand": John Marston to JQA, 8 July 1826, MHS AP reel
      476.

214 "ceased breathing as quietly": Jennings 1983, p. 51; for JM's death, see also
      Ketcham 1990, p. 669.

Selected Bibliography

Libraries of the Founding Fathers

Unless otherwise referenced, books that are mentioned as being owned by the founding fathers can be found through the following online sources, which provide searchable catalogs of the libraries (titles, authors, and subjects such as "agriculture").

Thomas Jefferson's Library.
http://tjlibraries.monticello.org
LibraryThing:
http://www.librarything.com/catalog/ThomasJefferson/yourlibrary

Benjamin Franklin's Library.
LibraryThing:
http://www.librarything.com/catalog/BenjaminFranklin/yourlibrary

John Adams's Library.
Library Thing:
http://www.librarything.com/catalog/JohnAdams/yourlibrary

George Washington's Library.
LibraryThing:
http://www.librarything.com/catalog/GeorgeWashington/yourlibrary

James Madison's Library.
LibraryThing:
http://www.librarything.com/catalog/JamesMadisonLibrary/yourlibrary

Online Sources and Internet Archives

MHS, Adams Family Papers. An Electronic Archive.
http://www.masshist.org/digitaladams/aea/

MHS, Thomas Jefferson Papers. An Electronic Archive. (For TJ's architectural drawings—please use the numbers provided in the endnotes to find the correct image.)
http://www.masshist.org/thomasjeffersonpapers/

USDA History Collection, Special Collections, National Agricultural Library.
http://www.nal.usda.gov/speccoll/collect/history/index.htm

Library of Congress (all images that are mentioned in the endnotes can be viewed online).
 Maps and Geography Division
http://memory.loc.gov/ammem/gmdhtml/gmdhome.html
 Prints and Photographs Division
http://www.loc.gov/rr/print/catalog.html

Journals of the Lewis and Clark Expedition. University of Nebraska–Lincoln Libraries—Electronic Text Center.
http://lewisandclarkjournals.unl.edu/

Papers of Benjamin Franklin online.
http://www.franklinpapers.org/franklin/

Marshall, A. Archaeological Investigations of the Madison North Detached Kitchen: Final Report. Seasons 2008–2009, draft (2009).
http://montpelier.org/explore/archaeology/reports/north_kitchen_2009.pdf

Reeves, Matthew. A Brief History of the Montpelier Landscape. With a Supplement Summarizing the Excavations of the 2006–2008 Field Seasons (2009).
http://montpelier.org/explore/archaeology/media/pdf/Brief_Landscape_History.pdf

Reeves, Matthew, Kim Tinkham, and Adam Marshall. Rear Lawn Report. Excavations for the Installation of the Mansion Bunker, 2004, 2005, and 2006 Seasons (2009).
http://montpelier.org/explore/archaeology/reports/rear_lawn.pdf

Reeves, Matthew, and Jim Barton. Report of the Madison Field Quarter Site, Phase II, Excavation Seasons 2004–2005 (2009).
http://montpelier.org/explore/archaeology/reports/hq_quarters.pdf

Trickett, Mark. South Yard Excavation Report, 2008 Season (2009a).
http://montpelier.org/explore/archaeology/reports/south_yard.pdf

Trickett, Mark. South Yard Excavation Report, 2008 Season (2009b).
http://montpelier.org/explore/archaeology/reports/south_yard.pdf

Diderot's and d'Alembert's *Encyclopédie,* ARTFL Encyclopédie Project.
http://encyclopedie.uchicago.edu/

Lily Fox Bruguiere's research on the Botanic Garden at the University of Virginia.
http://www.virginia.edu/president/kenanscholarship/work/archive_files/lily_fox_bruguiere/Site/Home.html

UNPUBLISHED AND PUBLISHED REPORTS

Beiswanger, William L. Report on Research and a Program for the Restoration of the Monticello Grove, February 1977. Monticello: Thomas Jefferson Library.

———. Report on Research and a Program for the Restoration of the Monticello Vegetable Garden Terrace, November 1978. Monticello: Thomas Jefferson Library.

Brown, C. Allan. Visualizing the Madisons' Landscape at Montpelier (Preliminary Report), Archaeology Department, Montpelier.

Coxe Toogood, Anna. Cultural Landscape Report. Independence Square: National Park Service, 2004.

John Miller Associates. Mount Vernon Cultural Landscape Study. Mount Vernon Library.

Lacy, Katharine. Cultural Landscape Report: Adams National Historic Site. Boston: National Park Service, 1997.

Miller, Anne. The Madison Family's Land in the Region of "Montpelier." Unpublished manuscript held at Montpelier Foundation, 1985.

MV Folder. Early Descriptions ante 1800. Mount Vernon Library.

National Park Service. Historic American Landscape Survey of John Bartram House and Garden. HALS No. PA-1.

Reeves, Matthew. Contested Space by the Main House: Montpelier's Service Complex. Unpublished manuscript, Archaeology Department, Montpelier, 2008.

———. Archaeology at a Presidential Plantation: James Madison's Montpelier. Conference paper, SHA Conference on Historical and Underwater Archaeology, Amelia Island Plantation, Florida, 2010.

Reeves, Matthew, and Jim Barton. Phase II, Report of the Madison Field Quarter Site, Excavation Seasons 2004–2005.

Wenger, Mark, and Alfredo Maul. Architectural History of the Montpelier Mansion. Unpublished manuscript, Archaeology Department, Montpelier, 2008.

Wheeler, Richard. Icons and Emblems. Unpublished conference paper, Stowe Estate Office (n.d.).

BOOKS

Adams, Abigail. *Letters of Mrs. Adams, the Wife of John Adams. With an Introductory Memoir by Her Grandson, Charles Francis Adams.* Boston: Wilkens, Carter, 1848.

Adams, Charles Francis (ed.). *Memoirs of John Quincy Adams.* Philadelphia: J. B. Lippincott, 1874–77.

———. *The Works of John Adams.* Boston: Little, Brown, 1850–56.

Adams, John. *Warren-Adams Letters, 1743–1777.* Boston: Massachusetts Historical Society, 1917.

Adams, William Howard. *The Eye of Thomas Jefferson.* Washington, D.C.: National Gallery of Art, 1976.

Allan, D. G. C. " 'Dear and Serviceable to Each Other' ": Benjamin Franklin and the Royal Society of Arts." *Proceedings of the American Philosophical Society,* vol. 144, no. 3, 2000.

Allen, David Grayson (ed.). *Diary of John Quincy Adams.* Cambridge: Harvard University Press, 1981.

Allen, W. B. (ed.). *Works of Fisher Ames.* Indianapolis: Liberty Fund, 1983.

Allgor, Catherine. *A Perfect Union: Dolley Madison and the Creation of the American Nation.* New York: Henry Holt, 2006.

Ambrose, Stephen. *Undaunted Courage: Meriwether Lewis, Thomas Jefferson, and the Opening of the West*. New York: Simon & Schuster, 2005.

Appleby, Joyce. *Capitalism and a New Social Order: The Republican Vision of the 1790s*. New York: New York University Press, 1984.

Aristotle. *The Politics*. Translated by Thomas Alan Sinclair. London: Penguin Books, 1992.

Armstrong, Alan W. (ed.). *Forget Not Me & My Garden: Selected Letters 1725–1768 of Peter Collinson, F.R.S.* Philadelphia: American Philosophical Society, 2002.

Arnebeck, Bob. *Through a Fiery Trial: Building Washington, 1790–1800*. Lanham, Md.: Madison Books, 1991.

Audubon, John James. *Delineations of American Scenery and Character*. New York: G. A. Baker, 1970 (first published 1826).

Axelrod, Jacob, and Philip Freneau. *Champion of Democracy*. Austin and London: University of Texas Press, 1967.

Baatz, Simon. *Venerate the Plough: A History of the Philadelphia Society for Promoting Agriculture, 1785–1985*. Philadelphia: Philadelphia Society for Promoting Agriculture, 1985.

Bailyn, Bernard. *The Ideological Origins of the American Revolution*. Cambridge: Harvard University Press, 1992.

Bartram, Moses. "Observations on Native Silk Worms of North-America." Transactions of the American Philosophical Society, vol. 1, 1769–71.

Bear, James A. (ed.). *Jefferson at Monticello: Recollections of a Monticello Slave and of a Monticello Overseer*. Charlottesville: University of Virginia Press, 1967.

Beeman, Richard. *Plain, Honest Men: The Making of the American Constitution*. New York: Random House, 2009.

Beiswanger, William L. "Dedication of the Garden Pavilion at Monticello," 12 April 1984, Monticello Keepsake, no. 34.

———. "The Temple in the Garden: Thomas Jefferson's Vision of the Monticello Landscape." In Robert P. Maccubbin and Peter Martin. *British and American Gardens*. Charlottesville: University of Virginia Press, 1983.

Bell, Whitfield J. *Patriot-Improvers: Biographical Sketches of the Members of the American Philosophical Society*. Philadelphia: American Philosophical Society, 1997.

Berg, Scott W. *Grand Avenues: The Story of Pierre Charles L'Enfant, the French Visionary Who Designed Washington, D.C.* New York: Vintage Books, 2008.

Bergon, Frank. "Wilderness Aesthetic." In Kris Fresonke and Mark Spence (eds.). *Lewis and Clark. Legacies, Memories, and New Perspectives*. Berkeley, Los Angeles and London: University of California Press, 2004.

Berkeley, Edmund, and Dorothy Smith Berkeley. *The Correspondence of John Bartram, 1734–1777*. Gainesville: University of Florida Press, 1992.

Berkin, Carol. *A Brilliant Solution: Inventing the American Constitution*. Orlando: Harcourt, 2002.

Betts, Edwin M. *Thomas Jefferson's Farm Book*. Charlottesville: University of Virginia Press, 1987.

———. *Thomas Jefferson's Garden Book, 1766–1824*. Philadelphia: American Philosophical Society, 1944.

Betts, Edwin M., and Hazlehurst Bolton Perkins (revised and enlarged by Peter Hatch). *Thomas Jefferson's Flower Garden at Monticello.* Charlottesville: University of Virginia Press, 1986.

Betts, Edwin M., and James Adam Bear (eds.). *The Family Letters of Thomas Jefferson.* Charlottesville: University of Virginia Press, 1986.

Betts, Richard J. "The Woodlands." *Winterthur Portfolio,* vol. 14, no. 3, 1979.

Birch, William. *Birch's Views of Philadelphia,* facsimile. Philadelphia: Antique Collector's Club, 2000.

———— (ed. Emily T. Cooperman). *The Country Seats of the United States.* Philadelphia: University of Pennsylvania Press, 2009.

Boorstin, Daniel J. *The Lost World of Thomas Jefferson.* Chicago: University of Chicago Press, 1993.

Bordewich, Fergus M. *Washington: The Making of the American Capital.* New York: Amistad, 2008.

Bowen, Catherine Drinker. *Miracle at Philadelphia: The Story of the Constitutional Convention May to September 1787.* Boston: Little, Brown, 1986.

Bowling, Kenneth. *The Creation of Washington, D.C.: The Idea and Location of the American Capital.* Fairfax, Va.: George Mason University Press, 1991.

Branch, Michael P., and Daniel J. Philippon (eds.). *The Height of Our Mountains: Nature Writings from Virginia's Blue Ridge Mountains and Shenandoah Valley.* Baltimore and London: Johns Hopkins University Press, 1998.

Brandt, Anthony. *Thomas Jefferson Travels: 1784–1789.* Washington, D.C.: National Geographic Books, 2006.

Brant, Irving. *James Madison.* Indianapolis: Bobbs-Merrill, 1941–61.

Breeden, James O. (ed.). *Advice Among Masters: The Ideal in Slave Management in the Old South.* Westport, Conn. and London: Greenwood Press, 1980.

Brissot de Warville, Jacques Pierre. *New Travels in the United States of America, performed in 1788.* New York: Augustus M. Kelly, 1970 (facsimile of 1792 edition).

Brookhiser, Richard. *George Washington: Founding Father.* New York: Free Press, 1997.

Brown, C. Allan. "Thomas Jefferson's Poplar Forest: The Mathematics of an Ideal Villa." *Journal of Garden History,* vol. 10, no. 2, 1990.

Brown, Everett Somerville. *William Plumer's Memorandum of Proceedings in the United States Senate 1803–07.* New York: The Macmillan Company, 1923.

Brown, Ralph Adams. *The Presidency of John Adams.* Lawrence: University of Kansas Press, 1975.

Browne, D. J. "American Forest Trees." *North American Review,* vol. 35, 1832.

————. "American Forest Trees." *North American Review,* vol. 44, 1837.

Brownell, Charles E., and Jeffrey A. Cohen. *The Architectural Drawings of Benjamin Henry Latrobe.* New Haven and London: Yale University Press, 1994.

Bryan, Wilhelmus B. "The Name *White House.*" *Records of the Historical Society of Columbia,* vols. 33–34, 1932.

Budka, Metchie J. E. (ed.). *Under Their Vine & Fig Tree: Travels through America in 1797–99 by Julian Ursyn Niemcewicz.* Elizabeth, N.J.: Grassmann, 1965.

Burk, Kathleen. *Old World, New World: The Story of Britain and America.* London: Little, Brown, 2007.

Burke, Edmund. *A Philosophical Enquiry*. Oxford: Oxford University Press, 1998 (first published 1757).

Busey, Samuel Clagett. *Pictures of the City of Washington in the Past*. Washington D.C.: W. Ballantyne & Sons, 1898.

Butterfield, L. H. (ed.). *Diary and Autobiography of John Adams*. Cambridge: Harvard University Press, 1961.

—— (ed.). *Letters of Benjamin Rush*. Princeton: Princeton University Press, 1951.

Butterfield, L. H., Marc Friedlander, and Wendell Garrett. *The Adamses at Home: Accounts by Visitors to the Old House in Quincy, 1788–1886*. Boston: Colonial Society of Massachusetts, 1970.

Cappon, Lester J. (ed.). *The Adams-Jefferson Letters*. Chapel Hill: University of North Carolina Press, 1987.

Carr, Robert Col. "Personal Recollections of Benjamin Franklin." *Historical Magazine*, August 1868.

Catalogue of Plants and Seeds, sold by Kennedy and Lee, Nursery and Seedsmen at the Vineyard. Hammersmith, London, 1774.

Chambers, Neil. *The Scientific Correspondence of Sir Joseph Banks, 1765–1820*. London: Pickering & Chatto, 2007.

Chaplin, Joyce E. *The Scientific American: Benjamin Franklin and the Pursuit of Genius*. New York: Basic Books, 2006.

Chapman, William. "Slave Villages in the Danish West Indies: Changes of the Late Eighteenth and Early Nineteenth Centuries." *Perspectives in Vernacular Architecture*, vol. 41, p. 991.

Charlesworth, M. (ed.). *The English Garden: Literary Sources and Documents*. Mountfield, East Sussex: Helm Publishing, 1993.

Chernow, Ron. *Alexander Hamilton*. New York: Penguin Books, 2004.

Chinard, Gilbert. "The American Philosophical Society and the Early History of Forestry in America." *Proceedings of the American Philosophical Society*, vol. 89, 1945.

——. *Honest John Adams*. Gloucester: Little, Brown, 1976.

Clarke, George. "The History of Stowe—X: Moral Gardening." In *Stoic*, vol. 24, no. 3, July 1970.

Cohen, I. Bernard. *Science and the Founding Fathers: Science in the Political Thought of Thomas Jefferson, Benjamin Franklin, John Adams, and James Madison*. New York and London: W. W. Norton, 1995.

Coke, Lady Mary. *The Letters and Journals of Lady Mary Coke*. Bath: Kingsmead Reprints, 1970.

Colden, Cadwallader. *Letters and Papers of Cadwallader Colden*. New York: New York Historical Society, 1918–37.

Coleman Sellers, Charles. "Charles Willson Peale with Patron and Populace." A Supplement to "Portraits and Miniatures by Charles Willson Peale." *Transactions of the American Philosophical Society*, New Series, vol. 59, no. 3, 1969.

Communications to the Board of Agriculture on the Subject Relative to the Husbandry and Internal Improvement of the Country. London: W. Bulmer, vol. 1, 1797.

Conway, Moncure Daniel. "George Washington and Mount Vernon. A Collection of Washington's Unpublished Agricultural and Personal Letters." *Memoirs of the Long Island Historical Society*, vol. 4, 1889.

Cook, Olive. *English Cottages and Farmhouses*. London: Thames & Hudson, 1982.

Cooke, Jacob E. "Tench Coxe, Alexander Hamilton and the Encouragement of Manufactures." *William and Mary Quarterly*, Third Series, vol. 32, no. 3, 1975.

Cornett, Peggy. "Encounters with America's Premier Nursery and Botanic Garden." *Twinleaf*, 2004.

———. "The Horticultural Potential of Lewis and Clark Plants." *Twinleaf*, 2003.

———. "Thomas Jefferson's 'Belles of the Day' at Monticello." *Twinleaf*, 2001.

Coues, Elliott (ed.). *The History of the Lewis and Clark Expedition*. New York: Dover Publications, 1970 (reprint of the 1893 edition).

Coxe, Tench. *A View of the United States of America, 1787–1794*. Reprints of Economic Classics. New York: A. M. Kelley, 1965.

Craige, Burton. *The Federal Convention of 1787: North Carolina in the Great Crisis*. Richmond: Expert Graphics, 1987.

Crèvecoeur, J. Hector St. John de. *Letters from an American Farmer*. Oxford: Oxford University Press, 1998 (first published in 1782).

Cullen, Charles T. "Jefferson's White House Dinner Guests." *White House History*, no. 17, 2005.

Cunningham, Noble E. *The Presidency of James Monroe*. Lawrence: University of Kansas Press, 1996.

———. *In Pursuit of Reason: The Life of Thomas Jefferson*. New York: Ballantine Books, 1987.

Custis, George Washington Parke. *Recollections and Private Memoirs of Washington*. Philadelphia: J. W. Bradley, 1861.

Cutler, William Parker, and Julia Perkins Cutler. *Life, Journals and Correspondence of Rev. Manasseh Cutler*. Athens: Ohio University Press, 1888.

Cutright, Paul Russell. *Lewis and Clark: Pioneering Naturalists*. Lincoln: University of Nebraska Press, 1989.

Dalzell, Robert F., and Lee Baldwin Dalzell. *George Washington's Mount Vernon: At Home in Revolutionary America*. Oxford: Oxford University Press, 1998.

Daniel, John S., Daniel L. Druckenbrod, and Susan Solomon. "Revolutionary Minds." *American Scientist*, vol. 95, 2007.

Darlington, William (ed.). *Memorials of John Bartram and Humphry Marshall*. Philadelphia: Lindsay & Blakiston, 1849.

Davis, Richard Beale (ed.). *Jeffersonian America: Notes by Sir Augustus Foster*. San Marino: Huntington Library, 1954.

Deforest, Elizabeth K. *The Gardens and Grounds at Mount Vernon*. Mount Vernon: Mount Vernon Ladies' Association, 1982.

Delano, Judah. *The Washington Directory*. Washington, D.C., 1822.

Delle, James A. *An Archaeology of Social Space: Analyzing Coffee Plantations in Jamaica's Blue Mountains*. New York and London: Plenum Press, 1998.

Dézallier d'Argenville, Antoine-Joseph. *The Theory and Practice of Gardening* (first publ. as *La Théorie et la pratique du jardinage*, 1709). Translated by John James. London: Geo. James, 1712.

Dickson, Harold E. " 'Th.J.' " Art Collector." In William Howard Adams (ed.). *Jefferson and the Arts: An Extended View.* Washington, D.C.: National Gallery of Art, 1976.

Dickson, R. W. *Practical Agriculture.* London: Richard Phillips, 1805.

"Dodsley's 'Description of The Leasowes.' " In M. Charlesworth (ed.). *The English Garden: Literary Sources and Documents.* Mountfield, East Sussex: Helm Publishing, 1993.

Donnan, Elizabeth (ed.). "The Papers of James A. Bayard, 1796–1815." *Annual Report of the American Historical Association,* vol. 2, 1913.

Dougherty, J. P. "Baroque and Picturesque Motifs in L'Enfant's Design for the Federal Capital." *American Quarterly,* vol. 26, no. 1, 1974.

Druckenbrod, Daniel L., and Herman H. Shugart. "Forest History of James Madison's Montpelier Plantation." *Journal of the Torrey Botanical Society,* vol. 131, no. 3, 2004.

Dumbauld, Edward. *Thomas Jefferson: American Tourist.* Norman: University of Oklahoma Press, 1946.

Dunn, Susan. *Dominion of Memories: Jefferson, Madison and the Decline of Virginia.* New York: Basic Books, 2007.

Duyker, Edward, and Per Tingbrand (eds.). *Daniel Solander: Collected Correspondence, 1753–1782.* Oslo, Copenhagen and Stockholm: Scandinavian University Press, 1995.

Elkins, Stanley, and Eric McKitrick. *The Age of Federalism.* New York and Oxford: Oxford University Press, 1993.

Ellis, Joseph J. *American Creation: Triumphs and Tragedies at the Founding of the Republic.* New York: Alfred A. Knopf, 2007.

———. *American Sphinx: The Character of Thomas Jefferson.* New York: Vintage, 1998.

———. *Founding Brothers: The Revolutionary Generation.* New York: Vintage, 2002.

———. *His Excellency George Washington.* London: Faber & Faber, 2005.

———. *Passionate Sage. The Character and Legacy of John Adams.* New York and London: W. W. Norton, 2001.

Everly, Elaine C., and Howard H. Wehman. " 'Then Let Us to the Woods Repair.': Moving the Federal Government and Its Records to Washington in 1800." In Kenneth R. Bowling. *Establishing Congress: The Removal to Washington, D.C., and the Election of 1800.* Athens: Ohio University Press, 2005.

Ewan, Joseph, and Nesta Dunn Ewan (eds.). *Benjamin Smith Barton. Naturalist and Physician in Jeffersonian America.* St. Louis: Missouri Botanical Garden, 2007.

Fallen, Anne-Catherine (ed.). *A Botanic Garden for the Nation: The United States Botanic Garden.* Washington, D.C.: United States Botanic Garden, 2006.

Farrand, Max (ed.). *The Records of the Federal Convention of 1787.* New Haven: Yale University Press, 1911.

Fazio, Michael, and Patrick Snadon. "Benjamin Latrobe and Thomas Jefferson Redesign the President's House." *White House History,* no. 8, 2000.

Ferling, John. *John Adams: A Life*. Knoxville: University of Tennessee Press, 1992.
———. *Setting the World Ablaze: Washington, Adams, Jefferson, and the American Revolution*. Oxford: Oxford University Press, 2000.
Finch, John. *Travels in the United States of America and Canada*. London: Longman, 1833.
Flannery, Tim. *The Eternal Frontier: An Ecological History of North America and its Peoples*. London: Penguin Books, 2001.
Fletcher, Whitcomb Stevenson. *The Philadelphia Society for Promoting Agriculture, 1785–1955*. Philadelphia: Philadelphia Society for Promoting Agriculture, 1976.
Ford, Paul Leicester (ed.). *The Autobiography of Thomas Jefferson, 1743–1790*. Philadelphia: University of Pennsylvania Press, 2005.
——— (ed.). *The Writings of Thomas Jefferson*. New York and London: G. P. Putnam's Sons, 1892–99.
Ford, Worthington Chauncey (ed.). *Statesman and Friend: Correspondence of John Adams with Benjamin Waterhouse*. Boston: Little, Brown, 1927.
Ford, Worthington Chauncey, Gaillard Hunt, John C. Fitzpatrick, and Roscoe R. Hill (eds.). *Journals of Continental Congress, 1774–1789*. Washington, D.C.: U.S. Government Printing Office, 1904–37.
Fortune, Brandon Brame. "Portraits of Virtue and Genius: Pantheons of Worthies and Public Portraiture in the Early American Republic, 1780–1820." Dissertation, Chapel Hill, University of North Carolina Press, 1987.
Fothergill, John. *Some Account of the late Peter Collinson*. London: 1770.
The Foundation of the Massachusetts Professorship of Natural History. Boston: Russell and Cutler, 1805.
Freeman, Douglas Southall. *George Washington: A Biography*. New York: Charles Scribner's Sons, 1948–57.
Friedenberg, Daniel M. *Life, Liberty and the Pursuit of Land: The Plunder of Early America*. Buffalo: Prometheus Books, 1992.
Froncek, Thomas (ed.). *An Illustrated History: The City of Washington*. New York: Alfred A. Knopf, 1977.
Fry, Joel T. "Archaeological Research at Historic Bartram's Garden." *Bartram Broadside*, 1998.
———. "An International Catalogue of North American Trees and Shrubs: The Bartram Broadside, 1783." *Journal of Garden History*, vol. 16, no. 1, 1996.
Furtwanger, Albert. *Acts of Discovery: Visions of America in the Lewis and Clark Journals*. Urbana and Chicago: University of Illinois Press, 1999.
Fusonie, Alan, and Donna Jean Fusonie. *George Washington: Pioneer Farmer*. Mount Vernon: Mount Vernon Ladies' Association, 1998.
Fussell, G. E. *The English Rural Labourer: His Home, Furniture, Clothing and Food from Tudor to Victorian Times*. London: The Batchworth Press, 1949.
Gandy, Joseph. *Designs for Cottages, Cottage Farms and Other Rural Buildings*. London: John Harding, 1805.
Gawalt, Gerard W. "Jefferson's Slaves: Crop Accounts at Monticello, 1805–1808." *Journal of the Afro-American Historical and Genealogical Society*, vol. 13, 1994.
Gordon-Reed, Annette. *Thomas Jefferson and Sally Hemings: An American Controversy*. Charlottesville: University of Virginia Press, 1997.

Gray, Ralph D. (ed.). "A Tour of Virginia in 1827: Letters of Henry D. Gilpin to His Father." *Virginia Magazine of History and Biography*, vol. 73, no. 3, 1968.

Green, Bryan Clark, and Ann Miller. *Building a President's House: The Construction of James Madison's Montpelier*. Orange, Va.: The Montpelier Foundation, 2007.

Greenberg, Allan. *George Washington, Architect*. London: Andreas Papadakis, 1999.

Griffin, Appleton P. C. *A Catalogue of the Washington Collection in the Boston Athenaeum*. Cambridge: Boston Athenaeum, 1897.

Griswold, Mac. *Washington's Gardens at Mount Vernon*. Boston and New York: Houghton Mifflin, 1999.

Hallock, Thomas. *From the Fallen Tree: Frontier Narratives, Environmental Politics, and the Roots of a National Pastoral, 1749–1826*. Chapel Hill: University of North Carolina Press, 2003.

Hallock, Thomas, and Nancy Hoffmann (eds.). *William Bartram: The Search for Nature's Design*. Athens: University of Georgia Press, 2010.

Hamilton, Alexander. *Concerning the Public Conduct and Character of John Adams*. New York: John Lang, 1800.

Hamilton, John C. *History of the Republic of the United States of America*. New York: D. Appleton, 1859.

Handler, Edward. " 'Nature Itself is all Arcanum': The Scientific Outlook of John Adams." *Proceedings of the American Philosophical Society*, vol. 120, no. 3, 1976.

Harlan, Richard. "Tour to the Caves in Virginia." *The Monthly American Journal of Geology and Natural Science*, vol. 1, no. 2, 1831.

Harper, Francis. "William Bartram and the American Revolution." *Proceedings of the American Philosophical Society*, vol. 97, no. 5, 1953.

——— (ed.). "John Bartram: Diary of a Journey through the Carolinas, Georgia, and Florida from July 1, 1765, to April 10, 1766." *Transactions of the American Philosophical Society*, New Series, vol. 33, no. 1, 1942.

——— (ed.). *The Travels of William Bartram: Naturalist's Edition*. New Haven: Yale University Press, 1958.

Harris, C. M. "Jefferson, the Concept of the Modern Capitol, and Republican Nation-Building." In Kenneth R. Bowling. *Establishing Congress: The Removal to Washington, D.C., and the Election of 1800*. Athens: Ohio University Press, 2005.

———. "The Politics of Public Buildings: William Thornton and the President's Square." *White House History*, no. 3, spring 1998.

———. "Washington's Gamble, L'Enfant's Dream: Politics, Design and the Founding of the National Capital." *William and Mary Quarterly*, Third Series, vol. 56, no. 3, 1999.

——— (ed). *The Papers of William Thornton*. Charlottesville: University of Virginia Press, 1995.

Harris, Wilhelmina. "Historic Furnishings Report: The Birthplaces of Presidents John Adams and John Quincy Adams." Adams National Historical Park, National Park Service 1966–69.

Hatch, Peter. "African-American Gardens at Monticello." *Twinleaf*, 2001.

———. "Bernard McMahon, Pioneer American Gardener." *Twinleaf*, 1993.

———. *The Fruits and Fruit Trees of Monticello.* Charlottesville: University of Virginia Press, 1998a.

———. "McMahon's Texas Bird Pepper: A Pretty Little Plant." *Twinleaf,* 1996.

———. " 'Public Treasures': Thomas Jefferson and the Garden Plants of Lewis and Clark." *Twinleaf,* 2003.

———. "We Abound in the Luxury of Peach." *Twinleaf,* 1998b.

———. "The Work is very Heavy." *Twinleaf,* 2005.

Haw, John. *John and Edward Rutledge.* Athens and London: University of Georgia Press, 1997.

Hayden, Peter. *Russian Parks and Gardens.* London: Frances Lincoln, 2005.

Hayes, Kevin J. *The Library of Benjamin Franklin.* Philadelphia: American Philosophical Society, 2006.

Hellman, George S. (ed.). *Letters of Washington Irving to Henry Brevoort.* New York: G. P. Putman's Sons, 1915.

Higman, B. W. *Jamaica Surveyed: Plantation Maps and Plans of the Eighteenth and Nineteenth Centuries.* Barbados: University of West Virginia, 2001.

Hillard, George S. (ed.). *Life, Letters, and Journals of George Ticknor.* Boston: James R. Osgood, 1876.

Hiltzheimer, Jacob. "Extracts from the Diary of Jacob Hiltzheimer, of Philadelphia, 1769–1798." *Pennsylvania Magazine of History and Biography,* vol. 16, no. 2, 1892.

Hindle, Brooke. *The Pursuit of Science in Revolutionary America 1735–1789.* Chapel Hill: University of North Carolina Press, 1956.

Hines, Christian. *Early Recollections of Washington City.* Washington, D.C.: Junior League of Washington, 1981 (first published 1866).

Hirschfeld, Fritz. *George Washington and Slavery: A Documentary Portrayal.* Columbia and London: University of Missouri Press, 1997.

Hogan, Margaret A., and C. James Taylor (eds.). *My Dearest Friend: Letters of Abigail and John Adams.* Cambridge and London: Harvard University Press, 2007.

Hosack, David. *A Biographical Memoir of Hugh Williamson.* New York: New York Historical Society, vol. 3, 1821.

Howard, Hugh. *Dr. Kimball and Mr. Jefferson: Rediscovering the Founding Fathers of American Architecture.* New York: Bloomsbury, 2006.

———. *Thomas Jefferson, Architect: The Built Legacy of Our Third President.* New York: Rizzoli, 2003.

Hunt, Gaillard (ed.). *The First Forty Years of Washington Society, Portrayed by the Family Letters of Mrs. Samuel Harrison Smith.* New York: C. Scribner's Sons, 1906.

Hunt-Jones, Conover. *Dolley and the "great little Madison."* Washington, D.C.: American Institute of Architects Foundation, 1977.

Hunter, Clark (ed.). *Life and Letters of Alexander Wilson, Clark Hunter.* Philadelphia: American Philosophical Society, 1983.

Hutchins, Catherine E. (ed.). *Shaping a National Culture. The Philadelphia Experience, 1750–1800.* Winterthur: Henry Francis du Pont Winterthur Museum, 1994.

Huth, Hans. "The American and Nature." *Journal of the Warburg and Courtauld Institutes,* vol. 13, 1950.

Hyland, Matthew G. *Montpelier and the Madisons*. Charleston: History Press, 2007.

Idzerda, Stanley J. (ed.). *Lafayette in the Age of the American Revolution: Selected Letters and Papers, 1776–1790*. Ithaca: Cornell University Press, 1977–83.

Isaacson, Walter. *Benjamin Franklin: An American Life*. New York: Simon & Schuster, 2004.

Jackson, Donald. *Thomas Jefferson and the Stony Mountains: Exploring the West from Monticello*. Norman: University of Oklahoma Press, 1993.

——— (ed.). *Letters of the Lewis and Clark Expedition, with Related Documents, 1783–1854*. Urbana and Chicago: University of Illinois Press, 1978.

Jacobs, James A. "William Hamilton and the Woodlands: A Construction of Refinement in Philadelphia." *The Pennsylvania Magazine of History and Biography*, vol. 130, no. 2, 2006.

Jefferson, Thomas. *Notes on the State of Virginia* (edited by William Peden). New York and London: W. W. Norton, 1982.

Jennings, Paul. "A Colored Man's Reminiscences of James Madison." *White House History*, vol. 1, 1983.

Jillson, Cal. "Fighting for Control of the American Dream: Alexander Hamilton and Thomas Jefferson, and the Election of 1800." In Kenneth R. Bowling. *Establishing Congress: The Removal to Washington, D.C., and the Election of 1800*. Athens: Ohio University Press, 2005.

Judd, Richard W. "A 'Wonderful Order and Balance': Natural History and the Beginnings of Forest Conservation in America, 1730–1830." *Environmental History*, vol. 11, no. 1, 2006.

Kelly, Donna, and Lang Baradell (eds.). *The Papers of James Iredell*. Raleigh: North Carolina Department of Cultural Resources, 2003.

Kelly, James C., and William M. S. Rasmussen. *The Virginia Landscape: A Cultural History*. Charlottesville: Howell Press, 2000.

Kent, Nathaniel. *Hints to Gentlemen of Landed Property*. London: J. Dodsley, 1775.

Ketcham, Ralph. *James Madison: A Biography*. Charlottesville: University of Virginia Press, 1990.

———. *The Madisons at Montpelier: Reflections on the Founding Couple*. Charlottesville: University of Virginia Press, 2009.

——— (ed.). "An Unpublished Sketch of James K. Paulding." *Virginia Magazine of History and Biography*, vol. 67, 1959.

Knapp Engle, Corliss. "John Adams, Farmer and Gardener." *Arnoldia*, vol. 61, no. 4, 2002.

Knobloch, Frieda. *The Culture of Wilderness: Agriculture as Colonization of the American West*. Chapel Hill: University of North Carolina Press, 1996.

Labaree, Leonard W. "Benjamin Franklin's British Friendships." *Proceedings of the American Philosophical Society*, vol. 108, no. 5, 1964.

Laird, Mark. *The Flowering of the Landscape Garden*. Philadelphia: University of Pennsylvania Press, 1999.

Langford, Paul. *A Polite and Commercial People, England 1727–1783*. Oxford: Oxford University Press, 1989.

Langley, Batty. *New Principles of Gardening.* London: A. Bettesworth and J. Battey, 1728.

Larkin, Jack. *The Reshaping of Everyday Life, 1790–1840.* New York: Harper & Row, 1988.

Larson, Edward J. *A Magnificent Catastrophe: The Tumultuous Election of 1800.* New York: Free Press, 2007.

Lavender, David. *The Way to the Western Sea: Lewis and Clark Across the Continent.* Lincoln, Neb.: Bison Books, 2001.

Lee, Jean B. *Experiencing Mount Vernon: Eyewitness Accounts, 1784–1865.* Charlottesville: University of Virginia Press, 2006.

Leighton, Ann. *American Gardens in the Eighteenth Century: For Use or for Delight.* Boston: University of Massachusetts Press, 1988.

———. *American Gardens of the Nineteenth Century: For Comfort and Affluence.* Boston: University of Massachusetts Press, 1987.

Levasseur, Auguste. *Lafayette in America in 1824 and 1825, Or, Journal of a Voyage to the United States.* Philadelphia: Carey and Lea, 1829.

Lewis, W. S. (ed.). *Horace Walpole's Correspondence.* New Haven and London: Yale University Press, 1937–61.

Louis Philippe, King of France. *Diary of My Travels in America, 1830–1848.* Translated by Stephen Becker. New York: Delacorte Press, 1977.

Maclay, Edgar S. (ed.). *Journal of William Maclay, United States Senator from Pennsylvania 1789–1791.* New York: D. Appleton, 1890.

Madison, James. *Letters and Other Writings of James Madison.* Philadelphia: J. B. Lippincott, 1865.

Magee, Judith. *The Art and Science of William Bartram.* Philadelphia: Pennsylvania State University Press, 2007.

Magoon, E. L. "Scenery and Mind." In *Home Book of the Picturesque, or American Scenery, Art and Literature.* New York: G. P. Putnam, 1852 (no author).

Malone, Dumas. *Jefferson and His Time.* Boston: Little, Brown, 1948–81.

Manwaring, Elizabeth Wheeler. *Italian Landscape in Eighteenth-Century England.* London: Frank Cass, 1965.

Mare, Margaret, and W. H. Quarrell (trans. and eds.). *Lichtenberg's Visits to England as Described in his Letters and Diaries.* Oxford: Clarendon Press, 1938.

Marsh, Philip M. "The Jefferson-Madison Vacation." *The Pennsylvania Magazine for History and Biography,* vol. 71, 1947.

Marshall, Humphry. *Arbustrum Americanum: The American Grove.* Philadelphia: J. Crukshank, 1785.

Martin, Edwin T. *Thomas Jefferson: Scientist.* New York: Henry Schumann, 1952.

Martin, Peter. *Pleasure Gardens of Virginia: From Jamestown to Jefferson.* Princeton and Oxford: Princeton University Press, 1991.

Martineau, Harriet. *Retrospect of Western Travel.* London: Saunders and Otley; New York: Harper & Brothers, 1838.

Marx, Leo. *The American Revolution and the American Landscape.* Washington, D.C.: American Enterprise Institute for Public Policy Research, 1974.

———. *The Machine in the Garden: Technology and the Pastoral Ideal in America.* London: Oxford University Press, 1978.

Massachusetts Society for Promoting Agriculture. Centennial Year of the Massachusetts Society for Promoting Agriculture 1792–1892. Boston, 1892.

Mattern, David (ed.). *James Madison's "Advice to my Country."* Charlottesville: University of Virginia Press, 1997.

Mattern, David B., and Holly C. Shulman (eds.). *Selected Letters of Dolley Payne Madison.* Charlottesville: University of Virginia Press, 2003.

Matthewson, Tim. "Jefferson and Haiti." *The Journal of Southern History,* vol. 61, 1995.

———. "Jefferson and the Nonrecognition of Haiti." *Proceedings of the American Philosophical Society,* vol. 140, 1996.

McCoy, Drew R. *The Elusive Republic: Political Economy in Jeffersonian America.* New York and London: W. W. Norton, 1980.

———. *The Last of the Fathers: James Madison and the Republican Legacy.* Cambridge University Press, 1989.

McCullough, David. *John Adams.* New York: Simon & Schuster, 2001.

———. *1776: America and Britain at War.* New York: Penguin Books, 2006.

McDonald, Forrest. *The American Presidency: An Intellectual History.* Lawrence: University of Kansas Press, 1994.

McDonald, Travis. "The Private Villa Retreat of Thomas Jefferson." *White House History,* no. 18, 2006.

McDougall, Walter A. *Freedom Just Around the Corner: A New American History, 1585–1828.* New York: Perennial, 2005.

McEwan, Barbara. *Thomas Jefferson: Farmer.* Jefferson, N.C.: McFarland, 1991.

———. *White House Landscapes: Horticultural Achievements of American Presidents.* New York: Walker, 1992.

McLane Hamilton, Allan. *The Intimate Life of Alexander Hamilton.* New York: Charles Scribner's Sons, 1911.

McLean, Elizabeth. "Town and Country Gardens in Eighteenth-Century Philadelphia." In Maccubbin, Robert P., and Peter Martin. *British and American Gardens.* Charlottesville: University of Virginia Press, 1983.

McMahon, Bernard. *The American Gardener's Calendar.* Philadelphia, 1806.

Michaelis-Jena, Ruth, and Willy Merson (trans. and eds.). *A Lady Travels: Journeys in England and Scotland from the Diaries of Johanna Schopenhauer.* London: Routledge, 1988.

Middleton, Charles. *Picturesque and Architectural views for cottages, farmhouses and Country Villas.* London, 1795.

Miller, Charles A. *Jefferson and Nature: An Interpretation.* Baltimore: Johns Hopkins University Press, 1988.

Miller, J. *The Country Gentleman's Architect.* London: I. & J. Taylor, 1787.

Miller, Lillian B. (ed.). *The Selected Papers of Charles Willson Peale and His Family.* New Haven and London: Yale University Press, 1983–2000.

Miller, Philip. *Gardeners Dictionary.* London, 1731, and subsequent editions.

Mitchell, Samuel Latham. "Dr. Mitchell's Letters from Washington: 1801–1813." *Harper's New Monthly Magazine,* vol. 58, April 1879.

Mitchell, Stewart (ed.). *New Letters of Abigail Adams.* Boston: Houghton Mifflin, 1947.

Moffat, L. G., and J. M. Carrière. "A Frenchman Visits Norfolk, Fredericksburg, and Orange County, 1816." *Virginia Magazine of History and Biography,* vol. 53, no. 3, 1945.

Morales-Vasquez, Rubil. "George Washington: The President's House and the Projection of Executive Power." *Washington History,* vol. 16, no. 1, 2004.

Morgan, Edmund S. *Benjamin Franklin.* New Haven and London: Yale Nota Bene, 2003.

Morison, Samuel Eliot (ed.). *Of Plymouth Plantation, 1620–1647, by William Bradford.* New York: Alfred A. Knopf, 1952.

Morton Smith, James. *The Republic of Letters: The Correspondence Between Thomas Jefferson and James Madison, 1776–1826.* New York and London: W. W. Norton, 1995.

Münchhausen, Otto von. *Der Hausvater.* Hanover, 1770.

Munger, Susan H. *Common to This Country: Botanical Discoveries of Lewis and Clark.* New York: Artisan, 2003.

Nash, Roderick. *Wilderness and the American Mind.* New Haven and London: Yale University Press, 1982.

Nelson, E. Charles. "Australian Plants Cultivated in England before 1788." *Telopea,* vol. 4, no. 2, 1983.

Nelson, Lynn A. *Pharsalia: An Environmental Biography of a Southern Plantation, 1780–1880.* Athens and London: University of Georgia Press, 2007.

Nettel, Reginald (trans. and ed.). *Carl Philip Moritz: Journeys of a German in England in 1782.* London: Jonathan Cape, 1965.

Nichols, Frederick Doveton, and Ralph E. Griswold. *Thomas Jefferson, Landscape Architect.* Charlottesville: University of Virginia Press, 1978.

North, Douglass C. *Growth and Welfare in the American Past.* Englewood Cliffs, N.J.: Prentice-Hall International, 1974.

Norton, Paul F. "Thomas Jefferson and the Planning of the National Capital." In William Howard Adams (ed.). *Jefferson and the Arts: An Extended View.* Washington, D.C.: National Gallery of Art, 1976.

Nygren, Edward. *Views and Visions: American Landscape Before 1830.* Washington, D.C.: The Corcoran Gallery of Art, 1986.

O'Malley, Therese. "Charles Willson Peale's Belfield." In Lillian B. Miller and David C. Ward (eds). *New Perspectives on Charles Willson Peale.* Pittsburgh: University of Pittsburgh, 1991.

———. " 'Your Garden Must Be a Museum to You': Early American Gardens." *The Huntington Library Quarterly,* vol. 59, no. 2–3, 1996.

Osborn, James M. (ed.). *Joseph Spence's Observations, Anecdotes, and Characters of Books and Men.* Oxford: Clarendon Press, 1966.

Otis, Denise. *Grounds for Pleasure: Four Centuries of the American Garden.* New York: Harry N. Abrams, 2002.

Pace, Antonio (ed). *Luigi Castiglioni's Viaggio: Travels in the United States of North America 1785–87.* Syracuse: Syracuse University Press, 1983.

Padover, Saul K. *Thomas Jefferson and the National Capital.* Washington, D.C.: U.S. Government Printing Office, 1946.

Parkyns, George Isham. *Six Designs for Improving and Embellishing Grounds.* London, 1793.

The Parliamentary History of England (1765–71). London: Hansard, vol. 16, 1813.

Parr, Marilyn K. "Chronicle of a British Diplomat." *Washington History,* vol. 12, no. 1, 2000.

Pattee, Fred Lewis (ed.) *The Poems of Philip Freneau: Poet of the American Revolution.* Princeton: Princeton Historical Association, 1907.

Pauly, Philip P. *Fruits and Plains: The Horticultural Transformation of America.* Cambridge: Harvard University Press, 2007.

Peterson, Merrill D. (ed.). *James Madison. A Biography in His Own Words.* New York: HarperCollins, 1974.

———— (ed.). *Visitors to Monticello.* Charlottesville: University of Virginia Press, 1993.

Plaw, John. *Sketches of Country Houses, Villas and Rural Dwellings.* London: J. Taylor, 1800.

Pocock, William Fuller. *Architectural Designs for Rustic Cottages, Picturesque Dwellings, Villas, &c.* London: J. Taylor, 1807.

Pogue, Dennis J. "The Domestic Architecture of Slavery at George Washington's Mount Vernon." *Winterthur Portfolio,* vol. 37, 2002

————. "Giant in the Earth: George Washington, Landscape Designer." In Rebecca Yamin and Karen Bescherer Metheny (eds.). *Landscape Archaeology: Reading and Interpreting the American Historical Landscape.* Knoxville: University of Tennessee Press, 1996.

Pollan, Michael. "The Food Movement, Rising." *The New York Review of Books,* 10 June 2010.

Price, Uvedale. *Thoughts on the Defence of Property.* Hereford, UK, 1797.

Prince, William. *Catalogue of Fruit Trees and Shrubs.* New York, 1790.

Prussing, Eugene E. *The Estate of George Washington Deceased.* Boston: Little, Brown, 1927.

Radbill, Samuel X. (ed.). "The Autobiographical Ana of Robley Dunglison." *Transactions of the American Philosophical Society,* vol. 53, 1963.

Ramsay, David, ed. by Lester H. Cohen. *The History of the American Revolution.* Indianapolis: Liberty Classics, 1990.

Randall, Henry S. *The Life of Thomas Jefferson.* New York: Derby & Jackson, 1858.

Randolph, Sarah N. *The Domestic Life of Thomas Jefferson.* New York: Frederick Ungar, 1976.

Regis, Pamela. *Describing Early America: Bartram, Jefferson, Crèvecoeur and the Rhethoric of Natural History.* DeKalb: Northern Illinois University Press, 1992.

Reps, John William. *Washington on View: The Nation's Capital since 1790.* Chapel Hill: University of North Carolina Press, 1991.

Rice, Howard C. "Jefferson's Gift of Fossils to the Museum of Natural History in Paris." *Proceedings of the American Philosophical Society,* vol. 95, no. 6, 1951.

Rink, Evald. *Technical Americana: A Checklist of Technical Publications Printed Before 1831.* New York: Kraus International Publications, 1981.

Roberts, Octavia. *With Lafayette in America.* Boston and New York: Houghton Mifflin, 1919.

Rochefoucauld-Liancourt, François Alexandre Frédéric de la. *Travels through the United States of North America in 1795, 1796 and 1797.* London: R. Phillips, 1799.

Rodenbough, Charles D. *Governor Alexander Martin: Biography of a North Carolina Revolutionary War Statesman.* Jefferson, N.C.: McFarland, 2004.

Ronda, James P. "Dreams and Discoveries: Exploring the American West, 1760–1815." *William and Mary Quarterly,* vol. 46, no. 1, 1989.

Ross, Earle D. "Benjamin Franklin as an Eighteenth-Century Agricultural Leader." *The Journal of Political Economy,* vol. 37, no. 1, 1929.

Saltzberg Saltman, Helen. "John Adams's Earliest Essays: The Humphrey Ploughjoggers Letters." *William and Mary Quarterly,* Third Series, vol. 37, no. 1, 1980.

Sambrook, James. "Wooburn Farm in the 1760s." *Garden History,* vol. 7, no. 2, 1979.

Schama, Simon. *Citizens: A Chronicle of the French Revolution.* London: Penguin Books, 1989.

Schlesinger, Arthur M. "Liberty Tree: A Genealogy." *The New England Quarterly,* vol. 25, no. 4, 1952.

Schöpf, Johann David, trans. and ed. by Alfred J. Morrison. *Travels in the Confederation, 1783–1784.* Philadelphia: William J. Campbell, 1911.

Schutz, John A., and Douglass Adair (eds.). *The Spur of Fame.* Indianapolis: Liberty Fund, 2001.

Scott, Pamela. "The City of Living Green: An Introduction to Washington's Street Trees." *Washington History,* vol. 18, nos. 1, 2, 2006.

———. "L'Enfant's Washington Described: The City in the Public Press, 1791–1795." *Washington History,* vol. 3, no. 1, 1991.

———. "Moving the Seat of Government." *Washington History,* vol. 12, no. 1, 2000.

———. *Temple of Liberty: Building the Capitol for a New Nation.* Oxford: Oxford University Press, 1995.

———. " 'This Vast Empire': The Iconography of the Mall, 1791–1848." In Richard Longstreth (ed.). *The Mall in Washington, 1791–1991.* Washington, D.C.: National Gallery of Art, 1991.

Scott, W. *A History of Orange County, Virginia.* Richmond: Everett Waddey Company, 1907.

Seale, William. *The President's House.* Washington, D.C.: White House Historical Association, 1986.

———. *The White House: The History of an American Idea.* Washington, D.C.: The American Institute of Architects Press, 1992.

———. "The White House in John Adams's Presidency." *White House History,* no. 7, 2000.

Semmes, John E. *John H. B. Latrobe and His Times, 1803–1891.* Baltimore: The Norman Remington Co., 1917.

Shaw, Peter. *The Character of John Adams.* Chapel Hill: University of North Carolina Press, 1976.

Shenstone, William. *The Works in Verse and Prose.* London: R. and J. Dodsley, 1764.

Shuffelton, Frank (ed.). *The Cambridge Companion to Thomas Jefferson.* Cambridge and New York: Cambridge University Press, 2009.

Silliman, Benjamin. *Remarks made on a short tour between Hartford and Quebec.* New Haven: S. Converse, 1824.

Silver, Bruce. "William Bartram and Other Eighteenth Century Accounts of Nature." *Journal of the History of Ideas,* vol. 39, no. 4, 1978.

Simpson, Henry. *The Lives of Eminent Philadelphians*. Philadelphia: William Brotherhead, 1859.

Slaughter, Jane C. "Anne Mercer Slaughter: A Sketch." *Tyler's Quarterly Magazine*, vol. 19, no. 1, July 1937.

Slaughter, Thomas (ed.). *Bartram: Travels and Other Writings*. New York: Library of America, 1996.

Smith Loughton, William. "Journal of William Loughton Smith, 1790–91." *Proceedings of the Massachusetts Historical Society*, Third Series, vol. 51, 1917.

Smith, Abigail Adams. *Journal and Correspondence of Miss Adams*. New York and London: Wiley and Putnam, 1841–42.

Smith, Murphy D. *A Museum: The History of the Cabinet of Curiosities of the American Philosophical Society*. Philadelphia: American Philosophical Society, 1996.

Smith, Page. *John Adams*. New York: Doubleday, 1962.

Smith, Paul H. (ed.). *Letters of Delegates to Congress, 1774–1789*. Washington, D.C.: Library of Congress, 1976–2000.

Smith, Robert C. "A Portuguese Naturalist in Philadelphia, 1799." *Pennsylvania Magazine of History and Biography*, vol. 78, 1954.

Soane, John. *Sketches in Architecture, Containing Plans and Elevations of Cottages, Villas and Other Buildings*. London, 1793.

Sowerby, Millicent E. (ed.). *Catalogue of the Library of Thomas Jefferson*. Charlottesville: University of Virginia Press, 1983.

Spence, Joseph. *Observations, Anecdotes, and Characters, of Books and Men*. London: John Murray, 1820.

Stahr, Walter. *John Jay*. New York and London: Hambledon, 2005.

Stanton, Lucia. *Free Some Day. The African-American Families of Monticello*. Monticello: Thomas Jefferson Foundation, 2000.

———. "Jefferson's People: Slavery at Monticello." In Frank Shuffelton (ed.). *The Cambridge Companion to Thomas Jefferson*. Cambridge and New York: Cambridge University Press, 2009.

———. *Slavery at Monticello*. Monticello: Thomas Jefferson Foundation, 1996.

———. "'Those Who Labor for My Happiness': Thomas Jefferson and His Slaves." In Peter S. Onuf (ed.). *Jeffersonian Legacies*. Charlottesville: University of Virginia Press, 1993.

Stein, Susan, R. *The Worlds of Thomas Jefferson at Monticello*. New York: Harry N. Abrams, 1993.

Stetson, Sarah P. "The Philadelphia Sojourn of Samuel Vaughan." *Pennsylvania Magazine of History and Biography*, vol. 78, 1949.

Stoll, Steven. *Larding the Lean Earth: Soil and Society in Nineteenth-Century America*. New York: Hill and Wang, 2002.

Strickland, William. "Observations on the State of America." In *Communications to the Board of Agriculture on the Subject Relative to the Husbandry and Internal Improvement of the Country*, vol. 2. London: W. Bulmer & Co., 1800.

Swem, Earl G., (ed.). "Brothers of the Spade: Correspondence of Peter Collinson, of London, and of John Custis, of Williamsburg, Virginia, 1734–1746." *Proceedings of the American Antiquarian Society*, vol. 58, pt. 1, 1948.

Switzer, Stephen. *Iconographia Rustica*. London, 1718.

Taylor, John (M. E. Bradford, ed.). *The Arator. Being a Series of Agricultural*

Essays, Practical and Political: In Sixty-Four Numbers. Indianapolis: Liberty Fund, 1977.

Terra, Helmut de. "Alexander von Humboldt's Correspondence with Jefferson, Madison, and Gallatin." *Proceedings of the American Philosophical Society*, vol. 103, no. 6, 1959.

Thomas, Keith. *Man and the Natural World: Changing Attitudes in England 1500–1800.* London: Penguin Books, 1984.

Thomson, Keith. "Benjamin Franklin's Lost Tree." In Keith Thomson (ed.). *The Common but Less Frequent Loon and Other Essays.* New Haven and London: Yale University Press, 1993.

———. *The Legacy of the Mastodon: The Golden Age of Fossils in America.* New Haven and London: Yale University Press, 2008b.

———. *A Passion for Nature: Thomas Jefferson and Natural History.* Monticello: Thomas Jefferson Foundation, 2008a.

Thornton, Anna Maria. "Diary of Mrs. William Thornton," 1800. *Records of the Columbia Historical Society*, vol. 10, 1907.

Thornton, Tamara Plakins. *Cultivating Gentlemen: The Meaning of Country Life Among the Boston Elite.* New Haven and London: Yale University Press, 1989.

Ticknor Curtis, George (ed.). *Life of Daniel Webster.* New York: D. Appleton and Company, 1872.

True, A. C. *A History of Agricultural Education in the United States 1785–1925.* New York: Arno Press and New York Times, 1969.

True, Rodney. "Early Days of the Albemarle Agricultural Society." *Annual Report of the American Historical Association*, 1918.

———. "Early Development of Agricultural Societies in the United States." *Annual Report of the American Historical Association*, 1925.

True, Rodney H. (ed.). "Minute Book of the Albemarle Agricultural Society." *American Historical Association*, vol. 1, 1921.

Trumbull, John. *Autobiography, Reminiscences and Letters from 1756 to 1841.* New York and London: Wiley and Putnam, 1841.

Uglow, Jenny. *The Lunar Men: The Friends Who Made the Future.* London: Faber & Faber, 2002.

Van Doren, Carl. *Benjamin Franklin.* New York: Penguin Books, 1991.

Van Horne, John C. (ed.). *The Correspondence and Miscellaneous Papers of Benjamin Henry Latrobe.* New Haven and London: Yale University Press, 1984–88.

Wade Martins, Susanna. *A Great Estate at Work: The Holkham Estate and Its Inhabitants in the Nineteenth Century.* Cambridge: Cambridge University Press, 1980.

Walpole, Horace. "The History of Modern Taste in Gardening, 1780." In M. Charlesworth (ed.). *The English Garden: Literary Sources and Documents.* Mountfield, East Sussex: Helm Publishing, 1993.

Wansey, Henry. *An Excursion to the United States of North America in the Summer of 1794.* Salisbury, UK: J. Easton, 1798.

Waterhouse, Benjamin. *The Botanist.* Boston: Joseph T. Buckingham, 1811.

Watson, John F. *Annals of Philadelphia and Pennsylvania in the Olden Time.* Philadelphia: Elijah Thomas, 1857.

Wayson, Billy Lee. "Martha Jefferson Randolph: The Education of a Republican

Daughter and Plantation Mistress, 1782–1809." Dissertation, University of Virginia, 2008.

Webster, Daniel. *The Writings and Speeches of Daniel Webster.* Boston: Little, Brown, 1903.

Weigley, Russell F. (ed.). *Philadelphia: 300-Year History.* New York and London: W. W. Norton, 1982.

Weintraub, Stanley. *General Washington's Christmas Farewell: A Mount Vernon Homecoming, 1783.* New York: Free Press, 2003.

Weld, Isaac. *Travels Through the States of North America, and the Provinces of Upper and Lower Canada during the Years 1795, 1796 and 1797.* London: J. Stockdale, 1807.

West, Gilbert. *Stowe: The Gardens of the Right Honourable Richard Lord Viscount Cobham.* London: L. Gilliver, 1732.

Whately, Thomas. *Observations on Modern Gardening.* London, 1770.

Williamson, Hugh. "Change of Climate, Which Has Been Observed in the Middle Colonies in North-America." *Transactions of the American Philosophical Society,* vol. 1, 1769–71.

Willich, A. F. M. *The Domestic Encyclopaedia.* London: Murray and Highley, 1802.

Wills, Garry. *Cincinnatus: George Washington and the Enlightenment.* New York: Doubleday, 1984.

————— (ed.). *The Federalist Papers by Alexander Hamilton, James Madison and John Jay.* New York: Bantam Books, 1982.

Willson, E. J. *West London Nursery Gardens.* London: The Fulham and Hammersmith Historical Society, 1982.

Wilson, Gaye, and Elizabeth V. Chew. "Fashioning an American Diplomat: The Mather Brown Portrait of Thomas Jefferson." *Dress,* vol. 29, 2002.

Wolcott, Oliver. *Memoirs of the Administrations of Washington and John Adams.* New York, 1846.

Wood, Gordon S. *Creation of the American Republic, 1746–1787.* Chapel Hill: University of North Carolina Press, 1987.

Wood, John. *A Series of Plans, for Cottages and Habitations of the Labourer.* London: J. and J. Taylor, 1781.

Woodward, Carl R. "Benjamin Franklin: Adventures in Agriculture." *Journal of the Franklin Institute,* vol. 234, no. 3, 1942.

Woys Weaver, William. *Heirloom Vegetable Gardening.* New York: Henry Holt, 1997.

Wright, Frances. *Views of Society and Manners in America.* New York: E. Bliss & E. White, 1821.

Wulf, Andrea. *The Brother Gardeners: Botany, Empire and the Birth of an Obsession.* New York: Alfred A. Knopf, 2009.

—————. *"Franklinia alatamaha." The Garden,* June 2008.

Wulf, Andrea, and Emma Gieben-Gamal. *This Other Eden: Seven Great Gardens and 300 Years of English History.* London: Little, Brown, 2005.

Young, Alfred F. *The Democratic Republicanism of New York: The Origins, 1793–1797.* Chapel Hill: University of North Carolina Press, 1967.

Young, Sterling James. *The Washington Community 1800–1828.* New York and London: A Harvest/HBJ Book, 1966.

ILLUSTRATION CREDITS

Once again I would like to thank the Wellcome Library, London, for their (almost free) database and for digitalizing some more illustrations to use in this book, and the Linnean Society of London, for waiving the reproduction fees for the illustrations from their collection. Many other organizations and individuals listened to my pleas and generously provided their illustrations at a discount, for which I'm very grateful.

Prologue: Benjamin Franklin, engraving by E. Savage after a painting by David Martin, 1767. Reproduced with permission of the Wellcome Library, London.

Chapter 1: Plan of Mount Vernon by Samuel Vaughan, 1787. Courtesy of the Mount Vernon Ladies' Association.

Chapter 2: The Temple of Modern Virtue and The Temple of Antient Virtue at Stowe. *A Description of the Gardens of Lord Viscount Cobham at Stow in Buckinhamshire,* by B. Seeley, 1749. Reproduced with permission of the Wellcome Library, London.

The Temple of British Worthies at Stowe. *A Description of the Gardens of Lord Viscount Cobham at Stow in Buckinhamshire,* by B. Seeley, 1749. Reproduced with permission of the Wellcome Library, London.

Chapter 3: A Draught of John Bartram's House and Garden as it appears from the River, 1758. Watercolor on paper by William Bartram. © Earl of Derby.

Chapter 4: View on Lake George, N.Y., Currier & Ives, 1866. Prints and Photographs Division, DLC.

Chapter 5: View of the Residence of John Adams and John Quincy Adams, Presidents of the United States, drawing by Eliza Susan Quincy, c. 1831. Courtesy of the Adams National Historical Park.

Chapter 6: Thomas Jefferson, Plan of the Federal District, 1791. Thomas Jefferson Papers, Manuscript Division, DLC.

William Thornton, Sketch of the White House, c. 1793–1805. Prints and Photographs Division, DLC.

Chapter 7: Meriwether Lewis, photographic print, c. 1903. Prints and Photographs Division, DLC.

View on the Potomac near Harpers Ferry, Currier & Ives, c. 1866. Prints and Photographs Division, DLC.

Chapter 8: Thomas Jefferson's drawing of fields at Monticello, HM 9396. Reproduced with permission of The Huntington Library, San Marino, California.

Chapter 9: Model cottage in the *Communications of the Board of Agriculture,* 1797, volume 1.

Magnolia virginiana, Mark Catesby's *Natural History of Carolina, Florida, and the Bahama Islands* (1731–1748). Reproduced with permission of the Wellcome Library, London.

George Washington, by Gilbert Stuart, oil on canvas, 1797. Reproduced with permission of The White House Historical Association (White House Collection).

John Adams, by Mather Brown, 1788. Reproduced with permission of The Boston Athenaeum.

Thomas Jefferson, by Rembrandt Peale, 1805, oil on canvas. Accession no. 1867.306, Collection of The New-York Historical Society.

James Madison, by Catherine A. Drinker after Gilbert Stuart, 1875. Reproduced with permission of Independence National Historical Park.

West Façade of Mount Vernon, attributed to Edward Savage, c. 1792. Courtesy of the Mount Vernon Ladies' Association.

East Façade of Mount Vernon, attributed to Edward Savage, c. 1792. Courtesy of the Mount Vernon Ladies' Association.

Magnolia tripetala, Mark Catesby's *Natural History of Carolina, Florida, and the Bahama Islands* (1731–1748). Reproduced with permission of the Wellcome Library, London.

Chionanthus virginicus, Mark Catesby's *Natural History of Carolina, Florida, and the Bahama Islands* (1731–1748). Reproduced with permission of the Wellcome Library, London.

State-House Garden, Philadelphia, by William Birch, from *The City of Philadelphia, in the State of Pennsylvania North America: as it appeared in the Year 1800.* Courtesy of Monticello/Thomas Jefferson Foundation.

George Washington at Bartram's Garden, reprint from Calendar, *The Philadelphia Bulletin Historical Series* No. 23, 1929, after a painting by Jean Leon Jerome Ferris.

Franklinia alatamaha, F. Andrew Michaux, *The North American Sylva, or a description of the forest trees, of the United States, Canada and Nova Scotia* (1819). Reproduced with permission of the Linnean Society, London.

View of Hudson River, by William Winstanely, c. 1793. Courtesy of the Mount Vernon Ladies' Association.

Acer saccharum, F. Andrew Michaux, *The North American Sylva, or a description of the forest trees, of the United States, Canada and Nova Scotia* (1819). Reproduced with permission of the Linnean Society, London.

John Adams's house, drawing by E. Malcom, 1798. Courtesy of the Adams National Historical Park.

Life of George Washington: The Farmer, Claude Regnier, after Junius Brutus Stearns, 1853. Courtesy of the Mount Vernon Ladies' Association.

Plan of the City of Washington, Pierre L'Enfant, 1791. Maps and Geography Division, DLC.

Plan of the White House Garden, probably Henry Benjamin Latrobe with additions by Jefferson, c. 1807. Maps and Geography Division, DLC.

George Town and Federal City, or City of Washington, by T. Cartwright after George Beck, 1801. Prints and Photographs Division, DLC.

Robinia hispida, Mark Catesby's *Natural History of Carolina, Florida, and the Bahama Islands* (1731–1748). Reproduced with permission of the Wellcome Library, London.

Liriodendron tulipifera, Mark Catesby's *Natural History of Carolina, Florida, and the Bahama Islands* (1731–1748). Reproduced with permission of the Wellcome Library, London.

Kalmia angustifolia, Mark Catesby's *Natural History of Carolina, Florida, and the Bahama Islands* (1731–1748). Reproduced with permission of the Wellcome Library, London.

The Passage of the Pato'k thro' the blew mountain at the confluence of that river with the Shan'h, by George Beck, 1796. Courtesy of the Mount Vernon Ladies' Association.

Natural Bridge, copy after William Roberts, by Joseph Constantine Stadler, 1808. Courtesy of Monticello/Thomas Jefferson Foundation.

Monticello, West Front and Garden, by Jane Pitford Braddick Peticolas, 1825. Courtesy of Monticello/Thomas Jefferson Foundation.

View from Monticello looking towards Charlottesville, by Jane Pitford Braddick Peticolas, 1825. Courtesy of Monticello/Thomas Jefferson Foundation.

Montpelier. Watercolor by William Thornton, 1802. Private collection.

Montpelier at the time of Madison's retirement. The Institute for Advanced Technology in the Humanities, University of Virginia, rendered by Chad Keller, 2010.

MAPS

Mount Vernon, modern map of the historic landscape, c. 1786. Courtesy of the Mount Vernon Ladies' Association, rendered by Curt Breckenridge, 2010.

Adams Seat in Quincy, modern map of the historic landscape, 1787. Courtesy of the Adams National Historical Park.

Monticello, modern map of the historic landscape, c. 1809. Courtesy of Monticello/Thomas Jefferson Foundation, rendered by Derek Wheeler, 2010.

Monticello, modern map of the historic landscape, c. 1809. Courtesy of Monticello/Thomas Jefferson Foundation, rendered by Derek Wheeler, 2010.

Montpelier, modern map of the historic landscape, 1818–1848. Courtesy of Archaeology Department, The Montpelier Foundation, rendered by Matt Reeves, 2010.

Acknowledgments

The founding fathers lived in a "republic of letters" in which they were able to share their scientific, political and philosophical thoughts and observations with a community of thinkers across the world. During the research and writing of *Founding Gardeners* I have encountered the twenty-first-century version of such a "republic of letters"—never before have I learned so much from so many inspiring, fabulous and helpful people. Without them I would not have been able to write this book. Thank you all for sharing so generously.

My first (and huge) thank-you goes to the International Center for Jefferson Studies at Monticello, where I was a three-time fellow for four months at the most enchanting place a writer can possibly find. My stay at the ICJS allowed me to become part of an academic community that has opened my eyes, broadened my horizons and helped me to understand the founding fathers. I would like to thank all the staff at the ICJS, the Jefferson Library, and at Monticello who have all given me so much of their time, as well as sharing their knowledge and passion for the subject. In particular, I would like to thank William Beiswanger, Lucia Stanton and Gaye Wilson for answering all my questions and for reading and commenting on some of my chapters (and for pointing out my mistakes), as well as Joan Hairfield, Andrew O'Shaughnessy, Peggy Cornett, Endrina Tay, Anna Berkes, Eric Johnson, Jack Robertson, Leah Stearns, Leni Sorensen and Elizabeth Chew; and Derek Wheeler for his great maps. Monticello would not be the same without the formidable Peter Hatch, whose official title, Director of Grounds and Horticulture, doesn't even come close to describing what he does. Thank you, Peter, for bringing Jefferson alive in his own landscape, for long walks across the estate, for generously sharing your horticultural knowledge, reading some of my chapters and for letting me read parts of your forthcoming book, *Thomas Jefferson: Revolutionary Garden*—thank you for taking me under your wing and becoming a friend. Thank you also to Lou Hatch for your wonderful hospitality and family dinners.

In Charlottesville and Albemarle County, I would also like to thank Billy Wayson for sharing his knowledge on eighteenth-century farming as well as reading and commenting on one of the chapters; Reuben Rainey for his clever comments on some of the chapters and for lending me Whately's *Observations;* and Sara Lee Barnes for a lovely tour of the farmland between Shadwell and Gordonsville.

The wonderful Dean Norton, Director of Horticulture at Mount Vernon, invited me to stay on the estate for an inspiring week in which I had the run of the place after the tourists had left. Nothing can describe the joy of sitting alone on Washington's porch with a glass of red wine and looking over the majestic Potomac. Thank you for your warm hospitality, friendship, your comments on the Mount Vernon chapter—and for letting me drive a John Deere across the estate (certainly one of the highlights of this entire project). I would also like to thank Curt Breckenridge for his great map of Mount Vernon, Dawn Bonner for her help with the illustrations, the staff at the Mount Vernon Library and in particular Mary Thompson for her assistance and comments on some of the chapters.

At Madison's Montpelier I would like to thank Tom Chapman for opening his files so that I could copy and transcribe as much as I liked—and for answering my many, many questions as well as reading and commenting on the Montpelier chapter. A big thank-you to Matt Reeves, whose question "Why do you think Madison put a slave village in the middle of his garden?" shaped the chapter on Montpelier. Thank you for talking, walking and sharing your archaeological results and reports as well as the wonderful map—this chapter would have been impossible without the fantastic archaeology at Montpelier.

At John Adams's Old House in Quincy and the National Park Service I would like to thank Robert Mackenzie for showing me around the garden and Kelly Cobble for helping me with my queries and illustrations.

This book would have been impossible to write without the help of the editors of the founding fathers' letters: I would like to thank Ed Lengel at the George Washington Papers; Lisa Francavilla at the Thomas Jefferson Retirement Papers for dealing with all my many queries with such delight and efficiency; David Mattern at the James Madison Retirement Papers, who allowed me to read and copy his transcripts of Madison's letters a year before the fabulous first volume of the Retirement Series was published and who patiently answered all my questions (again and again)—thank you for all your invaluable help and for your erudite comments on three chapters; Margaret Hogan at the John Adams Papers, who provided me with all the transcriptions—thank you for this amazing generosity, which saved me (and my eyes) from reading handwritten letters on microfilm, and for your great comments on some of the chapters; also a big thank-you to Sara Sikes who checked the Adamses' quotes from these transcriptions against the originals.

The White House Historical Association and OAH awarded me with a very generous one-month travel grant that allowed me to work in the National Archives in Washington, D.C. Thank you also to Bill Allman at the Office of the Curator at the White House for a tour and Jonathan Pilska for sharing his knowledge on the White House landscape.

I would also like to thank: the staff at the London Library, Linnean Library (in particular Ben Sherwood for once again helping with the illustrations) and the British Library; the staff at the Library of Independence National Historical Park in Philadelphia, in particular Karen Stevens for sending me a digital copy of the entire Independence Day Book and her assistance with other queries; the staff at the Massachusetts Historical Society; the staff at the National Archives in Washington, D.C.; the staff at the Washington Historical Society; the staff at the American Philosophical Society, in particular Roy Goodman; Beth Prindle at the John Adams Library Project at Boston Public Library for immediately putting Adams's garden books online when I contacted her; Beth Carroll-Horrocks at the American Academy of Arts and Sciences; Diane Richards for her research at the North Carolina State Archive in Raleigh; Marianne Hansen at the Bryn Mawr College Library; Cornelia King at the Library Company in Philadelphia; Paula Manzella at Burlington County Library; Michelle Schneider at National Park Service;

Catherine Medich at New Jersey State Archives; Kathryn Braund at Auburn University; Thomas Hallock and Nancy Hoffmann for their kind help on William Bartram; Sigrid Perry at Northwestern University Library; David Haugaard at the Historical Society of Pennsylvania; Elise Bernier-Feeley at Forbes Library; Robert Peck McCracken for showing me his flowering Franklinia; John Styles; Drew Newman for sending out a Bartram query to his colleagues at the Society of Early Americanists; and Hermann Düringer. My thanks also go to Joel Fry at Bartram's Garden in Philadelphia, for all his help and for his comments on the Bartram chapter.

And once again, I would like to thank Rebecca Carter, who despite her incredibly busy schedule came to my rescue when I got stuck . . . thank you so very much!

For the permission to quote from their manuscripts I would like to thank: Albany Institute of History and Art; American Antiquarian Society; American Philosophical Society; Connecticut Historical Society; Historical Society of Pennsylvania; Massachusetts Historical Society; New England Historic Genealogical Society; Princeton University Library; Rutgers University Libraries; University of Virginia Library.

I would like to thank the wonderful team at William Heinemann: Jason Arthur, Emma Finnigan, Laurie Ip Fung Chun for their continuing support and, of course, Drummond Moir, who has been a fantastic and patient editor. At Knopf I would like to thank an equally wonderful team: Edward Kastenmeier, Timothy O'Connell and Sara Eagle; and my copy editor, Anne Cherry.

I have encountered the most generous and charming hospitality during my stay in the United States: thank you to Alisa and David Dolev in Boston, Mia Sorgi in Washington, Annabel White in New York, Joy de Menil and Laird Reed for a delightful weekend in Virginia, the lovely Keith and Linda Thomson who invited a total stranger to their house and have since then been looking after me whenever I'm in Philadelphia (and even at the ICJS)—and thank you, Keith, for the clever comments on some of the chapters. One of the greatest joys of writing this book has been to meet Regan Ralph, who has not only given me a second home in the States (of which I have made—and will make—extensive use!) but who also has become a very special friend—thank you for your love, joy, generosity and energy . . . and thank you, Sam, for making me feel part of the family and teaching me about Popsicles and the real America . . . oh really!

Closer to home, I would like to thank Tom Holland who remains the greatest help for Latin emergencies; Saskia Manners for emergency photography and all those other things; Shefali Malhoutra for reading the first chapters and her steadfast encouragement; Mark Goldman for patiently explaining fiscal policies and for reading and commenting on the entire manuscript; Constanze von Unruh for so much—emotional support, cocktails and dinners, and for your honest and clever comments on the manuscript . . . poor old Ben Franklin, though; Patrick Walsh, my lovely friend and brilliant agent (in this order!) for who you are and what you do . . . thank you for always looking after me and for holding my hand when all went downhill. And Adam Wishart . . . your hand and mind is everywhere in this book—I will always be grateful that you encouraged me to be a writer—nothing will ever take that away. Thank you to my parents who were as always wonderful, supportive and clever. Thank you, Brigitte

Wulf, for battling through French letters and Diderot, and to Herbert Wulf for reading all chapters in their many versions.

Founding Gardeners would have not been completed had it not been for my grown-up, beautiful, lovely, gentle and wise daughter, Linnéa, who picked me up when my world tumbled down. Thank you—you truly are the best daughter in the universe.

This book is my "anniversary present" to Julia-Niharika Sen . . . to forty years of friendship . . . because we will last forever.

Index

Page numbers in *italics* refer to illustrations. Page numbers beginning with 221 refer to endnotes, and those followed by *n* refer to footnotes.

A NOTE ABOUT THE AUTHOR

Andrea Wulf was born in India and moved to Germany as a child. She trained as a design historian at London's Royal College of Art and is coauthor (with Emma Gieben-Gamal) of *This Other Eden: Seven Great Gardens and 300 Years of English History* (2005). She has written for *The Sunday Times* (London), *The Wall Street Journal* and *The Financial Times,* and she reviews for numerous newspapers, including *The New York Times, The Guardian, The Times Literary Supplement,* and *The Mail on Sunday.* She appears regularly on BBC television and radio. *The Brother Gardeners* was longlisted for the Samuel Johnson Prize in 2008, and won the 2010 American Horticultural Society Book Award and the 2010 CBHL Annual Literature Award.

A Note on the Type

The text of this book was set in Sabon, a typeface designed by Jan Tschichold (1902–1974), the well-known German typographer. Based loosely on the original designs by Claude Garamond (c. 1480–1561), Sabon is unique in that it was explicitly designed for hotmetal composition on both the Monotype and Linotype machines as well as for filmsetting. Designed in 1966 in Frankfurt, Sabon was named for the famous Lyons punch cutter Jacques Sabon, who is thought to have brought some of Garamond's matrices to Frankfurt.

COMPOSED BY *North Market Street Graphics, Lancaster, Pennsylvania*

PRINTED AND BOUND BY *Berryville Graphics, Berryville, Virginia*

DESIGNED BY *Iris Weinstein*